ENIGMA

How the German Machine Cipher Was Broken,
and How It Was Read by the Allies in World War Two

Foreign Intelligence Book Series
Thomas F. Troy, General Editor

ENIGMA

**How the German Machine Cipher Was Broken,
and How It Was Read by the Allies in World War Two**

Wladyslaw Kozaczuk

Edited and Translated
by Christopher Kasparek

UNIVERSITY PUBLICATIONS OF AMERICA, INC.

W kręgu Enigmy originally published by Książka i Wiedza, Warsaw 1979.

Copyright © by Władysław Kozaczuk 1984.

English-language translation Copyright © by Christopher Kasparek 1984.

Library of Congress Cataloging Publication Data

Kozaczuk, Władysław.

    Enigma: how the German machine cipher was broken, and how it was read by the Allies on World War Two.

    (Foreign intelligence book series)

    Translation of: W kręgu Enigmy.

    Bibliography: p. 321

    Includes index.

    1. World War, 1939-1945—Cryptography. I. Title.

II. Series.

D810.C88K6813 1984   940.54'85   83-16691

ISBN 0-89093-547-5

Printed in the United States of America.

CONTENTS

ILLUSTRATIONS

Plates

Figures

Pronunciation guide

Below are approximate pronunciations for some of the more prominent Polish names and terms appearing in this book. The Polish spellings are always used, except in the case of Warsaw, *Warszawa*—Var-SHAH-vah.

Biuro Szyfrów	BURE-oh SHIF-roof
Ciężki, Maksymilian	Mahx-ih-MEEL-yahn CHEN-shkee
Danilewicz, Ludomir	Loo-DOM-ere Dah-nee-LEV-eech
Fokczyński, Edward	ED-vard Fok-CHIN-ski
Kabackie (Woods)	Kahb-AHTS-kyeh
Kraków	KRAH-koof
Krzesławice	Kshes-wah-VEE-tseh
Langer, Gwido	GVEE-doh LANG-er
Palluth, Antoni	An-TOH-nee PAH-loot
Pyry	PIH-rih
Rejewski, Marian	MAR-yahn Rey-EF-ski
Różycki, Jerzy	YEZH-ih Roozh-IT-ski
ulica	oo-LEETS-ah
Wicher	VEE-her
Zygalski, Henryk	HEN-rik Zig-AHL-ski

Introduction

The fact of the German Enigma machine cipher having been "broken" by Polish cryptologists before World War II was first made public in my book published in 1967.[1] That book was subsequently reprinted in part in German by an association of former Abwehr workers in their publication *Die Nachhut* (The Rear Guard). In 1970 Heinz Bonatz, in his book, *German Naval Radio Intelligence, 1914-45*,[2] questioned whether the Poles had in fact solved Enigma, or, at any rate, the more complex variant of it that was used by the German Navy.

Three years later, in his *Enigma: The Greatest Enigma of the War of 1939-45*,[3] France's Gen. Gustave Bertrand supplied ample corroboration for the Polish claims and highlighted the French connection with Enigma. Finally, in 1974, Group Capt. F.W. Winterbotham's best-selling *The Ultra Secret*,[4] while valuable as a source on British involvement with Enigma, laid an ill-advised claim, since discredited, to British priority in the breaking of Enigma and triggered an avalanche of further accounts, some enlightening, but many spurious.

In this manner Poland, France, and Britain documented their involvement with Enigma in the same sequence in which it had occurred historically.

Enigma's breaking was perhaps the most spectacular event, in terms of difficulty and of consequences, in the entire several-thousand-year history of cryptography ("secret writing") and cryptology (the study of secret writing, especially for purposes of decryptment—the "breaking," or "reading," of secret correspondence by a third party).

Cryptology deals basically with ciphers, which either transpose (shift) or substitute letters for the original letters in a message, and with codes, which substitute arbitrary symbols most commonly consisting of letters or numbers for entire words and phrases.

The roots of cryptography and cryptology reach back at least to ancient Greece. The history[5] of this field is strewn with such names as Julius Caesar (inventor of "Caesar ciphers"), Leon Battista Alberti (famous architect and author of the earliest Western theoretical work on cryptology, 1467), Girolamo Cardano (sixteenth-century physician and mathematician who first formulated certain principles of probability theory), Blaise de Vigenère (French diplomat whose *Treatise on Ciphers* is still valued by specialists), John Wallis (greatest English mathematician before Newton, who, during Britain's Civil War in the mid-seventeenth century, read for Parliament the enciphered correspondence of King Charles I), Thomas Jefferson (the Father of American Cryptography, whose "wheel cypher," invented at the turn of the nineteenth century, came into use only after its reinvention in 1922), Edgar Allan Poe (who demonstrated that any simple substitution cipher can be solved, given a long enough cipher text), Charles Babbage (nineteenth-century precursor in computer theory, who first attempted to apply algebra to the solution of ciphers), Friedrich W. Kasiski (whose watershed book of 1863 was largely ignored until near the end of the century), Charles Wheatstone (inventor of the Wheatstone bridge and of the "Playfair" cipher, who stirred interest at the Paris Exposition of 1867 with his Cryptograph device), August Kerckhoffs (noted linguist who codified knowledge about ciphers up to that time and who emphasized that the strength of a cipher rests not in the physical security of the device used but in the variability of the key).

Cryptography and cryptology have developed in parallel with the evolution of science and technology. The use of telegraphy in war, first in the American Civil War and later in the Franco-Prussian War of 1870-71, spurred the theoretical study of ciphers. At the turn of the twentieth century, radio brought a new quantum jump; radio communications were to become essential to navies and air forces, which lacked other means of long-range operational communication. Measures prompted countermeasures. As early as 1908, the German Navy established on the island of Helgoland the first regular radio-monitoring station, and soon thereafter installed such equipment aboard its ships at sea. The British, confident in their naval superiority, did not introduce more secure crypto-systems until after their costly experiences in the early months of World War I.

The First World War also saw important applications of cryptology to political, as distinct from strictly military, purposes. The entry of the United States into the war was hastened by Britain's decryptment and communication to President Wilson, and by Wilson's publication of, a telegram of 17 January 1917 from German Foreign Minister Arthur Zimmermann to his ambassador in Washington, Count Johann von Bernstorff. Zimmermann informed the ambassador of Germany's intent to open unrestricted submarine warfare as of 1 February. Should it prove impossible to keep the U.S. neutral, Germany would propose to Mexico the joint prosecution of war against the U.S. Mexico's prize would be several states of the western and southwestern U.S. that Mexico had lost to the U.S. in the mid-nineteenth century. A few weeks after Wilson's publication of the Zimmermann telegram, on 6 April 1917, the U.S. declared war on Germany.

Early in the twentieth century, the only cipher system known to be in principle absolutely secure was the "one-time pad." This was not put into universal use, however, because it requires enormous quantities of pads that must be distributed periodically to all the users. Use of this kind of cipher was limited to the most important communication nets, especially in diplomacy and intelligence.

Germany's armed forces faced the problem of reconciling the requirements of security with the imperatives of speed and convenience. As early as the spring of 1918, the German Navy contemplated the use of cipher machines. A number of designs were considered, including one by Dr. Arthur Scherbius. Later, that German engineer would develop the "Enigma" machine that had been patented in Holland in the fall of 1919 by the inventor Hugo Koch, who subsequently sold the patent to Scherbius. Scherbius would improve Koch's design, introducing several ideas of his own, such as an unequal rhythm of movement in the rotors, something that other designers had vainly racked their heads over. He hoped to win a market for this machine in the world business community, but ultimately his company's best customer would be the German government, especially the armed forces.

Meanwhile, Germany's defeat in the fall of 1918 had interrupted the armed forces' experiments with automatic ciphers. The monarchy of Kaiser Wilhelm II fell, the Weimar Republic came into being, and soon the idea of equipping the armed forces with machine ciphers found realization. In 1926 the navy, and in 1928 the army, introduced cipher machines that at first were modified versions of the "civilian" model Enigma. Two years later, in 1930, a military version of the device was constructed, whose most essential innovation was a commutator, a "plugboard" with twenty-six plugs and plug connections, that vastly increased the number of possible cipher combinations.

Adoption of the cipher machines was connected with plans of the Weimar government to throw off Versailles Treaty limitations and transform the hundred-thousand-man professional Reichswehr into an army several times that size. Even before Hitler's accession to power, in the summer of 1932, a decision was made to increase the number of divisions. The armored and motorized "rapid armies" and air force, which were to become the key instruments of "lightning war,"[6] required new systems of radio communication, and that, in turn, entailed secure ciphers. To be sure, the German Air Force did not exist as yet, but when, in March 1935, Hitler broke the Versailles Treaty and officially created the Luftwaffe, it too was equipped with cipher machines. In 1933-34, Enigma was adopted by the Germans as a basic, unitary cipher system for the armed forces as well as military intelligence (the Abwehr), S.S. formations, the Nazi Party security and political intelligence service (S.D.), and other agencies of the Third Reich.

To cryptologists, an Enigma cipher was easily recognizable by its nearly perfect dispersal of letters. There were no correlates with natural language, and so statistical calculations of frequencies of the letters of the alphabet, such as had been described, for example, by Poe and Arthur Conan Doyle, were completely useless. The German machine cipher alarmed the general staffs of neighboring countries, especially those of Poland and France. Military monitoring stations—Polish at Starogard in the Polish Corridor, at Poznań, and at Krzesławice outside Kraków, and French at Metz, Strasbourg, and Mulhouse—and cryptologists charged with decrypting German ciphers s. work.

NOTES

1. Kozaczuk, *Bitwa o tajemnice,* 125f.

2. Bonatz, *Die deutsche Marine-Funkaufklärung 1914-1945,* 116. Hereafter referred to as *Funkaufklärung.*

3. Bertrand, *Enigma ou la plus grande énigme de la guerre 1939-1945.*

4. Winterbotham, *The Ultra Secret.*

5. The reader interested in a thorough historical treatment is referred to David Kahn's classic, *The Codebreakers.* A much briefer survey is Bruce Norman's *Secret Warfare: the Battle of Codes and Ciphers.*

6. One of the early framers of blitzkrieg doctrine was the Briton, J.F.C. Fuller (1878-1966), whose planning of the stunning tank attack at Cambrai, France, 20 November 1917, laid the foundation of modern armor tactics. Subsequently, Fuller played a major role in the conduct of the Allied armored operations of 1918, contributing significantly to Germany's defeat in World War I. After the war, Fuller launched a crusade for the mechanization and modernization of the British Army; in 1933 he retired as a major general in order to write, which he did voluminously. Fuller's tactical concepts of using tanks closely supported by aircraft and motorized infantry to break through enemy lines and disrupt rear areas influenced the British military writer B.H. Liddell Hart and Russian and German armor exponents. Gen. Heinz Guderian, one of the fathers of the German blitzkrieg that would overrun much of Europe in World War II, was thoroughly familiar with Fuller's teachings. The Briton's lectures (*Field Service Regulations III,* 1937) were adopted for study by the German, Soviet, and Czechoslovak armies. Fuller, who was considered extreme by conservative British military circles, saw his teachings largely vindicated by World War II.

1.

Poznań

In the first days of January 1929, the students at Poznań University's Mathematics Institute, which was housed in the Castle,[1] were preparing for their examinations. In the group tutored by the director of the institute, Prof. Zdzisław Krygowski, there was no counting on luck. The professor was not to be satisfied with rote memorization; he demanded of his students a facility in using their knowledge, an ability to formulate hypotheses, and skill in testing them. He also set a premium on the ability to reduce abstruse problems to their simplest, conceptually most tangible forms. The professor had developed this trait in earlier years when, as a lecturer at the Lwów Polytechnic Institute, he had emphasized the application of theory to the solution of practical problems.

At the beginning of January 1929 Professor Krygowski had a list drawn up of those third- and fourth-year mathematics students who knew German and had grades of at least "good" in their course work. Subsequently, selected students were asked to assemble at the Institute, where two officers from the Polish General Staff in Warsaw, Maj. Franciszek Pokorny and Lt. Maksymilian Ciężki,[2] in mufti, informed them that a cryptology course was being organized and invited them to participate. Twenty-odd students were pledged to secrecy concerning both the existence of the course and their participation in it. The classes were held twice weekly, in the evenings, and conducted by Cipher Bureau cryptologists commuting from Warsaw.[3]

The choice of Poznań for the site of a course in solving German ciphers was perfectly logical. The students at the Mathematics Institute came predominantly from western Poland (Wielkopolska) or from Pomerania (Pomorze) on the Baltic Sea and had attended German-language schools,

1

since the Polish language had been banned from schools in those parts of Poland that, from the late eighteenth century until 1918, had been occupied first by Prussia and later by Germany. Knowledge of one or more foreign languages, in addition to mathematics, was indispensable for a cryptologist.

Already then, in the late twenties, everything indicated that in favorable circumstances the small, hundred-thousand-man Reichswehr would quickly be transformed into a modern million-man army. The German government hardly concealed its intentions to take away from Poland the "lost territories" in the east: Pomerania, western Poland, Upper Silesia (Górny Śląsk). All the German political parties that came to power, regardless of their differences, voiced the same program, including the increasingly aggressive National Socialist German Workers' (Nazi) Party, or NSDAP, of Adolf Hitler.

The covert military build-up could not have been followed except through secret intelligence operations. An important source of information was the monitoring of German military radio stations, central and local, on condition that the messages could be decrypted to yield comprehensible plain texts.

There were few persons adept at cryptology in Poland at this time. At the General Staff's Cipher Bureau in Warsaw, trained specialists, as distinguished from clerks who enciphered and deciphered messages, could be counted on the fingers of one hand. Such a state of affairs led to the German ciphers and codes monitored at Starogard, Poznań, and Krzesławice being only partially tapped for their intelligence.

Germany's military preparations on the threshold of the thirties were causing mounting anxiety. In defiance of the Versailles Treaty of 1919, Germany was strengthening her military forces from year to year. For the time being in skeletal form, armored, air, and heavy artillery units were coming into existence. The Reichswehr staffs were drawing up contingency plans for war with Poland, Czechoslovakia, and France. In border areas, Grenzschutz units were secretly being enlarged, thereby reinforcing the superbly armed and trained hundred-thousand-man army.

Despite clauses of the Versailles Treaty forbidding Germany to conduct intelligence operations abroad, the Reichswehr had established numerous intelligence offices—disguised as permissible Abwehr counterintelligence—near the borders with Poland and Czechoslovakia. In early 1919, it had also commissioned a radio intelligence organization that employed numerous monitoring personnel and decryptment specialists from the Kaiser's old army and navy.

Little is known about the initial phase of the Polish-German cryptological duel, which began immediately following World War I and the re-emergence of Poland as an independent state. An interesting episode is recounted by a German historian who justifies the expansion of the Abwehr:

> Just how indispensable an organized intelligence service was, would be learned immediately after the conclusion of the war, in the summer of 1919. At that time, a military adviser with the cipher department of the Reich government was a certain Dr. Winiker, supposedly a professor at

the Berlin Polytechnic Institute and a specialist in radio communications. At the cipher department he soon came to know the entire military cipher and radio service—a fact that was of special importance in view of his working for Polish intelligence. One day Winiker disappeared without a trace, and thereafter there was a notable improvement in the radio and cipher service of the Polish armed forces.[4]

In the mid twenties, as surviving documents attest, German radio intelligence managed to read about six thousand messages between the staffs and regiments of the Polish Air Force. The blow was a severe one: German intelligence gained accurate information about the locations of most of the units, as well as about the plans of the air force command (the Aeronautics Department of the Ministry of Military Affairs) for the air force's development. Poland's Section II (military intelligence) learned of the setback through painstaking analytical work: Section II headquarters noticed on the basis of reports from its field offices that for some time the instructions for German agents in Poland had carried hardly any assignments concerning air force units, whereas the Polish Air Force and air defenses had previously been objects of lively interest to German intelligence. This suggested the possibility that information on the air force had gotten out some other way. An energetic search for the leak was ordered, including use of contacts in Germany. The investigation showed that the Abwehr had obtained information on the Polish Air Force from radio intelligence, allowing the Abwehr to shift its agents in Poland to other assignments.

Remedial action had to be taken. Polish agents in Germany's Abwehr were assigned to interest their German principals in purchasing the Polish Air Force code, "Port," used between the Aeronautics Department of the Ministry of Military Affairs and the air force regiments. German intelligence decided to avail itself of this opportunity and bought the code through its intermediaries. What remained was to satisfy the Abwehr's curiosity by broadcasting a series of messages between air force units and the Aeronautics Department. Besides genuine information mostly known to German intelligence, the messages contained disinformation. Over a period of a couple of months, several hundred messages were broadcast in "Port," while the real correspondence was conducted by courier and in coded telephone messages inaccessible to enemy monitoring. Operation Port was never detected by the Abwehr and to a considerable degree neutralized the damage that had been sustained.[5]

The cryptology course organized at Poznań years later, in early 1929, was meant to help Polish radio intelligence against its difficult German adversary, who had on his side the experiences of the world war of 1914-18.

A couple of weeks into the course, the lecturer passed out authentic Reichswehr ciphergrams for the students to solve. This system, he said, had already been broken, although for a time consultants, including Professor W. at Warsaw University, had considered it to be insoluble. The Germans called it Double Dice (Doppelwürfelverfahren), and it was currently in use. To make the problem easier, the lecturer added that it was a circular letter from the Berlin Reichswehr Ministry concerning winter quarters and bivouacs on Reichswehr training grounds. The latter hint was a relevant one, since it indicated the area of vocabulary in which the solution was to be sought.

A couple of hours later, some of the students, including Marian Rejewski, Henryk (Henry) Zygalski, and Jerzy (George) Różycki presented their solutions. For the others, the work was rougher going, and they failed this first, already fairly difficult test. There followed ever harder cipher texts and tests. Some of the students dropped out after concluding that they lacked the necessary talent or that they felt more at home in pure mathematics. Others simply could not keep up with the pace of the course, especially since Professor Krygowski still required the enrollees to take their regular examinations as scheduled.

The three students named above managed to reconcile the cipher course with their normal work. Marian Rejewski was then finishing up his master's thesis and preparing for his comprehensive examination.

On 1 March 1929 Rejewski received his master of philosophy, the degree conferred upon mathematics graduates, and found himself faced with a choice. He was a prime candidate to become a teaching assistant at the Mathematics Institute, but teaching held little attraction for him. Graduates in mathematics usually began their careers as high school teachers. A few managed to land assistantships at institutions of higher learning. There were few governmental and business institutions that employed mathematicians. Rejewski's family, which originally came from the Poznań area but several decades earlier had settled in Bydgoszcz, had traditionally taken up practical professions. Toward the end of the nineteenth century, a relative had established in Poznań a Polish insurance company called Vesta. Harassment by Prussian authorities and the struggle for survival had fostered in Poles a stance of active social involvement and hard work, which could enable them to resist the pressures of Germanization. Rejewski had intended upon graduation to go into actuarial mathematics. Professor Krygowski recommended a period of training in Göttingen, since the Polish universities at that time had no chair of high standing in this field. A few weeks later, without having completed the cryptology course, Rejewski went to Germany.

At Göttingen, the newcomer from solid, somewhat sleepy Poznań was struck by the international character of the renowned university. In the nineteenth century, such illustrious mathematicians as Gauss,[6] Dirichlet, and Riemann had lectured there, and later so had visiting scientists of such stature as Henri Poincaré and Max Planck. Rejewski wasted no time, but strove to keep abreast not only of his chosen specialty but of the state of mathematics in general. He studied the *Göttingische Gelehrte Anzeigen*, the *Crelles Journal für reine und angewandte Mathematik*, the *Rendiconti del Circolo Matematico di Palermo*, and other journals. He also participated in scholarly associations and delivered a couple of papers.

Apart from its genuine student population, Göttingen swarmed with assorted globetrotters and eternal students who squandered their money on an endless pursuit of amusements. True, the quiet university town was not the seat of such decadence as Berlin, but here too exceedingly free manners held sway. Loud—literally as well as metaphorically—libations and parties were held in the quarters of wealthy students from Britain, France, and overseas. Americans, especially, felt at home; the modern buildings of the mathematics institute and mathematics library had been built by the Rockefeller Foundation.[7] In this cosmopolitan tower of Babel, Rejewski soon found that the self-assured and seemingly carefree milieu was riddled with contradictions and conflicts. Nazi propaganda, with its racist slogans, was not yet strongly in evidence, but it was there; the subject frequently came up in Rejewski's conversations with other graduates from Poland, Zygmunt Birnbaum, Henryk Schaerf,[8] and Władysław Orlicz, later one of the directors of the Poznań University Institute of Mathematics.

In the summer of 1930, Rejewski concluded a year's stay at Göttingen. As he was leaving for home in Bydgoszcz, he could see that the successive political crises in Germany never altered the persistent, underlying enmity toward Poland. He also felt that the famous German school of mathematics was now largely a thing of the past. Among the professors whom he had come to know at Göttingen were no luminaries of such stature as Poland's Stefan Banach and Wacław Sierpiński, whose work had paved the way for twentieth-century mathematics.[9] Later, when Hitler came to power, professors from Göttingen such as Edmund Landau and Richard Courant would be removed from their chairs and hounded out of Germany.

A new academic year was beginning. In October 1930, Marian Rejewski was back at Poznań University's Mathematics Institute, ready to take up duties as a teaching assistant.

Poland's great National Exposition, held in Poznań from May to September 1929, had been a major event not only for the inhabitants of that city. The first exhibition of Poland's achievements in the ten years since the recovery of independence in 1918, after 123 years of foreign rule, had also had a broad impact outside Poland. In Berlin, the significance of this show in the metropolis of western Poland had been correctly read: Poles would never discuss revision of their western borders—a constant objective of the postwar governments of Germany, from 1919 on called the Weimar Republic. The German demands had been encouraged by the irresolute stance of the western powers, which in 1925 at Locarno had seen only to guaranteeing for themselves their own borders with Germany.

As Poznań had been living through the great exposition, the cryptology course organized there by the General Staff's Cipher Bureau had ended quietly. In the underground vaults of the Command Post (Komenda Miasta) on St. Martin's Street (ulica Świętego Marcina) a large room had been suitably outfitted, and the best students in the course had set to work solving German ciphers. This was a sort of laboratory that afforded the young cryptologists broad opportunities for experimentation.

This Poznań outpost of the Cipher Bureau, at which in the fall of 1930 Marian Rejewski likewise began working, had been so conceived as to permit its young workers to reconcile cipher work with university classes. They worked on intercepted German radiograms some twelve hours a week, selecting their own hours of the day or night. After showing their passes to the duty officer and descending the stairs into the vaults, they could work in total seclusion.

Installation of the "black chamber"—they often joked at the pretentious term—in the cellar of the Command Post had not been prompted by a fondness for mystery, but by practical considerations. From there to the Mathematics Institute at the Castle, it was literally but a few paces; thus, even a couple of free hours could be used for decrypting.

The Poznań outpost did not read long dispatches but only worked out methods of breaking German cipher keys, which were changed periodically. Radio intercepts were supplied by courier from Warsaw and from the nearest monitoring stations (one of them was in a Poznań suburb). When time was of the essence, solved messages were sent to Warsaw by airplane.

Solution of some of the more often used German military ciphers became a matter of routine. The small team of young cryptologists learned to exploit mistakes made by the German cipher clerks, as well as certain regularities that they discovered. One of these was a rule observed by German cipher clerks that a cipher text must contain at least fifty letters. The cryptologists soon determined that in the preliminary preparation the Germans were padding out short messages with the letter X in order to draw them out to fifty letters. Thus a short text such as "2 Oktober 1931 Zug mit Munition angekommen" ("2 October 1931 train arrived with ammunition"), would be altered to: 2XXOK TOBER X1931 XXZUG XMITX XXMUN ITION XXANG EKOMM ENXXX, and upon encipherment would read: LQREH BWXLF CNAPS PWLZY ARNCK PGMQT JOPBD SNZIT YPTCA AYDHC (fifty letters).[10]

Discovery of such rules made it easier to deal with a cipher. But increasingly messages appeared with which even the Cipher Bureau in Warsaw was helpless: something akin to the work of a blind man who reaches into a printer's cases and takes out pieces of type at random. Could it be that the Germans were putting fake ciphers on the air in order to occupy opponents with unproductive labor? This conjecture had to be discarded, because such messages were being broadcast with increasing frequency. Finally, they almost completely replaced other kinds of ciphers in the Reichswehr's radio communications.

At last there could be no more doubt: this was an intricate machine cipher that was impervious to standard methods of breaking.

NOTES

1. The Poznań Castle had been built, in a pseudo-Teutonic Knights style, at the beginning of the twentieth century by Kaiser Wilhelm II to be the official residence of the German crown prince. Poznań was purposely chosen as the site in order to bolster the effort to Germanize this German-occupied part of partitioned Poland.—ED.

2. Pokorny was then chief of the Cipher Bureau of Section II (Oddział II, or Intelligence) of the General Staff, and Ciężki was chief of the bureau's German section, B.S.[for Biuro Szyfrów, Cipher Bureau]-4. Pokorny's last name, in Polish, literally means "Humble," and Ciężki's, "Heavy."

3. The course was based, as Rejewski would discover in France during World War II, on a textbook available in ordinary bookstores: Marcel Givièrge, *Cours de cryptographie.*

4. Buchheit, *Der deutsche Geheimdienst: Geschichte der militärischen Abwehr,* 32.

5. Kozaczuk, *Bitwa o tajemnice,* 111-24, describes this in discussing disinformation.

6. At Professor Krygowski's request, Rejewski on arrival in Göttingen placed a bouquet of flowers on Gauss's grave.

7. Robert Jungk states, "Nearly all the Americans who became well known later...for the development of atomic energy had been at Göttingen at various times between 1924 and 1932." Göttingen's American alumni included Edward U. Condon, Norbert Wiener, Robert B. Brode, R. Richtmyer, Linus Pauling, and J. Robert Oppenheimer, the future "father of the atomic bomb," who, in May 1927, two years before Rejewski's arrival at Göttingen, had there obtained his doctorate in physics. Other alumni of German universities who would later become involved with U.S. atomic weapons included the Hungarian Jews Eugene Wigner, Leo Szilard, John von Neumann (who worked in mathematics at Göttingen) and Edward Teller, the future "father of the hydrogen bomb"; Jungk ascribes to their experience of anti-Semitism in Germany the fact that only a few years later they would become the most active champions of the construction of the U.S. atom bomb, in order to head off Hitler's Germany. Jungk, *Brighter than a Thousand Suns,* 21, 23, 32-33 and passim.—ED.

8. Now professors of mathematics in the U.S.: Z. William Birnbaum, at the University of Washington, Seattle; Henry M. Schaerf, at Washington University, St. Louis, Missouri. Asked over half a century later about his recollections of Rejewski at Göttingen, Professor Schaerf wrote the editor-translator (16 September 1982):

> While we were fellow students in Göttingen, we frequently took long walks together during which we discussed—among other things—a matter which was then of great interest to Rejewski. It was the question of what policies the Polish government should adopt with respect to ethnic minorities in Poland. I then thought that Rejewski's strong feelings on this question were based on press articles reflecting the views of [Poland's] National Democratic Party [Stronnictwo Narodowo-Demokratyczne]. However, he was quite tolerant of contrary arguments which I presented to him.—ED.

9. An excellent source on the development of the renowned twentieth-century Polish school of mathematics is *A Half Century of Polish Mathematics*, by Prof. Kazimierz Kuratowski (himself one of its leading lights, who died in Poland on 18 June 1980), 1980. The title is chronologically misleading, as the book is an English version of *A Half Century of Polish Mathematics, 1920-1970*, published in Polish in 1973. An alumnus of the Polish school of mathematics is Stanisław Ulam—student of the above-mentioned Kuratowski and friend of the famous mathematician John von Neumann (*see* note 7, above)—who himself gained celebrity for his brilliant work on U.S. atomic weapons, especially the hydrogen bomb. *See also* S.M. Ulam, *Adventures of a Mathematician.*—ED.

10. This is an arbitrary example fabricated by Rejewski to illustrate the German method of padding out manual ciphers. It is not an example of a double transposition cipher.—ED.

2.

The Enigma

In the summer of 1932, the Poznań cipher office was disbanded. Evidently the course at the Mathematics Institute and the Cipher Bureau branch temporarily active there had been set up in order to find talent and train specialists to work on the new German machine cipher.

On 1 September 1932, Marian Rejewski, who, following his return from Göttingen had taught for two years at Poznań University, and Jerzy Różycki and Henryk Zygalski, who had just graduated, began work as regular employees at the Cipher Bureau in the general staff building (the "Saxon Palace") on Warsaw's Saxon (later Piłsudski, and since World War II—Victory) Square.

If one were to hazard a characterization of the little team, its strength might be said to have stemmed from the diversity of the men's personalities. Marian Rejewski's penetrating mind and skill in formulating questions and advancing far-reaching hypotheses from scarce information were supported by the precision, energy, and perseverance of Henryk Zygalski, who was from Poznań (such qualities being ascribed in Poland to inhabitants of this region), and Jerzy Różycki, born in the Ukraine and educated in Russian and Polish schools, contributed elements of vivid imagination and intuition.

In the latter half of 1932, Polish-German relations were particularly strained. For some years Germany had been waging tariff and economic war against Poland. Revisionist attacks upon Poland's western border did not cease and, in the international forum of the League of Nations, the delegates of the Weimar Republic did all in their power to weaken the position of Poland, which was scornfully termed a Saisonstaat, seasonal state. Much useful information on German diplomatic and military plans was to be gleaned from radio monitoring, provided that methods were developed for solving German codes and ciphers, but that was becoming harder all the time, since the Germans were increasingly using machine ciphers.

The new game on the airways had been opened in 1926 by radio stations of the German Navy. Later, army staffs in Berlin, Königsberg, Breslau, and other military districts had increasingly joined in. Efforts undertaken in the years 1928-32 to solve the new crypto-system had led nowhere.

In their first weeks at the Cipher Bureau, however, the three mathematicians were given a different problem: a four-letter German naval code.

Codes and ciphers of the Kriegsmarine were considered to be particularly resistant to breaking. They had been worked out by experienced specialists who, during the First World War, had been responsible for the security of radio communications with U-boats.[1]

A few months after the German Army's collapse and the armistice in November 1918, the chief of the naval cipher office, Comdr. Martin Braune, had reactivated the cipher service and radio intelligence. The "E" (Entzifferung) branch set to work on solving foreign ciphers.

The Polish cryptologists' work on the four-letter German naval code was at first slow going.[2] Frequencies were drawn up for the code groups, and recurring longer fragments were compared. But there was still no point of entry.

"Suppose we try one of these short messages picked up over the last few days? They look as though they could be training signals."

This casual suggestion made by one of the trio did not seem too promising. The vocabulary in training messages had to be even broader than in routine service messages on naval matters. A code, as opposed to a cipher, involved the substitution of symbol groups for entire words and phrases. The solution of a code, therefore, rested to a greater degree on linguistics and logic than on mathematics.

Finally, from a dozen short messages, one was selected for closer study. It consisted of only six groups, each of four letters. The choice of message had apparently been intuitive: the first group, "YOPY," for some reason seemed more promising than those in the other signals. But the appeal of the message to the cryptologists had not been completely irrational. If the choice had fallen on precisely this signal, then something must have lodged in the men's minds as they had looked over countless four-letter code groups.

At last the reason dawned: the something was the letter Y. It occurred at the beginning of a sufficiently large number of code groups to preclude chance. Were these interrogatory sentences? In German, many interrogatory expressions (Wer? Wo? Wohin? Wann? Welcher?) begin with the same letter, and this regularity could have been duplicated in the code.

Next they noticed that, following this six-group message, another station had broadcast on the same wavelength a short signal of only four groups. Assuming that the first message had been a question, the second might be a reply. And such a short reply would probably be a number.[3]

"Four figures? Maybe it's a year?"

"If so, then what does it refer to? History?"

"Probably."

"What question could a code clerk pose on the spur of the moment that his colleague on another ship or at a naval base in Kiel or Swinemünde could answer with a date? The human mind has a lot of inertia to it. And let's not overrate the historical knowledge of our Kriegsmarine operator, and let's assume that he followed the line of least resistance."

"What can he ask his correspondent in six words, that can be answered with a date? It's probably easier to think of people than of things—of historical figures rather than events...."

"Luther? Goethe? Beethoven? Who starts?"

"What about, 'Wann wurde _____ geboren?' "

"No, that's no good. It has to be six words."

"Then how about, 'Wann wurde Friedrich der Grosse geboren?' "(When was Frederick the Great born?)

Suddenly, everything was simple.

Solution of this six-word signal led to the gradual reconstruction of the entire German naval code used in the second half of 1932. Over the next couple of months, the Poles could read German naval signals almost simultaneously with their addressees. When the next change came, a similar effort had to be undertaken all over again. With every week, however, the number of card files indispensable for a decrypting operation increased. They contained such things as abbreviations of naval terms and cryptonyms for ships, their captains, and ports and naval bases on the Baltic and North Seas. This information was augmented by the reading of a dozen or so signals pertaining to a long cruise to the Indian Ocean by a Kriegsmarine training ship. The messages referred to equipment (Sonnensegel mitnehmen), places (the ship was to call, among other places, at the Ceylonese port of Trincomalee), and so on. Even half a century later,[4] Marian Rejewski remembered that YOPY meant "when," YWIN—"where," BAUG—"and," and KEZL—"cancel the final letter."

After breaking a code or cipher, the mathematicians would not ordinarily read incoming texts.

Every so often, the Germans tried to make things difficult. They departed from alphabetical order, omitted certain letters of the alphabet, or from time to time broadcast bogus code groups.

The breaking of the German naval code could not have been timelier. In late 1932 and early 1933, tensions with Germany were mounting by the week. Earlier, in the summer of 1932, in violation of an existing agreement between Poland and Danzig, the Free City's senate had forbidden Polish naval vessels to accompany British destroyers visiting Danzig. Thereupon the Polish Navy had sent the destroyer O.R.P. (Polish Naval Ship) *Wicher* into the Danzig harbor, with instructions to open fire upon the seat of the Danzig authorities in the event of any insult to the Polish flag. The Free City, despite its support by Berlin, had had to back down.

The endless attempts at undermining Poland's rights by the Danzig authorities and the German government pointed to a likelihood of similar incidents in the future. The breaking of the German naval code allowed the

Poles to follow the movements of the German fleet in the Baltic and thereby avoid surprise.

Even before work on the naval code had been completed, one of the mathematicians received instructions to take up an urgent new problem. "At first I worked alone in the evenings," recalls Marion Rejewski. "Later, when I had obtained the first positive results, [I worked] together with my colleagues J. Różycki and H. Zygalski."[5]

The earliest Polish work on the German machine cipher had begun in 1927-28,[6] soon after the system's introduction by the German Navy and Army.[7] Attempts had been made to solve Enigma by resorting to leading mathematicians and to parapsychology, but not even the clairvoyant Stefan Ossowiecki could help.

Now, apart from mathematical analysis, there was no starting point. Clues had to be sought in the cipher texts, in the endless, meaningless sequences of letters. The frequencies of the letters in all the signals were almost perfectly uniform, hence the usual statistical and linguistic methods would be useless. Nor were there any notable repetitions that might offer a starting point.

The ultimate mathematical solution of Enigma is given at the end of the book. Let us note here but one of the preliminary findings that, taken together with others, helped form a starting point:

> If we write two cipher texts with identical beginnings one below the other, identical letters in the same places will occur on the average twice as often as when we juxtapose in the same manner texts with at least partly different beginnings.
>
> For example:
>
> 1. rfowl dpcai hwbgx empto btvgg infgr ojvdd zluws jurnk ktehm
>   rfowl dnwel scapx oazyb byzrg gcjdx ngdfc mjupi mjvpi tkely
>
> 2. wkxwf ixjwt okisc wgapd rebdw lfvgk wzjub cojhs vuemh oxhon
>   wdxwg gusdt oherk udegl swfpv fgmre ylrmz yarzj mgepw afnug

The above samples of Enigma cipher are, of course, too short to provide statistically valid conclusions, but they may serve as an illustration. Additional clues were obtained by studying the occurrence of a similar correspondence in average German texts. The regularities observed were expressed in mathematical formulae.

The work of Enigma required enormous concentration and at least eighty intercepts collected on the same day, using the same setting on the German cipher devices.

Soon after Rejewski had obtained his first preliminary results, he was given a cipher machine that had been acquired in Germany. It was an Enigma of the commercial type, used by business firms.

Externally, the machine resembled a typewriter, with an additional panel built into the lid. In the panel were twenty-six little circular glass windows bearing, like the keyboard, the letters of the alphabet; on the panel's underside were a corresponding number of glowlamps. Inside the machine was a set of three rotors, or rotating drums, and a "reversing drum" or "reflector," all mounted on one axle and forming part of an intricate system of wiring. The machine could be powered by a battery or by regular current passed through a small transformer.

With every stroke of a key, one or more rotors revolved.[8] At the same time, a glowlamp beneath the panel lit up, illuminating the letter in the window above it. The machine was so designed that when one struck the keys, "typing" a plain text, the letters of the cipher text lit in the appropriate windows and, conversely, when one tapped out a cipher text, the letters illuminated in turn spelled out the plain text. In order to conduct a secret dialog, both parties had to have identical devices set, using various knobs and levers, to the same cipher key.

However, the commercial Enigma solved nothing. At most, it provided a general insight into the machine's construction and operation. The device was produced on much the same principle as a Yale door lock, mere familiarity with which hardly enables one to open another such lock. One still needs the key. Besides that, the military version of the machine would probably have not only totally different wiring, but also additional components.

The cryptologists would have to continue studying the system from the mathematical side, on the basis of the intercepts. One of the divisions of higher mathematics is group theory, concerned among other things with the properties of permutation groups; this division of mathematics would prove especially useful in studying the military Enigma.

NOTES

1. Britain's World War I cryptological successes against the German Navy (Admiralty Room 40) had largely been based on *captured* material. For example, in the autumn of 1914, the British had received a Kriegsmarine codebook that had been taken by Russian divers out of the cruiser *Magdeburg*, grounded in the Baltic. (Some of the *Magdeburg*'s sailors had subsequently been buried in Danzig—now Gdańsk—where, each year, German naval vessels put in for the ceremonial laying of wreaths on their graves. This tradition was to serve the Germans as pretext for sending to Danzig, on 25 August 1939, the battleship *Schleswig-Holstein*, whose salvos, directed against the adjacent Polish peninsular bastion of Westerplatte at dawn on 1 September 1939, were to signal the opening of World War II.) Between 1914 and 1918, British divers had searched about eighty sunken U-boats and other German naval vessels, thereby obtaining cryptographic materials.

Similarly, Marian Rejewski observed about the British and Enigma: "They [the British] got the connections [wirings] of the first five drums from the Poles [in the summer of 1939], and subsequent ones (in the Navy) when they managed to capture a submarine with intact drums. They did not discover any connection in the drums on their own by cryptological means. Their effort [during World War II], to be sure an enormous one, concentrated mainly on recovering keys on the basis of a machine that they already had." Rejewski, "Uwagi do Appendix 1 . . . książki: *British Intelligence in the Second World War* prof. F.H. Hinsley'a, 494." Hereafter referred to as "Uwagi do 'Appendix 1.' "

Jürgen Rohwer comments that just how important the wirings in the rotors were is indicated by the fact that Britain's Bletchley Park, which had an incomparably greater staff of specialists and enjoyed much greater technical resources than Poland's B.S.-4, did not succeed in 1940, or right up through April 1941, in recovering the wiring in the German naval (type "M") Enigma, though Bletchley had, for a year, been freely and currently reading German Army and Air Force Enigma, which worked according to the same basic principles. It was only after the British captured an intact type "M" Enigma, complete with its set of eight rotors, in a naval commando operation in the vicinity of the Lofoten Islands northwest of Norway, that they began to make headway against naval Enigma. Rohwer and Jäckel, *Die Funkaufklärung und ihre Rolle im Zweiten Weltkrieg*, 84-86. Hereafter referred to as *Die Funkaufklärung*.

2. The solution of the naval code is presented after Rejewski, *Wspomnienia z mej pracy w Biurze Szyfrów Oddziału II Sztabu Głównego 1932-1945*, supplemented by oral accounts. Hereafter referred to as *Wspomnienia*.

3. In a code, to avoid error, the figures were usually transmitted as whole words (null, eins, zwei . . .).

4. The last living member of the cryptological trio who vanquished Enigma, Marian Rejewski (born at Bydgoszcz on 16 August 1905), died, apparently of a heart attack, at his home in Warsaw, Poland, on 13 February 1980.

5. Rejewski, *Wspomnienia*.

6. Rejewski, "Uwagi do 'Appendix 1,' " 488.

> [T]he Poles had been working since [at least] 1928 at solving Enigma, but these had not been mathematicians, only one regular Army officer [Capt. Mak-

symilian Ciężki, head of B.S.-4, the Cipher Bureau's German section] and one [civil] engineer [Antoni Palluth]. It was not until October 1932 that one mathematician began working [on it, that is Rejewski], and from the beginning of 1933, three mathematicians [Rejewski, Różycki, and Zygalski].

7. Ibid., 487, 491.

On June 1, 1930, the *final* model of military Enigma was introduced, complete with "plugboard" [commutator]. What was later changed pertained only to changes in accessories such as exchange of the reversing drum [reflector] (November 2, 1937), addition of drums [rotors] IV and V (December 15, 1938), a gradual increase in number of plug connections to as many as 13, ever more frequent changes of daily keys (during the war, every 8 hours), a gradual increase in the number of nets, each using different keys, but above all several changes in *the manner of enciphering the message key*.

. . . The German Navy used the same type of Enigma as the army and air force, except that [the navy's Enigma] earlier [than the army's and the air force's] had five drums [rotors] instead of three. We were unable to read the navy at first due to lack of [cipher] material.

8. Gordon Welchman, Cambridge mathematician who worked on Enigma decryptment at Bletchley Park, north of London, during World War II, explains:

The right-hand wheel ["rotor" or "cipher drum"—ED.] moves on one position every time a key is pressed. When the right-hand wheel reaches one particular position, known as its "turnover position," the left-hand [*sic:* should be "middle"—ED.] wheel also moves ahead one position. In due course the middle and right-hand wheels may both be in their turnover positions, at which time pressing a letter-key will cause all three wheels to move. [Welchman's footnote: "The three wheels would have to go through a cycle of $26 \times 26 \times 26 = 17{,}576$ successive positions before they would return to their starting position. . ."] Each time a key is pressed, encipherment takes place when the wheels have reached their new position.

Welchman, *The Hut Six Story*, 45.

3.

The Break

France and Czechoslovakia, like Poland, threatened by German expansionism, were natural allies for Poland in collecting intelligence on German armaments and war plans. Nevertheless, cooperation among the respective intelligence services depended on many factors, including the foreign policies of the several countries. Notwithstanding their alliance of 19 February 1921, Poland and France had frequent disagreements. The Poles, alarmed at the clandestine rearmament of the Reichswehr, as early as August 1925 proposed to the French the coordination of their intelligence gathering in Germany. Postulated was a demarcation line that would have run roughly through Stettin, Berlin, and Leipzig, with Germany's capital to be operated in by both intelligence services. The French General Staff rejected the proposal, nor would it consent to a Polish military intelligence post in the Rhineland, where the German armaments industry was concentrated. There was disagreement in other fields of intelligence concerning the Weimar Republic and, from 1933 on, concerning the Third Reich.

Particularly valuable in this situation was the initiative taken in 1932 by then Capt. Gustave Bertrand, chief of French radio intelligence.[1] Ignoring the politicians and generals, whom he does not spare sharp criticisms in his book, Bertrand established direct cooperation with his opposite number in the Polish General Staff, principally for work aimed at solving Enigma. He had concluded that, of the possible allies, the Poles had the best chance of success.

In October 1932, French military intelligence could credit itself with a coup. This was the result not of a protracted and intricate intelligence game, but of an extraordinary opportunity. A French intelligence officer had reported that a man had come to him, introducing himself as an employee of the Reichswehr cryptographic agency and offering his intelligence services in return for monetary compensation. In such cases, one may be 90 percent sure that the walk-in is an impostor or an *agent provocateur* and, at first, that is how the man was treated. Still, the reflection prevailed that perhaps he really was an unscrupulous individual who was out for money. This could not be ruled out in advance, even if he was a highly paid employee of the Reichs-wehr's Chi-Stelle (Chiffrierstelle—Cryptographic Agency). A check of French intelligence files dispelled the first doubt. The man was what he said he was, and his brother was a highly placed Reichswehr officer. It was decided to keep up the contact, and further probing was entrusted to Captain Ber-trand, responsible for technical and scientific intelligence and for ciphers. He was a cautious officer, but courageous and capable of making quick decisions. He accepted the German's offer and gave him the assignment of supplying a trial consignment of documents. When the man furnished the samples, they were recognized as being authentic—or as having been superbly fabricated by the Abwehr. The newly recruited agent[2] received the pseudonym "Asche" (German for "ashes") and a sizable advance, and to the next meeting he brought further material. This time, any remaining doubts were dispelled. The documents were certainly authentic, and of great importance to intelli-gence on the Chi-Dienst (Chiffrierdienst, the German cryptographic service).

The first two meetings, on the Dutch- and Belgian-German borders, were followed by further ones. Asche could leave Berlin only on weekends and therefore met with his new principals on Saturdays and Sundays. The mate-rials had to be picked up from him somewhere near the German border, in Holland, Belgium, Denmark, or Czechoslovakia. The meetings were held in a different place each time, and secrecy was carried to an extreme. For example, Captain Bertrand would take a passenger boat to England and from there embark for Denmark, where Asche would be waiting. The sole exception was in August 1938, when Asche was invited to Paris, where, as reward for "services well and loyally performed," he was given an opportunity to sample the great city's nightlife.

An ex-Abwehr officer has volunteered a singular opinion concerning compatriots of his who have fallen into the toil of foreign intelligence services. It is hard to say whether it is flattering or ironic. Even as paid agents, he writes, they are "reliable and capable" (zuverlässig und tüchtig).[3] In this case, it was so. Asche not only supplied the French with everything he could get without incurring exposure, but actually proposed to his German employ-ers ideas for codes and ciphers that would be easier to break. However, that did not advance the solution of the machine cipher, until finally he did gain access to documents on Enigma.

The total intelligence supplied by Asche included the following:

- Materials on the organization of the Reichswehr Cryptographic Agency (ten documents).
- Various codes (Satzbücher) used in the German armed forces: A, B, C, D, E, and Code "Black" (Schwarzes Satzbuch).
- Documents concerning keys to manual ciphers used by staff (Stabschlüs-sel), army signals service (Heeres-Nachrichtenmittelschlüssel), for liaison

between military and civil authorities (Zivchi-Zahlenschlüssel), and with railway police (Bahnschutz), and others.

- Documents on machine ciphers: operating instructions for Enigma (Gebrauchsanweisung, H. Dv. g. 13 and L. Dv. g. 13); keying instructions (Schlüsselanleitung, H. Dv. 14, L. Dv. 14 and M. Dv. Nr. 168); and monthly tables of army keys for December 1931, 1932, 1933, and the first half of 1934.
- Materials on an earlier Engima model of 1930, ten documents in all, including one cipher text with corresponding plain text.

In addition to valuable information on Chi-Stelle operations, Asche also supplied nine obsolete or fake documents, in case someone should propose them to the French.

Unfortunately, Asche never had an opportunity to get his hands on the most important materials: the dossier on Enigma, containing the scheme of the machine's wiring, which reposed in the safe of the chief of the Chi-Stelle.

Theoretically, there still remained the possibility of learning about the machine's works in another way: from persons who worked on its assembly. Bertrand obtained a list of such persons, but this turned out to be a dead end. The various Enigma components were produced at different plants, and final assembly took place in a special workshop of the Enigma firm, each worker being under constant surveillance by an Abwehr officer. Leaving aside the difficulty of reaching these few persons engaged in assembly, it would have been impossible for them to make notes or to smuggle anything out.[4]

On receipt of Asche's Enigma materials, Captain Bertrand contacted the Polish Cipher Bureau and arranged to visit Warsaw. When he arrived to sound out the possibilities of cooperation with the Poles, principally on the German machine cipher, he did not arrive empty-handed. But he could not have expected that the materials he brought would arouse such interest. The Polish Cipher Bureau had been working on the Enigma cipher since 1927, but all they had to go on was intercepts; hence, anything that broadened their knowledge of the machine was welcome indeed.

If Bertrand describes his first meeting with the Poles on 7-11 December 1932 in Warsaw as "historic," this is no mere courtesy. To that time, he says, the French had had no contacts with radio intelligence specialists from the Polish General Staff, excepting the sporadic exchange of German military radio intercepts. "A reliable and durable collaboration (it was in the interest of both parties) was established, which was to be transformed into friendship and, quite unawares, to enter History."[5]

During the Warsaw meeting in December 1932, a division of tasks was established between Bertrand and his Polish opposite number. The head of the Polish Cipher Bureau, which had been thoroughly reorganized a year earlier, was Maj. Gwido Langer.[6] The French were to concentrate on furnishing intelligence from Germany that might facilitate the breaking of the machine cipher, the Poles on theoretical studies of Enigma intercepts. Procedures were set up for exchange of German radio intercepts, radiogoniometric data, and other intelligence. It was also decided to establish closer ties with the corresponding unit of the Czechoslovak General Staff, thereby creating a triple entente of cryptological services. (Bertrand would go to Prague on the matter.) Captain Bertrand was to use the pseudonym "Bolek" (the diminutive of the Polish name Bolesław), Major Langer—"Luc" (French for "Luke"), and the Czechoslovak officer—"Raoul." In the later thirties, the B-L-R triangle would be active in practice only on the Bolek-Luc line, due chiefly to the unsatisfactory Polish-Czech relations prevailing at that time.[7]

Bertrand gives high marks to the Warsaw Cipher Bureau and its personnel. In contrast to the French staff, the Poles were already employing outstanding mathematicians who had been properly trained in cryptology on the German ciphers.

Such, in barest outline, was the situation in Polish-French collaboration on German ciphers at the end of 1932. The foregoing, of course, refers to relations between the directors of the two cryptological agencies, who were responsible for organizing that cooperation. The matter presented itself differently to the actual executors of the Polish-French plans. The principle of strict secrecy and compartmentalization meant that even the most trusted radio intelligence and decryptment workers learned only as much as was indispensable to their own work about the materials supplied to them. The three mathematician-cryptologists who were the brains of the German-cipher office knew nothing of the Polish-French contacts or of the origin of the information supplied to them in the course of their work on Enigma, including the German documents which they received in December 1932.[8]

The final fragment in the story of Enigma's theoretical solution can now be reconstructed from Polish and French accounts that were written independently, but that are strikingly in accord on the salient points. According to Polish cryptologist Marian Rejewski, he received four documents: operating instructions (Gebrauchsanweisung) for the cipher machine, keying instructions (Schlüsselanleitung), and obsolete tables of daily keys (instructions for setting the machine in its starting position) for September and October 1932.[9] According to Bertrand, the materials passed to the Poles also contained further key tables and an Enigma cipher text with corresponding plain text.

The difference is not a crucial one since, in any case, the materials by themselves would not have afforded the slightest chance of vanquishing Enigma—particularly of reconstructing the wiring and components. Nor did they provide any starting point for elaborating a reliable system for finding the variable keys, which could be recovered only on the basis of German intercepts.

Nevertheless, it would be incorrect to conclude that these intelligence materials played no significant role in the studies on Enigma. In conjunction with the mathematical analysis that had already been carried out on intercepts, they gave new momentum to the work, permitting rapid verification of hypotheses and bringing the ultimate result closer. The French assist was particularly valuable as it came at just the right moment, when the work had entered its decisive final phase.

Particularly helpful was a photocopy of the operating instructions to the E-Eins cipher machine. Superficial inspection of the instructions sufficed to show that this was the military version of Enigma. The document was signed by Lt. Col. Erich Fellgiebel,[10] later general and chief of Wehrmacht signals.

The E-Eins, as was evident from Fellgiebel's instructions, differed fundamentally from the commercial Enigma. The most important difference was the presence of a commutator, a kind of plugboard with twenty-six sockets and several plug connections,[11] located behind a special lid in the lower part of the machine. The sockets were not numbered, but one could guess that the numbering began with the one marked with a concave dot.

It was a complicated business setting the machine to the key, which comprised several elements that changed periodically.[12] The probability of accidentally striking upon the setting was practically nil. After setting the main part of the key, the operator closed the metal lid and brought the Enigma to the basic position. Only then did he type out on the keyboard his own key, different for each message.

The instructions brought by Bertrand gave a general idea of Enigma's appearance and operating principles but said nothing about its inner structure: about the electrical connections within the rotors, the variable contacts, or the other components that, all together, raised the number of possible combinations to astronomical magnitudes.[13] Yet solution of Enigma depended on the detailed reconstruction of absolutely all these elements; with but one of them missing, the entire effort would have been in vain.

Characteristic of the work on Enigma was the linking of precise mathematical analysis with the "intuitive" reconstruction of individual parts. Useful in this regard—trite as it may sound—was a knowledge of the German mentality. It was thanks to this that one of the important parts, the "entry ring" (Eintrittswalze), of the sight-unseen military Enigma was solved.

Rejewski had found that in the commercial Enigma the letters of the alphabet were represented on the circumference of the entry ring in the same order in which they appeared on a German typewriter keyboard. What could be their order in the entry ring of the *military* Enigma? Since both models had their keyboards ordered the same way, Rejewski assumed the military model had its entry ring organized the same way as the commercial model. This assumption cost him much futile labor and nearly led to suspension of work on Enigma. Finally, in December 1932 or the first days of 1933, he took a wild guess: since the keyboard wasn't wired to the entry drum in keyboard sequence, maybe the wiring was in alphabetical order? The hypothesis proved correct: from his pencil, "as by magic, began to issue numbers designating the connections in rotor N," the right-hand rotor that turned one twenty-sixth of a revolution each time a key was depressed. The German fondness for Ordnung, order, had triumphed again!

An erroneous view has been reiterated in numerous publications that the breaking of Enigma was a one-time feat, following which the cryptologists could rest on their laurels. This necessitates the following observation.

Solution of the Enigma system, which took about four months altogether, involved two distinct matters:

First, the theoretical reconstruction of the cipher device itself. The most important matter was determining Enigma's wiring. The cryptologists first discovered the function of the reflector, or "reversing drum" (Umkehrwalze), then, step by step, reconstructed all the connections in the machine, whose most essential components were a system of rotors (Chiffrierwalzen) revolving about a common axle, and the commutator (Steckerverbindungen) with its plug connections. This enabled the Poles to build doubles of Enigma that made it possible to read German ciphers, assuming that one could find the keys, that is, the machine's initial settings prior to encipherment of a message.

Second, the elaboration of methods for reconstructing the Enigma keys exclusively on the basis of the intercepts that were supplied daily by monitoring stations.

Both these basic problems, in all their many aspects, were solved theoretically and practically by the trio of mathematicians at B.S.-4, the Cipher Bureau's German section, by twenty-seven-year-old Marian Rejewski, twenty-five-year-old Henryk Zygalski, and twenty-three-year-old Jerzy Różycki. General Bertrand writes:

> As for the Polish cryptologists, to them alone belongs all the credit and all the glory for having successfully carried through this incredible technical feat, thanks to their knowledge and their perseverance, unequalled in any country in the world.
> They overcame difficulties that the Germans had thought to be "insurmountable," of which it is hard to give an idea....[14]

The chief breakthrough came in the final days of December 1932. The practical reading of messages began during the second ten days of January. Success, once again, could not have been more timely. Just under way in Germany was the Nazi campaign that on 30 January 1933 would deliver power into Hitler's hands. Neither the French nor the British, as it later turned out, despite their long-standing traditions of black chambers with experienced cryptological teams and large financial outlays, managed to solve the German cipher system.

NOTES

1. In the twenties, French radio intelligence had been decentralized. Solution of foreign ciphers and codes (chiefly German and Italian) had been the business of a cryptology department in the general staff, and radio monitoring had been conducted by the intelligence service, Service de Renseignement, or S.R. At the end of 1930, decrypting was turned over to S.R., creating a section "D" (Decryptement), of which Bertrand became chief; later he took over all radio intelligence.

2. He has been identified by David Kahn as Hans-Thilo Schmidt. (According to other versions, Asche's real name was different, and the pseudonym Asche was the German phonetic transcription of the French pronunciation of his actual initials, H.E.: "Ash-eh.")

Further information about Hans-Thilo Schmidt and his putative high-ranking brother is provided in the following notes, evidently by French Gen. P. Renauld, which were published in the *Bulletin Trimestriel de l'Association des Amis de l'École Supérieure de Guerre.*

Concerning the German Hans-Thilo Schmidt (pseudonym "Asché") who in 1931 delivered to Major Bertrand, of the French S.R., documents on the Enigma cipher machine, we have indicated (B.78 [*Bulletin* no. 78, *2ᵉ trimestre 1978*] - p. 53) that he seems to have been a brother of Gen. Rudolf Schmidt. Information obtained recently on the career of Rudolf Schmidt reinforces this hypothesis.

Born on 12 May 1886 in Berlin, he [General Schmidt] is in 1914 a lieutenant in telegraph battalion no. 5, in 1918 at the headquarters of the 4th Army, next at the Inspectorate of Signals, then in 1924 major in a company of signals battalion no. 4.

In 1925, he is director (Leiter) of the Cipher Bureau (Chiffrierstelle). In 1928 he attends the Lehrgang für Führergehilfe ["course for assistant directors"], camouflage for the banned Kriegsakademie [War Academy], then as a lieutenant-colonel becomes chief of the headquarters of the Inspectorate of Signals. Appointed a colonel, he takes command on 1 December 1933 of the Kriegsakademie that has been set up by Hitler.

After having commanded IR 13 he becomes Oberquartiermeister III (Organization and technical matters) at OKH [Supreme Command of the Army]; named a major-general on 1 December 1936, he takes command of the 1st Pz. Div. at Weimar.

General-Leutnant as of 1 June 1938, he commands on 1 February 1940 the XXXIX AK [Army Corps] which is to be part of Guderian's group in June 1940. General der Panzer Truppen on 1 June, he will become the following year, on the Eastern front, commander of the 2d Army, then on 26 December 1941 commander of the 2d PZ Army in place of Guderian, dismissed by Hitler.

On 10 July 1943 he is relieved of command of the 2d PZ Army [and], pensioned off on 30 September retires to Weimar, his garrison of 1939, and dies at Krefeld on 1 April 1955.

This officer of importance had thus been Director of the Chistelle, where he had engaged Hans-Thilo, who in 1931 had delivered to Major Bertrand documents relating to Enigma; he had commanded the Kriegsakademie, then had been at OKH the deputy chief for "Organization and technical matters" at the time that Hans-Thilo had conveyed to Captain [Henri] Navarre [of French intelligence] information on the courses and training at the Kriegsakademie and on the organization of the German armed forces. He had commanded a Panzerdivision, as Bertrand indicates for the brother of "Asché." The latter, denounced by Lemoine [a French agent who had been present at the meetings with Asché], had been shot in Berlin in July 1943 [Renauld's footnote 1: "and not in October as I erroneously state in Bulletin 78, page 53"]. General Oberst [Colonel General] Rudolf Schmidt had been relieved of his command on 10 July 1943 at the height of the Kursk offensive and while fearing a Russian counter-offensive against the Orel salient held by his 2d PZ Army.

Certain accounts suggest that Colonel General Schmidt, before being pensioned off on 30 September 1943 at the age of 57, a victim of the acts of a wayward brother, had been hailed before the military High Tribunal of the Reich.

A. The work *"Heeres einleitung 1939"* [Introduction to the Army 1939] gives the order of battle of the [German] Army [Heer] prior to mobilization; General von Kurowski, who had it published in 1954 by Verlag Podzun at Bad Nauheim, has indicated in a note, page 140, that Rudolf Schmidt had been seized and carried away forcibly in 1947 at Weimar by the Russians. He was repatriated in 1955 together with other officer prisoners and then retired at Krefeld. —ED.

3. Reile, *Geheime Ostfront.*

4. Bertrand, *Enigma*, 32ff.

5. Ibid., 37. From 1932 to the outbreak of World War II, Bertrand visited Warsaw thirteen times, the last time in July 1939. Representatives of the Polish Cipher Bureau went to France an equal number of times.

6. The Cipher Bureau, formed in mid-1931 by merger of the Radio Intelligence Office (Referat Radiowywiadu) and the Polish-Cipher Office (Referat Szyfrów Własnych), between 1932 and 1936 took over additional responsibilities, such as organizing radio communication between military intelligence posts in Poland and abroad and radio counterintelligence (mobile radioloca-tion-and-monitoring stations for uncovering the transmitters of foreign intelligence networks and fifth columnists on Polish soil). Major Langer, after a tour of duty as chief of staff of the First Infantry Division, on 15 January 1929 became head of the Radio Intelligence Office, and subsequently of the Cipher Bureau.

7. Close Polish-Czech cooperation in radio intelligence against Germany lasted until 1936. On the circumstances of its rupture, see Kozaczuk, *Bitwa o tajemnice*, 237-40.

8. They learned of the documents' French provenance only during World War II, in 1940.

9. "I received no other documents, including any text given both in plain and in cipher, which would have been of no use to me anyway." Rejewski, "Uwagi do 'Appendix 1,' " 488.

10. Erich Fellgiebel, 1886-1944: during World War I a signals officer, in the postwar Reichswehr held staff posts including director of signals and cryptography, in 1934 promoted to colonel and appointed inspector of signals in the Army High Command (In. 7 OKH) and later commander of the signal corps, in 1938 a major general, in 1940 general of signal corps, associated with the military conspirators who made the abortive bomb attempt on Hitler's life 20 July 1944, arrested the same day, on 8 August sentenced to death, executed 4 September 1944.

11. The plug connections, which could number up to a total of thirteen, served to interconnect in pairs the sockets corresponding to given letters of the alphabet, and thus interchange ("commu-tate") those letters in the course of encipherment.—ED.

12. The full Enigma key included the sequence (and, later, also selection from a larger number) of the rotors in the machine, the settings of the rotors' adjustable rings, the connections in the commutator, and the individual message key given at the commencement of a message.—ED.

13. The number of possible cipher combinations with the type "W" (Wehrmacht) Enigma, considering only the commutator, which initially exchanged six pairs of letters, came to 100,391, 791,500; considering only the reflector ("reversing drum"), 7,905,853,580,625; considering only each rotor ("cipher drum"), 403,291,461,126,605,635,584,000,000. To indicate Enigma's full

potential, the last figure would have to be raised to the third power and multiplied by the two previous figures, giving 5×10^{103} possible cipher combinations. Hence the great confidence of the German cipher-machine experts in the unbreakability of their system.

Rejewski observes:

> "[Hinsley], to be sure, says how many possibilities there are of setting the machine ["one hundred and fifty million million million," or 1.5×10^{20}], but he does not say how many possibilities there are for the internal connections within the drums. Given three drums, those possibilities come to 500 million million million... million [the word "million" being written a total of 15 times—and the whole number thus being 5×10^{92}, and that after all is the most important matter, because it is synonymous with reconstruction of the machine. More generally, I have noticed that all the British publications avoid this very question, as though taking it for granted that the connections within the drums could have been obtained only by the theft, capture, or otherwise illicit acquisition of the machine."

Rejewski, "Uwagi do 'Appendix 1,' " 487.

14. Bertrand, *Enigma*, 61.

Two mathematicians, I.J. Good (who worked with Alan Turing during World War II) and Cipher A. Deavours, wrote afterwords to an (inadequate) English translation of Rejewski's (title mistranslated) "How Polish Mathematicians Deciphered the Enigma." (A competent translation of the paper appears in this book as Appendix D.) Deavours comments (229, 232):

> No doubt practitioners of group theory should introduce this property of permutations [exploited by Rejewski] to students as "the theorem that won World War II." [S]olving the Enigma traffic via statistical analysis, table lookups, or mechanical computation (the Poles used all these methods) was an immense undertaking—one that no other country was up to at that period of history. At the same time Rejewski and his compatriots were busting Enigma traffic on an ongoing basis, the only cryptanalytic technique available [outside Poland] was a method known as "cliques on the rods" to the British or the "baton" method to the French. This technique was perfected during the Spanish Civil War and was really useful only for the nonplugboard model of the Enigma that was used in that conflict.

I.J. Good writes (232): "Because of the security principle of the 'need to know' I was not aware, during the war, of the details of the Polish work, although I knew they had made a contribution to the breaking of the Enigma. It was therefore an eye-opener for me when I read Rejewski's paper."

4.

The Double

At the beginning of February 1933, the Cipher Bureau commissioned the AVA Radio Manufacturing Company (Wytwórnia Radiotechniczna AVA) at 34 New World Street (ulica Nowy Świat 34) in Warsaw to build fifteen doubles of the military Enigma.[1] The duplicates were to be made up of the same components and, by virtue of identical wiring, to work in the same way as the original military machine known to German cipher personnel as Schlüsselmaschine E-Eins.

In the hot political period just before the Nazi takeover in Germany, the effort that had been invested in the cracking of Enigma had to be made to pay off quickly. The cryptologists had only one machine, and it was not the military but the commercial model, lacking a commutator. Theoretically, it was unsuitable for decrypting military signals. However, a way was found to read Enigma ciphers pending delivery by AVA of the military doubles. Caps were fitted onto the typing keys, and the upper part of the machine was altered, the illuminated windows being covered with cellophane on which the letters were written in the appropriate order.

Construction of the first batch of Enigmas at AVA did not proceed altogether without a hitch. When the first two devices were delivered and cipher text was put through them, the result was anything but German. What emerged resembled some exotic Polynesian language abounding in vowels and diphthongs.

The cause, as the mathematicians soon discovered, was fairly ordinary. In passing the order on to AVA, their superiors had forgotten about the caps, which were slipped over the keys only for reading signals. This completely altered the order of internal connections in the first Polish-made doubles. Before long the defect was remedied, and reading of the accumulated ciphers proceeded on an assembly line basis. Meanwhile, AVA built further Enigmas, reliable and even more convenient in use than the German prototype.

The small AVA firm, which applied technology that was modern for its time, had for a couple of years been filling commissions for the general staff, especially for the Cipher Bureau. AVA had come into being in 1929-30 on the initiative of persons who in subsequent years were to be associated with the German-cipher office.

One of AVA's directors, Edward Fokczyński, a cipher machine specialist, was a classic autodidact, his formal education not having extended beyond four grades of primary school in Pabianice, where he had worked as a journeyman locksmith. In 1913 he had moved to Łódź, where he had gotten a job in the electrical engineering firm of Knapik and Company. In 1919 he had enlisted in the Polish Army, serving in a radio battalion and later in Field Wireless Station Number Four. Mustered out in 1922, he worked for a couple of years as a technician in the infant Polish broadcasting industry. "Very bright and capable. Intelligent, somewhat phlegmatic. . . extremely gifted in radio work. . . independent, requires absolutely no supervision": phrases like these recurred in appraisals of him. In 1927 he opened a small radio work-shop in a single cramped room. Sporadically he received orders from the Cipher Bureau: Major Ciężki, director of its German section, had known him since his army years. During 1929-32, Fokczyński's modest shop on New World Street, Warsaw's most elegant thoroughfare, ten minutes' walk from the General Staff Building, was transformed into AVA, a specialized manu-facturing firm, which subsequently moved to newly built facilities in southern Warsaw's Mokotów district.

All four of AVA's directors were unusual men. A second founder of AVA was Antoni Palluth, a civil engineer by education and a full-time employee of the Cipher Bureau, where in the late twenties he worked on German ciphers (he had also lectured in the Poznań cryptology course). During the thirties he did design work at AVA. Finally, Ludomir Danilewicz and his brother Leonard were, when the company was being formed, polytechnic students and short-wave hams. The call signal of their ham radio station later gave rise to the company's name. The germ of AVA, recalls Leonard Danilewicz,[2]

> came into being while I was in school, when T[adeusz] Heftman[3] and I set up an amateur radio club in the eleventh grade at Stanisław Staszic High School, in [the coal-district city of] Sosnowiec in 1924. My brother, who was then a student in the electrical department at the Warsaw Polytechnic, supported us in our endeavors. A visit to Sosnowiec, in 1924, by Lt. Groszkowski[4] and Lt. Noworolski, who gave a lecture on radio with a demonstration receiver, settled our future. Our little group was invited by Lt. Groszkowski to Warsaw, where we visited the radio station at the Citadel,[5] C.B.O. [Centralne Biuro Operacyjne—the Central Operational Bureau], and the radio station of the Ministry of Posts and Telegraphs near Wawrzyszew; also the modest radio laboratory of the Warsaw Polytechnic, which seemed to us a storehouse of treasures.
>
> During 1925, our mania deepened; we turned out primitive two-tube receivers which we sold to the unwary. In spite of these distractions, Heftman and I graduated from high school and naturally entered the Warsaw Polytechnic. In the period 1925-27, there collected around the only publication devoted to radio a group of "radiots" who sought

something more than the official knowledge of those times had to offer. The editors and publishers of this magazine (*Radio-amator* [The Radio Ham]), the Odyniec brothers, supplied much-desired information on the short-wave movement, its worldwide organization, the technology, equipment, etc.

They also initiated the registration of short-wave operators and the assignment of callsigns. My brother and I had a common callsign, "TPAV," and A. Palluth—"TPVA." From the combination of these signs arose the trademark "AVA." Using this name, in 1928, even before the establishment of the firm, we undertook to produce two short-wave transmitting-receiving radio stations for the local railroad managements in Warsaw and Lwów. The enterprise was premature both for the railroad and for us, and so despite the successful establishment of communication between the local managements, it died a natural death.

[After the official formation of AVA] difficulties began from the first day, since the firm's assets comprised: compensation in the event of giving up our lease, 5,000 *złotych* [about $1,000 at that time]; machines and tools, 2,000 *złotych*; cash in the till, zero. Fortunately, we did not need to draw any profits from the firm, since all four of us had other jobs. Shortly the Cipher Bureau came to our rescue with an order for eight very primitive 10-watt short-wave radio stations, which became the embryo of Section II's future radio network. In addition, we had orders for press receivers from Agencja Express and were winning a client in the person of Prof. Lugeon, director of W.I.M. [Warsaw Meteorological Institute], for whom we built a device of his own design called an *atmoradiograf* that picked up and registered disturbances in the atmosphere. This was the embryo of future radio astronomy, though at the time neither the inventor nor we were aware of it.

We also produced low-frequency transformers, rotary condensers, and later radio receivers in short series. In 1929 we proposed to the General Staff a device of my design for secret radio telegraphy which fortunately did not win acceptance, as it was a truly barbaric idea consisting in constant changes of transmitter frequency. The commission did, however, see fit to grant me 5,000 *złotych* for executing a model and as encouragement to further work.

Our firm made a very good showing in the short-wave exhibition on [Warsaw's historic] Senator Street (ulica Senatorska) in 1930. At great effort and financial sacrifice we displayed a 50-watt radio transmitter and receiver, designed by my brother and very avant-garde. The total working personnel of the firm at that time consisted of the four co-owners and two apprentices. Our displays inspired great interest, and as a result we received orders for six sets from the Cipher Bureau and two sets from the Navy, which were to be adapted to seafaring conditions and installed on the [two new destroyers] *Wicher* [*Gale*, commissioned 1930] and *Burza* [*Storm*, commissioned 1932]. . . . Section II's radio communications were completely on the Cipher Bureau's responsibility. The Cipher Bureau entrusted the design and execution of all the equipment, along with its later modifications, to our firm. Since we were operating mostly in little-known fields and were doing work that had no precedent, precise cost estimates were virtually impossible . . . Therefore we had an inspector from the Cipher Bureau who watched over both the quality of the equipment and the costs. On completion of the work a reckoning would be made, and the firm would get 15 percent over costs as profit. The results showed this [cost-plus] system to be advantageous for both parties, since due to good organization our overall costs were low, and overhead negligible. Thus the [General] Staff had an inexpensive product, and we had a lot of worries off our minds.

AVA was one of the first industrial plants in Poland to have its production process put on a scientific basis when in 1932 Stanisław Guzicki,[6] one of the pioneers in organization science,[7] was hired by the company. Thus engineer Guzicki, although he was associated with the Communist movement, came to be employed at an industrial establishment that was supervised by the military and engaged in secret projects. In speaking for the first time with the director of the Cipher Bureau, Maj. Gwido Langer, the engineer had himself brought attention to his leftist views which, in the eyes of the major's superiors, might disqualify him. Undismayed, Langer had answered: "I know that they want to pin a Red label on you, but that is of no concern to me. I need an expert to organize the work. If you're for a planned economy and industrialization, so much the better. You'll have a chance to show what you can do."[8] No doubt it will sound apocryphal but, as Professor Guzicki has told it,[9] he was advised at the Cipher Bureau to subscribe for a time to National Democratic[10] periodicals in order to dispel the suspicions of the police, whose written permission was necessary for employment.

When in January 1933 the mathematicians had solved Enigma, AVA[11] was already so far developed that in a very short time it was able to produce a double of the complicated machine. Several Polish Enigmas were built—by mid-1934, over a dozen.

A few weeks after the first Enigma doubles had been constructed, the cryptologists received a series of German military signals whose bearings indicated them to be correspondence between districts number 1 in Königsberg and number 2 in Stettin. Methods of reading that had been reliable until then proved useless. Signals enciphered on the mysterious machine continued to come in for several weeks, then vanished as suddenly as they had appeared. This was merely another in the series of Enigma mutants, but the Germans had named it E-Zwo (Enigma II).[12] Some time later, it was determined to be an Enigma equipped with eight rotors and an automatic writing device. It had been used only by the highest military commands and had proven unreliable. E-Zwo's works often jammed and required complicated repairs. This was probably why after several weeks it had been withdrawn from use.

In late February 1933 the world learned about the burning of the Reichstag and about the mounting terror being directed against leftists and others who refused to submit to Hitler's new regime. In this period the Warsaw Cipher Bureau was augmented with a hastily trained six-person team of deciphering operators. Work proceeded around the clock, in three shifts. Still there were backlogs, and thought had to be given to mechanizing certain tasks.

Recovery of the settings (starting positions) and keys in the various Enigma nets was by the method of elimination. First, using the grill method, the connections in the commutator would be found (there were 100,391,791, 500 different possibilities). During the first months after Enigma's solution, further elements of the key were obtained manually, by turning the metal rotors as many as 17,576 ways—there being that many (26^3) possible settings for each of the six possible sequences of the three rotors. This was a tedious, time-consuming job and, on account of the work's secrecy, the mathematicians could not delegate it to the Cipher Bureau's technical personnel. In their haste the men would scrape their fingers raw and bloody.

At first the Germans changed the commutator connections in the Enigma infrequently, once a quarter. In 1934, when they began changing them monthly, later daily, and finally every eight hours, thought had to be given to other means of finding the commutator connections.

The situation was vastly improved when Rejewski invented what he dubbed the cyclometer. This was a device, based on two sets of Enigma rotors linked together electrically, that served to determine the length and number of cycles in the "characteristic" for each position of Enigma's rotors. The cyclometer enabled the cryptologists to set up a catalog of characteristics encompassing the 105,456, or 6×26^3, possible settings of the rotors. After that, comparison of intercepts with the catalog of characteristics gave much faster recovery of the keys. Among other things, the cyclometer "annihilated" the connections in the commutator, which constituted one of Enigma's strong points.

Other inventions included the clock, devised by Jerzy Różycki, which made it possible in certain cases to determine which rotor was at the far right side on a given day in a given Enigma net.[13]

During the first year and a half after Hitler's takeover, Germany buzzed like a beehive. In addition to numerous military transmitters, new radio stations were going on the air all the time at the staffs of Ernst Roehm's two-and-a-half-million-strong brown-shirted S.A. (Sturmabteilung, or Storm Troops) and Heinrich Himmler's black-shirted S.S. (Schutzstaffel, originally Hitler's elite bodyguard). Separate radio nets were also set up by the Gestapo (Geheime Staatspolizei, or Secret State Police, founded in 1933, and headed until 1936 by Hermann Goering) and the S.D. (Sicherheitsdienst, or Security Service), the Nazi party's political intelligence organization.

In late June 1934, the three young mathematicians, although they did not ordinarily read entire signals but only broke the keys, experienced some exciting moments. As they were decrypting the beginning of a message, reading: "To all commandants of airfields throughout Germany," they surmised that this was a dramatic communication heralding important events. Further on, the signal ordered the "apprehension and transportation to Berlin, alive or dead, of Oberfuehrer Karl Ernst, adjutant to S.A. chief of staff Roehm."

Hitler, backed by Gestapo chief Goering and S.S. chief Himmler, had just embarked on his bloody showdown with rivals within the Nazi party. On June 30 and over the next several days S.S. and Gestapo bullets killed the powerful Roehm, virtually all his staff, and several hundred S.A. functionaries. The occasion was also taken to brutally murder many politicians and members of opposition parties, including the former Reich chancellor Gen. Kurt von Schleicher and former intelligence chief Gen. Ferdinand von Bredow.

Succeeding reports from Germany spoke of further acts of terror, intensive armament, and clandestine build-up of the army. In the first days of August 1934, with the death of President Hindenburg and the Wehrmacht's swearing loyalty to Hitler as the nation's Fuehrer and head of state, power passed completely into the hands of the criminal dictator and his party.

Thanks to the solution of Enigma, the Cipher Bureau in Warsaw could read simultaneously with German addressees many of the messages that were being transmitted in these tense hours of Roehm's Putsch and the "Night of the Long Knives."

While dramatic events were taking place in Germany, the mass of intercepts contained some messages that resisted solution. They resembled the language of Enigma, but when hitherto reliable methods were applied to them the result was an incomprehensible babble. After several unsuccessful tries, it was decided to set this cipher aside for the time being. It was taken up again a month later, when the situation in Germany had simmered down.

The cryptologists split the tasks up among themselves, and results did not require a long wait. The cipher was found to be based on a hitherto unknown system of keys. In addition, Ueberschlüsselung (superencipherment) had been used: before encipherment, the texts had been coded. First to be solved were the openings of these messages, many of which began with the stock phrase, Hoeherer S.S. Fuehrer (Higher S.S. Commander). These proved to be orders broadcast to S.S. and S.D. units from Himmler's Berlin headquarters. Though the cryptography was complex, the primitive vocabulary made the cryptologists' work easier: it was mostly police jargon concerning arrests, surveillance, trials, and sentences. In some dispatches the names of cities in which the terror was known to have reached a particular pitch recurred. These were the great industrial centers in the Rhineland, as well as Hamburg, Rostock, and other port cities. Solution of this system, which was given the working name "S.D. cipher," was made possible by the recurring expressions.

The S.D. correspondence pertained not only to internal affairs. A message later intercepted reported that certain foreign dignitaries would not in the opinion of the Nazis be "insensitive to the sound of money, and might even agree to collaborate." A minister of a western country was mentioned by name.[14] Did the Polish General Staff or Ministry of Foreign Affairs use this information, and if so, how? The mathematicians never found out.

Received with mixed feelings by them, as it was by the majority of the Polish people, was the Polish-German Declaration of Nonaggression of 26 January 1934, which generated much domestic and international confusion. It inspired suspicions, especially in the French and the Soviets. The Russians suspected that there might be secret codicils to the declaration in which the two parties had agreed to combine against Russia. To assuage the Soviets, Polish Minister of Foreign Affairs Józef Beck went to Moscow in February 1934, between the signing and the ratification of the Polish-German declaration—the first official visit by a western foreign minister to Moscow since the Soviet Revolution. In France, aside from politicians genuinely concerned over a loosening of the Polish-French alliance, there were those who saw Poland merely as a pawn to be used for keeping Germany in check or as a *cordon sanitaire* against the Soviet Union. Moreover, part of the French and British press, inspired and paid by German intelligence, stirred up anti-Polish feeling. This, of course, was grist for the mill of German demands for revision of that country's borders with Poland and France.[15]

In addition to ciphers of the German Army (Heer) and the S.D., the B.S.-4 cryptological office in Warsaw solved, as has been mentioned, codes and ciphers of the German Navy. The Kriegsmarine employed three kinds of Enigma keys: operational (Marineschlüssel), staff (Stabschlüssel), and admirals' (Admiralsschlüssel). The latter, exceptionally complex key resisted breaking for a long time. Only certain messages of the German Navy were read at B.S.-4, due to limited Cipher Bureau personnel and because knowledge of army and air force correspondence was deemed more important to the national defense.[16]

NOTES

1. Rejewski, "Uwagi do 'Appendix 1,' " 488. Rejewski notes:

As soon as I had gotten the connections [wiring] in the drums [rotors], the AVA factory received an order to make a dozen or so copies of the military machine, based on the commercial-model machine bought considerably earlier, on photographs of the military machine to be found in the Gebrauchsanweisung document supplied by Bertrand, and on the connections in the drums given by me on a scrap of paper.

2. Danilewicz, *Memoirs About the Founding of the AVA Radio Manufacturing Company.* Manuscript in Marian Rejewski's files.

3. Later, chief engineer at AVA. During World War II, he was director of the Polish Military Radio Works (Polski Wojskowy Warsztat Radiowy) in Great Britain, which, among other things, produced miniature radio transmitters for use by Allied intelligence and sabotage groups acting in countries occupied by Germany.

4. Janusz Groszkowski (born 1898), from 1929 professor of electronics at the Warsaw Polytechnic, from 1952 a member, and in 1962-71 president, of the exclusive Polish Academy of Sciences. During World War II, he analyzed the radio guidance system of the German V-2 rockets, and his vital information was sent to the Allies in London. (*See* notes, chapter 13.)

5. A fortress in Warsaw built in 1832-34, following suppression of the Polish Uprising of 1830-31, by the Czarist Russian army. The list of Poles imprisoned and/or executed there up through World War I reads like a "Who's Who" of eminent patriots and revolutionaries and includes persons as diverse as Romuald Traugutt, leader of the 1863 Uprising against Czarist Russia; Jarosław Dąbrowski, later military head of the 1871 Paris Commune; Feliks Dzierżyński, a leader of the Soviet Revolution of 1917 who founded the Cheka secret police; Rosa Luxemburg, and Józef Piłsudski.—ED.

6. Stanisław Guzicki (1894-1975): during World War II, a member of the resistance and the Polish Workers' Party (Polska Partia Robotnicza, a Communist party); after the war, professor at the Warsaw Polytechnic.

7. A field generally cognate with what is now known by such more recent names as systems management, operations analysis, cost-effectiveness analysis, administration, and so on. Another Polish pioneer in this field was Prof. Karol Adamiecki (1866-1933) of the Warsaw Polytechnic. Both Guzicki and Adamiecki published papers in *Przegląd organizacji* (Organization Review: a Monthly on the Organization and Administration of Economic Life; a Publication of the Scientific Organization Institute, Warsaw), founded, evidently, in 1926.—ED.

8. In view of comparisons that have been drawn between the secret of Enigma decryptment by the Allies in World War II and the secret of the atom bomb, for instance by David Kahn (who, in the *New York Times Book Review* of 29 December 1974 called the former "the greatest secret of World War II after the atom bomb"), it may be of interest to note that the military head of the Manhattan Project, Gen. Leslie Groves, like Lt. Col. Gwido Langer pressed to find competent specialists to carry out his project, like Langer overlooked the earlier Communist flirtations of some of his personnel. See Davis, *Lawrence and Oppenheimer.*

Actually, of these two great secrets of World War II, Enigma decryptment was not only much less expensive and kept much longer—indeed, much longer than necessary—but was incomparably the more important to the conduct of the war, since it played a crucial role throughout the duration, whereas the atom bomb merely put the seal on the foregone conclusion. It may also be argued that the mirror image of the Enigma secret's positive importance in the Second World War (Eisenhower termed it "decisive") has been the negative effect of its too-long-continued secrecy since the war—a secrecy that has made Allied victory seem *too much* a foregone conclusion and consequently has distorted the United States's and western Europe's perceptions of their power to determine more recent world history. Thus, Winterbotham warns,

> Let no one be fooled by the spate of television films and propaganda which has made the war seem like some great triumphant epic. It was, in fact, a very narrow shave, and the reader may like to ponder. . . whether or not we might have won had we not had Ultra.

Similarly, he cautions "all those who have been brought up in the belief that the Allied victory over the Fascist powers was accomplished with some ease plus the will of Allah. . . ." Winterbotham, *The Ultra Secret*, chapter 3 and Conclusion.—ED.

9. Guzicki, 16 January 1975, oral account.

10. National Democracy (Narodowa Demokracja) was a right-wing political party.—ED.

11. In later years known as Wytwórnia Radiotechniczna AVA, Spółka z ograniczoną odpowiedzialnością (AVA Radio Manufacturing, a Limited Liability Company), located at ulica Stępińska 25, Warsaw.

12. The name was determined by breaking an emergency manual cipher and reading the brief message: "Enigma II out of service" (E-Zwo ausser Betrieb).

13. According to Col. Tadeusz Lisicki the device's name, "clock,"

> comes from an analogy between the turning of the drums [or "rotors," in the Enigma] and the turning of the hands of a clock. If the right-hand drum turns by 26 cogs (that is, 360 degrees), then the middle drum will move by one cog. After 26 movements of the middle drum, the left-hand drum will move by one cog. In a similar way turn the hands of a clock, indicating the seconds, minutes and hours.

Lisicki, Materials enclosed with a letter to the editor-translator.—ED.

14. Rejewski, *Wspomnienia.*

15. Sobczak, *Propaganda zagraniczna Niemiec weimarskich wobec Polski.*

16. Rejewski's *Wspomnienia*, and oral explanations to the author. Additional light is thrown on this matter by a subsequent comment of Rejewski's:

> The reading of messages enciphered on Enigma proceeded currently from the beginning of 1933. It depended only on the number of messages intercepted. To break a given net's key for a given day, one needed about 60 messages. [In some sources, Rejewski gives the number as 80.—ED.] Thus it also depended on the number of nets being formed and the number of messages broadcast by each of the nets. That is why initially only messages in the Wehrmacht net were read; there were too few Navy messages and Air Force messages; but in the final years before the war there appeared a new S.D. net with an adequate number of messages, and for that reason this net was then regularly read. The Navy likewise in the final period before the war began broadcasting more messages, and that is why messages in the Navy net were also sporadically read at this time. . .
>
> In general, during [the] period [from the first breakthrough until 1938], the recovery of a key was a matter of 10-20 minutes.

Rejewski, "Uwagi do 'Appendix 1,' " 490.

5.

The Duel

In the first three years of Hitler's power, the strength of Germany's armed forces increased eightfold, from about one hundred thousand to nearly eight hundred thousand. After Germany's repudiation of the Versailles Treaty in March 1935, the New Wehrmacht was quickly saturated with modern weapons and equipment. Ever stronger units of air force (Luftwaffe) and armor (Panzertruppen) came into being. Cadres, technical personnel, and hundreds of thousands of recruits were trained. Draftees in the blank classes that had not been subject to military service under the Weimar Republic were inducted into special "E" (Ergänzung) units for accelerated training.

The stationary military radio communications network grew in similar fashion. At first it comprised the two central stations of the Reichswehr ministry and a radio station at each of the seven military districts. But already by 1935 the number of districts had grown to twelve and subsequently increased to seventeen, and the number of divisions went from seven to thirty-six. The Wehrmacht also made use of underground cables, which were inaccessible to monitoring, but increasingly orders and reports were being transmitted by radio, with which lower-echelon units were also being equipped. Radio was the basic signals medium during the great Wehrmacht maneuvers and exercises conducted near the borders with Poland and Czechoslovakia. It was also, of necessity, the means of communication in the naval and air forces. The Luftwaffe network, apart from the central radio stations, included six, later ten, air district commands (Luftgaukommandos) controlling ever more numerous bomber, fighter, and reconnaissance squadrons, ground ordnance and support units, supply depots, and airfields. In secret correspondence, the Luftwaffe used the same E-Eins Enigmas as the army. Only the navy continued to operate its own Enigma, with a larger number of rotors for selection.

The struggle against the German machine cipher did not end in 1933, with the solution of Enigma and the building of its double. In order to read the messages of the German Army, Air Force, and Navy, it was not enough to break the system once. Changes in it had to be detected and reacted to. In the ceaseless duel between the Polish and German cryptological services, the latter had the advantage in technology and personnel. German intelligence, including radio monitoring and decryptment, drew not only on the government's budget but also on the resources of great concerns such as Krupp and I.G. Farben-Leverkusen, which were authorized to run their own secret operations, supervised by the Abwehr.

Meanwhile, the numbers of intercepts were growing proportionally to the rapid pace of the Wehrmacht's expansion. Several Polish lieutenants and captains were sent to the Cipher Bureau for training. In the event of war, they were to man cipher units. There still was not much talk of war in Europe, but the Italian aggression in Ethiopia, begun in the fall of 1935, and the overt intervention of both Fascist powers, Germany and Italy, in Spain not quite a year later in the summer of 1936, made it necessary to expect the worst. Consequently, a flow of reliable, up-to-date information from Germany was becoming extremely important for the Polish General Staff, and the role of radio intelligence in this was increasingly essential.

After World War I, despite Versailles Treaty restrictions banning any kind of German intelligence activity abroad, the German secret services had been reborn with amazing speed. These had included radio intelligence units together with cryptological sections. In early 1919 there came into being in the Foreign Office (Auswärtiges Amt) the Referat I Z, embracing a German-cryptography and a decryptment section. It was directed by an intelligence officer, Kurt Selchow, who employed in the newly organized service the ablest experts from the war years. The name "I Z" survived to 1936, when it was changed to Pers Z. The bureau's personnel included experienced cryptologists such as Rudolf Schauffler and Adolf Paschke. The head of the mathematical team was Werner Kunze, who had his doctorate in mathematics from Heidelberg, where he had also studied philosophy and physics. In 1923 Kunze had solved a French diplomatic cipher, and reputedly thirteen years later he managed to crack a Japanese cipher. The cryptologists developed the one-time pad for use by the Foreign Office and other German ministries. The specialist in Polish codes and ciphers was Hermann Scherschmidt, who held the title of Regierungsrat (Government Counsellor). The staff of the I Z-Pers Z Bureau quickly grew after Hitler's rise to power, from thirty cryptologists in 1933 to over eighty. The number of ancillary employees tripled.[1]

Independently of the Foreign Office, the German Army and Navy developed their own radio intelligence and decryptment. As early as 1919, Lieutenant Colonel Buschenhagen had organized, in a rented apartment on Berlin's Friedrichstrasse, a twelve-man center of radio intelligence and cryptology. In 1920 its personnel had been incorporated into the Reichswehr Ministry. The Reichswehr High Command, in an order issued in the fall of 1921, had directed a search for officers possessing knowledge of radio engineering, mathematics, geography, and foreign languages (English, French, or east European). Their training had at first been nonresident, with the ablest officers later being enrolled in cryptology courses. The German Army's cryptology service grew rapidly after March 1935, when the Versailles Treaty was openly repudiated in order to transform the Reichswehr into a million-man Wehrmacht.

German naval intelligence (Marine-Nachrichtenabteilung), headquartered in Berlin, had a network of posts not only on the coast, but also deep inland. Seven Kriegsmarine radio monitoring posts were active on the Baltic coast—at Felsheft, Neumünster, Kiel, Arkona, Swinemünde, Stolp, and Pillau—and four on the North Sea. In 1937 another monitoring station was organized deep inland, in the little town of Langenargen on the Bodensee. This listening post was directed at Italy. Despite their close alliance, Hitler and Mussolini spied on each other. After the takeover of Austria in March 1938, an additional radio intelligence post came into being there. It was organized at Neusiedl am See, and its assignment, together with the post at Pillau, was to locate and monitor Soviet ships, especially those coming out of the Gulf of Finland into the Baltic Sea.

Cipher solution in the navy was the business of the A III B Service, cooperating closely with the Abwehr. It comprised five separate departments: "A" (coordination and evaluation), "E-1" (Great Britain), "E-2" (France), "E-3" (U.S.S.R. and Poland), and "E-4" (research and training).[2]

It is difficult to estimate the size of the radio intelligence establishment as a whole in the Third Reich. The navy's A III B Service by itself, smaller than the others, by itself employed over five hundred military and civilian specialists in peacetime. The Gestapo's "Research Office" (Forschungsamt) had about two thousand personnel even before the war. Counting the radio intelligence staffs of the Foreign Office, OKW (Oberkommando der Wehrmacht, the supreme command of the German armed forces beginning in February 1938), army, and air force, the total is an estimated four to five thousand specialists working in Germany's radio intelligence and cryptological services before World War II. These personnel fell into four categories: cryptologists, operators, researchers, and auxiliary personnel.

Strange as it may seem, the heads of German cryptological agencies took a skeptical view of the utility of scientists in work on foreign codes and ciphers. The chief of the navy's radio intelligence, Commander Bonatz, has stated that the German General Staff engaged outstanding archeologists who had made their marks by reading unknown writing systems found in Mesopotamian excavations. The results of their work with codes and ciphers were mediocre. German radio intelligence, he says, had no trouble finding capable engineers, but great difficulties in finding gifted cryptologists. Candidates—differently than in Poland—were sought not among young graduates of institutions of higher learning, but among called-up reserve officers, commissioned and noncommissioned, who possessed knowledge of foreign languages. Businessmen with foreign experience and teachers proved the most useful. Some of them, after acquiring experience, were promoted to be directors of units.

As traits valuable in decryptment Bonatz names, in the first place, a keen mind and a combinatorial sense, a knowledge of languages, and a good acquaintance with military terminology and problems. As far as mathematical training goes, pure mathematicians (reine Mathematiker) were not well suited to the E-Dienst (Entzifferungsdienst, decryptment service), since they tended to get lost in theoretical abstractions. Their speculative investigations would strike against an impenetrable barrier when it was necessary to go beyond formulas to solve a problem that was insoluble from the standpoint of pure mathematics. Apparently the Germans found few mathematicians who, in addition to theoretical knowledge, had fluency in foreign languages and innate cryptological talent. Shortages in the E-Dienst, adds Bonatz, became especially acute after the outbreak of the war.

Having obtained no great achievements in the mathematical and scientific solution of codes and ciphers,[3] German intelligence acted persistently and aggressively by other means, including espionage. In late 1935, the Abwehr obtained the complete French naval alert code (Code d'Alerte) by recruiting a young naval officer who turned traitor from financial motives.[4] Reading of French naval dispatches with the aid of this code lasted only a few months, however. The officer, who had proceeded to conduct an intemperate life, was unmasked, the first signal having come to the Deuxième Bureau from across the English Channel. The British had informed French counter-intelligence that they were afraid that French naval Lieutenant Aubert was an agent of German intelligence. Surveillance confirmed the suspicion. Aubert was in the service of the Abwehrstelle in Hamburg, which specialized in naval intelligence, and maintained contact with it in a roundabout way through a German agent who lived in Dublin. He sent in his reports by means of mailed books, periodicals, and so on, pricking appropriate letters with a pin. The reports were of course encrypted, but French specialists managed to make fairly quick work of them.

The damage done by Aubert's espionage was considerable. He had furnished the Abwehr with the mobilization plans of the French Mediterranean fleet as well as much information on naval bases, communications systems, and so on. Just determining everything that the Germans had gotten from him took a couple of months. For a time he was left at large, in order to learn the thrust of the Abwehr's interests. After Aubert was finally arrested in the fall of 1936, the correspondence was kept up in his name. The Germans accepted the reports as authentic, and the last message from Hamburg, in the final days of August 1939, read: "Congratulations. Thank you."

The French secret service in the thirties, the Second Bureau (Deuxième Bureau), was a central state institution subordinate to the premier.[5] It included two basic departments: intelligence (Section de Recherches des Renseignements—S.R.R.) and counterintelligence (Section de Centralisation des Renseignements—S.C.R.). Information acquired by S.R.R. was studied by the intelligence bureaus of the army, air force, and navy staffs. Thus, French intelligence was organized differently than in Poland, where all military intelligence—the collection of information and its study, as well as counterintelligence—was concentrated in Section II of the general staff.

The head of French intelligence in the second half of the thirties was Colonel Roux, and his deputy was Lt. Col. Louis Rivet, who, after the outbreak of war, became the head of a new, joint intelligence service, the Fifth Bureau.

In the France of the thirties, as the deputy chief of counterintelligence in that period recalls, anti-espionage laws were lax.[6] As a result of legal loopholes and procedural machinations, Nazi agents were often acquitted by the courts. The situation in Germany in this respect was diametrically the opposite, especially after the Nazi takeover in 1933 when, for helping the Polish intelligence agent Capt. Jerzy Sosnowski obtain Reichswehr documents, two women were, without any qualms, sentenced to death and executed.

Paillole cites examples of flagrant impunity involving evident traitors and spies, as in the well-known case of a certain Frogé, a French army officer recruited by the Abwehr post in Lindau, and in the affair of a noncommissioned officer who sold to German intelligence the newest model of hand machine gun. The maximum penalty for an offense of this kind was five years in prison, but as a rule the courts' sentences were still lower. Thus S.D. and Abwehr agents could operate in France without risking much, as could French informers who had been bribed or who acted from other motives.

French military authorities seemed utterly helpless.[7] In the face of frequent changes of government cabinets, ranking army, navy, and air force commanders were entangled in political intrigues that absorbed much of their time and attention. Additionally, the armed forces were strongly influenced by Nazi propaganda which fomented pacifist sentiments, understood as peace at any price and as indifference to all that did not directly involve France or her overseas possessions.

French counterintelligence had to combat not only German agents but native pro-Fascist groups. In the years before the war, a secret organization was active in the armed forces, the Secret Committee for Revolutionary Action (C.S.A.R.), also known as the Hooded Ones (La Cagoule). The goal of the Cagoulards was overthrow of the republican system and establishment of a dictatorship and, in foreign policy, the creation of a bloc of Fascist states in which France would find herself at the side of Germany, Italy, and Spain. Cagoulard groups, small but vigorous, constituted a serious threat to republican institutions. Both Premier Édouard Daladier and General Maurice Gamelin knew about their existence in the forces. The ranks of the organization took in about 1,200 officers, including some in intelligence.[8]

German intelligence penetrated even the highest echelons of the French government. The minutes of the strictly secret session of the senate that was held on 16 March 1939, the day after the entry of Nazi troops into Prague, reached Abwehr hands almost immediately.[9]

Beginning in May 1939, questions concerning the fortifications of the Maginot Line disappeared almost entirely from the questionnaires for Abwehr agents that were intercepted from time to time by French counterintelligence. It turned out that after March 15 the Germans had found, in the files of the Czechoslovak General Staff, French plans that the Czechs had made use of in building their own fortifications on their western border, modeled after the Maginot Line.

German intelligence succeeded before 1939 in obtaining, with the help of the military attaché in Stockholm, four Hagelin cipher machines built in Sweden on a French military contract. While the machines were altered and adapted in France, having acquired them, the Germans could attempt to solve the French machine cipher. Still, nothing indicates that they succeeded.

The foreign ties of the German E-Dienst were broad. Potential cryptological allies with whom contacts were established included Italy, Finland, Sweden, Spain, Portugal, Hungary, Bulgaria, and Turkey. Close cooperation was established only with Italy (Ufficio B) and Finland. In the mid thirties, work was also well along on setting up a German radio intelligence station on Portuguese soil. For unknown reasons, the plan was never realized.

German cryptological cooperation with Japan dated from 1929 and lasted to the end of World War II. This collaboration is particularly interesting on account of the celebrated Magic operation—the reading by the United States of the Japanese machine cipher "Purple."

We have considered the development of the B-Dienst (Beobachter Dienst), the radio intelligence organization of the Kriegsmarine, which in this field—as in the introduction of Enigma machines—led the way. After the Nazi takeover in January 1933 and the start of intense preparations for war, the army likewise developed its own radio intelligence organization. In addition to the already existing fixed foreign-radio-monitoring posts, in mid-1935 seven mobile monitoring companies (Horchkompanie) were formed. On 18 March 1936 their assignments were set out in a secret directive from the chief of Wehrmacht signals, Erich Fellgiebel, the "Assignment of Radio Monitoring Zones."[10] German monitoring was ready in peacetime to precisely study the radio systems of bordering states, in order to, upon the outbreak of war, "apprehend them over the full range." Six Horchkompanie units (one was kept in reserve) were assigned monitoring zones designated, in order of priority, by the numbers I, II, and III—the first and second zones to be monitored particularly intensively.[11]

Radio Intelligence Unit	Monitoring Range	Degree of Importance
Number 41	Poland, Lithuania	I
	U.S.S.R.	II
	Latvia, Estonia	III
18	Poland	I
	Czechoslovakia	II
	U.S.S.R.	III
7	Czechoslovakia	I
	Italy	II
	France, Austria, Switzerland	III
25	France, including North African possessions	I
	Switzerland	II
	Spain	III

9	Metropolitan France	I
	Belgium	II
	Great Britain, Holland	III
26	France, Belgium	I
	Great Britain	II
	Holland	III

Monitoring companies in the signal corps (Nachrichtentruppe) were to work together closely, exchanging intercepts and observations, with the seven fixed radio intelligence centers (Feste Funk-Empfangsstelle—FFE): Königsberg, Jüterbog (the great Wehrmacht training grounds), Breslau, Dresden, Munich, Stuttgart, and Münster, each of which had teams of cryptologists. Active near the frontiers with bordering states were forward radio direction-finding posts (Grenzpeilstelle).

The range of radio intelligence covering foreign states ordered in Fellgiebel's directive of 18 March 1936 (just after Germany's remilitarization of the Rhineland) was very broad. It was to encompass "all the radio correspondence of fixed and mobile radio stations of land and air forces" as well as all transmissions by semi- and paramilitary (halbmilitärische and militärähnliche) organizations in Poland, the Soviet Union, Czechoslovakia, France, Belgium, Great Britain, and other countries.

Documents necessary for work on foreign codes and ciphers, as the same directive indicates, were supplied by the central cryptological service (Chi-Dienst) of the Ministry of War.[12] Sets of documents that made it possible to shift immediately to a war footing had also been prepared for the number III zones. And finally, Fellgiebel's directive ordered the intensification, as of 1 June 1936, of monitoring of maneuvers by foreign armies. Each radio intelligence unit was each year to conduct in border areas two major intelligence operations that were to prepare it for mobile action under combat conditions.

In creating as early as 1935, four years before the war, mobile radio intelligence units integrated with the already existing system of radio monitoring and decryptment (the FFE), the Wehrmacht command was far distancing its chief adversaries on the European continent.

The Polish radio intelligence system, comprising merely the three fixed monitoring stations at Starogard, Poznań, and Krzesławice, and a German-cipher office (B.S.-4) at the general staff that employed several persons, was disproportionately small, compared with the enormous German organization. Nevertheless, it took up the unequal—but as it was to prove, very effective—struggle, attacking the Germans' most important nervous system: the Enigma ciphers.

This universal system for encrypting the communications of key agencies of the Third Reich had, meanwhile, been expanding and changing in numerous ways.

By the beginning of 1936, the Germans were using six kinds of keys to Enigma machines, earmarked for the following:

• the supreme civil authorities (Behördenmaschinenschlüssel);
• the staffs of the Armed Forces (Wehrmacht-Stabs-Maschinenschlüssel);
• the Army (Heeres-Maschinenschlüssel);

- S.S. staffs (SS-Stabs-Maschinenschlüssel);
- S.S. operational units (SS-Frontschlüssel);
- special situations (Sonder-Maschinenschlüssel "A").

As of 8 February 1936, the last mentioned, the special "A" key, had been introduced into secret correspondence, no doubt in connection with the army's preparations to enter the western zone that had been demilitarized by the Versailles Treaty. The remilitarization of the Rhineland was the first of a series of Hitler's "accomplished facts" that would lead to the territorial expansion of the Third Reich.

Surviving documents from the period include an order to destroy the tables of Enigma keys for February 1936, issued for use by the army, on account of their having been compromised.[13] No explanation is given as to whether the secret documents had been stolen or lost. Other Chi-Dienst documents of the period also show that the Nazis were vigilant and immediately reacted to the slightest suspicion that their ciphers may have been compromised. Precautions were sharpened as war approached. While the conviction about Enigma's insolubility remained unshakable, the Germans kept careful records of machine starting positions (the Kenngruppensystem) so as to prevent the repetition of the same combinations, remote as that possibility was. Beginning on 1 February 1936 the sequence of the machines' rotors was changed not quarterly but monthly, and beginning 1 October 1936, daily. Likewise, on the latter date, the number of plug connections in Enigma's commutator was made to vary between five and eight (before that, it had invariably been six).

However, Enigma operators, though now generally better trained, from time to time committed errors that B.S.-4 was quick to take advantage of.[14] The experienced cryptologists of the Polish Cipher Bureau's German section also used standard cryptological tricks. Thus, encrypted messages might refer to mobilization preparations, to the deployment and composition of units, to armaments, to preparations for maneuvers. They might contain the recurring names of commanders or training grounds. Sometimes they would refer to S.D. or Abwehr operations on foreign soil. Thus, chances were that certain elements of a code or cipher could simply be guessed by substituting in probable words or phrases.

The cryptologists at B.S.-4 had a variety of reference aids at their disposal, including the Rangliste, an annual German Army publication that gave the names of all regular army officers, listed by rank and seniority (date of last promotion). A starting point could sometimes be obtained by studying the endings of enciphered messages, where the sender's signature usually appeared. But after 1932 the Germans discontinued publication of the Rangliste so that its swollen lists of officers would not give away Germany's military build-up to foreign intelligence, and so it was necessary to seek other sources of information on the personnel of German military staffs. Such information was collected in Germany by deep intelligence, which sometimes reached to the highest echelons of the Wehrmacht. Information from border areas was supplied by shallow intelligence posts Number 3 in Bydgoszcz and Number 4 in Katowice.

Section II of the Polish General Staff did not, however, up to 1938 have access to information from German cipher bureaus or posts, which were kept under exceptionally rigorous surveillance by German counterintelligence (Abwehr III). Likewise, the French source on Wehrmacht ciphers had dried up when Asche had been transferred in 1934 from the military Chi-Dienst to the Gestapo's Research Office—Forschungsamt—which was largely occupied with wiretapping.[15] Hence all the innovations and changes introduced into the Enigma machines and into the procedures for their use in the proliferating Wehrmacht, S.S., S.D., police, and other signals nets had to be studied exclusively on the basis of monitored cipher texts.

The entire prewar history of the duel between Poland's B.S.-4 and the Nazi Chi-Dienst, 1933-39, may roughly be divided into three periods.

In the first period, 1933-35, relatively little changed on the German side, and the methods and apparatus that had been developed by the Poles in the first few months following the Nazi seizure of power (the grill method, Różycki's clock, Rejewski's cyclometer, and others) sufficed to assure continuous decryptment of Enigma.

In the second period, 1936 to November 1938, each change came fast upon the heels of the last and, to keep pace with them, the Polish cryptologists had to throw into the balance all their knowledge and experience, while having basically the same tools and resources at their disposal.

Finally, in the third period, from late 1938 to September 1939, there lasted a tense confrontation with a new, wartime generation of Enigmas, following the introduction by the Chi-Dienst of further complications that had been planned for mobilization (Mob.-Fall) and war.

In the business of cipher and code breaking, as in other fields that unite theory with practice, it is concrete achievements that count. And these are not assured by even the greatest erudition and industry. Also required is an ounce of luck, a favorable coincidence. This thought will occur irresistibly to anyone who traces the struggles of the Polish cryptologists with Enigma in the years 1932-39. He will conclude with all due respect for science that, given a somewhat different sequence of events, Enigma probably would never have been solved. Whatever one may call it now, fate itself seemed to smile upon the Polish enterprise and to conspire against the Nazis.

When in November and December 1932 the most intensive work had been in progress in Poland on Enigma, German cipher clerks had committed outrageous blunders. They had often selected message keys (the first six letters at the beginnings of messages) in a perfectly stereotypic manner. For example, they would strike the same letter three times (AAA) or they would strike letters in alphabetical order (ABC). Or again, they would use letters that lay next to each other down or diagonally across the keyboard—which was also against regulations. Perhaps the cipher personnel were still imperfectly trained and the supervision by their bosses superficial. But the crux of the matter would seem to have been blind faith in Enigma, a belief that it could transform *anything* into an absolutely unbreakable cipher text.

Nonetheless, the Polish mathematicians at B.S.-4—thanks to the cycle principle discovered by Marian Rejewski, which a contemporary German researcher has called a stroke of genius—were able to quickly distinguish total chaos from the merely ostensible chaos that resulted when initially ordered impulses flowed through the machine's innards.

About mid-January 1933, after Enigma had been solved, these German shortcomings disappeared. "So if we had set to work not in October 1932 but just a couple of months later, we would have had a lot more trouble. In fact we had the impression that the Germans had gotten jittery, as if they sensed intuitively that something had happened," says Marian Rejewski.

There were more coincidences that favored the Poles, beginning with French recruitment of Asche and Bertrand's turning over to the Polish Cipher Bureau in early December 1932 documents furnished by the German. In themselves Asche's materials were of little value, but when combined with the mathematical analysis that had already been done in Poland, they helped to form a completely new quality, reducing the number of unknowns in the equations that Rejewski had derived. Not long after that, Asche had been transferred to a different job and had lost all contact with Enigma.

When the Germans exchanged the reflector in their Enigmas on 2 November 1937, they would make the mistake of not changing the wiring in the three rotors at the same time. The Poles' work would also be facilitated by the S.D.'s tardiness in switching (finally, on 1 July 1939) to new procedures for enciphering message keys that had been adopted by other German Enigma nets on 15 September 1938.

Meanwhile, on 5 November 1937, Hitler announced to his generals that "idleness" would soon end, that the armed forces were to be ready at a moment's notice to solve the problems of Austria and Czechoslovakia. If diplomatic pressure failed, military means would prevail.

In 1937, important changes were being made in the Polish Cipher Bureau. Its German section, B.S.-4, was separated from headquarters and moved out of the city. In the specially constructed new facilities hidden in woods not far from Pyry, south of Warsaw, working conditions were incomparably better than in the cramped quarters at the general staff in Warsaw.[16]

The transfer of the German section, however, was dictated not only by a need to relieve cramped conditions. Another purpose was to better protect the secrecy of B.S.-4 operations. Decrypted German messages suggested that the Abwehr never rested in its efforts to find potential traitors among the hundreds of military and civilian workers at general staff headquarters. Strolling agents, even if lacking access to the staff building, could observe personnel entering and leaving, photograph them with hidden miniature cameras, and send the photos to Berlin. This was not merely conjecture. Every so often, Section II acquired German instructions for agents in Poland. In these intelligence assignments (Arbeitsplan für Aufklärungsgebiet Polen) drawn up for each calendar year at Abwehr headquarters on the Tirpitzufer in Berlin, securing informants in the Polish General Staff was always a priority assignment.

At B.S.-4, a categorical prohibition was in force against talking to anyone, even to fellow Cipher Bureau workers, about Enigma. Snatches of conversation on technical matters, or contacts with the AVA Company, could have alerted German agents. If this did not happen, it was not due to Abwehr dereliction but to 100 percent secrecy—not only on the part of the mathematician-cryptologists and operators at the Cipher Bureau, but of the dozens of people who collaborated on the building of the Polish Enigmas and other equipment. The transfer of B.S.-4 out of Warsaw was intended to make things still more difficult for the Abwehr.

The move cannot be said to have been greeted by the staff of B.S.-4 with enthusiasm. To be sure, the trip to work was facilitated by a dark blue official bus that departed for Pyry punctually at 7 a.m. from the Theater Square (Plac Teatralny) near the general staff building. But often it was necessary to work nights, and then the trip was tedious. There was also another, perhaps a somewhat irrational, reason why it was hard for the mathematicians to leave their old quarters in the great eighteenth-century general staff building (remodeled in the nineteenth century) adjacent to the Saxon Gardens (Ogród Saski), so called because of their having been established in the early eighteenth century by Poland's elected Saxon kings. It was there that they had begun working for B.S.-4, there too that in September 1932 they had solved the German naval code and, just before the Nazi takeover in Germany, in January 1933, the "unbreakable" Enigma. From the windows of their office in the northeast wing they could see the Tomb of the Unknown Soldier under the colonnade-topped arcade that joined the two wings.[17] Taking a break from mathematical formulas and ciphers, they could look down from their third-floor perch at foreign delegations laying beribboned wreaths. They derived a peculiar, perhaps slightly perverse, satisfaction from watching the dignitaries of the Third Reich. The awareness that they—anonymous workers in one of the Polish General Staff backroom units—could penetrate the German dignitaries' most secret plans prejudicial to Poland's defense and independent existence, gave them a sense of intellectual and moral superiority. The pompous Goering, aglitter with gilt medals and badges, the demonically grimacing Goebbels, and other emissaries from Germany who in the years 1934-38 were fairly frequent visitors to Warsaw, seemed like characters out of some wretched wandering theater. Could foreknowledge of the adversary's designs but have redressed the imbalance of forces!

The politicians failed to draw conclusions from the Nazis' false game. To be sure, it was not easy to get one's bearings in the situation, with Hitler threatening and making conciliatory gestures by turns, and other governments erred as well. But even the tactical agreements with Germany seemed to Rejewski and Zygalski, who came from the part of Poland that for over a century had been occupied by Prussia and later by Germany, to be incomprehensible and dangerous.

After a lull of a few months there again appeared, in the final quarter of 1937, signs of frantic movement in the Enigma nets, indicating a new wave of international tensions.

The changes which again made decryptment difficult were not yet as far-reaching as those which were to follow. All the same, they indicated that the ever-vigilant Chi-Dienst was intent on bringing its universal machine cipher to what it perceived as perfection. Improvements in the Enigmas included exchange of the reflector, or reversing drum (a new type "B" was introduced). This change was not as effective as the Germans had anticipated, however. Though they did not know it, Enigma signals continued to be read in Poland.

The year 1938 arrived, and with it a sharp turn for the worse in international relations. In February, Hitler eliminated the rather weak tendency toward insubordination among his generals. He removed from their high posts Field Marshal Werner von Blomberg, Gen. Werner von Fritsch, and Gen. Ludwig Beck. The first territorial annexations of the Third Reich were approaching, in which the chief role would still be played by intimidation.

In January 1938 the Polish General Staff ordered an experiment to be carried out, designed to show how efficiently B.S.-4 could read intercepted Wehrmacht ciphers. The test, conducted over a two-week period, showed that the ten-man team of cryptologists and operators was able to solve and read from beginning to end about 75 percent of all intercepted Enigma messages. This was a remarkable result, considering that part of the intercepts were garbled or incomplete due to interference.[18]

On 10 March 1938, before noon, Hitler took the final decision to make the Anschluss (merger) with Austria, concentrating on her borders an army of 105,000 men. Included were Wehrmacht troops and newly formed S.S. regiments (Standarten): the Germania, the Deutschland, the Adolf Hitler guard regiment, and a Totenkopfstandarte (Death's Head Regiment) from Dachau in Bavaria. "Any resistance," proclaimed the order issued on the eve of the march on Vienna, "is to be broken mercilessly with armed force." If any groups in the population offered resistance, the German forces were to act ruthlessly, applying military law, and the same went for any form of passive resistance to the decrees of the German Army.[19] If such methods were ordered for an operation that was billed as a "reunion" (Wiedervereinigung), then how would unfriendly countries be treated?

On 12 March 1938, at 0800 hours, German troops crossed into Austria, along her entire border from Schärding to Bregenz, and at 0915 Luftwaffe squadrons landed in Vienna. On 14 March Austria ceased to exist as an independent state, and her army (Bundesheer) was incorporated into the Greater German Wehrmacht and swore loyalty to the Fuehrer.

From 12 to 15 March 1938, while these dramatic events were taking place, France—following the resignation of Chautemps's cabinet—was experiencing a governmental crisis. The Austrian envoy in Paris could speak only with the departing minister of foreign affairs, Delbos, who was unwilling to make any decisions concerning possible assistance to Austria. Eventually the governments of France and Britain lodged a protest with Hitler, although —as the Austrian envoy was told—they were convinced that this would not alter the course of events.[20]

Meanwhile, in Poland, military counterintelligence had detected mounting interest among German agents as well as diplomats assigned to Warsaw in the military installations located on the outskirts of the city. This interest included the new center in the Kabackie Woods. As Polish-German relations became increasingly strained, the frequency of the quasi-diplomatic travels grew. One day, the car of the Reich's ambassador, Hans von Moltke, was found parked in a glade near the B.S.-4 facility. This was probably a coincidence, as ambassadors seldom engage personally in outright spying that could compromise them. Still, it caused a tightening of security at B.S.-4. Surveillance was strengthened, a new system of passes was adopted, and the center's contacts with the outside world were further restricted.

What were Polish-French relations like in the tense period following the German occupation of Austria in March 1938? In radio intelligence, they were considerably closer than they were in the great political sphere. Bertrand recalls that it was during one of his trips to Warsaw, via Switzerland and Austria, that his train arrived in Vienna just as German troops were entering. When he telephoned his superiors, proposing to stay on in order to observe the Anschluss and collect fresh information, he was ordered to return home at once. Austria had been written off by the French politicians and general staff. The high command was not interested in the actual course of this first annexation by the Third Reich, which had already upset the balance of power in Europe.

Bertrand's Polish opposite number, Lt. Col. Gwido Langer, expressed the mood in Polish General Staff circles that took a pessimistic view of the chances for peace. "What [will come] after the Saar and Austria?" he wondered in a letter to Bertrand of 11 April 1938, a month after the Anschluss. "[Will it be] the colonies, Czechoslovakia, us? One can but see that a great deal of explosive material has gathered in Europe. And [what will follow] the explosion?" After considering the unpleasant prospects, Langer added philosophically: "That is history, to be sure, but it is not the object of humanity." The chief of the Polish Cipher Bureau next thanked his French colleague for his "great efforts" (in establishing closer liaison with the Czechoslovak General Staff. In view of approaching war, it was urgent to ensure reliable communication in the Warsaw-Paris-Prague triangle). He also sent word that "the station in the woods is already functioning"—meaning that the new B.S.-4 post outside Warsaw was operational. In closing, Langer wrote: "You are a hard worker, and for men of your kind life is not very easy—one eats his bread in the sweat of his brow, very often there are disillusionments—but the end crowns the work."[21]

It was only in the second half of May 1938, when the situation had simmered down, that Bertrand could once again set out for Poland. This time, he arrived without incident. On 27 May, after several days of consultations and just before his departure, Langer invited him to see the B.S.-4 center at Pyry which was code named Wicher (Gale).[22] There, the French officer later recalled, "everything was in concrete bunkers, from the radio station to the cryptologists' offices: this was the brain of the organization, where work went on day and night in silence."[23]

That was Bertrand's next to last visit to Poland. On his way home he stopped by Prague, where on behalf of himself and Poland's B.S.-4 he spoke with representatives of the Czechoslovak General Staff, which at that time still looked to the future with hope.

In France, Bertrand's service—having left Enigma entirely to the Poles—during the final year of peace concerned itself with nonmachine ciphers, chiefly those of Germany and Italy. As a result of efforts going back several years, the French were now able to read the secret radio correspondence of over a dozen countries, most importantly that of the two Fascist states. Intelligence games were also conducted, in which adversaries were fed false information about French codes and ciphers. In this way the Germans obtained the "mobilization code" of the S.R., France's military intelligence, and the Italians obtained the French B.G.D. 30 naval code and the British N.I.C. 1 (Naval Intelligence Code No. 1). Later during the war, false information transmitted in the latter code, accepted by the Italian naval command as being authentic, contributed to the success of a raid by British torpedo planes on the Italian naval base at Taranto, with the resultant sinking of several Italian Navy ships.

In the subterranean world of the European intelligence services, an exchange was known to exist in Rotterdam where, for sizable quantities of cash, one could buy, of course at his own risk, various codes and ciphers allegedly used by diplomats, the military, industry, business, and so on. The overwhelming mass of material sold was fake or obsolete; nevertheless, transactions continually took place, and intelligence services anticipated that the real thing just might turn up in the mass of trash. Bertrand visited the exchange from time to time, using the pseudonym Victor Hugo.

However, the goal that had to be attained, cost whatever it might, the "supreme hope and supreme idea," was the universal Enigma cipher machine that was used by the German armed forces with the exception of the navy, which used a different version of it.

After the annexation of Austria by Germany in March 1938, the British began to show more interest in intelligence contacts with their future allies. Shortly after the Anschluss, Bertrand was invited to London, where for the first time he was able to meet the British cipher experts. His bargaining counters were the documents from Asche, which he turned over to the British piecemeal, rationing them out in proportion to reciprocal services.

The British cryptological service in the thirties was part of the Foreign Office, although it also contained some military sections. Officially known as the Government Code and Cypher School, or G.C.C.S. for short, it was also referred to as Room 47 of the Foreign Office until early 1939 when it was called Station X or Bletchley Park (after its transfer from 56 Broadway, Westminster, London, to the secluded country house about fifty miles north of London, and about midway between Oxford and Cambridge).

The long-time chief of the G.C.C.S., Comdr. Alastair Denniston, was a professional naval intelligence officer who, during the years 1914-18, had worked at breaking German codes and ciphers in the famous Room 40 at the Admiralty. The chief cryptologist at G.C.C.S., the civilian Alfred Dillwyn Knox, had also worked at Room 40 during World War I.

It is now known—although British sources remain scanty—that, beginning in the mid thirties, G.C.C.S. had worked hard at breaking the German machine cipher but had failed to make headway. Knox did manage, most likely in 1938, to solve the cipher of General Franco's army, based on the commercial version of Enigma. But the latter bore about the same relation to the highly refined German military Enigma as the Spanish rebel army bore to German military might. Thus the signals of the Wehrmacht, S.S., and other German agencies remained for the British experts through all these years a tantalizing riddle.

The reason for the British failure, aside from the methods used (about which little is known) appears to have been loss of the race for time. The Poles, in addition to using the more precise tools of mathematical analysis, had started out several years ahead of the British, due to the far-sightedness of the officers in the Polish General Staff who were responsible for decryptment efforts, and more especially of the Cipher Bureau's German section.

In mid-1938 and the next tension-filled months, Enigma became a mounting concern to Britain's G.C.C.S., since nothing indicated that in the event of a new conflict they would be able to repeat the World War I successes of Room 40. Still, the British showed great reserve toward Bertrand's proposals that they join forces with his organization and with the Poles.

Following the liquidation of Austria's sovereignty and that country's incorporation into the Thousand-Year Reich as Ostmark, the full fury of German propaganda and subversion was directed against Czechoslovakia. In April 1938, a secret order from Berlin caused the Sudeten German Party (S.D.P.), headed by Konrad Henlein, to present Prague with demands of broad autonomy for the region. In September 1938, the German government itself joined in the campaign of pressure, demanding that a plebiscite be held in the Sudetenland. And as had been the case in Austria, a Nazi fifth column set about stirring up trouble. Multiplying acts of sabotage, which the Czechoslovak authorities naturally sought to counter, deepened the tensions, chaos, and confusion in the country that had been singled out by Hitler to be the next object of aggression.

During this period, in view of the sharp deterioration in the international situation, B.S.-4 reckoned seriously with the possibility of the German cryptographic service switching over to wartime procedures.[24]

It was a peculiar invisible game that was being played out on the European chessboard. The German Chi-Dienst knew of the opponent only that he certainly existed and acted (for example it knew, as did Poles, the locations of the three Polish monitoring stations at Starogard, Poznań, and Krzesławice, and probably also the locations of the main French and British stations). That, insofar as Enigma was concerned, this was strictly a Polish-German duel, and that they had been losing it for several years running, probably never occurred to them.

In any case, so as to assure foolproof security and deny their adversaries any insight into the Wehrmacht's war preparations, the Germans decided on a grand castling operation. At midnight on 15 September 1938, two weeks before the Munich conference, before their first eastward march and their occupation of the Sudetes, the Germans radically altered the rules for enciphering message keys on the by then twenty thousand Enigmas used by Hitler's army, air force, navy, and key civil agencies. Henceforth the Enigma operator himself would select the basic position, a new one each time, for enciphering the individual message key.

The stream of information that had ceaselessly flowed from Enigma nearly dried up. However, the Polish cryptologists found, to their amazement, that a readable trickle continued to flow. These signals originated from an S.D. radio net that continued to use the old keying procedures. But while the S.D. signals gave the Polish General Staff and government much valuable data about internal relations within Germany, a more important matter in the fall of 1938 was military information. An attempt had to be made to reestablish as quickly as possible the decryptment of Wehrmacht correspondence.

Meanwhile, events were gathering momentum. On September 23 Czechoslovakia declared general mobilization of men in the classes between twenty and forty years of age, raising the strength of that country's armed forces to a million and a half men. France carried out a partial mobilization, while Great Britain ordered a naval alert. Italy concentrated her troops in the north, in Sicily and in her North African colonies. Under way in London were British-French talks that revealed a lack of readiness to firmly resist prospective German aggression. On September 26 a British envoy conveyed to Hitler a letter from Prime Minister Neville Chamberlain appealing for calm consideration of the Sudeten question. That same day, Hitler ordered OKW chief General Keitel to mobilize five additional divisions and to concentrate them on the border with Czechoslovakia.

On 30 September 1938, the Munich conference, attended by Hitler, Mussolini, Chamberlain, and French Premier Daladier, ended in capitulation by the western powers before the German demands and the cession to the Reich, without the Czechoslovak government being consulted, of the Sudeten region complete with its vital zone of border fortifications, which were occupied by Hitler's troops in the first days of October.

From late October 1938 on, there were clear signs that the next object of German attempts at intimidation, possibly of open aggression, would be Poland.

NOTES

1. Kahn, *The Code Breakers*, 436-38.

2. Bonatz, *Funkaufklärung*, 73ff.

3. Which is not to say that the Germans solved no codes or ciphers, before the war or during it. There will be more later about their achievements in this field. For now, a few examples will suffice.

Since the early 1930s, the French Ministry of War had used a special codebook in communications with its military districts; the encoded messages were, additionally, superenciphered. This procedure was thoroughly broken by the Germans, who, during the years 1937-39, read the French signals. Only for communication with the military district bordering on Italy was a four-letter code used which the Germans long were unable to crack; this they succeeded in doing only at the turn of 1938-39, and from mid-1939 on they read the French ministry's signals to this district as well. After France's formal entry into the war on 3 September 1939, the French high command adopted the latter, previously local, system for the entire army, and it remained in use to the end of the Franco-German campaign in June 1940.

German cryptologists also solved a U.S. diplomatic cipher that was used until September 1944 in radio communications between Washington and nearly all the U.S. diplomatic posts abroad. After gradually cracking the cipher, the Germans, between 1942 and September 1944, read U.S. diplomatic correspondence on twenty-two lines of radio communication.Rowher and Jäckel, *Die Funkaufklärung*, 106-08.

German wartime decrypting triumphs also included the unscrambling of scrambled radio-telephone conversations, including a number between Churchill and Roosevelt. This eavesdropping, however, netted the Germans relatively little information, since as a rule the two statesmen spoke guardedly. Farago, *The Game of the Foxes*, chapter 48.

4. Nord, *L'Intoxication*, 139ff.

5. Second Bureau headquarters were in Paris, at 2 bis, avenue de Tourville, behind the Invalides. The Foreign Legion had a separate, small secret service (Bureau Special de la Legion Etrangère) headquartered in Marseilles.

6. Paillole, *Services Spéciaux 1935-1945*, 31.

7. New, stricter espionage laws were issued in France on 17 June 1938 and 29 July 1939.

8. Mazurowa, *Europejska polityka Francji 1938-1939*, 164ff. A leader of the Cagoulards, civilian and military, was Joseph Darnand, later a leading collaborationist and, from 1943 on, the chief of the Vichy militia established to combat the French resistance. After the war Darnand was sentenced to death and executed. See *also* Paillole, *Services Spéciaux*.

9. Paillole, *Service Spéciaux*, 115-16.

10. OKH. "Geheim. Betr.: Zuweisung von H.-Gebieten an die Horch-Kompanien und F.F.E.-Stellen," microfilm, series T-311, roll 42.

11. Ibid., series T-311, roll 42, point 5.

12. The name "Ministry of War" (Kriegsministerium) had been introduced on 21 May 1935.

13. The order read: "Heeres-Maschinenschlüssel blossgestellt. Sofort verbrennen." (Army machine key compromised. Burn at once.)

14. For example, S.D. messages sometimes mixed code and plain text: the word *einwandfrei* (faultless) was formed as *ein* + code group *wand* (wall) + code group *frei* (free). Even if this mixture *was* run through the "insoluble" Enigma prior to transmission, the procedure certainly was not cryptologically "faultless."

15. Bertrand, *Enigma*, 56.

16. The commandant of the new B.S.-4 center, responsible for working conditions and security, was Capt. K. Sobecki, formerly commander of the radio intelligence station in Poznań.

17. An evocative scene involving Rejewski in the last years of his life is painted by Strumph Wojtkiewicz at the end of his fictionalized book, *Sekret Enigmy*:

> [S]tanding before the Tomb of the Unknown Soldier in Warsaw, [Rejewski] pointed into space, as he spoke:
> "Over there...in the [nonexistent] left wing, next to the now nonexistent colonnade of the Saxon Palace [as the general staff building was also known], with its windows looking onto the inner courtyard, used to be the BS-4 office, and it was there at the end of 1932 that the three of us discovered the secret of the German Enigma..."
> He continued to reminisce: "Later we were transferred to the center at Pyry, but at this time next to our own room was room 13, which employees called the 'clock room.' The entrance to this room, like that to our cryptological office, was shrouded by a black curtain....Neither we [cryptologists] nor [the handful of other employees who had admittance] were permitted to speak about decryptment, about Enigma, about equipment or machines...Silence was obligatory..."
> Suddenly, as he was looking at the patch of sky, he had to break off his narrative. Unknown to anyone present, along with others he stepped aside, for a ceremony was just beginning at the Tomb of the Unknown Soldier.

Strumph Wojtkiewicz, *Sekret Enigmy*, 169-70.

The Tomb of the Unknown Soldier had been established at the general staff building, within the colonnade-topped arcade that joined the two wings, in 1925. Buried in it are the remains of a Polish soldier selected at random by the Ministry of Military Affairs from among anonymous graves on battlefields dating from World War I and from the postwar battles to establish Poland's borders.

The Saxon Palace, formerly a private residence, had been purchased and enlarged by Poland's first Saxon king, August II (reigned in Poland 1697-1706, and 1709-33). It was remodeled in 1842 and, following World War I, became the seat of the Polish General Staff.

The general staff building was totally destroyed during the Second World War, except for (by extraordinary chance) a small fragment of the arcade which to this day continues to shelter the Tomb of the Unknown Soldier.—ED.

18. Langer, from one of two wartime documents in Rejewski's files.

19. "Einsatzbericht der 8. Armee zur Wiedervereinigung Österreichs mit dem Deutschen Reich," cited in Schuschnigg, *Im Kampf gegen Hitler*, 307ff.

20. Schuschnigg, 321.

21. Bertrand, *Enigma*, 46.

22. About the codename Wicher, Marian Rejewski told Richard Woytak: "I never encountered the term 'Wicher,' I didn't need it. 'Wicher' may have been needed...when Bertrand and Langer talked to each other, or [when] Langer wanted to talk...with [somebody at the] AVA ...plant...." Rejewski, interview 24 July 1978.

23. Bertrand, *Enigma*, 52. His description, stating that at Wicher "everything" was in bunkers, is exaggerated.

Col. Stefan Mayer, from 1935 to 1939 the chief of the Intelligence Department in Section II (Poland's only intelligence service) of the Polish General Staff, told Richard Woytak that the Pyry center had a twenty-kilowatt transmitter which could easily reach Tokyo and could operate on twenty frequencies, as well as antennae that could be lowered so as not to be visible above the woods. Polish intelligence needed such powerful radio equipment to communicate with its outposts within and beyond the Soviet Union, including Mukden and Harbin in Manchuria. It spent equally as much on its Soviet as on its German operations, though the Soviet Union was incomparably the more difficult and dangerous country to work in (only about 10 percent of Poland's agents who went into the U.S.S.R., illegally across a closely guarded border, returned). The Soviets, on the other hand, had considerable ease in finding agents to work for them, including, in 1930, a Major Demkowski of the Polish General Staff's Section IV, who was recruited by the Soviet military attaché Bogovoy and was caught practically the first time that he attempted to pass a stack of general staff documents to the Soviet, was tried, and was shot; many persons volunteered their services to the Soviets, attracted by what Mayer characterized as the false ideological appeal of an ostensibly just and egalitarian new social system that seemed to be the wave of the future. (German intelligence, too, enjoyed a recruiting advantage over Polish intelligence.) The Poles broke Soviet manual ciphers (the latter had no machine ciphers) without difficulty. Polish intelligence suffered from chronic shortages of funds and personnel, and this was one reason why Mayer placed heavy emphasis on radio intelligence and cryptology, as the least expensive intelligence resources. Another reason was what he termed the "fragile" nature of the human element. "I always maintained: I have more confidence in radio monitoring and sound, scientifically based cryptology than in even the best agent. Because that best of agents can be inspired ["disinformed"]; [mis]information can be palmed off on him." A case in point is that of Jerzy Sosnowski, a Polish intelligence agent who worked in Germany: Sosnowski attempted to pass off authentic but obsolete German war plans, dating back to 1928, on his Polish employers, and for his less than undivided devotion to the Polish national interest received from them a fifteen-year prison sentence, finally dying in a southern Russian prison, in Rostov, at the mouth of the Don River. Mayer, Interviews recorded by Richard Woytak in London, January 1976.—ED.

24. Colonel Mayer writes:

> In [the] summer [of] 1938 [an agent] of . . . Polish Secret Service Station No. 3 (Ekspozytura nr 3) [headed by] Major Żychoń, reported that in [the event] of . . . imminent war the German [High] Command intended to put [into] use two additional drums [to] the "Enigma" machine. [This] was . . . reliable information, as [the] agent was a member of [the] signal section of a German Air Force detachment. [In the event] at the end of 1938 our [German-cipher] cryptologists . . . [did] face [a] sudden change in the "Enigma" . . . radiograms. They [ceased to be] readable. It was apparent that [the] additional drums [had been introduced].

The Germans brought the additional drums into use on 15 December 1938 (see next chapter) after first, on September 15, changing the procedure for enciphering message keys. Mayer, "The breaking up of the German ciphering machine 'ENIGMA,' " 3.—ED.

6.

The Bomb

The cryptological difficulties continually introduced by the Germans, especially those of 15 September 1938, created a need for further automation of decryptment. The Polish mathematicians had long been thinking of constructing a device superior to the cyclometer to take over the toilsome calculations. In mid-October 1938, Marian Rejewski worked out the mathematical model of an aggregate which, after thorough checking, was turned over to designers at AVA working under the direction of engineer Antoni Palluth.

The bomb (bomba), as the new device for recovering Enigma keys was christened by Jerzy Różycki,[1] was a true invention, even if the labor of its creators had to remain anonymous. Every advance was a closely guarded secret that could not be shared, even with one's immediate family. Within the Cipher Bureau itself, workers in other sections never knew what Rejewski, Różycki, and Zygalski were up to.

The path from plan to finished apparatus was a short one. General staff orders had to be filled by the AVA Company quickly and precisely. This particular order was completed in only a couple of weeks. The components, which had been produced at the AVA plant on ul. Stępińska in Warsaw, were brought to B.S.-4 at Pyry in the first ten days of November 1938 and assembled by technicians sworn to secrecy, including Czesław Betlewski.

The bomb was an electro-mechanical aggregate based on six Polish Enigmas, combined with additional devices and transmissions. An electrically driven system of rotors revolved automatically, creating in each bomb, successively, over a period of about two hours (100-120 minutes), 17,576 different combinations. When the rotors aligned in the sought-for position, a light went on, the motors stopped automatically, and the cryptologist read the indications. Thus, by setting in motion the bombs (six were built at once in November 1938), the daily keys could be recovered within two hours. Used in

53

the bombs were a number of ideas that constituted the acme of existing technology, such as semielastic axle shafts and transmission wheels, and special instantaneous glowlamps.

Almost simultaneously with the bomb, a method was worked out at B.S.-4 for breaking the doubly enciphered individual message keys, now (except in the S.D. net) being formed in accordance with the new procedures that the Germans had instituted on 15 September 1938. The new Polish method was based on using special series of perforated paper sheets with a capacity of fifty-one holes by fifty-one. Each series consisted of twenty-six sheets. Theoretically the method was based on so-called females (samiczki[2]), that is, on manipulating the sheets so as to match the coincident places in this preprogrammed system. Designed chiefly by Henryk Zygalski, the system was effective regardless of the number of plug connections in the German Enigma's commutator.

Using these new bombs and the perforated sheets, the cryptologists were once again able to find the keys to Wehrmacht signals. As soon as the key was broken, cipher clerks set several—sometimes a dozen or more—Enigma doubles into operation, turning the columns of intercepts into readable plain text. Sometimes, however, it was necessary to revert to slower and more laborious methods that had been used earlier, such as the grill, the Różycki clock, and others. During the several months after Munich, B.S.-4 not only continued reading the S.D. machine cipher but, thanks to the newly invented devices, was again solving German Army and Air Force Enigma, though with much greater effort.

This state of affairs did not persist for long. On 15 December 1938 the Germans once again revamped their Enigma ciphers. This time the change involved not operating procedures but components. The Germans introduced two additional rotors per device, thereby raising the number from three to five. (Only three rotors operated in the machine at any one time, but not only could the sequence of these three be altered,[3] as before, but now they were selected from among five rotors available for the purpose.)

This innovation, combined with the new keying procedure that had been introduced three months earlier, nullified any chance of decryptment by the methods so far used. At least, that would have been the case had it not been for the S.D. cipher.

A year earlier, in September 1937, Polish monitoring stations had discovered a new radio net of the S.D. (Sicherheitsdienst, the S.S. Security Service). This net included radio stations not only within Germany but also abroad. The better trained S.D. cipher clerks did not commit the errors that had occurred in earlier years. The key groups were selected more carefully and showed no frequency. Changes in enciphering procedures were introduced in the S.D. too, but with a certain delay. This delay would prove to be the undoing of the Germans.[4]

The S.D. cryptographic units received the additional, fourth and fifth, rotors for their Enigmas at the same time as the Wehrmacht, on 15 December 1938, but they continued until 1 July 1939 to use their machines in the old way, like the Wehrmacht prior to 15 September 1938. This lack of coordination between Wehrmacht and S.D. was immediately exploited by the cryptologists at B.S.-4. By mathematical and other operations during the second half of December and the first few days of January 1939, they reconstructed the internal connections in rotors four and five. Thus the S.D. ciphers continued to hold no secrets for the Polish cryptologists and, moreover, opened up possibilities of again reading the correspondence of the Wehrmacht's land and air forces. Nevertheless, even with the bomb and perforated sheets, the new keying procedure and the increased number of rotors posed some major problems.[5] And on New Year's Day, 1 January 1939, the Enigma picture became still murkier when, as though uncertain of the efficacy of all these measures, the Germans increased the number of plug connections in the commutator.

Thus, at the beginning of 1939, the Poles continued without great difficulty to read S.D. Enigma, but while the Wehrmacht's machine ciphers, with all their new complications, were again mastered theoretically, continuous decryptment would have required the investment of ever greater resources. A sharp escalation had taken place in the struggle for mastery of the already war-oriented Enigma cipher system. Continuation of this cryptological race would have required immediate possession not of six, as theretofore, but of at least sixty cryptological bombs[6] and as many series of perforated Zygalski sheets. To be sure, the sheets were inexpensive, but their programming and manual production would have required the training of many new skilled workers.[7] Concurrent with the expanding number of monitored German radio nets, there was a growth in the needs of the monitoring stations, which were to be supplied with modern equipment, including secure teletype lines for direct transmittal of intercepts to B.S.-4. Also necessary were the production, for current use, of large numbers of Polish Enigmas, which wore out from constant use, and the creation of a stockpile of the machines for wartime. The struggle for the secrets of the Third Reich, especially in the realm of scientific and technical intelligence, was becoming ever more expensive.

At the beginning of 1939, the Polish General Staff decided to broaden its exchange of information on Enigma with potential allies.[8] Constant liaison had been maintained with the French staff, but it still did not know that Enigma had been solved back in late December of 1932, that doubles had been created, and that the secret radio correspondence of the Wehrmacht had been read regularly for the past six years. General Bertrand's book, published in 1973, suggests that Enigma had been broken in Poland as late as 1939.

In December 1938, as no disclosures from Poland materialized, the French had begun to grow impatient. They had probably lost hope that the Poles would successfully conclude their studies of Enigma. Consideration was given to the possibility, in the event of war appearing inevitable, of at least for a time disrupting German secret communications. By an intentional leak the French would let the Germans know that the Enigma cipher had been broken. That would force the German High Command to make very time- and labor-consuming modifications in the machine or to change the system altogether. To lend weight to the allegations, it would be necessary to produce evidence. French intelligence could furnish such evidence, a single plain text obtained not through decryptment but through an agent.

A second possibility being weighed by the French was that of bringing about a "meeting of Polish and British experts at a single table in Paris at S.R." headquarters, relations between the Polish and British agencies at that time being rather cool. The meeting would be a kind of brainstorming session.

In the final weeks of 1938, Bertrand succeeded in realizing his goal of organizing a trilateral meeting in Paris of top officers of the cryptological services of Poland, France, and Great Britain. However, he first had to make a special trip to London in order to induce the chief of G.C.C.S., Commander Denniston, to take part in the meeting. Denniston apparently did not believe that it would contribute anything new. He had not been in touch with the Polish cryptologists and did not imagine that they could have any achievements in regard to Enigma.

This first meeting to be attended by British representatives took place on 9-10 January 1939 in Paris, at the French military intelligence offices. The French were represented by Major Bertrand, Capt. Henri Braquenié of the air force staff, and an army staff officer; the British by three of their experts; and the Polish General Staff by Lt. Col. Gwido Langer and Maj. Maksymilian Ciężki. The report of the conference stated:

> Each party presented its methods of research and the results obtained up to 15 September 1938, the date on which the system was modified by the Germans, probably by putting mobilization Walzen [rotors] into service. [This was not true: on 15 September 1938, the Germans had not introduced the additional fourth and fifth drums (this had occurred on 15 December), but had altered the procedure for forming message keys.—ED.]
>
> Although the methods used show some differences [in approach to the problem] and the exchange of views was useful to all [parties], the work seems to have arrived at an impasse, out of which only information from an agent can provide a way: to that end, a technical questionnaire has been drawn up, as simple as possible, to be given to such agent as may be judged capable of carrying out the assignment.
>
> Moreover the research work has been divided up insofar as possible, and these assignments shall be pursued by all the parties.
>
> In conclusion, it is the opinion of the best experts, who share an earnest desire of success, that this [problem] is not insoluble if certain external elements can be obtained, whereas reconstruction of the machine solely through study of [cipher] texts must be regarded as practically impossible: that is, moreover, the opinion of the German specialists who conducted the same work before putting the machine into service.[9]

At the Paris meeting it was agreed that the next conferences would be held in Warsaw and London, in that order, but only if there was "something new." Meanwhile, several tense months went by during which the political situation in Europe deteriorated further. On 15 March 1939, German troops marched into Prague, pursuant to Hitler's orders to "dispatch" the rest of the Czech lands ("Erledigung der Rest-Tschechil"). Even the most ardent advocates of appeasement, of whom there were many in western countries, had to concede the failure of their policy in face of Germany's now completely naked aggressions. One of the chief architects of Munich, British Prime Minister Neville Chamberlain, in a speech on March 17, wondered whether this was the end of Germany's aggressions or merely the beginning, whether it was a step toward world conquest.

Long-range Nazi objectives became plain during the next months, days, and even hours. Still, Germany continued to hope that she would achieve them piecemeal without a great armed conflict. A few days after the occupation of Prague on March 19-23 German forces occupied the Baltic port city of Klaipeda (Memel) in Lithuania.

On March 21 Hitler's foreign minister, Joachim von Ribbentrop, demanded through the Polish ambassador to Berlin that Poland acquiesce in the incorporation of the Free City of Danzig into Germany and the building of an "exterritorial highway and railroad line" across Polish Pomerania. That same day, the British government came forward with a proposal for a common declaration by Great Britain, France, and Poland opposing any aggression. On March 23 German forces, with the agreement of a puppet government formed nine days earlier, entered Slovakia. In this way, the deep strategic flanking of Poland on the north by East Prussia had been matched in the south.

In Poland on March 23 the commanders of the five field armies received orders to prepare the defense of their districts. A partial mobilization augmented the armed forces by four infantry divisions, a cavalry brigade, and several auxiliary units. Two additional divisions and a brigade were shifted from the east to strengthen the western border defenses. Meanwhile, since January 1939, the Wehrmacht command had been concentrating in the border areas even more divisions, both active and quietly mobilized ones. From deep intelligence within Germany and from shallow intelligence in German border areas the Polish General Staff was receiving fairly detailed reports about the gradually, but clearly growing, threat of attack. Still, almost to the end of August, the chief matter remained unclear. A military attack on Poland, as Hitler and Ribbentrop well knew, would mean assuming the risks of a major war whose nature and territorial extent could not be foreseen. Today, in retrospect, it is easy to evaluate the whole situation as it then existed. But at that time so many factors, only partially known, entered into the picture that both the Germans and their future opponents were groping in the dark. Even so, if one delves into the postwar accounts of former intelligence chiefs, he is struck by the enormous gulf between the quantity and quality of the information collected, on the one hand, and the incommensurately low degree of its utilization, on the other. The influence of intelligence findings on the decisions of leading politicians was often negligible.

A chief reason for this seems to have been a style of political thinking that was very widespread between the world wars, that centered around an outdated belief in the value of traditional diplomatic maneuvering, assurances and reassurances, balances of power, neutralization, and so on. Transient political configurations and formal pacts obscured for the politicians of parliamentary, as well as authoritarian, governments the hard material and strategic realities that in the final analysis would be decisive.

The solution of the Enigma cipher just as Hitler was taking power had secured a regular flow of reliable military, political, and other information from Germany. Apart from a few examples, for instance, the messages in the period of Roehm's Putsch, this book has generally not considered the nature or range of this information or the questions involving its preliminary evaluation at B.S.-4, its distribution, use, and so on. So far, little material has been unearthed relating to these questions. However, it appears that the stream of Enigma information was directed from B.S.-4 principally to the German Office (Samodzielny Referat "Niemcy") of Section II (Intelligence) of the Polish General Staff, which evaluated all the intelligence on Germany, especially its armed forces. How closely guarded the Enigma secret was is attested to by the fact that it was kept initially even from the deputy director, then Maj. Jan Leśniak, who was director of the German Office for a year, from April 1938. He states:

> [B]eginning in the fall of 1935 I received and worked up items of information and dispatches, usually brief, from "Wicher" ["Gale"— codename for B.S.-4], which was regarded as a reliable source. At the time, I did not know that this was information obtained by the Cipher Bureau from monitoring of German military and police radio transmitters. . . I think it was only not quite a year later that I was informed that these were messages solved by our Cipher Bureau, and from then on I was in personal contact with Col. Gwido Langer, Maj. Maksymilian Ciężki, and Capt. Wiktor Michałowski of the German section.
>
> The messages came in, in varying volume, until the fall of 1938. They contained orders and directives from the Ministry of War in Berlin to the various military districts, primarily Königsberg (Wehrkreis I). Reports going the other way pertained to personnel, transfers, training, exercises, allotments of weapons and equipment. There were also directives pertaining to mobilization, strengths, infrequently Air Force correspondence, often reports by German naval units on movements of ships at Kiel and on the Baltic. . . .
>
> From the beginning, this was one of the most closely guarded secrets of Section II of the General Staff. . . [10]

All the more stringently were the principles of security observed in contacts with the French and British. The Poles did not, up to the very summer of 1939, furnish decrypted Wehrmacht signals to their potential allies. Only summaries on the German armed forces were exchanged. Close contacts in radio intelligence between Poland and France did not mean sharing the secrets of the cryptological workshop, the methods of solving Enigma ciphers, and the apparatus used. Exchange of information and joint conferences in Warsaw and Paris took place at the level of the directors of the cryptological services and their deputies. The mathematicians Rejewski, Różycki, and Zygalski and the other B.S.-4 specialists had never spoken with their French or British opposite numbers. Only as war loomed did the general staff consent to making available to Poland's allies the methods and devices developed at B.S.-4. Bertrand writes:

> So it was, in July 1939, that the great event took place: a telegraphed invitation arrived from Luc, as "there was something new"...[11]
> Nevertheless, the Chief Cryptologist at London had to be hauled down by his ear: perhaps he was bent on arriving at the goal by himself in order to bask in the glory, and played for time. At my insistence and an order from his chief, he finally gave in.
> On July 24, 1939, we all arrived in Warsaw, some of us by Nord-Express (Branquenié and myself), some by plane (those coming from London), and all anxious about the morrow.

That same evening, Langer informed his French colleague that the efforts expended had not been in vain and that not only had Enigma's secret been plumbed, but the machine itself had been reconstructed. The French would receive one copy, the British another.

The next morning, the foreigners were driven to the B.S.-4 facility in the Kabackie Woods outside Warsaw. There the actual working meeting took place, during which a reconstructed Enigma was shown. The British representatives, Comdr. Alastair Denniston and Alfred Dillwyn Knox, were "left speechless, and it was there that, perhaps for the first time, the arrogance of the British experts collapsed, before the results obtained by the Polish experts."[12] Bertrand writes:

> They had to recognize ... that in six months' time Great Britain had profited gratuitously from a Franco-Polish friendship of eight years' duration, forged at the cost of a dozen visits by each side and sustained by mutual trust.[13]

It is possible that one of the participants in the Polish-French-British meeting in late July 1939 was, in fact, the deputy head of British military intelligence, Col. Stewart Menzies. The man in question appeared incognito as a "Professor Sandwich," a mathematician from Oxford.[14] He participated only in the official conferences, along with ranking Polish General Staff officers and the Cipher Bureau's directors, Langer and Ciężki, as well as Bertrand and Denniston. The nuts and bolts conferences involved the French Capt. Henri Braquenié, the Briton Knox, and the Poles Rejewski, Różycki, and Zygalski and, in discussions of technical details, engineer Antoni Palluth and other AVA specialists.

Upon seeing the Polish Enigma double, Denniston and Knox wanted to contact London at once and have mechanics and electricians sent down to draw up plans of the machine. They did not believe their own ears when Langer told them that there would be a machine each for Paris and London.[15]

The next day, Bertrand and Braquenié took a Polish flight to Cologne, where they transferred to a French airliner (the Polish LOT flight was continuing on to London).

The two Enigma machines soon arrived in Paris in diplomatic luggage. On August 16 Bertrand, accompanied by a British diplomatic courier, took one of them to London and at Victoria Station personally turned it over to Colonel Menzies, soon to be chief of Britain's Secret Intelligence Service (S.I.S.).[16]

Just after the Warsaw-Pyry conference on 24-25 July 1939, chief British cryptologist Alfred Dillwyn Knox sent to the three Polish mathematician-cryptologists a thank you note, dated 1 August 1939, on official stationery. In the note, Knox wrote in Polish: "Serdecznie dziękuję za współpracę i cierpliwość. A.D. Knox" (My sincere thanks for your cooperation and patience. A.D. Knox), and below that, in French:

Ci inclus   (a) des petits batons
               (b) un souvenir d'Angleterre
(Enclosed   (a) small batons
               (b) a souvenir from England).

Enclosed, for each of the Poles, was a set of little paper batons inscribed with the letters of the alphabet, and the souvenir, a beautiful scarf with a view of a derby horse race.

Knox, a veteran of Britain's famous Room 40 of World War I, had unsuccessfully attempted in the thirties, with his cryptological team, to break German Enigma ciphers. "I don't know how Knox's method was supposed to work," Marian Rejewski has commented. "Most likely he had hoped to vanquish Enigma with the batons. Unfortunately, we beat him to it."[17] In any case, Knox's gesture was a sporting one—something akin to handing over one's weapon in acknowledgement of another's success.

The final days of August 1939 were marked by feverish work by the Polish General Staff. Border incidents were multiplying, and the spotter network was noting ever more flagrant violations of Poland's western border by high-flying reconnaissance aircraft. The reports of Polish military intelligence were now speaking of a "buildup of forces in the eastern border areas of the Reich, chiefly in Silesia and northern Moravia." They also stated that fortifications begun by the Germans in mid-March 1939 along the entire Polish-German border to protect the forces preparing for offensive operations were going on without interruption and lately had been proceeding very intensively.[18]

At the same time, Section II's reports showed the enormous intensity of the war propaganda being whipped up in the German press. "Mobilization Begins in Poland," "Poland Plots Aggression on Gleiwitz," "Poland Fires on German Planes Outside Polish Air Space," "Warsaw Plans to Attack Danzig," "Germans Arrested on Train in Corridor," "German Patience at an End," "Idiotic Mosaic State," "Polish Sadists Run Amok": these are a few titles from among countless newspaper articles in the final days of August 1939.

On 24 August 1939 German radio stations in Königsberg, Gleiwitz, and Opava began broadcasting propaganda designed to weaken the will to fight of the Polish people and armed forces. Discussed were such topics as the inadequate security of Poland's borders (weak fortifications) and the alleged mass flight into the heart of the country of the population from Silesia.

In the Kabackie Woods, B.S.-4 was working around the clock. The operators and decipherers had been on three shifts since the spring of 1939. In the secluded building perfectly camouflaged in thick foliage, the bombs and Polish Enigmas clattered without pause, transforming enemy ciphers into plain language. The fact that in August 1939 the Polish General Staff identified 80 to 90 percent of all the Wehrmacht units assembled at Poland's borders was in no small measure due to the decryptment center.

Meanwhile, over the previous year and more, German radio intelligence had been evolving. Hitler's actions of 4 February 1938—dismissing Field Marshal Werner von Blomberg as minister of war and commander in chief of the armed forces, abolishing the War Ministry, and creating the high command of the armed forces (Oberkommando der Wehrmacht, or OKW), to which the three services, army, navy, and air force, were subordinated, with Hitler (as before) supreme commander—were followed by changes in the radio-intelligence and cryptology agencies. The former Chi-Stelle was split up into a cryptology department (Chi-Abteilung) subordinate to OKW, and a radio monitoring agency (Horchleitstelle) subordinate to the newly designated commander in chief of the army, Gen. Walther von Brauchitsch. The Luftwaffe kept its own monitoring service, but its cryptologists were turned over to Chi-Abteilung. The navy retained its B-Dienst (Baobachtungsdienst) intact. In this way, the bulk of the German cryptological service, henceforth incorporated into OKW, was separated from the radio-monitoring service, and both were separated from the Abwehr. All these innovations did not fundamentally alter the system of fixed and mobile radio-monitoring stations that had been formed several years earlier and which, as war approached, was refined, expanded, and redeployed.

Since the beginning of 1939, apart from radio-intelligence preparations for the campaign in Poland, the Wehrmacht signals command had been organizing war communication nets in the west. These were special nets (Sondernetze) of Army Group West, designated by the cryptonyms "Ottokar" and "Georg," in which an important role was played by intelligence units. They were directed by an evaluation unit (Auswertestelle der Heeresgruppen Kommando West), headed by Lieutenant Colonel Erzleben, comprising seventeen military and civilian specialists in radio intelligence and decryptment.[19]

As early as mid-June 1939, two and a half months before the aggression against Poland, the German Army command issued a document entitled "Instructions for Wartime Radio Traffic." It ordained a change in cipher keys as of 1 July 1939, the necessity for this being explained by the statement that "the previous keys were used during the operation against the former Czechoslovakia."[20]

At about the same time, an additional Enigma machine was issued from mobilization stocks to the command of every tactical formation and unit, thus nearly doubling the number of devices in army use, to an estimated forty thousand.

A subsequent version of "Instructions for Wartime Radio Traffic," dated 2 August 1939, was issued to unit staffs in sealed envelopes bearing the inscription "Molch" (Salamander). These were to be opened after radio transmission of the same code word, Molch, from the army high command (OKH). That took place a month later, on August 31, the day before World War II began.

On August 19, the Chi-Dienst had decided to reduce still further any risk of the Wehrmacht's ciphers being read, even though they were already regarded as 100 percent secure. The number of plug connections in Enigma had been increased to ten,[21] thus once again immensely increasing the number of possible cipher combinations.

A couple of weeks before the scheduled onslaught, a special signals intelligence staff was created in Oppeln (Arbeitsstab Oppeln), among the German armies massed in Silesia. The "special directive on communications" issued by the staff on 23 August 1939 contained instructions for scouting out and, after the outbreak of war, securing Polish telecommunications facilities. "It is especially important," stressed the document, "to seize the transmitting stations [Verstärkerämter] in Częstochowa, Piotrków, Kielce, Radom, Grójec, and Warsaw, as well as underground cable lines." Special detachments were formed within each army corps, consisting of signal troops which were to carry out the instructions of the chief of army signals.

The task of manning captured Polish broadcasting facilities was given to mixed teams prepared jointly by Goebbels's Ministry of Propaganda and the Wehrmacht High Command, which centrally planned all operations aimed at seizing—if possible, intact—cable and radio communications facilities on Polish soil.

The same directive of 23 August 1939 passed sentence on Poland's carrier pigeons: they were to be captured or killed ("sicherstellen bzw. töten").[22]

Separate instructions of the German High Command and Abwehr dealt with Polish military and civilian signals personnel, particularly those in radio-intelligence and cryptology units.

The day before the attack on Poland, on 31 August 1939, S.S. Sturmbann-führer Alfred Naujocks, a confidant of Heinrich Himmler, carried out an operation that was supposed to furnish a *casus belli*. Hitler did not much care whether the pretext were plausible. No one would judge the victor anyway. That evening, Radio Gleiwitz suddenly interrupted its scheduled programming. A manifesto by "insurgents," calling on Silesians to "take up arms," was read over the air in broken Polish. Shots rang out, and also faked sounds of battle. About 11 p.m. the radio station resumed its programs. The announcer informed his audience that Poles had attempted to take over the station, but the authorities had restored order and foiled the "perfidious plot." The bulletin was picked up by other German stations. Meanwhile, along Germany's eastern border, the Wehrmacht's motorized and armored divisions were already taking up their starting positions for the attack.

NOTES

1. According to Colonel Lisicki,

> The name "bomba" [Polish for bomb] was given [to the device] by [Jerzy] Różycki. [A]t [that] time there was...in Warsaw [a very popular] ice-cream [dessert] called [a] bomba which looked like a[n] old-fashioned..., round, with chocolate [on the] outside. [T]he idea [for] the machine came while they were eating it.

Lisicki, Materials enclosed with letter of 30 August 1982 to the editor-translator.

   B.S.-4 workers also referred to the device, irreverently, as a mangle (magiel) or washing machine (pralka), on account of the characteristic muffled noise that it produced (Oral account by Czesław Betlewski).—ED.

2. The Polish term *samiczki*, females, may have arisen as a play on words. In Polish, *te same* means "the same" (plural number), thus *samiczki* may have been short for "the same places," that is, an alignment of apertures, quite apart from the biological association.—ED.

3. "Daily keys, from the very outset to the beginning of the war, were changed once daily; during the war (I do not know the exact date) the Germans proceeded to change the key every eight hours. It was only one part of the key, the sequence of drums [rotors], that was changed at first once every three months, then beginning February 1, 1936, once a month, and from October 1, 1936, daily." Rejewski, "Uwagi do 'Appendix 1'," 490.

4. The foregoing remarks on the German cryptographic service are based on accounts by Marian Rejewski.

5. "[On] July 1, 1939 ... the S.D. net, which up to then had been using the old procedure for transmitting message keys...switched to the system used by the other nets.... We continued reading the SD net on a current basis until July 1, 1939. After December 15, 1938, we had read only 10 percent of the military net, after July 1, 1939 [we read] only 10 percent of the S.D. net." Rejewski, "Uwagi do 'Appendix 1,' " 492.

6. Production of sixty cryptological bombs would have cost an estimated 1.5 million *złotych* (then about $350,000). Yet the funds provided for new projects and development of radio intelligence, in the Cipher Bureau's budget for fiscal year 1937-38, did not exceed 100,000 *złotych*, or some $23,000.

7. Rejewski summarizes the foregoing admirably:

> We overcame very quickly the difficulties caused by the changes of September 15, 1938, by building 6 bombs and beginning production of perforated sheets. More serious difficulties arose on December 15 with the introduction of drums [rotors] IV and V. To be sure, we quickly found the connections [wirings] within the drums, but the introduction of the new drums raised the number of possible sequences of drums from 6 to 60, that is, ten-fold, and hence also raised ten-fold the work of finding the keys. Thus the change was not qualitative but quantitative. We would have had to markedly increase the personnel to operate the bombs, to produce the perforated sheets (60 series of 26 sheets each were now needed, whereas up to the meeting on July 25, 1939, we had only two such series ready) and to manipulate the sheets.

Rejewski, "Uwagi do 'Appendix 1,' " 492.

8. Rejewski comments:

No, it was not [as Hinsley suggests, cryptological] difficulties of ours that prompted us to work with the British and French, but only the deteriorating political situation. If we had had no difficulties at all we would still, or even the more so, have shared our achievements with our allies as our contribution to the struggle against Germany.

Ibid.

Col. Stefan Mayer writes:

From Gen. [Tadeusz] Pełczyński [before World War II a colonel and chief of Section II of the Polish General Staff], now resident in Great Britain, I know that . . . he [had] suggested [to the chief of the Polish General Staff, Gen. Wacław Stachiewicz] that in case of [impending] war the Enigma secret . . . be used as our Polish contribution to the common . . . defence and divulged to our future allies. [Pełczyński had] repeated [this] to Col. [Józef]   Smoleński when in [the] first days of January 1939 [Smoleński] replaced [him] as . . . head of [Section II].

That was the basis of [Lt. Col. Langer's] instructions . . . when he . . . represent[ed] the Polish side at the [Paris] conference . . . in January 1939 and then in Warsaw in July 1939. . . .

[W]e Poles had . . . reason to [believe] that . . . the British side . . . treated [these conferences] as [acts of] official . . . contact between [the] two intelligence services. Commander Denniston and Mr. Knox were introduced to us (Lt. Col. Langer) by then-Major Bertrand as acknowledged representatives of the British cryptological branch. Thus it was by no means a semiprivate intelligence affair but . . . formal contact between two services.

Mayer, "Supplement to the paper of 21.5. 1974," 2.—ED.

9. Bertrand, *Enigma*, 57-58.

The German cryptographic service, as indicated by recently unearthed documents, had already, in 1936, issued to division staffs and units that used Enigma, additional, fourth and fifth, rotors to be put into service in the event of mobilization and war. See Generalkommando II Armeekorps (Wehrkreiskommando II).

According to Mayer, at the Paris conference in January 1939, Langer and Ciężki had "instructions . . . not to disclose Polish achievements in this field unless the other participants of the conference [showed] that they had made some [progress] in solving [Enigma] and [were] ready to divulge their . . . knowledge. . . . Langer and Ciężki were under the impression that their [opposite numbers] were straightforward but had nothing" to contribute. Mayer, "The breaking up of the German ciphering machine 'Enigma,' "3.

10. Woytak, "Wywiad z Pułkownikiem Dyplomowanym Janem Leśniakiem."

Winterbotham, Calvocoressi, and others have noted that during World War II top Allied commanders had to be told what was the source of "Ultra" intelligence, so that they would give it the confidence and attention that it deserved. Hence, it is worth citing at greater length, from the interview recorded in January 1976 by Richard Woytak, Colonel Leśniak's analogous personal experience at a time when no one in Britain had yet dreamed of an "Ultra" operation (Leśniak died in Vienna three months after the interview, on 15 April 1976):

Already as deputy director of the German Office [in Polish intelligence], from the fall of 1935, I had been receiving and working up, in general, short . . . messages that, as I was officially informed, came from Station "Wicher" ["Gale"]. At the time, I had not been . . . told that this was information [obtained from] the Cipher Bureau's radio monitoring. That was a very closely guarded secret. It was only perhaps a year later that I was let in on it, because I was questioning the information: I said, "I'd like to know who supplied this, and when?" Some of the information was so important, about mobilization and so on, that . . . I questioned [it]: "I can't accept this until you tell me who supplied it, and how he was able to get it." [I challenged the information] right away, in '36 [and was told its source] shortly afterwards. They had no choice, because I told them, "I'm not taking this into account. . . . I'm discarding it . . . It's such important information, but I don't know where or when this information... [D]o you have a staff officer in the German ministry [of war]?"...I knew all [our] main intelligence officers in Germany; I knew where each of them was; I didn't know their sub-agents, but...I knew them all personally, and so I said, "Which of them supplied this? It's so important that I want to know." And that's why I was put in the know then, under a great pledge of secrecy. My subordinates didn't know about it. [In late 1938 and early 1939, at its largest, the German Office would have only eighteen officers, including seven general staff officers and two officers with civilian higher educations: one a doctor in philosophy, the other an economist.] [I was told] I think [by] the chief, Colonel Mayer...not [by] the Western Office [Referat Zachód, the branch of Department IIA (offensive intelligence) that was directed against Germany, while Leśniak's German Office was one of the two main branches (the other being the Russian Office) of Department III, or Studies] but personally [by] Colonel Mayer, under this pledge of great secrecy. And from that time on I had direct contact with Colonel Gwido Langer, the chief of the Cipher Bureau, and with the director of [its] German section, Major Ciężki, and with Captain Michałowski, and sometimes when there was something important they would actually bring the messages over; sometimes they would decipher something, and they wouldn't know whether a certain unit existed or not; or they would have half a name—of a detachment, or a last name or whatever—and sometimes I could help them out by telling them how the situation was. Mainly these were messages between the Ministry of War in Berlin and the command of the military district in Königsberg, Wehrkreis Number I, and with some of the other Wehrkreises...: information mostly of a military nature—transfers, postings...questions and directions concerning preparations for mobilization. The contents implied that it concerned preparations for mobilization or the build-up of the army. There was less information on the air force, a great deal...on the navy, for example the movements of naval ships putting out from Kiel, putting out into the Baltic: we would know about it the same day, because they [the Cipher Bureau] were reading...the messages. [T]his was valuable information, and once I knew that it was from such a reliable source, it helped us...in determining [German units and facilities and in] establishing mobilization and other preparations.... The messages came in in varying intensity: sometimes during a week there would be...say, several [of them], and sometimes there would be from ten to twenty. The greatest flow of messages was in 1938. In 1939, we hardly had any messages: very few. At that time, I made inquiries and learned that they were having troubles with decryptment [...At that time we were receiving] police [that is, Gestapo and S.D.] messages, fewer [Nazi] party messages—[I don't recall whether] the party [had] its own apparatus [that is, Enigma network]—and anyway, those matters were so open, the newspapers were so full of them, of the NSDAP [Nazi party], S.S. and so on, that we hardly needed it.... Oh yes, there was some air force information coming in. ... This flow of information came to an end, and in 1939, during the September Campaign, we had no information.... When there is no radio monitoring, there are no messages, and you can't work. It was only in France [in late 1939] that this source started up again, after the whole team...had been turned over to the French [general] staff.

Beginning about April 1938, as tensions with Germany mounted and the German military build-up grew enormously, Leśniak gave two to three briefings a week on the situation in Germany to the chief of the Polish General Staff, General Wacław Stachiewicz, whom Leśniak describes as a very capable and disarmingly unpretentious officer. From late June 1938 on, Leśniak delivered daily briefings on Germany, in the chief of staff's large conference room, which were attended by the chief of staff, the deputy chiefs of staff, the colonels who headed all the general staff's sections, a representative of the Ministry of Military Affairs, and a delegate of the inspector-general.

In mid-April 1939, after a year as its head, Leśniak turned the German Office over to Lt. Col. Stanisław Bień and formed a Situation Office (Samodzielny Referat Sytuacyjny), intended for wartime service, which he headed to and through the September Campaign of 1939. At first he was given only two officers, with whom he manned the office in watches around the clock, but gradually additional officers were detailed to the Situation Office from the German Office. (Later, Leśniak would head a German Office at the Polish General Staff in France and in London.)

In June 1939, Leśniak was shown a building on ulica Rakowiecka, in southern Warsaw's Mokotów district, that had been designated to be the headquarters of the commander in chief's staff in the event of war. The inside of the building and the ventilating system were still being finished. He was shown where his Situation Office would be located upon the outbreak of war and was instructed to arrange the room as a duplicate of his office in the general staff building on the Saxon Square (by then renamed Piłsudski Square, after Poland's Marshal Józef Piłsudski, who had died in 1935), every two to three days updating the situation map, and so on, in order, when war broke out, to move there at an hour's notice and forget about the Saxon Square. Of Leśniak's personnel, only his deputy was informed of these preparations.

In July 1939, Leśniak went to Berlin to observe a military review staged for the brother of Yugoslavia's king. Leśniak recalled to Richard Woytak that he watched the parade from the main reviewing stand, seated four meters behind Hitler: he would later regret not having taken the occasion to shoot Hitler.

When World War II broke out on 1 September 1939, Jan Leśniak and his colleagues in Polish intelligence had been working very intensively—often, well over a dozen hours a day—through the preceding two or three years in order to establish the German orders of battle, and had succeeded in working out nearly 95 percent of these. The German attack on Poland, at 4:30 a.m., on September 1, did not come as a surprise to the Polish General Staff, which had been expecting it through the previous week and had known that it could happen at any moment. The results obtained by Polish intelligence—thanks to the dedication, patriotism, skill, and unstinting effort of all its personnel—according to Leśniak, "absolutely exceeded what would normally have been possible."

Leśniak offers the following comparison between the Polish and German intelligence services:

> Considering Germany's enormous resources—in finances, technology, communications...people (a million and a half Germans in Poland...most of whom collaborated...with Germany), the vast amounts of money that Germany spent on intelligence—[their] achievements, [judging] from what I have read...were incomparably smaller than those of Polish intelligence, which operated with incomparably smaller resources in people, budget, and so on. [On the other hand] German intelligence and staffs in the field functioned very well, very efficiently, and were well prepared for their tasks.

Often, intelligence and counterintelligence are functionally inseparable. Colonel Mayer told Richard Woytak in January 1976 of an incident that both Mayer and Rejewski recalled from late 1938, shortly after the Wehrmacht introduced the new Enigma-enciphering procedures. Gero von Gersdorf, leader of the Deutsche Vereinigung (German Union) in Bydgoszcz, Rejewski's home town, had been under surveillance by Polish authorities, who determined that he was in possession of a short-wave transmitter; a search of his premises indeed turned up a transmitter cached in a barrel of sauerkraut, and von Gersdorf was arrested and put on trial. The defense claimed that the transmitter had been planted in an effort to discredit him; hence the case against him was, on its face, a weak one. To be sure, a Polish intelligence expert testified that there was incontrovertible evidence for von Gersdorf's involvement with German military intelligence, but it could not be produced in court. Inasmuch as the accused had, to the court's knowledge, at most been *preparing* to engage in espionage and there had been no hard evidence adduced to otherwise incriminate him, von Gersdorf received and served a sentence of only five months' imprisonment. Released just before the outbreak of World War II, immediately after Poland's occupation he received a high decoration from Hitler. Polish intelligence had indeed had strong evidence against von Gersdorf: while he had been in prison awaiting trial, the Königsberg Gestapo office in East Prussia had radioed in Enigma to the Gestapo-Amt in Berlin, complaining that the Abwehr-Amt (German military intelligence) was engaging in the extremely risky practice of recruiting for intelligence work leading political activists such as Gero von Gersdorf. Intercepted by the Poles, the message had been sent to the Cipher Bureau, decrypted, and passed on to counterintelligence; but the damning evidence had not been presented to the court, so as not to jeopardize the security of Poland's Enigma-reading operation.—ED.

11. Rejewski states: " 'Il y a du nouveau' [There is something new] was an agreed-upon code phrase. The only thing new was that the Chief of [the Polish General] Staff had given permission to reveal the secret of Enigma's solution." The Poles had, of course, broken Enigma in the final days of December 1932—over six and a half years earlier—but "Langer had not been authorized to disclose that we had long since broken Enigma." "Uwagi do 'Appendix 1,' " 491.

12. Bertrand, *Enigma*, 59.

13. Ibid., 60.

14. Rejewski wrote about "Sandwich":

> Another visitor to Pyry was a certain Sandwich, a descendant of the famous Lord John Montagu [fourth Earl of] Sandwich [1718-92, English politician, twice first lord of the Admiralty, whose mismanagement of the Royal Navy was a cause of British failure in the American War of Independence, for whom the Sandwich (Hawaiian) Islands and (supposedly) the sandwich were named], but he was not involved in cryptology but in questions of communications, and he only once paid a brief visit to our room.

Rejewski, *Wspomnienia*.

Mayer writes:

> I presid[ed] at [an] official lunch for the British delegation. Besides Comdr. Denniston and Mr. Knox, Lt. Col. Langer introduced to me...a third dele-gate...of the British team, a certain professor of...Oxford University who actually did not belong to the cryptological branch but [so Lt. Col. Langer had been told, and so he told me] closely cooperated with it. [A]fter the war I met on one private occasion M[ajor] Gen[eral] Menzies. I [immediately] recognised...him [as the] mysterious [Oxford] professor...When...I [said] that...we [had long ago] met...his reply was: 'Yes, it was [in the] Enigma [affair].' [General] Menzies [had been] at the time of the July 1939 conference [a colonel and] deputy head of the [British] S.I.S.

Mayer, "Supplement to the paper of 21.5.1974," 2-3.

On Menzies's presumptive presence in Warsaw in July 1939, see also Richard Woytak's conversation with Rejewski reproduced at the end of this book.

Mayer relates another "anecdotic detail" of the July 1939 Warsaw conference:

> Commander Denniston learned in conversation with me that my daughter (then 14) [was] taking English [in] school as [a] foreign language. He promptly and amiably suggested that we...exchange...daughters during long school holidays for language stud[y]. I would send my daughter to England to his family, and his daughter would come to Poland to [stay] with my family. Of course the outbreak of the war thwarted any...such...arrangement.

Mayer emphasizes that cooperation between the Polish and British intelligence services had by no means only recently begun.

> Since...Captain Derbyshire, the British Secret Service [resident] in Warsaw [had been] persuaded by us to abandon unnecessary espionage activities, the presence of successive S.I.S. [residents] in Warsaw ha[d] been formally notified to us. They loyally collaborated with us in...matters of mutual interest. They were Captain Ross and lastly, till the outbreak of war, Col. Shelley.

Mayer, "Supplement to the paper of 21.5.74," 3.—ED.

15. Some accounts of the July 1939 conference state that it was then decided that the British would concentrate on technical aspects of key-breaking, while the Poles worked on theory. About this, Rejewski comments:

> This was...wishful thinking. The closeness of [impending] war made it impos-sible even to think of theoretical work. All our effort during these few weeks up to the moment of our evacuation [in September 1939] was directed exclusively at recovering the greatest possible number of keys with the aid of the six bombs and two series of perforated sheets that we had. We had absolutely no time to even begin perforating a third series of sheets, much less to think of theoretical work.

Rejewski, "Uwagi do 'Appendix 1,' " 492.

16. Bertrand, *Enigma*, 60-61.

17. Reference is made to the "baton method" by C.A. Deavours. Deavours, "How the British Broke Enigma."—ED.

18. Cieplewicz and Zgórniak, *Przygotowania niemieckie do agresji na Polskę w 1939*.

19. The personnel roster of the Auswertestelle includes names such as Major Randewig, Captain Dr. Franz, and Regierungsinspektor Sernatinger.

20. "Funkregelung im Kriege," June 15, 1939, series T-311, roll 42.

21. Directive of Heeres-Gruppen-Kommando. 4. "Steckerverbindugen der Chiffriersmaschine 'Enigma'," Series T-312, roll 80.

22. Arbeitsstab Oppeln, "Besondere Anordnungen für Nachrichten-Verbindungen," Series T-312, roll 80.

7.

War Begins

The first of September 1939 came, and with it the first air raids on Warsaw, the first dead and wounded, the first ruins and burned-out buildings, aerial battles over the southern outskirts of the city, brief encouragement when a struck Heinkel bomber, trailing smoke, crashed in the woods outside Pyry.

An air defense bulletin on casualties and damage in Warsaw's Ochota district reported that German bombs had hit the new AVA production facilities on Szczęśliwicka Street (ulica Szczęśliwicka). These had been built and outfitted with modern equipment shortly before the war. Whether this was simple chance or whether the target had been picked in advance by Abwehr agents was never learned.

In addition to the well-known incident at Gleiwitz, which had been staged for political ends, the Germans employed several lesser-known stratagems meant to disorganize Polish defenses by inducing individual units to capitulate. One such attempt was made by Kriegsmarine intelligence, which had succeeded just before the war in working out a Polish four-letter naval code that was used by the Polish garrison at Westerplatte.[1] On the second day of the war the German naval radio-intelligence post (B-Dienst Leitstelle) at Swinemünde broadcast a bogus order in this code. Ostensibly from Polish military authorities, it called for Westerplatte to discontinue resistance and surrender. The attempt failed ("der gewünschte Erfolg blieb aus"), notes one of the former heads of German radio intelligence.[2]

B.S.-4 worked normally only in the first days of September. The situation at the front was getting worse daily. The thin zone of defensive positions was cracking under the massed blows of Nazi armor, and thousands of airplanes emblazoned with black crosses hung in the skies from dawn to dusk, attacking not only military units but open cities and civilian refugees fleeing the western parts of the country.

At the outbreak of war, Polish monitoring station number 5 at Staro-gard, twenty-five miles south of Danzig, was to have withdrawn to its designated new operations site at Włocławek, ninety miles farther south, on the Vistula River. But due to the rapidly developing German onslaught, it was evacuated southeast to Warsaw, then on to Siedlce, fifty-five miles east of the capital.

Station number 4 at Poznań, in western Poland, was to have withdrawn in the second phase of evacuation. But on account of the general situation, it broke off operations as early as September 2, and personnel and equipment were moved to Konin, sixty miles east. After the bombing of the railway station at Konin by the German Air Force, the local command ordered immediate evacuation to the east. The final stop for this station was Włod-awa, one hundred miles southeast of Warsaw, on the Bug (Boog) River in eastern Poland.

Station number 3 at Krzesławice, outside Kraków in southwestern Poland, evacuated in the first days of the war toward Tarnów, fifty miles east of Kraków.

It was impossible to observe the principle that only one of the three monitoring stations was to move at a time, while the remaining two operated as usual.[3]

On September 3, Britain and France declared war on Germany, but this did nothing to relieve the pressure on Poland. The French armed forces did not move, and Britain's Royal Air Force dropped propaganda leaflets on Germany instead of bombing troop transports and airfields.

The aggression against Poland, conducted with all of Germany's armored divisions, two Luftwaffe airfleets, and her best motorized and infantry divisions, had exposed her western frontier. No more than twenty to twenty-five Wehrmacht divisions remained there. Nevertheless, the French supreme command did not take advantage of the favorable situation to carry out operations in relief of the Polish front. The commander in chief of Allied forces on the western front, Gen. Maurice Gamelin, limited himself to ordering a diversionary attack at the Saar River on the Franco-German frontier. During the night of September 6-7, French units crossed the border without encountering resistance. The next day, they moved cautiously into a small wood called the Warndt Forest, from which the Germans had retreated. After advancing seven miles on a front twenty-five miles wide, the French ran up against the Siegfried Line, which was still unfinished. They then simply stopped and sniped at the German fortifications with rifles. The negligible French incursion caused the Germans not the slightest inconven-ience and certainly resulted in no forces being withdrawn from Poland.[4]

In view of the deteriorating situation at the front, on September 5 B.S.-4 at Pyry received an order to destroy part of its files and prepare to evacuate. Crates containing indispensable documents and apparatus were loaded onto trucks, which took them by night to Warsaw's Wilno Station (Dworzec Wileński). A special evacuation train, the Echelon F (Eszelon F), stood on a siding, waiting for the signal. All bureau personnel, stated the next order, were henceforth at the disposal of supreme headquarters, which had been transferred to Brześć (Brest Litovsk) on the Bug River.

Moving slowly due to track damage, and subjected to numerous air attacks, the Echelon F finally reached Brześć three days later, on September 10. Meanwhile, German Panzer spearheads, bypassing strongly defended Warsaw, had pushed on eastward, and the Polish Supreme Command had soon abandoned Brześć. The stage masters there indicated the subsequent direction of evacuation: south. The Cipher Bureau's personnel and secret equipment had to be kept from falling into enemy hands; nevertheless, it took some doing to convince the stage master that the heavy green crates were more important than the luggage of civilian dignitaries who were fleeing with their families and domestics. The crates contained Polish Enigmas, decrypting equipment, and Polish Lacida cipher machines that had been built by AVA.

The subsequent evacuation route led south-southeast through Kowel (September 11), Łuck (September 12),[5] Włodzimierz Wołyński (September 13), Trembowla and Husiatyn (September 15). The news at the successive stages was increasingly alarming. For lack of fuel, some of the trucks had to be abandoned; equipment and documents were gradually destroyed.

The Cipher Bureau received orders to evacuate, along with other units of the general staff, to Rumania. They now had only one battered truck left, its gasoline tank half empty. Half a mile southeast of the town of Kuty (population about four hundred), the B.S.-4 cryptologists, together with other military and civilian general staff personnel on 17 September 1939—the same day as the Polish government—crossed a bridge over the Czeremosz River into Rumania.[6] At the border a Rumanian officer confiscated their truck, then separated military from civilians and indicated a different direction of march to each group.

Taking advantage of the confusion caused by the arrival of the next wave of refugees, Rejewski, Różycki, and Zygalski, who kept together, ignored the Rumanian's instructions. They anticipated that in an internment camp they might easily be identified by the Siguranca (the Rumanian security police), in which the Abwehr and S.D. had informers. Therefore, they proceeded straight on, to the nearest railroad station at Adancata, where they managed to exchange money and buy tickets. They boarded the first train headed south and, at one of the larger stations, switched to an express train.

After a dozen or so hours they got off the train at Bucharest, at the other end of Rumania. On the way they had had ample time to think over their situation. Not much more water would flow down the Danube before Rumania would find herself under German domination. That much seemed certain. German intelligence outposts already active there would do all they could to pick out of the mass of refugees workers of the Polish General Staff, including its German intelligence units.

In Hitler's long-range plans, Rumania was meant to be a bridge over which German expansion would roll on to the Middle East, to Bagdad and beyond. Consequently, Rumania was increasingly being infiltrated by Germany. The task of Nazi intelligence in Rumania was made easier by the sizable German minority. In the central regions of Rumania alone, especially in Transylvania, lived about two hundred fifty thousand Germans, concentrated around the cities of Sibiu and Braşov. In the Bukovina area, near the border with Poland, lived eighty thousand Germans, and an approximately equal number lived in the Banat, in western Rumania. Moreover, in all the larger cities throughout Rumania, there were many Germans working in industry, the railroads, and commerce. With Hitler's rise to power, German political parties were activated in Rumania. In place of the Nationale Einheit party that had been dissolved by Rumanian authorities, a new party had been created in 1934 called the V.G.D.R. (Volksgemeinschaft der Deutschen in Rumänien) that intended to play a role there similar to that which Henlein's armed bands had played in Czechoslovakia.

In Bucharest, the war was nowhere in evidence. Amid the crowds of the big city it was easier to avoid notice by the Rumanian police, which had received orders to detain and send to internment camps any stray refugees from Poland. It was essential for Rejewski, Różycki, and Zygalski to speedily contact the Polish Embassy and military attaché, Lt. Col. Tadeusz Zakrzewski, whose office was in the embassy, not far from the city center, and a seedy hotel aptly named the Transit, where the three mathematicians had found accommodations. Polish agencies that were still operating assisted refugees in getting out of the German sphere of influence, but the three civilians, even if they were from the Cipher Bureau, were now at the bottom of the list. Military and government dignitaries were first in line. The military attaché, however, still found time to hear the cryptologists out. He was one of those officers who, even before the war, had appraised the situation more accurately than most. In the summer of 1938 he had tried to bring about closer cooperation between military circles in Poland and Czechoslovakia. His initiatives had been rejected by the Polish Ministry of Foreign Affairs and the general staff, which had ordered him to break off the secret talks with the Czechoslovak military attaché in Bucharest, Colonel Buda. When Zakrzewski learned from the three mathematicians about the close contacts that had been maintained in radio intelligence with Allied staffs, he recommended that they go directly to the British or French Embassy. "It's quite possible that these matters will be of interest to them and that one of the embassies will help you get out. For the time being, there is nothing that I can do."

After a brief consultation, the cryptologists decided to turn to the British. During the memorable final meeting at Pyry before the outbreak of war, the British had shown particular interest in working with the Poles. And just now most of the Poles' bitterness and disappointment was directed against France. Despite her powerful army, mobilized in the final days of August, she had not attacked the aggressor with even a few divisions, which would have forced the Germans to withdraw part of their forces, at least of their air force, from the Polish front.

The trio arrived at the British Embassy just as a bus carrying Britain's entire Warsaw embassy staff rolled into the yard. An official listened to the mathematicians but gave no definite answer. He promised to consult London "as time permits."

Time was pressing. It would have to be the French after all! Their embassy was also nearby, close to the city center, so Rejewski, Różycki, and Zygalski went there.

In the elegant lobby of the French Embassy, an official inquired as to the purpose of their visit. The Poles stated that they would like to speak with a representative of the French armed forces. "Please just tell your superior that we are friends of Bolek."

The official disappeared behind a leather-upholstered door. A moment later, he ran back in. "Mais oui, messieurs!" (Of course, gentlemen!) he said a number of times. "Please wait a moment, gentlemen, the colonel will see you just as soon as he has finished speaking with Paris."

The telephone conversation must have been a brief one, because a few minutes later the mathematicians were able to speak with the French colonel who was standing in for the absent General Musse. The instructions that he had received from Paris were unequivocal: to assist the Polish cryptologists in leaving at once for France. The word "Bolek" was not a prearranged code word, but was the pseudonym of French radio-intelligence chief Gustave Bertrand, who had been waiting several days to reestablish contact with the Poles, severed since their departure from Warsaw. The military attaché asked the three Poles no further questions but directed the official to see about passports and transit visas.

The preparations and formalities took less than two days. There were troubles with the Rumanian authorities, who had to consent to the Poles' departure, but their French guardian was familiar with the local customs, and after a 500-*lei* banknote had been slipped into the official papers, the difficulties vanished.

Since 1938 Rumania had been under mounting German pressure. Lieutenant Colonel Zakrzewski had reported on the growing influx of trade missions and tourists from Germany. Rumania's Fascist Iron Guard had many supporters in the armed forces who "did not shrink from passing Rumanian secrets to German intelligence."[7]

At the beginning of 1939, Polish military intelligence had set up an office in Rumania camouflaged as a mixed Polish-Rumanian manganese extraction company.

In the complex situation that existed in Rumania at the end of September 1939, an important assist to the new Polish government in exile was the $600,000 in assorted foreign currencies belonging to Section II that had been brought by the Section II treasurer, Maj. Franciszek Ptak, and turned over to Lieutenant Colonel Zakrzewski. Half of these funds, about $300,000 worth, were placed at the disposal of the new premier, Gen. Władysław Sikorski, and an equal sum was left in Rumania to cover the costs of evacuating Polish troops to France. Used in the latter process were legal, semilegal, and cloak-and-dagger means. In the vaults beneath the Polish attaché's offices, a special factory turned out exit documents and visas issued in fictitious names. The real names of the holders were sent to Paris in ciphered dispatches.

There was some friction in relations with the French. "I was obliged," recalls Lieutenant Colonel Zakrzewski, "to seek the warmest possible relations with the French and British embassies. This soon led to attempts at ordering me around... General Faury, recently chief of a military mission in Poland and until 1927 dean [dyrektor nauk] at the Polish Military Staff College [Wyższa Szkoła Wojenna] in Warsaw, tried to meddle in my affairs, and I was forced to... remind him that he could give orders only to his French officers."[8] Relations were, of course, better with the French military attaché in Bucharest, who expedited the departure of the B.S.-4 personnel, particularly the three mathematician-cryptologists.

The evacuation of Polish military and civilian refugees from Rumania, Hungary, and the Baltic countries was, at first, rather chaotic. Gradually, however, using Polish diplomatic posts, General Sikorski's government in exile organized a net of semilegal and secret outposts that transferred people—above all, flying, armored, and signals personnel. In time, the evacuation net came to include seven primary outposts (Bucharest, Constanţa, Budapest, Kaunas, Riga, Helsinki, and Stockholm), four secondary outposts (Belgrade, Rome, Helsinki, Stockholm), two transit-transport outposts (Athens and Split) and three terminal points (Marseilles, Modane, and Mentone).

Over the eight-month period from the end of September 1939 to May 1940, a total of 37,601 military and civilian personnel were evacuated to France, some 20,000 of them from Rumania alone (including 7,120 air force pilots, mechanics, and ordnance personnel). Over 60 percent were transported by sea. Embarcation posts were Constanţa in Rumania, Piraeus in Greece, and Split in Yugoslavia, with the ships sailing to Marseilles. The main route of evacuation by land ran across Yugoslavia and northern Italy to the French border station at Modane.

After quickly—for wartime conditions—obtaining passports and transit visas, Rejewski, Zygalski, and Różycki, toward the end of September, set out on their way. After over a dozen hours' train ride via Belgrade, Zagreb, and Trieste, they reached Turin. The Italian security police carefully questioned the three Paris-bound Poles. "Young, in good health, and you haven't served in the army? And you get visas for France so quickly? Extraordinary," a black-uniformed policeman said to them. Italy was not yet at war with Poland or France and, after inspecting their modest baggage, the Fascist police officer "generously" waved them through.

It was now less than two hours to the French border. Rivoli, Bussoleno, Susa, read the names of the successive Piedmont stations. The Poles could feel the tang of the sharper Alpine air. Finally, the little station at Bardonocchia in the Alps. In ten or twenty minutes, they would be at the border. Suddenly the train plunged into a several-kilometer-long tunnel running through Mont Cenis and came to a stop just outside the far end. They were in France.

At Modane, a little town on the Arc River, a mixed Polish-French evacuation center had been operating for a few days. The railroad station was full of military men and civilians waiting to get through the formalities. The military usually proceeded on to a collecting point organized at the great

Bessiers barracks in Paris, where they awaited assignment to units. The few higher officers summoned by name from Rumania by General Sikorski's newly formed government went to the Hotel Regina, where a new general staff and various auxiliary units were being formed.

The refugees were clearly depressed; they still remembered vividly the lost Polish campaign and their disappointment with Poland's passive Allies. But here in Modane, by contrast with Bucharest, Rejewski, Różycki, and Zygalski were no longer left to fend for themselves. They did not have to stand in the long line where permits were issued to remain in France. All the formalities were taken care of by a French officer, who supplied them with railroad tickets and saw them off to the platform. Then a few more hours by train, through Lyons, Nevers, and Orleans. Although the war had been in progress for several weeks, Paris was pulsing with the normal life of the great city of five million.

The first few days in the French capital were filled with formalities and talks with representatives of the newly formed wartime radio-intelligence organization, whose chief, Bertrand, had gone to Rumania to secure the release from internment camps of officer and civilian workers of the Polish B.S.-4. The cryptologists were put up temporarily at the Hotel Viator and later at the Hotel des Sèvres.

On September 29 they were summoned to the Polish Embassy, where they learned about the formation of Gen. Władysław Sikorski's new government and about negotiations being conducted with the French government concerning the creation of Polish armed forces in France. Bertrand returned on October 2, and soon other B.S.-4 personnel began to arrive in Paris: Maj. Maksymilian Ciężki, Antoni Palluth, Edward Fokczyński, and somewhat later Lt. Col. Gwido Langer and the others.[9]

Although before the war the French High Command had pledged large-scale air operations in the event of aggression against Poland, these solemn promises were not fulfilled. General Gamelin was, as he later wrote, irritated by the excessive obtrusiveness of the Polish ambassador and military attaché in Paris, who demanded immediate, effective action on land and in the air. The French and British staffs allegedly had no proof that Germany's Luftwaffe was, in fact, attacking open cities in Poland and massacring civilian refugees. On September 12, when the great Battle of the Bzura River[10] was just developing seventy miles west of Warsaw, French "Directive Number 4" to all commands practically meant abandonment of any large-scale offensive against Germany. It was decided to "dig in on native soil" (s'enterrir au sol paternel) and wait for the Germans to attack and bleed themselves white on the Maginot Line. The consequences of this passive strategy, which turned all the initiative over to the enemy, were within a few months to prove catastrophic.

Patriotic French officers, many of whom had participated in World War I and, in November 1918, had celebrated victory over the Kaiser, had taken seriously their high command's assurances about immediate actions to be taken in relief of their Polish ally and to be followed by a great offensive "with all available forces." Day after day went by, and all they could do was follow the rapid advances of the German armies through Poland, drawing the positions of the two sides on a scrupulously maintained situation map.

The chief of France's Second Bureau, Col. M. Gauché; the chief of the new wartime intelligence organization, the Fifth Bureau, Col. Louis Rivet; and the chief of radio intelligence, Lieutenant Colonel Bertrand, were among the ranking French officers whom the commander in chief, General Gamelin, regarded as excessive pessimists. The main battle, reasoned Gamelin, would be fought on the Franco-German front, and it would be a mistake to engage the Germans prematurely.

NOTES

1. Westerplatte is a small peninsula within the city limits of Gdańsk (formerly Danzig) at the outlet of the Wisła (Vistula) River. Before the war, Westerplatte was the site of a Polish military transit depot. On 1 September 1939, Westerplatte's bombardment by the German battleship *Schleswig-Holstein* signaled the opening of World War II. Despite overwhelming German superiority (3,500 men, sixty-five artillery pieces, and Luftwaffe and torpedo boat support) the 182 Poles commanded by Maj. Henryk Sucharski managed to defend Westerplatte until September 7. The stubborn defense of Westerplatte had great importance for the morale of the embattled Polish people.—ED.

2. Bonatz, *Funkaufklärung*, 116.

3. Sadowski. *Oddział II Sztabu Głównego.*

4. On the posture of Poland's allies, and for a lucid summary of the September Campaign generally, as well as of Poland's interwar history, see Watt, *Bitter Glory.*—ED.

5. Marian Rejewski told Richard Woytak:

> [S]omewhere near Łuck ["Wootsk"—ED.], at the edge of a wood, Langer, Ciężki [and] Palluth by their joint efforts buried some documents pertaining to [Enigma, in] a chest. . . . It was late in the evening. Someone could have seen it. . . . If [those notes] had gotten into Russian hands, . . . if they had [been] sent to specialists, say in Moscow, [the Russians] could have reconstructed [the principles and techniques of solving Enigma]. But. . . that is all speculation [?].

Rejewski, Interview.

The drama of those days is captured in a surviving diary of Henryk Zygalski's, containing brief notes on the successive stages and events in the evacuation:

5 IX	[September] 39 Burning of papers, preparations for evacuation. In the night, departure for the Vilno [Railroad] Station [Dworzec Wileński, on the east bank of the Wisła River—ED.].
6 IX 39	In the evening, departure.
7 IX 39	Stop at Miłosna [a town a short distance east of Warsaw—ED.]. At Mińsk Mazowiecki [25 kilometers east of Warsaw—ED.], air raid on the station. Outside Mińsk, a stop in the woods. . .
8 IX 39	During the night, collision between trains. Cars pushed off [tracks]. Opaleń before Siedlce [50 kilometers farther east—ED.]. Air raids and bombings. . . Captain Zawadzki wounded. During the night, we go through burning Siedlce.
9 IX 39	Several stops (Luków [30 km. south of Siedlce—ED.], Terespol [90 km. east of Luków—ED.]. In afternoon, arrival in Brześć [8 km. east of Terespol—ED.]. Air raids on railroad station. Taking out of wounded. . .
10 IX 39	Air raids on Brześć before noon. Leave by truck for Wielkoryty. In evening, departure by special [direction finding] auto with Major's family.
11 IX 39	We arrive outside Kowel [120 km. southeast of Brześć—ED.]. A stop in woods. Drive through Kowel, air raid. A stop outside Kowel.

13 IX 39   In Łuck [40 km. southeast of Kowel—ED.] we lose [our] authorities. We race on toward Włodzimierz [70 km. to the west—ED.]. We turn back, and once more toward Włodzimierz. Meet Major [Ciężki], [who] orders [us] to turn back. We lose our way and drive toward Łuck. A bad day. In Łuck, search for gasoline. Night with watches by turns.

14 IX 39   We drive toward Włodzimierz... We return and drive toward Dubno [110 km. east-southeast of Włodzimierz—ED.]... Take on gasoline. Air raid. We drive on through Krzemieniec [35 km. south of Dubno—ED.]. Special auto breaks down...

15 IX 39   We transfer to special vehicles. Downpour. Ride toward Trembowla [85 km. south of Krzemieniec—ED.]. My car breaks down. Bivouac in grove. News about bombing of echelon (13 IX). Change in direction of travel—toward Husiatyn [40 km. southeast of Trembowla—ED.]... News about death of Cybulski and Butkiewicz. Drive south.

16 IX 39   Drive across Dniestr [River]. Kołomyja [100 km. west-southwest of Husiatyn—ED.]... A stop in a field... In evening, billet in Utoropy.

17 IX 39   Sunday... News from the East. Drive on. In the night, arrival in Kuty [about 50 km. southeast of Kołomyja—ED.]. Crossing of border on 17/18 IX...

Zygalski, Diary.

6. At 4 a.m. that morning, the Soviet Army had entered eastern Poland. The Polish-Soviet border was only sixty miles east of Kuty (KOO-tih), and that afternoon Soviet tanks had entered Śniatyn, a town just twenty-five miles away. The bridge at Kuty was now the only point at which Poles could cross into Rumania; the Red Army held all the others. All day long, remnants of the Polish Air Force, now numbering no more than a hundred planes, had been flying low over Kuty, headed for internment at the Rumanian military airfield at Cernauti. At a meeting in Kuty that began at 4 p.m., the Polish cabinet decided to withdraw to Rumania. Thousands of Polish soldiers were crossing the bridge and as they did so, to prevent confiscation of their rifles by the Rumanians, throwing them over the parapet of the bridge into the shallow Czeremosz River. Almost none of the government leaders or officials, and few of the soldiers, would ever set foot on Polish soil again. Watt, *Bitter Glory*, 7-9—ED.

7. *Relacja attaché wojskowego w Bukareszcie (1939-1940) ppłka dypl. T. Zakrzewskiego.*

8. Ibid.

9. According to Mayer,

On 26 [September] 1939... French Army [Captain] de Winter [had] arrived at Calimanesti [a Rumanian spa in the southern Carpathian Mountains of northern Rumania, on the Aluta River, a tributary of the Danube; population in 1970: 7,500—ED.] where...part of the officers of the Polish General Staff [were being] detained by [the] Rumanians. He came to me and even stayed in my [hotel] apartment... He was looking for some Polish officers [including] Lt. Col. Langer [for] whom he had a message from Bertrand... Next day he met Langer and [proposed that Langer] go to France with all his...cryptologists...to continue...work. Lt. Col. Langer immediately...reported this to me and asked for my advice. [In view of the impossibility of reestablishing] in the nearest future [an] independent Polish radio interception service, which was absolutely indispensable for...cryptological work, I advised Langer to accept Bertrand's invitation...go to France and [there] settle...with the new Polish authorities the matter of further Polish-French collaboration in this field. According to Langer's papers [that are] in my possession [that is what] he did...

When at the end of December 1939 I was at last allowed to [leave Rumania for] France, Major Bertrand found me...and invited me to..."P.C. Bruno." There I was received with full military honours. But the most important thing which I noticed then was...that Major Bertrand [had organized] his post with full recognition of the Polish participation in its functioning (Polish emblems, Polish papers, etc.).

Mayer, "Supplement to the paper of 21.5.1974," 3-4.—ED.

More detail about B.S.-4's evacuation from Warsaw to Paris were provided by Marian Rejewski in conversation with Richard Woytak:

[T]o Brześć we rode the so-called Echelon F evacuation train.... At Brześć...the three of us, Zygalski, Różycki, and I, [were] detailed to...Headquarters and therefore...continued the journey...by automobile [instead of train]. [S]ometimes [we rode] in a passenger car—we had a tiny car—the three of us, plus the driver, and there were also some—spare batteries—it was awfully uncomfortable. I was seated very badly, I was sprawled on top of all these batteries—it was awful.... Later we rode in... Poland had these...mobile stations for ciphers— probably they had been produced by AVA. [I]nside...was a [radio] station [and] one or two cots. It had been intended to accommodate several—maybe two, three, four—persons. In this we rode, along with...a dozen or more people—it was stuffed beyond any normal capacity—and in this fashion we rode all the way to the [Polish-]Rumanian border.... At the border...civilians were separated from military—the military [went] one way, civilians another. In this way, we lost contact with our military authorities, with Langer and Ciężki. [O]f necessity, we became...our own bosses—A [Rumanian] lieutenant told us to go that way, to the camp. He pointed out the direction. I tried to remonstrate with this...Rumanian, but he said: "Befiel ist Befiel!" [properly "Befehl ist Befehl!"—German for "An order is an order!"]—Straight on, we were supposed to go straight on. So go we did—but...not...to the camp. Along the way there was a railroad station, so instead of going to the camp [the three of us] went to the station, waited for the next train, got on board, and rode to Bucharest.... In Bucharest [we went] straight to...the Polish embassy, [and] I reported to the [Polish] military attaché, Colonel Zakrzewski, and told him that we...had been in touch with the French and the British, that they were probably expecting us, that we were cryptologists, and so on. And he...said that if we'd like to get in touch with [them], he agreed to it.... So my colleagues and I went to the British embassy.... And there, as chance would have it, *just* as we got there—I was asking the usher where I could find—I don't know whether I was asking for the ambassador or the military attaché .... "There he is!" [A] bus had just pulled in, [carrying] the entire...British embassy from Warsaw. Well, this...man—I don't know whether he was the ambassador or the attaché—he was rather preoccupied. Here I was trying to explain in my broken English what I wanted, and he says: "All right, but I don't have time just now...I'm not going to wire...I can...write, or something like that. Come back in a few days." Well, I took that...like the Spanish *mañana*...that is, [as] a rebuff.... And so I went to the French. And they [were very attentive]: "Yes, certainly, right away—may we have your passports...ah, you have no passports? ...That's no problem." There was a young man...secretary of the French embassy, probably his name was de Victor...he went right away to the Polish embassy. [The Polish embassy] was besieged [by] thousands of people...who wanted to get passports too. He squeezed through them all...we went in...and they immediately gave us passports. We wrote out all the information ourselves just as we wanted it [and] they stamped them. We had [our] passports; then...we still had to get other visas ...Yugoslavian...that took a day or so, and we immediately set off by train from Bucharest to Paris.... On the way we made one stop, I think it was in Trieste, because...we were tired, and then again [at] the border station in Modane, France—there we also made a brief stop, but a colonel phoned—I gave him a phone number to call: *dix-huit, dix-huit, dix-huit* [eighteen-eighteen-eighteen]— he phoned, then he went in,...bought [us] tickets, saw us off to the train, and we were on our way.

[Meanwhile, Langer and the others] were looking for us. Ha! [laughing] *they were looking for us....* when we arrived in Paris [and] reported in,...Bertrand's deputy received us [and] said that Bertrand was away—he didn't say [Bertrand was] out of France, that he was in Rumania—...he [only] said [that Bertrand] was away....[Most likely] he had just gone to Bucharest—to Rumania—to look

for us. Meanwhile they were looking for us high and low; later I found out
. . . Langer had told them . . . : "Well, . . . if we don't find Rejewski, there's no point
in our going to Paris." But apparently . . . they finally got word [laughing] *that
we're already in Paris, and they came* [to Paris].
Rejewski, Interview.

10. Known also as the Battle of Kutno (KOOT-noh), it was conducted in west-central Poland on
September 10-17 and was directed on the Polish side by Gen. Tadeusz Kutrzeba, with notable
initial successes. The Polish offensive brought to the scene the commander in chief of the
German Army, Gen. Walther von Brauchitsch, who personally conducted the German operations there, beginning September 14. The outcome of the battle was decided by Luftwaffe bomber
units.—ED.

8.

Paris

On October 20, barely two weeks after the Polish Army's last regular battle of 1939,[1] a small group of Poles resumed their interrupted struggle with the German ciphers. The mathematician-cryptologists who had been evacuated to France in late September, and the military and civilian B.S.-4 personnel who had subsequently been evacuated to France from Rumanian internment, were the first among the host of Polish refugees to again operate actively on the anti-Hitlerite front.

A credit to the French High Command, despite its posture during September 1939 and its disastrous military doctrines, was its appreciation of the importance of intelligence. This is bespoken by the creation of a smoothly functioning center for decryptment and radio intelligence. The animating spirit of that center was Maj. Gustave Bertrand, who was given a free hand and was not interfered with.

In accordance with mobilization plans for the French armed forces, the military intelligence service (S.R.), which until then had been directly subordinate to the Ministry of War, became a part of the general staff. Its official name henceforth was "Fifth Bureau of the Army General Staff" (5ᵉ Bureau de l'État Major de l'Armée). The Fifth Bureau comprised four sections: administration, offensive intelligence, information collection and preparation, and studies. The last, uncommunicative name (Section d'Examen, or S.E.) concealed radio intelligence and decryptment of enemy signals.

Named to head the S.E., the wartime radio intelligence service,[2] was Gustave Bertrand, who, henceforth, directed all of radio intelligence. Two separate monitoring systems now worked for his service: the former civilian Network for Monitoring and Radiogoniometry of Foreign Radio Broadcasting (Réseau d'Ecoute et de Radiogoniométrie des Emissions Radio-Electriques Etrangères, or R.E.G.), and the Network for Supervision of Domestic Radio Broadcasting and Investigation of Clandestine Stations (Réseau de Contrôle des Emissions Radioélectriques de l'Intérieur et de

Recherche des Postes Clandestins, or R.C.R.). Bertrand held, concentrated in his hands, an elaborate apparatus that supplied to the cryptologists signals traffic both from the Reich and from Nazi agents in French territory. French radio intelligence worked efficiently—which, as Bertrand writes, could not be said of other units in the high command and general staff. The Polish cryptologists and other specialists, without whom decryptment of Enigma would have been impossible, became the apple of his eye.

The central units of French military intelligence were moved out of Paris for the duration of the war to two spacious chateaux in the town of Gretz-Armainvillers, about forty kilometers northeast of the capital. The seat of offensive intelligence and evaluation was the Château Péreire, code named P.C. [Poste de Commandement—Command Post] Victor, and the radio intelligence and decryptment services were housed in the large, three-story Château de Vignolles, code named P.C. Bruno.

The Château de Vignolles, with numerous quarters and a guardhouse at the main entrance, was encompassed by a large park, in which stood several smaller buildings. One of these, at the other end of the park, housed a seven-man group of Spanish cryptologists who worked on Italian ciphers. They were fugitives from the Franco regime, Republican officers who had been reclaimed from French internment camps. The park grounds included a pond with sluice and a piece of meadow, as well as artificial grottos and rocks. The chateau's attic held something that resembled a painter's studio. The walls were covered with pretentious stylized landscapes, and a large fireplace of hewn stones completed the furnishings.

Bertrand had the clutter cleared out of the rooms and, under his provident eye, Château de Vignolles was transformed into a bustling, efficient radio intelligence center. By the end of October 1939 the Polish team that constituted the backbone of the operation was complete. In addition to the officers and specialists from the general staff Cipher Bureau who have been mentioned, there had arrived at Vignolles Capt. Jan Graliński, Maj. (reserves) Wiktor Michałowski, Lt. (reserves) Henryk Paszkowski, Sylwester Palluth (nephew of engineer Antoni Palluth), Piotr Smoleński, Bronisław Krajewski, and Kazimierz Gaca. The Poles formed Team Z,[3] which worked at breaking Nazi ciphers and codes.[4] French decipherers were detailed to help with the routine reading of signals.

In wartime, when governments and states collapse and are reborn in a different political shape, the legal status of soldiers and civilians who find themselves abroad, in a foreign if friendly country, becomes complicated. The position of the handful of Poles who were to take up the struggle against the Nazis in the sensitive field of cryptology likewise required clarification.

In October 1939, when Polish military authorities—a ministry of military affairs, and a general staff—were being formed in Paris, Polish recruiting offices were already active in France, enlisting volunteers. The legal basis for Polish military recruitment in France was the bilateral agreement of 9 September 1939, which envisaged the raising initially of "one Polish division, to be a part of the Polish armed forces."[5] Poland's defeat, and the unprecedented exodus of the Polish government and high command to Rumania while the country was still fighting, upset these plans. But already, beginning on September 12, the army camp at Coetquidan, in Brittany, which had been turned over to the Poles, rang with Polish voices and, in the evenings, Polish soldiers' songs. By 20 September 1939, about fifteen thousand resident Polish émigrés had reported as volunteers. The initial limit having been exceeded, enlisting was temporarily halted.

In the closing days of September 1939, when General Sikorski assumed command of the Polish armed forces (army and air force units) in France, the register of mobilization-age Poles took in some one hundred thirty thousand men, including one hundred three thousand fit for military service. Over two hundred recruiting boards came into existence. The French authorities, however, would not agree to such broad recruitment, since many of the Poles worked in industries vital to France's national defense. The quota granted to the newly organized Polish Army came to about sixty thousand men. More refugees and fugitives from internment camps kept arriving, however, from Rumania, Hungary, and Lithuania, and directly from occupied Poland.

The creation of a Polish Army in France, to continue the war with Germany, encountered numerous difficulties. Arms, equipment, and barracks were scarce. Nevertheless, Polish tactical units arose in record time: the First Grenadier Division (Pierwsza Dywizja Grenadierów), the Second Rifle Division (Druga Dywizja Strzelców Pieszych), the Highland Brigade (Brygada Podhalańska), the Light Motorized Brigade (Brygada Lekka Motorowa), and later the Third Infantry Division (Trzecia Dywizja Piechoty). About 20 percent of the Polish Army were veterans of the September campaign and Polish refugees; the remainder were newly recruited Polish émigrés resident in France. (All Polish Air Force personnel in France had been in the air force before the war.)

When the situation of the Polish military units in France was finally clarified in mid-October 1939, the legal status of the officers and civilians of the Polish General Staff's Cipher Bureau was also cleared up. On the basis of an agreement with the French High Command, the cryptologists were listed with Polish Army personnel and detailed for the duration of the war to the Franco-Polish Bruno center at Gretz-Armainvillers. This solution was only logical, for to break and read Nazi signals the specialists needed suitable facilities and enemy intercepts. These essentials could only be provided by the French High Command, which ran a suitably equipped radio monitoring system.

Beginning in November 1939, the Franco-Polish Bruno center became the chief headquarters and foundation of all Allied radio intelligence. It encompassed monitoring stations, fixed and mobile goniometric posts for direction finding of enemy radio stations, and other auxiliary facilities. All enciphered intercepts reached the Polish cryptologists, who had the use of three Enigma machines (two secretly taken out of Poland during the evacuation, plus the one that had been presented to the French after the Warsaw conference in July 1939).[6]

The work was made more efficient by some new ideas and discoveries. For example, it was found that the German encipherers, after setting their

Enigmas in the starting position and closing the metal lid, were selecting as the message key (Spruchschlüssel) the letters visible in the glass windows. Such carelessness cost the Nazis dearly. These letters were usually identical with the settings on the Enigma's internal rings. As a result, a few minutes past midnight the duty cryptologist would already know the cipher key for that day, and the French could read Wehrmacht orders and reports broadcast that day at the same time as their intended recipients.

During the Poles' first weeks at Bruno, toward the end of November 1939, the French deputy chief, Capt. Henri Braquenié, confided some news from across the English Channel. The British were building their own cryptological bomb, the plans for which chief British cryptologist Alfred Dillwyn Knox and Comdr. Alastair Denniston had become acquainted with on July 25, during their visit to Warsaw. They were also producing perforated (Zygalski) sheets. Indeed, of the latter, there were enough not only for their own needs but also for Bruno. In exchange, Bruno was supplying German Navy and Air Force signals, which were of particular interest to the British, who were not directly threatened on land. On 3-7 December 1939, Colonel Langer and Captain Braquenié were in London and at Bletchley on a working visit.

The changes that the Germans had introduced into Enigma cipher keys on 1 July 1939 were the main obstacle that the cryptologists had to overcome after getting to France and starting work at Bruno. Just before the outbreak of war, on 26 August 1939, they had broken the new, wartime version of the Enigma system (the messages of July 6 had been read, and the backlog quickly made up). On arrival in France, however, they had to reconstruct the entire process of breaking the new cipher, since all the relevant documents had been destroyed before the team had crossed the border into Rumania.[7] The first key to be solved in France was one for 28 October 1939.[8] Thereafter, the stream of fresh firsthand information about the enemy was once again flowing to the French High Command and to London. Liaison with the British was assured by a British officer detailed to Bruno, Capt. Kenneth "Pinky" McFarlan, as well as by mutual visits and contacts between Bruno and Bletchley Park.

> As a result, collaboration with Y [one of the cryptonyms for Bletchley] continued more than ever, and in December [1939 Bertrand] went to London to organize work "en pool," as well as diverse measures relative to interception and the rapid exchange of results: a procedure was set up for transmitting keys by teletype or radio.[9]

Another important matter was the production, on the basis of the Polish Enigmas, of a larger number of the machines, since they were wearing out from round-the-clock use. In November 1939 Bertrand ordered forty copies from a precision mechanics firm that had long been associated with S.R. To avoid construction errors, the Poles prepared detailed drawings of all the parts on a scale of 1:1.[10] In order to do this, they had to strip down one of the three machines that the Bruno center worked with. For a time, this cut down on the number of signals read, though it did not disrupt the cryptologists' work on reconstructing keys. Much as AVA had been in Poland, the French firm was obliged to deliver only the parts, while the assembly itself was to be carried out at Bruno. Unfortunately, the manufacture of the Enigma parts proceeded sluggishly, and by May 1940 Bruno had not received a single new Enigma. It was only after the fall of France in June 1940 and the opening of underground work in the free zone of the south that four machines were finally assembled from parts produced in occupied France.[11]

Information derived from Enigma decryptment at Bruno was printed on gold-colored paper, hence in staff intelligence parlance it was called Feuillettes Jaunes (Yellow Pages). Ministry of Foreign Affairs decrypts of manual ciphers were green, Ministry of Internal Affairs, pink.

Bruno's personal liaison with French headquarters was through Bertrand and Lieutenant Annequin. Three times daily, the Deuxième Bureau delivered reports to the commander in chief. At the same time, the Yellow Pages were supplied to Colonel Baril, intelligence chief of the Northeastern Command at La Ferté-sous-Jouarre. Baril then forwarded them to Colonel Gauché, intelligence chief of Allied ground forces at Montry. There were also teletype links, and plans to install a secure radio teletype (Belino), but up to the German assault on France, work on this most modern form of secret communication had not been completed. Bruno reports were also sent to the general staff and the air force high command.

Enigma decrypts were exchanged with Bletchley Park in England through a specially established teletype line. This was seen to personally by the British liaison officer, Captain McFarlan.

What was the content of the Enigma intercepts read by the Poles at Bruno?

Particularly important were ciphergrams that referred to the procedures of the German communications system. Every day before midnight, messages called Verkehrsabwieklung were broadcast, informing all radio stations in a given net about the transmission and reception hours, wavelengths, and call signs that would be in effect the next day. This information was used by French monitoring stations to prepare for intercepting enemy correspondence the next day.

Monitoring of the German radio nets and reading of their correspondence made possible the gradual reconstruction of the entire system of German radio communication in the west and, consequently, establishment of the disposition of Wehrmacht commands, higher formations, and units. A separate category of radiograms told of methods used by the Germans to camouflage radio correspondence (Verschleierung) and to actively mislead the adversary (Täuschung).

Bertrand lists twenty-odd categories of cipher intercepts. Following are only the most characteristic ones, indicative of the range of information available from this source:

- Funkbetrieb: Procedures in the German radio nets.
- Morgenmeldung: ⎧ Situation reports
- Tagesmeldung: ⎪ transmitted at
- Tagesabschlussmeldung: ⎬ the respective
- Abendmeldung: ⎩ times of day.

- Aufklärungsmeldung: Reports of intelligence collected by German staffs about the adversary.
- Gliederung: Order of battle of German higher formations.
- Frontverlauf: Detailed description of the front line (the forward edge of a German military grouping).
- Alarmbereitschaft: Directives for combat readiness.
- Lageorientierung: Information on the location of forces.
- Einsatzbefehl: Combat orders.
- Gefechtsmeldung: Combat reports.
- Meteo: Meteorological situation (for the air force).
- Flottenbefehl: Air fleet orders.
- Sonderunternehmen: Special operations.
- Flak: German antiaircraft orders and reports.
- Nachschub: Information on logistics.

In the west, through the winter and early spring of 1940, there lasted a *drôle de guerre* (phony war). The French Army sat back behind the powerful fortifications of the Maginot Line. The French General Staff, after studying the late Polish campaign, reached the ill-advised conclusion that its course held out no important warnings for France. The Polish armed forces, it was maintained, had been poorly armed and trained. The Poles had no chance of stopping the aggressor—but not because of some special strength of Germany's armor or air force. The Germans had had a disproportionately great advantage, which had been further increased by the disastrous configuration of Poland's borders. France's situation was altogether different. To generals peering through the loopholes and periscopes of a Maginot Line bristling with artillery and machine guns, the danger seemed rather unreal.

But even with the mistaken French doctrine of passive defense based on the Maginot Line, an important role was still ascribed to intelligence concerning German strengths and intentions. Radio intelligence and the reading of enemy signals acquired particular importance under wartime conditions, when the flow of secret-agent information had decreased. Bruno thus had its hands full of work. While the front was enveloped in the silence that preceded the storm, the intelligence war on the airwaves raged on uninterrupted.

At Château Vignolles, work proceeded around the clock, in three shifts. Intercept stations near the German border, at Metz, Strasbourg, and Mulhouse, equipped with teletype, sent endless strings of letters to Bruno, and the Polish specialists turned them into plain German.

The greatest concentration of work fell within the night hours. Between 0000 and 0020 hours, cipher operators with the Nazi army groups, armies, corps, and divisions deep within Germany and on the Siegfried Line changed their Enigma settings and keys. Rejewski, Różycki, and Zygalski, using methods tested out during the years 1933-39, broke the keys that were daily changed. They also reconstructed many German signals from beginning to end, because in France, unlike in Poland, they did not have experienced decipherers to help them. They often worked fifteen or sixteen hours a day, for example, in shifts from 3 p.m. to 6 or 7 a.m. In time, trained French noncommissioned officers took over the reading of the less important signals.

Marian Rejewski, who continued to work on the theoretical and mathematical aspects of cipher breaking, for a time was exempted from night duty and occupied himself with elaborating a methodology for solving ciphers. Produced as a secret handbook, this was a valuable aid in training new workers at the center.

In the early spring of 1940, the French radio-intelligence and decryptment service, thanks to the Polish specialists and Major Bertrand's energy, was probably the most efficient of all the Allied intelligence services. To make solution of Enigma keys still faster and more efficient, a Franco-British teletype link was established.

In 1975, shortly before his death, Henri Braquenié (one of the participants in the trilateral conferences of January and July 1939) divulged[12] some details about communications between Bruno and Bletchley in the first half of 1940. In December 1939, he had gone to Bletchley and established procedures for mutual exchange of information, especially of solved daily Enigma keys. Exchange of information about the keys took place after midnight, since the Germans set their Enigmas to the new key—the machine's new starting position—every day at 0000 hours. The Bruno-Bletchley teletype line ran across six hundred kilometers of French and British soil and the English Channel, so there was always a possibility of its being tapped by unauthorized parties, and the cipher used had to be absolutely secure. Therefore, according to Braquenié, for their correspondence the Allies used *Enigma itself!* Clearly, the Allies put as much faith in the German machine's unbreakability by the Germans as the Germans did in its unbreakability by the Allies.

A rule observed by cipher units, Allied as well as German, required that long messages be divided into separately transmitted parts, and that short ones be padded out. The purpose was to make it hard for the enemy to decrypt a message, for example, by substituting in presumed contents. As padding the Germans used X's or entire phrases such as Gurkensalat (cucumber salad) or Schweinefleisch (pork). Braquenié, who was personally responsible for the Bruno-Bletchley correspondence, observed the same rules, and in addition closed his messages to Britain with a "Heil Hitler!"

The Franco-British exchange of information, which prevented duplication of effort, worked efficiently during the fighting in Norway in April 1940. But even before the fighting had started on the craggy Norwegian coasts and fjords, the Polish-French team had broken an uncommonly hard three-letter code used by Nazi staffs for communication with fighter and bomber squadrons and also for exchange of meteorological information between aircraft and land.

The puzzling three-letter code had first made its appearance in December 1939, but the cryptologists, overburdened as they were with work on Enigma, had not given it much attention. With the German assault on the west impending, however, the breaking of the Luftwaffe code was taking on mounting urgency, and the trail of the elusive code (its system of letters changed every twenty-four hours) led back once again to Enigma. This time, the first clue came from Bletchley. The British had noticed that the letters in the code did not change in a random manner. If "a" changed to "p," then "p" was elsewhere replaced by "a." They had made no further headway, but this observation satisfied the Polish Enigma experts at Bruno. They knew that what was manifesting itself here was the "exclusivity principle" which they had discovered back in 1932. It was hard to believe that the Germans could be so careless.

The Germans' mistake meant that, having after midnight solved Enigma's daily setting, the Poles could with no further effort also read the Luftwaffe signals. In view of the intensifying war in the air, this was an important cryptological victory.

Meanwhile, at the French staff offices, the atmosphere was becoming increasingly jittery. Intelligence was registering more and more German divisions concentrating at the borders with Holland (three), Belgium and Luxembourg (eighteen), and France along the upper Rhine (ten to twelve). Additionally, the number of divisions in western Germany, in the Saar Basin and the Palatinate, was estimated at twenty-five, and in the Baden-Baden area, five. A further six to eight divisions were discovered east of the Rhine. Between October 1939 and April 1940, the Germans raised forty-three new divisions, bringing the total to one hundred ninety divisions, including ten to twelve armored. The French General Staff now wondered: when? It was already known that the Germans would have about one hundred divisions in the first wave, ten of them armored.

Before attacking France, Hitler decided to secure strong strategic positions on the sea by taking over Norway and Denmark. The French General Staff learned of the decision to attack these two countries four days before the event from decrypted Enigma signals. Information also came from Polish intelligence agents in Stettin, who reported troop embarkations.

At 5 a.m. on 9 April 1940, the invasion began, planned and executed by the OKW command staff (Wehrmachtsführungsstab) under Hitler's personal direction. Participating in the campaign against Norway and Denmark were forces under the command of Gen. Nikolaus von Falkenhorst: nine divisions, two hundred forty bombers and assault planes, ninety-five fighters, and five hundred forty-five transport and reconnaissance aircraft. Naval forces in the operation included three battleships, six cruisers (two of them heavy), thirteen destroyers, eight torpedo boats, and thirty submarines. While shielding the landing operation, this fleet sustained heavy losses, including the heavy cruiser *Blücher*, sunk in the Oslo Fjord.

In the course of the Norwegian operations, the German Army suffered heavy losses at Narvik, where units of the Polish Highland Brigade that had been formed in France also fought.

While fighting continued in Norway with variable fortunes, the Abwehr was conducting a large-scale deception campaign. Its agents in neutral countries were spreading rumors, and Nazi diplomats were committing intentional indiscretions. One version had it that before the conclusion of the fighting in Norway an offensive in the west was nonsense, but after subduing Norway, Hitler was ready to sacrifice half a million men and lose 80 percent of the Luftwaffe, if need be, to break through the Maginot Line. In the meantime, the German General Staff was elaborating a completely different version of the assault on France.

In the last days before the German general offensive in the west, alarming reports were reaching the French General Staff:

On 20 April 1940: Abwehr agents were withdrawn from Belgium, indicating that this country would soon become a theater of military operations.

On May 1: German forces would attack between May 8 and 10 along the entire front, including the Maginot Line. The Sedan area, Belgium, Holland, and northern France were to be occupied within ten days, all of France, within a month.

The night of May 5-6: The general offensive was to be expected at any moment.

On May 6: The attack was to be expected at any moment. German staff officers said that the French Army would not be able to stop the Wehrmacht's armor.

In May 1940, the French Army, although it had over 3,000 tanks, had but two armored divisions, recently formed and poorly trained; each contained about 150 tanks, less than half as many as a German division. The remaining tanks were dispersed among infantry units as direct support.

Claims about the ubiquitousness and extraordinary efficiency of the Abwehr and of Nazi intelligence generally were probably exaggerated. Many people in Poland, France, and later Britain as well, knew about Enigma having been broken, yet the Germans continued to use it right up to the final collapse of their Thousand-Year Reich in May of 1945.

To be sure, French intelligence, especially the prudent Gustave Bertrand, had not neglected precautions. After work had begun at Bruno in the late autumn of 1939, a supposed mathematical genius named Raffali had presented himself to representatives of the French General Staff in Paris, promising to solve the German and any other machine cipher if the general staff would grant him 200,000 francs to construct decrypting equipment. Bertrand succeeded, with some effort, in convincing his superiors that they should not begrudge the money. Let this genius—probably a German agent—work on his decrypting machine. Bertrand argued: we want the Germans to think that we are still grappling unsuccessfully with their cipher; giving him the money will be the best way of convincing them. Even with the modest value of the franc, it was still an expensive deception. But the military advantages that accrued to the Allies from the work of the Team Z cryptologists were incomparably greater. The phony war could not last forever, and in the face of the inevitable confrontation with Germany, precise information about that country's armed forces and war plans was beyond price.

Bruno received intercepts not only from the two French monitoring nets that have been mentioned, but also from the French Air Force, the French military command in North Africa, and a special post on Sainte-Margerite Island off the Riviera, manned by French and British personnel, that monitored the Italian Air Force.

An important part of Bruno's work was ferreting out clandestine radio transmitters in French territory. This operation was based on the prewar R.C.R. radio-monitoring net, whose peacetime task had been discovering radio operators who had not registered with the authorities, had not paid their fees, or broke broadcasting regulations. This task had been the business of the ministries of posts and telegraphs and of internal affairs. After war broke out, the monitoring net was turned over to the military, and secret messages intercepted by it were sent to Bruno for decryptment. Signals that were read were passed on to counterintelligence, which sought to locate and neutralize the spy transmitters.[13]

During the war, the Abwehr relied on three different cryptographic means for radio transmissions:[14]

The first: To addressees in countries under firm German security control and within the confines of their diplomatic missions, they employed Enigma.

The second: To agents at large or their outposts in countries where the security of crypto-systems could not be guaranteed, they used "paper and pencil" ciphers, keyed, for example, to published books, a different one being issued to each agent.

The third: In rare instances, they used code books (Satzbücher).

In addition to the main department at Bruno concerned with deep radio intelligence, a counterespionage department was created, whose task was to read the encrypted reports of German agents and the instructions transmitted to them by the S.D. and Abwehr in Germany. The cryptological work in this department was handled by two French officers, Captain Marlière and Captain Chadapaux, and by the Polish engineer Antoni Palluth, who, before the war, apart from his designing and technical duties, had worked in B.S.-4 on nonmachine ciphers. The counterespionage department had considerable achievements. Over a few months, 287 radio transmissions by German agents were read, contributing in no small way to combatting the German intelligence nets and fifth column before the start of the German general offensive in the west in May 1940.

With respect to the nature and quality of the information obtained about the enemy, the work of the Bruno cryptologists may be divided into three periods: from the solution of the Enigma cipher on 28 October 1939 to the start of the Norwegian campaign on 9 April 1940; from 10 April 1940 to the start of the German general offensive in the west on 10 May 1940; and the German-French campaign until the evacuation of Bruno and the capitulation of France on 22 June 1940.

The first period took in months of nearly total stagnation on the Franco-German front, a situation reflected in the term *phony war*. Nevertheless, beneath this mask of inactivity, while Germany's diplomats were probing the possibility of "peaceful solutions" at the price of recognition of conquests already completed, German staffs and commands were working feverishly, preparing new offensives and "lightning wars" patterned on the aggression against Poland. During this period, the German Army made broad use of cable communications; nevertheless, many messages sent by military radio stations were read. This made it possible to determine the order of battle of a considerable number of higher formations and units, their organizational structure, armaments and disposition, and the locations of weapon and equipment depots and other rear echelon facilities.

Apart from information about the Wehrmacht's preparations on German soil for further military operations, many messages pertained to Austria, Czechoslovakia, and Poland, where supply bases and weapon and ammunition depots were being established and airfields were being expanded and modernized. Some of the decrypts referred to the training of Luftwaffe cadre at the Air War Academy (Luftkriegsakademie) and in blind-flying schools (Blindflugschule), to training of antiaircraft artillery (Flak) units, and so on.

In the period just preceding the Norwegian campaign, numerous Enigma decrypts pertained to the intentions and concrete moves of the German commands. On April 6, three days before German forces began their invasion of Denmark and Norway (Operation Weserübung—Weser Exercise), Bruno read a directive from the chief censor of the Wehrmacht Supreme Command, implying the direction of the approaching attack. German press and radio coverage of these two countries was to be handled in such a way as not to prematurely alarm their governments and peoples or those of the Allies.

The forces that were to be used in the northern invasion were also known beforehand. They were determined from a decrypt that contained a special signal (Verfügungssignal) whose transmission would introduce new communications procedures. The message's distribution list—the army, air force, and navy units to which it was addressed—pointed to a new Wehrmacht grouping designated for a large-scale air-sea landing operation.

During the Norwegian campaign, Bruno discovered certain regularities in the German system of transmitting orders to combat units and battlefield reports back to headquarters. Most important were two categories of signals from which crucial information could be extracted for Allied staffs:[15]

First: Operational orders containing information about enemy positions (Feindlage) and about operations that German forces were to carry out (Einsatzbefehl).

Second: Various reports on the course and outcome of combat operations (Tagesmeldung), on air actions (Gefechtsmeldung), on readiness for operations (Einsatzbereitschaftsmeldung), on reconnaissance of enemy forces (Aufklärungsergebnisse), on their front line (Verlauf der vorderen Linie), and others.

All command and reporting lines for the Luftwaffe forces in the invasion of Denmark and Norway ran to the radio communications center of the Luftwaffe command set up immediately after the landing at Trondheim, Norway (Fliegführer Drontheim).

Very important to the planning of Allied air operations against the coming German invasion in the west was the breaking of the Meteo cipher used by the net of German meteorological stations (Wetterwarte, or Wewa for short) headquartered at Oslo, Norway, with field stations at Stavanger, Trondheim, and Bergen. Three times a day, they broadcast detailed information on air force operating conditions.

The determination during the Norwegian campaign of the German command and battlefield reporting system would facilitate the monitoring and decryptment of German signals during the coming period of Fall Gelb (Case Yellow), the Wehrmacht's general offensive against Holland, Belgium, and France that would begin on 10 May 1940.

NOTES

1. The Battle of Kock ("Kotsk") was fought in the vicinity of Kock, seventy miles southeast of Warsaw, from 2 to 5 October 1939, by Gen. Franciszek Kleeberg's Operational Group Polesie. Although Warsaw had fallen on September 28, the group (two infantry divisions, a cavalry division and a cavalry brigade) fought on for the honor of Polish arms. Kleeberg's army capitulated only after complete encirclement by German and approaching Soviet divisions, and after firing its last rounds.—ED.

2. As opposed to Poland's Cipher Bureau, French radio intelligence (the S.E.) had nothing to do with supplying its own armed forces with crypto-systems.

3. The Spanish cryptologists were called "Team D." The letters "Z" and "D" designated the sources of the "Bruno" information sent to the French High Command and General Staff; the fact that the information came from decryptment was not disclosed.

4. Apparently, not all of Team Z was concerned with German ciphers and codes. According to Mayer:

> The Polish group [at] "P.C. Bruno" consisted of fourteen persons besides Lt. Col. Langer. They were [German-cipher] cryptologists...Major M. Ciężki, Major W. Michałowski, Lt. H. Paszkowski, Lt. A. Palluth [and] civilian employees M. Rejewski, J. Różycki, H. Zygalski, S. Palluth, K. Gaca, R. [sic] Krajewski, E. Fokczyński [and Russian-cipher] cryptologists...Captain Graliński, Lt. S. [?] Szachno and civilian employee Smoleński.
>
> The total [number] of radiograms read...between 20 [October] 1939 and 23 [June] 1940 by the Polish group [at] Bruno [came to] 8,440. Of these, 1,151 were connected with the campaign in Norway. 5,084 deciphered radiograms concerned the campaign in France. 287 were from...clandestine radio stations working [for the] Germans. 1,085 were [Russian] radiograms... The remaining 833 radiograms came from various sources (Switzerland). Among those concerning the campaign in France were several of great operational importance. They contained information about [the] movements and O. de B. [order of battle] of German [higher formations], revealed...in [sufficient] time for undertaking ...counter-measures.
>
> On 24 [June] 1940...Bruno...ceased to exist. Its Polish personnel [were] evacuated by air to Oran and afterwards to Algiers. Lt. Col. Langer tried to get in touch with the Polish authorities and to evacuate his group [together] with [other] Polish troops to England. But he [failed to get] the necessary assistance from his French patrons.

Mayer, "The breaking up of the German ciphering machine 'ENIGMA,' " 4-6.—ED.

5. A new, expanded agreement was signed on 4 January 1940 by Gen. Władysław Sikorski and French Premier Édouard Daladier. It defined more precisely the status of the Polish armed forces that were being formed in France in the anticipated strength of one field army, including all the basic branches. Soldiers were recruited chiefly from the numerous Polonia (Poles living outside Poland) who had emigrated from the home country between the world wars, spurred by economic stagnation and unemployment.

6. According to Mayer:

> One of them was [the] one which [the Poles had] given to the French. . . in August 1939. Two others were brought by Lt. Col. Langer from the stock produced by [the] Poles which after [Poland's] defeat [in September] 1939 had [had] to be destroyed.

Mayer, "The breaking up of the German ciphering machine 'ENIGMA,' " 5.

7. Rejewski says: "[A]t first in France we could not solve Enigma messages. . . because we had destroyed all our work tools—the perforated sheets and bombs—before leaving Poland, and without them. . . work was. . . out of the question." Rejewski, "Uwagi do 'Appendix 1,' " 492.

8. This does not mean that it was solved *on* 28 October 1939. Mayer, relying on a wartime document by Gwido Langer, writes: "Langer [noted] that on 17 [January] 1940 they finally solved the key for 28 [October] 1939. . ." However, Hinsley, generally an unreliable source on matters involving Enigma, claims that G.C.C.S. records show that the Poles solved the October 28 key earlier, " '[a]t the end of the year' " 1939. Langer, Two Wartime Documents. Mayer, "The breaking up of the German ciphering machine 'ENIGMA,' " 5. Hinsley, *British Intelligence in the Second World War*, vol. 1, 493.—ED.

9. Bertrand, *Enigma*, 76.

10. This work was carried out by Antoni Palluth and Edward Fokczyński.

11. They were transported by Bertrand, who went to occupied Paris under false papers for that purpose.

12. Braquenié, Interview.

13. Bertrand, *Enigma*, 74.

14. Farago, *The Game of the Foxes*, chapter 18.

15. Bertrand, *Enigma*, 90.

9.

Ultra

Secure radio communications and foolproof cryptography, and the interception and decryptment of enemy codes and ciphers, held exceptional importance for Britain, greater than for other countries. The reason for this was simple: Britain's military potential rested primarily in her navy and air force; and in these, communications, and thus the entire command system, were based on radio and cryptography. Conversely, intelligence on enemy forces meant, for the British, chiefly a first-rate interception and decryptment service permitting constant surveillance of Axis, principally German, but also Italian, naval and air fleets.

Hence the uncommon doggedness with which the British attacked enemy codes and ciphers in the First, and still more in the Second, World War. It was a matter of survival, of getting an edge on an enemy who could deal the British Isles a mortal blow only from the sea or the air. The deficiencies of the third branch of Britain's armed forces, the army, would cost her dearly in 1940, when she had to participate in the continental war.

Britain's military radio intelligence and cryptology were an enterprise in which nothing was skimped: not qualified personnel, nor technical or material resources, nor money.

Two things should be distinguished here: first, a tendency to attribute the *entire* success to the British, and second, the actual achievements of British cryptologists during World War II, which, unquestionably, were considerable. As far as the first phase—fundamental to all further work—is concerned, it has been shown that the solution of Enigma, in all its evolving manifestations during the years 1933-39, was a purely Polish achievement. The mathematical methods, Polish Enigma doubles, and ancillary technology, when passed on to the British, enabled them to exploit this achievement in record time.

If the solution of Enigma can be presented here on the basis of comprehensive Polish sources, then information on the use that this was put to, its impact on Allied strategy and tactics during World War II, must largely be obtained elsewhere. Apart from Bertrand's book, which first broke silence in the matter, information is mainly to be found in British publications—most importantly those of F.W. Winterbotham, Patrick Beesly, Ronald Lewin, R.V. Jones, Peter Calvocoressi, Ralph Bennett, F.H. Hinsley, Gordon Welchman—and in articles and scholarly papers that significantly supplement their accounts.

How, then, does the British side of the matter present itself? Let us first recapitulate the most important facts concerning the years 1939-40, when the British operation that Winterbotham christened Ultra paralleled the decryptment efforts of the Polish-French Bruno center.

Despite all that has been written about it, the picture of the British decryptment service in the first months of the war is somewhat confused. It can, however, be roughly reconstructed, and encountered are some familiar names such as Comdr. Alastair Denniston and Alfred Dillwyn ("Dilly") Knox, who had visited Warsaw in July 1939. Between the world wars, Britain's chief cryptological center, the Government Code and Cypher School (G.C.C.S.), had been subordinate to the Foreign Office, which, during the early twenties, had taken over the personnel of the famous Room 40, the Royal Navy's World War I black chamber. In mid-1939, the Foreign Office's communications department, and with it the cryptology section, were transferred to Bletchley Park, north of London, where they remained to the end of World War II.[1]

After the outbreak of war, some of Britain's most valuable minds were concentrated at Bletchley, and work proceeded at full speed. Apart from the Enigma double, the British used a number of equipment designs that they had also received from the Poles, including those of the perforated (Zygalski) sheets and the cryptological bomb. Peter Calvocoressi, a leading Bletchley specialist, describes the bomb as a kind of electromechanical computer which subsequently underwent further evolution and gave rise to the first electronic computers, but which retained its Polish name.[2]

When the B.S.-4 workers had been evacuated from Poland to France and the Polish-French Bruno center had been set up outside Paris, the British quickly established contact with it, sending Capt. Kenneth McFarlan, a cipher officer, there as liaison. Meanwhile they were building their own cryptological bomb modeled on the Polish device and producing Zygalski sheets (in mid-December 1939, they delivered to France, for the Poles, one set of sixty series of twenty-six sheets each).[3]

The designer of the first British bomb was a young mathematician, Alan Turing (hence some publications speak of the Turing Bomb). Before the war, he had worked in the United States under Prof. John von Neumann, a pioneer in information science and computers, who, during the war, participated in the Manhattan Project. In the first months of 1940, Turing would come down to Bruno to exchange experiences in Enigma decryptment with the Poles.

Following Alan Turing's premature death in 1954 by cyanide poisoning, his mother corresponded with Henryk Zygalski, who settled in England after the war and died there on 31 August 1978.

Marian Rejewski recalls:

We treated [Turing] as a younger colleague who had specialized in mathematical logic and was just starting out in cryptology. Our discussions, if I remember correctly, pertained to the commutator and plug connections (Steckerverbindungen) that were Enigma's strong point. Turing was also interested in the three-letter code used by the Luftwaffe.

Decades later, in 1975, Rejewski recalled scenes from his wartime odyssey that—given a knowledge of the subsequent fates of principal actors—take on a new, even symbolic, meaning. For example, he remembered with almost photographic precision the farewell supper given before Alan Turing's return to England after several days' visit to the Bruno center.

In a cozy restaurant outside Paris staffed by Deuxième Bureau workers, the cryptologists and the chiefs of the secret decryptment center, Bertrand and Langer, wished to spend an evening in a casual atmosphere free of everyday concerns. Before the dishes ordered and the choice wine selected for the occasion had been served, the attention of the diners was drawn to a crystal flower glass with flowers, placed on the middle of the tablecloth. They were delicate rosy-lilac flowers with slender, funnel-shaped calyces. It was probably Langer who uttered their German and then their Polish names: "Herbstzeitlose...Zimowity jesienne...."

This meant nothing to Turing, as he gazed in silence at the flowers and the dry lanceolate leaves. He was brought back from his reverie, however, by the Latin name, *Colchicum autumnale* (autumn crocus, or meadow saffron), spoken by mathematician-geographer Jerzy Różycki.

"Why, that's a powerful poison!" said Turing in a raised voice.

To which Różycki slowly, as though weighing each word, added: "It would suffice to bite into and suck at a couple of stalks in order to attain eternity."

For a moment there was an awkward silence. Soon, however, the crocuses and the treacherous beauty of the autumnal flowers were forgotten, and an animated discussion began at the richly laid table. But despite the earnest intention of the participants not to raise professional questions, it proved impossible to get completely away from Enigma. Once again, there was talk of the errors committed by German operators and of the perforated sheets, now machine- rather than handmade, which the British sent in series from Bletchley to the Poles working at Gretz-Armainvillers, outside Paris. The inventor of the perforated sheets, Zygalski, wondered why their measurements were so peculiar, with each little square being about eight and a half millimeters on a side.

"That's perfectly obvious," laughed Alan Turing. "It's simply one-third of an inch!"

This remark in turn gave rise to a dispute as to which system of measures and currency, the traditionally chaotic British one or the lucid decimal system used in France and Poland, could be regarded as the more logical and convenient. Turing jocularly and eloquently defended the former: What other currency in the world was as admirably divided as the pound sterling, composed of 240 pence (20 shillings, each containing 12 pence)? It alone enabled three, four, five, six, or eight persons to precisely, to the penny, split a tab (with tip, generally rounded off to a full pound) at a restaurant or a pub.

Still, the very close and friendly collaboration between the cryptologists at Armainvillers and at Bletchley did not mean that all secrets and experiences were shared by the two groups. Thus, during his visit to France at the beginning of 1940, Turing did not say a word about the British having already, in mid-September 1939 soon after the memorable visit to Warsaw and Pyry, set to work not only on the mechanized production of Zygalski sheets, but also on the design and construction of an improved bomb based on the cryptologic bombs that had been built in Poland in the fall of 1938—the precise plans and diagrams for which the British had received just before the outbreak of war. In the design and construction of the British bomb Alan Turing played—as one learns from Welchman—the leading role.

The Poles hardly could have supposed that their young British colleague would some day figure in textbooks on information science as an outstanding theoretician of computers. Yet the beginnings of this new field, as has become known only recently,[4] were in Bletchley, at the Enigma-reading center created for wartime needs; and still earlier, at B.S.-4 in Warsaw and Pyry, where, beginning in 1938, several cryptological bombs had been in operation that, taken together with the unimpressive-looking, hand-perforated sheets, would give rise at Bletchley to the world's first electronic computers. (According to Marian Rejewski, inventor of the cryptological bomb, the perforated sheets that the Poles had used since 1938 were ideally suited to computerization.)

As has been mentioned, another of the luminaries at Bletchley was Alfred Dillwyn Knox, the chief British cryptologist, who had participated in the trilateral Warsaw conference in July 1939.

In relations among the several national Allied intelligence services, the prevailing tone was set by overriding considerations represented not by the cryptologists but by their high commands and general staffs. The latter decided moves and tactics that sometimes disregarded countries that were soon to be allies in war against Germany. At first it may seem hard to fathom why the Polish General Staff did not make Enigma, which had been solved at the end of 1932, available to the French until July 1939. Possibly the chief of French radio intelligence, Gustave Bertrand, did in fact know about it much earlier, privately. In any case, when—after his book came out in 1973—Polish publications disclosed the actual date of Enigma's breaking, he did not seem in the least surprised or resentful.[5] Maybe he had decided that in those dramatic and traumatic years when Hitler was repudiating the Versailles Treaty, building up the Wehrmacht, remilitarizing the Rhineland, and finally annexing Austria and the Sudetes, the secret would more safely be left in Poland. This would accord with his highly critical assessment of the policies of the prewar French governments and the French High Command's passive military doctrine, which he held responsible for France's military debacle in May-June 1940.

As for the British, they would repay the Poles' discretion—or distrust— when Rejewski and Zygalski arrived in Britain in 1943.

Concerning the date when Enigma reading was first mastered in Britain, with the aid of Polish equipment and techniques, there are discrepancies in the sources. Winterbotham writes that the first German (Luftwaffe) machine ciphers were read in their entirety at the end of February 1940. Polish and French sources, however, indicate that the British had been actively collaborating with Bruno at least since December 1939, exchanging solved daily keys and intercepts by teletype.

Winterbotham treats this early phase of Britain's Enigma operation (Ultra) marginally. During this period, only the less important German Air Force, practice, logistical, and other signals are supposed to have been solved at Bletchley. During these early days, he writes,

> the Bronze Goddess was still somewhat immature and intermittent in operation, and, I believe, it was our good fortune in obtaining an Enigma machine complete with operational keys from a shpt down German aircraft off Norway. Later the same useful material was captured from a German Tank Signals unit which had got too far ahead in the Battle of France, and again in May of 1941 the Navy's capture of a German U boat, complete with its Enigma and chart of operating keys intact, not only gave us direct access to much of the naval, military and air Enigma traffic but was also invaluable in helping the brains of Bletchley to bring the Bronze Goddess to maturity.[6]

In sliding as he does over this first, decisive stage of the Ultra operation (and, incidentally, passing over Ultra's Polish connection), Winterbotham is far too modest. Documents from the period include a report by Lt. Col. Gwido Langer giving dates of keys solved during the period from January to June 1940 and stating that, of the total of 126 keys solved in this period, 83 percent were broken with British participation.[7]

Bletchley's major participation in the day-by-day solution of German ciphers as early as the first half of 1940 is reflected in another surviving document, likewise drawn up by Langer in France. A fragment of this document illustrates well the relations existing in this unique Polish-French-British triangle, not always single-minded and free of discord.

> When I was in England in December of 1939 [writes Langer] there was also discussion of establishing cooperation. The British asked that [our] specialists be turned over to them. At that time I personally took the position that we must remain where our [Polish] armed forces were being formed. The French rejected the British proposal to create a common unit at P.C. [Poste de Commandement] Bruno. The upshot was that we were to conduct the research, and the British to do the technical and day-by-day work.[8]

Such, in the first months of the war, was the order of battle in the struggle with Enigma. The Poles still led in theoretical and mathematical work, in basic research.[9] The French, at that time the strongest partner of the alliance in terms of land forces (with their fully mobilized, 5.4-million-man army), guarded their primacy in intelligence concerning the Wehrmacht forces that were making ready for the great offensive in the west. Apparently they considered closer integration in radio intelligence and decryptment with Britain to be unnecessary. Yet, even in this area, despite the boundless energy and organizational talent of Gustave Bertrand, the indolence of the French military authorities made itself evident. At first, states Langer, "We had the use of three [Enigma] machines. Already in January one of these was taken apart to make technical drawings. On another worked the [three-man] research team."[10] That left only one machine for reading Enigma ciphers. It would be the end of July 1940, and Bruno would have been evacuated to North Africa, before the firm that had contracted to make copies of Enigma would produce any machines.

As for the British, from the fall of 1939 up to May 1940, while the phony war was being waged only by the intelligence services on the two sides, considerable progress was made at Bletchley toward mastering the techniques and procedures for reliable, regular reading of Enigma. At the same time, an extensive net of Special Liaison Units (SLUs) was created that eventually spanned nearly all the continents on the globe.

The task of the SLUs was to convey the substance of solved enemy radio messages to Allied high commands and staffs in Great Britain, the European continent, Africa, Asia, and Australia. The very existence and function of the SLU system was one of the best-kept secrets of World War II.

The system for ensuring security of information from Enigma decrypts rested on the following principles:

1. The smallest possible number of persons was to have access to Enigma information.

2. The list of recipients was to be limited to four or five persons at each of the following main headquarters: supreme headquarters, army groups, principal army and air commands in Europe and Southeast Asia, and British and U.S. air force commands operating from Britain.

3. The addition of a name to the distribution list required the permission of British intelligence chief Gen. Stewart Menzies' deputy, F.W. Winterbotham.

4. Commanders, or members of their staffs, cleared for Enigma information were to receive it from their SLU officers personally; the latter were then to destroy the documents.

5. No Ultra recipient was to transmit or repeat an Ultra signal.

6. Any action taken by a commander on Ultra information was to be by way of an operations order, command, or instruction that in no way referred to the Ultra signal or could lead the enemy to believe his messages were being read.

7. Combat operations undertaken on the basis of Enigma information were to disguise the source of the information (for example, reconnaissance aircraft were to be sent out prior to an attack on enemy convoys in the Mediterranean).

8. No recipient of this information was to voluntarily place himself in a situation that might lead to his capture.

The last point sometimes brought protests from commanders who liked to be in the front lines, for example, Maj. Gen. George S. Patton and Maj. Gen. Jimmy Doolittle, who liked to go on bombing missions. A senior Royal Air Force officer who read Enigma material was shot down over France, creating panic at the air staff. Everyone calmed down only after he had been smuggled back to Britain.[11]

In handling such valuable intelligence, it was also essential to use the most secure cipher possible in putting Ultra transmissions on the air. Hence, Winterbotham insisted that they be in a one-time pad cipher, the only absolutely secure kind, and that if any government department that received Ultra material wished to put it on the air, this be done through the SLU organization.

NOTES

1. According to Peter Calvocoressi, Bletchley Park was supervised by a ranking Foreign Office official through nearly all the war. Rohwer and Jäckel, *Die Funkaufklärung*, 88f.

2. Calvocoressi, "The Secrets of Enigma."

3. Rejewski explains that the "help from GC and CS" that Hinsley says enabled the Poles to make "the first war-time break into the Enigma...in Paris at the end of 1939" consisted merely in the British copying the Poles' perforated sheets and sending one set to the Poles. Rejewski further emphasizes, in view of Hinsley's vague implication that the British had invented the perforated sheets, that the British had "adopted this from us [Poles]; the only difference was that we used millimeter-ruled paper and they used paper divided into inches, that our paper was white and theirs was cream-colored, that we cut the holes out laboriously with razor blades and they used a perforator." Rejewski, "Uwagi do 'Appendix 1,' " 492, 494.

4. Randell, "The COLOSSI—Britain's Secret Wartime Computers."

5. Oral account by Marian Rejewski, who corresponded regularly for over two years with General Bertrand before the latter's death in southern France at the age of 79, on 23 May 1976.

6. Winterbotham, *The Ultra Secret*, 28. Rejewski notes in this regard:

> According to what Winterbotham states and according to our other sources, it was only in May of 1941 that the British obtained from a sunken submarine (I believe, the U-110) the set of five drums [rotors] that we had supplied them in July 1939.

Rejewski, "Uwagi do 'Appendix 1,' " 494.

7. Langer, Two wartime documents. These include a five-page list of keys solved. Rejewski comments on the fairly large British role:

> The situation is perfectly obvious: How could it be otherwise, when there were three of us Poles, later two [Rejewski and Zygalski], and [there were] at least several hundred British cryptologists, since about 10,000 people worked in Bletchley and the environs. Besides, recovery of keys also depended on the amount of intercepted cipher material, and that amount was far greater on the British side than on the French side. Finally, in France (by contrast with the work in Poland) we ourselves not only sought for the daily keys, but after finding the key also read the messages. In such circumstances, conceptual work really was out of the question. One can only be surprised that the Poles had as many as 17 percent of the keys to their credit.

Rejewski, "Uwagi do 'Appendix 1,' " 493.

8. Langer, Two wartime documents.

Mayer adds, "when...Lt. Col. Langer visited London [in December 1939] he learnt that [the British had already allocated] twelve thousand pounds...for construction of additional replicas of 'Enigma.' [R]esearch [on] 'Enigma' was in full swing." Mayer, "The breaking up of the German ciphering machine 'ENIGMA,' " 5. According to Welchman, however, the British did not construct Enigma replicas, but used modified British Type-X cipher machines. Welchman, *The Hut Six Story*—ED..

9. However, compare Rejewski's comments cited in note 7, above: "there were [only] three of us Poles, later two [and] we ourselves not only sought for the daily keys, but. . .also read the messages. In such circumstances, conceptual work really was out of the question."

10. Langer, Two wartime documents; document number two.

11. Winterbotham, *The Ultra Secret*, 88-90.

10.

Collapse of France

A few days before the opening of the German offensive against France, a conference of French and British intelligence representatives took place, presided over by Colonel Gauché. The date of the German offensive was predicted accurately, but the conferees were unable to establish its strategic goal or main direction. In this respect, Polish military intelligence had done better in the summer of 1939.

On 10 May 1940, precisely at 5:35 a.m., the German Army opened a powerful offensive, trampling Belgium, Luxembourg, and Holland in order, soon thereafter to reach the borders of France.

> Soldiers of the western front! [proclaimed the Fuehrer's order on the first day of the offensive]. The hour of decisive combat has arrived. For three centuries, the rulers of England and France have striven to thwart the idea of European unity ... In a few weeks, the armed forces of Germany brought to her knees Germany's chief adversary abetted by England and France, Poland, thus eliminating the danger in the east. Now the time has come for you. The struggle that begins today will settle the fate of the nation for a thousand years. The German people stand by you with their wishes of godspeed.

Participating in the offensive, whose prime objective was the defeat of France, were the following forces: 118 infantry divisions, 1 cavalry division, 10 armored divisions, and 7 motorized divisions (including two and a half S.S. divisions). They formed three army groups:

- Col. Gen. Gerd von Runstedt's Army Group A (the Fourth, Twelfth and Sixteenth Armies, plus Col. Gen. Ewald von Kleist's armored group),
- Col. Gen. Fedor von Bock's Army Group B (the Sixth and Eighteenth Armies), and
- Col. Gen. Wilhelm von Leeb's Army Group C (the First and Seventh Armies).

Army Groups A and B, supported by Gen. Albert Kesselring's Second Air Fleet and Gen. Hugo Sperrle's Third Air Fleet, moved in the first operational wave and, after regrouping on June 5, were reinforced by the Second and Ninth Armies and Gen. Heinz Guderian's armored group. Army Group C constituted the second wave and went into action on June 14, its assignment being to breach the Maginot Line. In the campaign against France, the Second Air Fleet conducted the first large-scale airborne landing operation of World War II.

In the first days of the German offensive, part of Bruno's personnel were moved from Gretz-Armainvillers to the Paris intelligence headquarters at 2 bis, avenue de Tourville.[1] This was a long, drab building, behind the Invalides, similar to the entire complex of nineteenth-century buildings. On seeing the Deuxième Bureau headquarters for the first time, the Poles were a little disappointed with its ordinary appearance. Rejewski and his colleagues were first lodged in S.R.-secured rooms at the Hotel Vauban, but were soon moved to rooms at the French intelligence headquarters itself.

After a couple of days of conflicting reports on the situation at the front, each bulletin, as during Poland's September campaign of 1939, was worse than the last. Army Group A's massed armor went through the Ardennes to strike at the flank and rear of the Franco-British forces in Holland and Belgium, forcing them into retreat.

After installing themselves on avenue de Tourville, the Polish cryptologists and their French colleagues did all they could to keep up the normal work routine. That was not easy. Just before opening their general offensive in the west on 10 May 1940, the Germans had changed the procedures for using the Enigmas in all their armed forces. Though Enigma was still considered insoluble, these changes were designed to preclude even a chance reading that might jeopardize German surprise.

If the surprise did come off, it was not because of a lack of warning to the Allies, but because of a lack of belief by the French High Command. Gen. Maurice Gamelin, who dwelt conceptually in the World War I era, refused to entertain the idea that the adversary could plan and undertake so reckless a maneuver. The situation had been different in Poland, where the striking disproportion in forces, the configuration of borders, and the ineptitude of the Polish command had allowed the German Army to make deep armored incursions in contempt of genuine military craft.

That there was no shortage of warning is attested to by the reminiscences of numerous ranking commanders and intelligence officers. The concentration of German armor in the Ardennes was detected in its general outlines, and only a mistaken assessment of the German strategic grouping led to the equally mistaken decision to send the left wing of the Allied forces far forward—a move that was to be decisive in the outcome of the French campaign.

The Germans' modifications of their Enigma ciphers proved effective. For the first several days of the offensive, the Allies were unable to look over the shoulders of the principal German commanders. But this situation did not last long. By the tenth day of war, the Polish cryptologists were once again reading Enigma. According to Bertrand, "It took *superhuman*, day-and-night effort to overcome this new difficulty: on May 20, decryptment resumed."[2]

It also proved possible to improve upon the already broad intelligence that had been available during the Norwegian campaign. In addition to the standard operational orders, daily situation reports, front line reports, and so on, timely information became available on special operations (Sonderunternehmen) set in motion by ad hoc decisions of Hitler, army Commander in Chief Gen. Walther von Brauchitsch, or air force Commander in Chief Field Marshal Hermann Goering. This created unique opportunities for counter-operations that might have thwarted enemy plans. But not even the most superb intelligence could, by itself, have done the trick.

During these busy days, the Polish cryptologists and technicians worked around the clock in three shifts, never leaving the building on avenue de Tourville. The monitoring posts continued to work efficiently, supplying masses of Wehrmacht orders, directives, and reports. After decryptment, intelligence summaries were prepared for the Allied high command and the staffs of individual armies. As the front disintegrated and other sources of intelligence shrank, Enigma information became increasingly vital. Its authenticity and accuracy soon came to be appreciated. The Yellow Pages printed on thin paper in a score of copies were eagerly snapped up by generals and colonels of the French High Command, some of whom waited at the entrance to the cryptologists' quarters and even spent nights in the building in order to get their hands on the hot information.

But the Yellow Pages could not reinforce the French positions or stop the massed tanks and airplanes that the Case Yellow of Hitler and his chief strategist, Gen. Erich von Manstein, had pitted against France. German armored spearheads were going around the Maginot Line from the northwest and were tearing deep into the rear of the French armies.

Events were moving ever faster. On May 13, the front had been breached at the Meuse River, followed by the encirclement of Allied armies in Belgium, north of the Somme, and on May 15 Holland had capitulated. On May 19, French Premier Paul Reynaud had requested Marshal Philippe Pétain, the now eighty-four-year-old hero of Verdun from an earlier world war, to "strengthen the government" by his person. Gen. Maxime Weygand had replaced the incompetent Gen. Maurice Gamelin as commander in chief. The next day, on May 20, the advancing German divisions had reached the English Channel. On May 28, Belgium capitulated.

The Polish cryptologists experienced some bitter moments. In supplying precise information, they expected enemy intentions to be appropriately counteracted. Unfortunately, this was not so. An example of a chance passed up was the French High Command's reaction to information about the German High Command organizing—not at all with "lightning" speed, but over a fairly long time and with some hesitation—a massive air raid on Paris.[3] The first data on the planned special operation, Sonderunternehmen P. (Paula), were obtained from Enigma at 0035 on May 26, and subsequent

German orders were followed with the greatest attention. Implementing orders by Luftwaffe commands, detailing plans for the bombing raid on Paris, with additional raids on other localities, were read on May 29 (one message), May 30 (six messages), May 31 (three messages), and June 1 (five messages). In this way, the French High Command received full data on the Luftwaffe forces designated for Sonderunternehmen P.—the order of battle of bombers and fighter escorts, their flight routes to the concentration area, the route and altitude of the whole group to target, and return routes to home bases.[4]

The Allied air command was kept abreast of German plans and preparations for Operation Paula. In spite of that, it took no countermeasures because, according to the commander in chief of the French Air Force, Gen. Joseph Vuillemin, "he did not have the hundred fighter aircraft necessary unless he stripped the front of that number."[5]

At 3 p.m. on 3 June 1940, formations of Heinkels and escorting Messerschmitts, black crosses emblazoned on their fuselages and wings, appeared over the greater Paris area. Bombs were heard detonating. The French Air Force did nothing. The main targets of the raid were Renault and Citroën plants, but bombs also fell on residential districts. This scene, observed by the Poles with impotent rage, reminded them of the situation in September 1939. But the dimensions of the catastrophe that was soon to occur could not yet be conceived.

The fifteen-man Polish group remained at the posts that the vicissitudes of war had allotted to them. There was still hope that the Germans would break their teeth on the Maginot Line and that France would survive the period of adversities, as during World War I, to launch a counteroffensive.

Meanwhile, the authorities had ordered the evacuation of women, children, and the aged from Paris, and the vast city of five million lived in an atmosphere of great chaos. Scenes out of Dante were played out in the streets and the jammed railroad and Métro stations. Strings of vehicles and mobs of pedestrians pushing handcarts loaded down with furniture and bedding blocked the streets. People camped in the railroad stations, waiting for the few trains that ran. The nervous atmosphere imparted itself as well to the armed forces which, like the country as a whole, were entering the shooting war psychologically disarmed after months of phony war.

During the final days of May, and up to June 3, about three hundred thousand British and thirty thousand French troops were evacuated from Dunkirk on the French coast to the British Isles. Some French units, after a short rest, were shipped back to France, to the Cotentin peninsula and Brittany, to be thrown back into battle.

On June 5, changes took place in the French government. Yves Bouthillier became minister of finance, Prouvost minister of propaganda, and the little-known Gen. Charles de Gaulle took charge of the armed forces.

On June 7 the Germans began a massive, four-pronged attack against France, meeting little resistance. On June 10, Italian forces struck France from the Alps. The Italian offensive, though it made no headway, increased the chaos and confusion.

On June 10 the evacuation of the French General Staff to southern France also began. The first stage was at Bon Encontre, near Agen. The French High Command prepared a new defense line along the Loire River, which runs more or less across the middle of France. This was no easy task. Masses of troops and crowds of refugees from the north were encamped in the vicinity of the bridges and, to make things worse, a new wave of refugees from the greater Paris area began to arrive, blocking the already clogged roads. Meanwhile, the German Air Force ceaselessly attacked bridges and ferries between Tours, Orleans, and Gien on the Loire. Stukas, Heinkels, and Messerschmitts ruled the skies over France as they had done eight months earlier over Poland, and with the same savagery massacred the retreating columns of troops and refugees heading south down all the roads. Signs of breakdown of civil administration appeared with the radio announcement that the departments along the Loire had been declared a combat zone.

The headquarters of the commander in chief, Gen. Maxime Weygand, were now at Clermont-Ferrand, and Lieutenant Colonel d'Ales of the Fifth Bureau went there to find out the high command's plans and its instructions for the intelligence services. Word had gotten out that Pétain was considering capitulation. General Weygand was unable to tell the emissary of military intelligence much. He directed that the Fifth Bureau be ready to "continue operations," but how he envisaged those operations was not made clear.

When the order came on June 9 to evacuate Bruno from Gretz-Armainvillers, it turned out that the general staff lacked adequate transportation for the purpose. German forces were getting dangerously close to Paris, and there was not a moment to lose. It was essential to keep Bruno's personnel and secret equipment out of German hands. Colonel Bertrand decided to act on his own and, at one of the suburban transport depots, commandeered a bus and a five-ton truck. These had to accommodate over a hundred French, Polish, and Spanish personnel as well as indispensable equipment and files. The fixed monitoring facilities and radio stations were blown up. In a few hours, Bruno was ready to move.

The Bruno staff set out from Gretz-Armainvillers on June 10, soon after midnight (0140 hours), heading south. The town of La Ferté-Saint Aubin, about thirty kilometers south of Orleans, was designated by the general staff as the new operations site. On arrival, the Poles activated their Enigmas and once again read German signals. These were mostly messages from armored divisions approaching the Loire. The decrypts, alas, bore testimony to the enemy's triumph. One Luftwaffe message (June 12) heralded another raid on Paris by heavy bombers.[6] Bruno's liaison with the French High Command, to which the results of decryptment were delivered, began to be increasingly unsatisfactory. After three days of improvised work, the unit had to pack up its radio station and monitoring equipment to leave La Ferté.

The next stopovers for Bruno were the town of Le Chatelet (June 15) and Vensat (June 16) in the western part of the Massif Central. Here again decryptment resumed, but the general staff was no longer responding. Contact with it was secured on June 17 at the town of Larches, but only to receive orders for continued evacuation toward Agen on the Garonne River, and next to Bon Encontre. Here, on 22 June 1940, the Polish team was informed that Pétain—now premier—had signed an armistice.

A new period of clandestine operations began. In the terms of armistice, the Germans stipulated that all radio intelligence facilities were immediately to be turned over to them, together with lists of personnel. A split appeared among the French officers. "Loyalists" rigidly stuck by their oaths and kept faith with Pétain; they believed in his political "good sense," which was expected to save the country from complete catastrophe. Others, including Bertrand, at once took a position decidedly opposed to seeking accommodation with the Germans. Their first impulse was to try to get out of the occupied zone, and next to evacuate to North Africa. After arriving in Toulouse, in tremendous haste, Bertrand, on June 24 (at 1005 hours), managed to fly Bruno's international personnel—fifteen Poles and seven Spaniards—in three planes to Algeria. The aircraft landed in Oran at 1525 hours. The British liaison officer, Captain McFarlan, had been driven to Cazaux, where he had managed to catch the last RAF plane for England.[7] In Algeria, on June 28, Bruno established its last radio contact with London.

During the Franco-German campaign of 1940, the Germans had once again encountered Polish front-line troops. These were antitank batteries on the outskirts of Paris and, later, armored and monitored units in southern Champagne, the First Division in Lorraine, and the Second Division in the Belfort Gap. In each of these engagements, the Germans sustained heavy losses.

Up to May of 1940, the Polish Army in France had attained a strength of over eighty thousand men—thirty thousand who had arrived from occupied Poland (chiefly via Rumania and Hungary) and fifty thousand recruited from local Polonia. Only part of these troops were adequately armed and trained for combat.

When, in late May, enemy pressure was mounting along the entire front, in the atmosphere of panic and retreat, Polish units distinguished themselves in heavy defensive fighting. There was no lack, too, of successful offensive operations, including some by units of the Polish Armored-Motorized Brigade, acting as part of the French Fourth Army. On June 13, in the Champaubert area, they threw back superior German forces and launched a successful counterattack, forcing a crack German division to retreat with losses. Nightfall found burning German tanks and armored cars strewing the battlefield. But the attack at Champaubert drew attention to the Poles. The next day, June 14, Luftwaffe formations struck furiously at the Polish unit, which retreated; a day later, communications with the French command broke off. No one now seemed to be interested in the Polish brigade, except the enemy. The armored battalion—thirty-odd slow but powerfully armed tanks—was now entirely on its own. The tanks were running out of fuel, but an abandoned French fuel dump was found. Though German Stukas dropped incendiary bombs, the Poles managed to roll out a score of drums and refuel. Meanwhile, patrols determined that neighboring French units were surrendering to the Germans, rumors having reached them of capitulation. A decision had to be made quickly: should the Poles fight on and try to break through to the south, or lay down their arms? They decided to fight.

Before evening, the Polish armored unit approached Montbard. The town had been occupied by the enemy. Even without field glasses, the tank men could see antitank guns and machine gun emplacements on the streets and in brick buildings in the outskirts. German sappers were laying mines, and signals troops were busy with wire drums, laying telephone lines to their superior staff.

Without stopping, the Polish column deployed into battle array and charged Montbard. The Germans opened fire on the oncoming tanks and the foot soldiers who followed in their wake. But the momentum of the attack carried the Poles through the fortifications, and the Germans withdrew to the other end of town. The Poles captured a score of antitank and antiaircraft guns, a large quantity of machine guns, motor vehicles, and an ammunition dump. The retreating enemy managed to blow up one bridge, but another was captured intact. The Poles had lost seventeen men and had nearly thirty wounded; German losses were several times higher. Statements of German prisoners indicated that the city had been defended by troops securing the flank for a higher Wehrmacht formation.

Of course, such local victories could not stem the broader tide of events. The capitulation of France and the creation of the Vichy government were consequences of a years-long policy of appeasement toward Germany, of British and French indifference toward German remilitarization, of the Munich Pact, of the failure to come to Poland's aid in September 1939.

On the same day that Polish units were fighting at Champaubert, on 13 June 1940, at the chateau of Cangé-en-Tourenne, on the way from Paris to Bordeaux, Marshal Pétain was speaking of the coming capitulation. "Whatever happens," he declared, "it is the duty of the French government to remain in France. . . . To deprive France of her natural defenders in time of misfortune is to deliver her into the hands of the enemy. France's renewal may be expected sooner from our remaining here than from the help of Allied guns. . . . France's eternal durability is conditional on armistice."

These highflown words could not obscure reality. Despite opened negotiations, German forces pushed ahead to seize as much territory as possible so as to weaken Pétain's bargaining position. On June 17, immediately after Pétain's offer of armistice had been conveyed through the Spanish government, Hitler put a secret order on the air to the commanders of all three army groups. They were "emphatically to continue pursuit of the defeated enemy forces. A particular duty of honor for the Army must be the swiftest possible seizure of the old German territories of the Reich to the line Verdun-Toul-Belfort, as well as the coastal cities of Cherbourg and Brest and the central district of the armaments industry at Le Creusot."[8]

On 22 June 1940, the act of capitulation was finally signed. Pétain placed himself at the mercy of the enemy, but Hitler did not reciprocate the gesture of the old marshal who "as one soldier to another" put his country's fate into Hitler's hands. "France," declared a Fuehrer flushed with triumph, "has met with well deserved punishment. She bears the full blame for the war, and any courtesies or considerations are out of the question." Three weeks later, on July 12, at a secret conference in the German Ministry of Propaganda, Dr. Goebbels put matters bluntly: "Our sole interest is in keeping France for the future, too, as weak as possible. We must stir, in the French, hatred for the English, as that will make our situation easier."[9]

The last Allied forces in France to lay down their arms, when further struggle was hopeless and adjacent French units had disintegrated at rumors of armistice, were Polish units, including the First Grenadier Division under Gen. Bolesław Bronisław Duch. As the French retreated in disorder or surrendered, Duch declared that the Polish Army in France had not been formed in order to capitulate to the enemy. When, finally, the Poles did discuss terms with the Germans, a sizable part of the division, including General Duch, disappeared, in civilian or other disguise. The general, with a red ink-splotched head bandage, and dressed as a private, went to a Paris hospital, from which he fled the same day.[10]

France was reduced to a rump state comprising about two-fifths of her former area. The two-million-man French Army was reduced to one hundred thousand men. Close to a million prisoners of war were penned up in camps or sent to forced labor in Germany.

Even as France was collapsing, on June 18, General de Gaulle, in his first speech over the BBC, proclaimed the Free French movement and a continuation of the struggle. But in the occupied north as well as in the unoccupied southern zone, centers of resistance were expiring and apathy had swept over most people.

The armistice signed on 22 June 1940 divided France's territory into several parts. Three-fifths of the country was occupied, Alsace and part of Lorraine were annexed by Germany, and two *dèpartements* in the northwest were attached to the German Army administration in Belgium. A very limited autonomy was retained only by the unoccupied zone, later called L'Etat Français (the French State), which was ruled dictatorially by Pétain. On 10 July 1940, the terrified deputies to the National Assembly adopted, by a vote of 569 to 80, Pierre Laval's proposal giving all powers to Pétain. The marshal's vice premier, Laval, had intended to be the strong man in the new regime, but Pétain, though eighty-four years old, was not senile. He saw through Laval, who was conducting his own private negotiations with the Germans, and on 13 December 1940 dismissed him from the Vichy government and clapped him under house arrest. To be sure, on December 17, Otto Abetz, Hitler's representative to Vichy, obtained Laval's release, but it would be over a year (17 April 1942) before Pétain would reappoint Laval as vice premier (or the effective head of the government) under himself, the chief of state.

Bertrand succeeded in withdrawing not only the Bruno center, but also the radio-monitoring stations in northern and central France, before the approaching Germans. Also evacuated was the British-French monitoring station on Sainte Marguerite Island, when Italy entered the war on 10 June 1940.

The Poles of Team Z, evacuated to Algeria, were first registered under fictitious names and quartered at the Hotel Royal in Oran, then at the Touring Club Hotel in Algiers. They tried not to draw the attention of the French-Algerian authorities, among whom were many supporters of accommodation with Germany. They avoided any contact with both the local French and the Moslem inhabitants of the city. Only once during their nearly three-month stay in Algiers did their French hosts arrange for the Poles an excursion out of the city, to the nearby oasis of Bu Saada. There the hospitable Bedouins treated the Poles to their specialty, a dish called cous-cous, cooked with mutton and spices.

Meanwhile, ever larger Nazi teams were arriving in North Africa. Apart from outposts of the German branch of the Armistice Commission and various German offices, the Abwehr and S.D. were setting up their own networks of agents. The political situation in Algeria was getting increasingly complicated. The French inhabitants of North Africa and refugees from France could not get over the shock of an attack by Britain's Royal Navy on the French Atlantic squadron anchored at the Mers-el-Kebir naval base near Oran.

This had taken place a few days after the arrival of the evacuated Poles. On 3 July 1940, a Royal Navy task force under Adm. Sir James Somerville had arrived at Oran. An ultimatum had been sent to French Admiral Gensoul commanding the Atlantic squadron at Mers-el-Kebir: either join us in fighting the Axis, sail with reduced crews to a British or French West Indian port, or be sunk. Gensoul had cabled Admiral Darlan for instructions and been ordered to resist any aggression. The French squadron was consequently crushed in fifteen minutes, all ships being disabled except the battle cruiser *Strasbourg* and three destroyers which escaped the bombardment. Over sixteen hundred French sailors were killed or wounded. At the same time, French warships in English ports were seized and those in the harbor of Alexandria blockaded.

Was the sinking of the French squadron at Mers-el-Kebir necessary? The British feared the Germans might seize the ships; still, the opinions of historians on this tragedy are divided. Indisputably, the events at Mers-el-Kebir worsened Franco-British relations and prompted disaffection, even hatred, among the French for their former ally. The British attack delayed the development of a resistance movement and decreased enlistments in de Gaulle's Free French units.

The underground military organization that came into being in the postarmistice French Army included many patriotic officers who decided to rebuild in southern France the anti-German intelligence and counterintelligence organizations, reactivate surviving networks, and form new ones. For the fifteen Poles of Team Z and the seven-man Spanish group, this would mean going underground. The S.D. and Abwehr would give a great deal to get their hands on the cryptologists and other intercept personnel.

As early as 8 July 1940, Colonel Bertrand presented his superiors with a proposal to resume radio intelligence. Such operations could proceed only in deep secrecy, since, in the event of exposure, the Germans would accuse the

Vichy government of violating the terms of armistice, with incalculable consequences.

Bertrand's position was, therefore, very delicate. He and his French superiors knew that the Polish cryptologists could render valuable services to the Allies and that they could do this best working in France, right under the enemy's nose. Gen. Juliusz Kleeberg, the semiofficial representative in southern France of the Polish government in exile, in consultation with London, concluded that Bertrand's plan had chances of success, and that the Polish group should continue working together with the French. Organizationally, Colonel Langer's unit would be subordinate to Section II (Intelligence) of the Polish commander in chief's staff in Great Britain, and would receive the code name Ekspozytura 300 (Field Office 300).[11]

The Franco-Polish plan was, thus, to work in the territory of unoccupied France, using German wireless ciphergrams intercepted and forwarded to the clandestine decryptment center by patriotic officers at the Vichy government's monitoring system (Groupement des Contrôles Radioélectriques de l'Intérieur—G.C.R.). The decryptment center would also solve German wire ciphergrams supplied by members of the resistance movement working in the French postal system.

The main outlines of the plan were approved by General Weygand. All this happened in the first weeks after the armistice, while Pétain's regime was still being formed. The French military command was secretly trying to secure a flow of information for itself about Wehrmacht staffs and units as well as German civil authorities in the occupied part of the country. Courageous and trustworthy people were needed to conduct sensitive radio intelligence operations and break the ciphers of an adversary who was separated only by a demarcation line and was ready at any moment to exercise military power.

The armistice agreement contained a clause forbidding the French to engage in any intelligence operations involving the German armed forces or German affairs generally. The ban included not only the conduct of intelligence but even the use of codes and ciphers. French institutions, whether civil or military, could use only those codes and ciphers that had earlier been reported to the German authorities and thus could be read by them. That the defeated French would resume offensive radio intelligence almost immediately apparently never occurred to the Germans.

Nevertheless, it was necessary to act quickly, since German intelligence and police were wrapping southern France ever more tightly in their tentacles. The offices of the Armistice Commission, which were also a cover for the Abwehr and S.D., were watching the moves of the reduced French Army more and more closely. A favorable circumstance, on the other hand, was the fact that in July-August 1940 the Germans' attention was absorbed by the great aerial Battle of Britain and preparations to invade the British Isles. Consequently, they were unable to keep track of everything that was happening in France, even as they ruthlessly exploited her economic resources.

Meanwhile, in July and August, Major Bertrand, alias Monsieur Barsac,[12] was readying in southern France new facilities for a clandestine radio-intelligence center that was to act jointly with the Allies and the emerging French Résistance. Finally selected as the site was the Château des Fouzes near the historic little town of Uzès (about four thousand in population) and not far from the Mediterranean coast. This site for "P.C. [Command Post] Cadix" was chosen so that, in case of discovery by Nazi intelligence, the center's personnel could readily be evacuated to North Africa. By virtue of a special authorization from General Weygand, the chateau became the property of the French S.R. (military intelligence). Monsieur Barsac purchased the large chateau, all the necessary false papers being drawn up so as to avoid suspicion.

The chateau had to be adapted to its new purposes. In secret, generally by night, short-wave transmitters were installed on the second floor and in the attic. Openings and niches were hollowed out in the walls; boxes of lime, sacks of cement, and tools were hidden next to these, for walling-up the equipment, should the need arise. Quarters for the cryptologists were arranged on the ground floor; their work tools were the least troublesome and could be cleared away at a few minutes' notice.

1. Two views of a military-model Enigma, equipped with plugboard. Right: the wooden flap at bottom is dropped, revealing plugboard with two cables, each plugged into two sockets in order to exchange the respective letters. The operator's finger, at right, is depressing the "O" key. See Figure 17 for a view of another military Enigma, with the plugboard again revealed and also the metal lid lifted, showing the drums and light bulbs. (From the author's files.)

2. Set of three military Enigma rotors. Top, viewed on end. Bottom, placed in series, ready for operation. Note that these military-model rotors have *numbers* instead of letters about the circumferences of their rings. (From the author's files.)

3. The Polish General Staff building (the Saxon Palace) in Warsaw, in a prewar view from the Saxon Square. After World War II, the Saxon Square would be renamed Victory Square—in honor of a victory that was largely made possible by the cryptologists who, from 1932 to 1937, had worked in the General Staff building.

  The Saxon Palace had been developed from a private residence, beginning about 1724, by Poland's Saxon King August II. In 1804-16, the building had housed a secondary school at which Frederick Chopin's father had taught French, living with his family in one of the out-buildings. After World War I, the Saxon Palace had become the seat of renascent Poland's General Staff. (Reprinted from *Stolica* magazine.)

4. Entrance to Poznań University's Mathematics Institute, attended by future cryptologists Rejewski, Zygalski, and Różycki. Photo taken in late September 1939; the soldiers are German. The Castle had been built by Kaiser Wilhelm II to be the official residence of the German Crown Prince; Poznań had been chosen as its site in order to bolster the effort to Germanize this German-occupied part of the then-partitioned Poland. (Reprinted from *Stolica* magazine.)

5. Major Maksymilian Ciężki in the 1930s. In early 1929 he, along with engineer Antoni Palluth—a civilian employee of the Polish General Staff's Cipher Bureau—and the then-chief of the Bureau, Major Franciszek Pokorny, conducted a secret cryptology course at Poznań University that eventually led to recruitment of the mathematicians Rejewski, Zygalski, and Różycki to the Cipher Bureau in Warsaw.

A chief of B.S.-4 (the fourth, or German, section of the Biuro Szyfrów, or Cipher Bureau), Ciężki was the immediate superior of the three civilian mathematician-cryptologists. Courtesy of Richard Woytak, who received this photo from Marian Rejewski.

6. Henryk Zygalski (1907-78) in a photo taken about 1930. He had begun work at B.S.-4, together with Marian Rejewski and Jerzy Różycki, on 1 September 1932. (From the author's files.)

7. Marian Rejewski with his son Andrzej, perhaps two-and-a-half years old, in the Bielański Wood (Lasek Bielański) of northern Warsaw's Żoliborz district, near where the Rejewskis lived on Gdańsk Street (ulica Gdańska). Photo taken in the spring of 1939, only a few months before the outbreak of World War II. Andrzej was to die of poliomyelitis in Bydgoszcz in the summer of 1947, just a few months after Rejewski's return to Poland. (From Rejewski's files.)

8. Jerzy Różycki (1909-42) in a document photo taken about 1928. He was the youngest of the three mathematicians, all graduates of Poznań University, who broke Enigma; and he was to die the youngest, in the sinking of the French packet-boat *Lamoricière* in January 1942, as he was returning to Cadix in southern France from a tour of duty in Algiers. (From the author's files.)

Edward Fokczyński

Antoni Palluth

Ludomir Danilewicz

Leonard Danilewicz

9. The four founders of the AVA Radio Manufacturing Company, of Warsaw, which produced equipment for the Polish General Staff's Cipher Bureau, including Enigma doubles, cyclometer, and cryptological bombs. During World War II, Fokczyński and Palluth—and with the latter, his nephew Sylwester—would be with Lieutenant Colonel Langer's cryptological unit in France. The brothers Danilewicz would be in Britain, where together with Tadeusz Heftman—Leonard's high school mate, and later chief engineer at AVA—at the Polish Military Radio Works, they produced highly praised and prized miniature radio transmitters for use by Allied intelligence and sabotage groups, like Cadix acting in countries occupied by Germany. (From the author's files.)

10. General Gustave Bertrand. This is a postwar photograph which he sent to Rejewski, dedicated on the reverse "To my dear friend Marian REJEWSKI, one of the three 'discoverers' of ENIGMA, as a memento of times past and with my best regards, General G. Bertrand (C.R.)."

Tajne !

WEDŁUG ROZDZIELNIKA

Przedstawiam / przesyłam / Komunikat Nr.19 za

okres październik - grudzień 1938 o sytuacji wewnętrznej

Niemiec.

SZEF ODDZIAŁU II SZTABU GŁÓWNEGO

PEŁCZYŃSKI

Płk.dypl.

Otrzymują :   L.ew.

Pan Generalny Inspektor Sił Zbrojnych 1

Pan Minister Spraw Wojskowych 2

Grupa G.I.S.Z. i Sztabu Głównego :

P.P. Inspektorowie Armii i P.P.Generałowie do prac
     G.I.S.Z. / przez Biuro Inspekcji G.I.S.Z./ ....3 - 18

Pan Szef Sztabu Głównego 19

Pan Sekretarz Komitetu Obrony Rzeczypospolitej 20

Szef Oddziału II Sztabu Głównego ....21 - 41

Szef Oddziału III   "   "   ....42 - 43

Grupa M.S.Wojsk. :

Pan I Wiceminister Spraw Wojskowych 44

Pan II Wiceminister Spraw Wojskowych 45

11. Secret distribution list for "Communiqué no. 19, for the period October-December 1938, on the internal situation in Germany," dated Warsaw, 28 January 1939 and signed by Colonel Tadeusz Pełczyński, chief of Section II of the General Staff. At right are record numbers of copies issued to: the Inspector General of the Armed Forces (number 1); the Minister of Military Affairs (number 2); the Inspectorate General of the Armed Forces, and the General Staff (numbers 3 through 43); and the First and Second Vice Ministers of Military Affairs (numbers 44, 45). (From the author's files.)

August 1 1939

Szan,

*Serdecznie dziękuję za współpracę
i cierpliwość.*

A. D. Knox

*(a) inclus (a) des petits bâtons
(b) un souvenir d'Angleterre*

12. Letter dated 1 August 1939, from British chief cryptologist Alfred Dillwyn Knox to the Polish mathematician-cryptologists, written following the trilateral Warsaw-Pyry Enigma conference of 24-25 July 1939, at which the Poles revealed their achievements. Knox writes (in Polish), "My sincere thanks for your cooperation and patience. A.D. Knox," and below that (in French): "Enclosed (a) *petits bâtons*, (b) a souvenir from England." The souvenir was a scarf picturing a Derby horse race—evidently emblematic of the cryptological race that Knox had hoped to win using the little paper batons, and whose loss he was acknowledging. The embossed seal on the official stationery has been rubbed lightly with pencil to make it visible in reproduction. (From the author's files.)

13. Hitler on Warsaw's Saxon Square, before the Polish General Staff building and the statue of Prince Józef Poniatowski, during victory parade in October 1939. Little did he realize that the doom of his Third Reich had been sealed years earlier in the very building he is facing. (Reproduction from a Nazi propaganda publication.)

14. The chiefs of the Polish-French Bruno center established in October 1939 at Gretz-Armainvillers, outside Paris—Lieutenant Colonel Gwido Langer (left) and Major Gustave Bertrand (center)—and (right) the British liaison officer, Captain Kenneth McFarlan. Bruno would operate for eight months, until 10 June 1940 (well into the Battle of France), when it would be evacuated less than two weeks short of the Franco-German armistice (22 June). (From the author's files.)

15. Marian Rejewski taking his ease at Bruno. (From Rejewski's files.)

16. Panzer Gen. Heinz Guderian and Enigma operators in command vehicle during Battle of France, 1940.

NOTES

1. Dr. Tadeusz Lisicki writes: "the Russian [-cryptology] team did not move to Paris." Lisicki, Letter of 19 September 1982, to the editor-translator.—ED.

After several days' intense work on renewing Enigma decryptment at Bruno, the cryptologists left for Deuxième Bureau headquarters in Paris on 16 May 1940. The technical staff had left Gretz a little earlier, in order to prepare quarters for the cryptologists and to install equipment. Zygalski, Diary.

2. Bertrand, *Enigma*, 88-89. According to Langer, the interruption in decryptment was shorter, from 13 through 19 May 1940; he also noted "change in encipherment" next to the two consecutive dates, May 14 and 20. Hence, the cipher system was, in fact, changed either just before May 10 or in the first days of war. Langer, Two wartime documents.

3. A German unit showed confusion as to the meaning of the cryptonym Paula, and this led to disclosure of the target. Bertrand cites a German message, 101 0110 5060 Kcs: "An Fliegerkorps VIII Angriff Paula hier unbekannt. Erbitte hierzu Befehle. Kampfgruppe 77" (To Air Corps VIII: Raid Paula unknown here. Request orders. Combat Group 77) and the reply: 101 0110 5060 Kcs: "Zu [To] 0110. Paula = Paris." Bertrand, *Enigma*, 91-93.

The editor-translator is indebted to Dr. Lisicki for bringing the incident to his attention. Lisicki, Letter of 19 September 1982.

A similar, but controversial, instance of German failure to maintain the anonymity of a targeted enemy city is described by Winterbotham, involving the Luftwaffe raid on Coventry that was to take place over five months later, on 14 November 1940. Winterbotham, *The Ultra Secret*—ED.

4. For example, a message broadcast at 10:45 a.m. on 31 May 1940 read: "Bei Durchfuehrung Paula ueberfliegt Geschwader mit einer Marschtruppe (3 Kampfgruppen) Sankt Marie in 1500 Meter, Wackelflugzeug 10 Minuten voraus. Wahre Aufnahmezeit folgt zeitgerecht. Flugweg suedl. Reims. Zielanflug (Ziele sind Corbeil, Melun, Nangis). Nach Angriff nach Sueden abbiegen und Rueckflug ueber Sedan." Bertrand, *Enigma*, 93.

5. Ibid., 95.

6. It was to have been a "special operation similar to Paula" (Sonderunternehmen aehnlich Paula), but never took place because Paris was occupied on June 16.

7. A fellow passenger of McFarlan's was a French lieutenant whose manner seemed peculiar to Major Bertrand, for the man clicked his heels when introducing himself. This was the Fascist, Prince Ernst Rüdiger von Starhemberg (1899-1956) of Austria, former vice chancellor (1934-36), who had fled the Nazis at the time of the Anschluss and had joined the French Army. Bertrand recalls inquiring about Starhemberg's wife, the beautiful film actress Nora Grégor.

8. The full text of Hitler's message:

An Heeres-Gruppen A, B, und C. Geheime Kommandosache. 17 6 1940.—Die neugebildete französische Regierung hat durch Vermittlung Spaniens wissen lassen, dass sie die Absicht habe, die Feindseligkeiten einzustellen und bäte, ihr die

Friedensbedingungen bekanntzugeben. Ich werde meine Antwort erst geben, nachdem ich mit dem Duce des faschistischen Italiens Fühlung genommen habe.—Die Operationen der Wehrmacht sind unter schärfster Verfolgung des geschlagenen Feindes mit Nachdruck fortzusetzen.—Eine besondere Ehrenpflicht des Heeres muss es sein, die alten deutschen Reichsgebiete bis zur linie Verdun-Toul-Belfort sowie die Küstenplätze Cherbourg und Brest und das Rüstungszentrum Le Creusot so rasch als möglich zu erobern.

9. Boelcke, *Kriegspropaganda 1939-1941*.

10. Incident recounted by Lt. Józef Kasparek, who heard of it from General Duch ("Dookh") at Hodgemoor Camp, 20 miles northwest of London, 1947. Kasparek, Communication.

11. Mayer writes:

At the end of September 1940, under the persistent persuasion of Lt. Col. Bertrand, Langer returned with his group to France ([the Château] Fouzes near Uzés, Dep. Gard). He again received...permission [from] Polish authorities to work [together with the] French, but this time as...Polish Secret Service Station [No.] 300 (Ekspozytura Nr. 300). According to [a] note in Langer's papers, the French cover-name for...Station [No.] 300 was Cadix. Its post in Algiers, which existed from April 1941 till January 1942 [and was] called...P.O. 1 [by the Poles], had the French cover-name Post "Z".

The result of the work [at] Station [No.] 300 in 1941 was: 4,158 German radiograms and 2,435 Russian radiograms deciphered. The German radiograms [included] interesting [machine-enciphered] material from the Balkan campaign coming [in over] the "Luftwaffe" network... From September 1941 the intercept[s were] mostly of routine exercise character. [S]canty material was intercepted from the Russian front.

The Russian radiograms in codes of 2, 3, and 4 digits produced little information of use. It was apparent that...discipline [in] radiocommunication [had been] strengthened. Less irresponsible garrulity was observed, more cover-names for commanders and units and coordinates for localities were in use. No detailed information was adduced in Lt. Col. Langer's papers about the cryptological results achieved by...Station [No.] 300 in 1942. He mentioned only that in general they were similar to those [in] 1941.

Besides the cryptological work which was the main task of...Station [No.] 300, it performed another, marginal but nevertheless extremely important, role. As from 7 [March] 1941 the Station [maintained] direct radio [communication] with...Polish Secret Intelligence [Headquarters] in London, which operated in close contact with...Commander Dunderdale of the British S.I.S. [Secret Intelligence Service, also known as MI 6]. This line of communication was used for liaison between Lt. Col. Bertrand (Bolek) and Commander Dunderdale (Dun).

The role of...Station [No.] 300 as...intermediary between the Polish secret intelligence...station "Rygor" in Algiers and [Headquarters] in London was of no less importance. "Rygor's" task was gathering information on which [O]peration "Torch" [the coming Allied landings in North Africa] was to be based. The transmission of data collected by "Rygor," which mostly concerned the French position in Algeria and Morocco, had to be done behind [the back of] Bertrand...(Bolek)...whose attitude to [the] British was typically French, halfhearted. For instance, according to Lt. Col. Langer's papers, Bertrand did not hide his dissatisfaction that the British had got[ten] from the Poles [a] Polish replica of "Enigma." He would [have] prefer[red] to [have] monopoli[zed] this field. In 1939/40 he [had] opposed the proposition made by the British to form in France a joint cryptological group. [Apparently] he [had been] afraid of the...British [dominating] such a group. In 1942, when the British ceased to send...keys to "Enigma"[-en]ciphered radiograms, he wanted to break contact with them. He even emotionally threatened [to] sell the "Enigma," which after all was not [a] French but a Polish achievement. Lt. Col. Langer convinced him, however, that...contact with "Dun" should not [be] broken.

Mayer, "The breaking up of the German ciphering machine 'ENIGMA,' " 6-8.

Col. Lisicki comments in a letter to the editor-translator (30 August 1982):

Col. Mayer, in writing that the British ceased in 1942 to send [Enigma] keys [see above], was somewhat in error; [Col.] Langer's papers, on which Mayer relied, indicate that the British refused a request to send [keys]—which hardly means that in 1941 they had sent them, as I rather doubt.

In the same letter, Lisicki writes:

Rejewski in one of his letters conceded that Bertrand was doubtless right that at Cadix they had read Enigma, and that the number given by Bertrand, of 673 [Wehrmacht] telegrams, was correct. . . . The British did not send keys to Cadix; these were found using various tricks such as the sillies [and] Herivel tip described by Welchman, Knox's method, as well as others that Rejewski no longer remembered.

In an enclosure to this letter, Lisicki writes concerning "Knox's methods":

In early 1940 the British shared with the Polish cryptologists two methods of reconstructing daily keys [Lisicki's footnote: "Langer, 1946, 107"] informally known as Knox's methods. Both these methods exploited German errors. The first relied on the observation that short meteorological telegrams transmitted by German airfield radio stations were first encoded and then enciphered in a substitution cipher that used the letters in the [Enigma] plug connections for the given day. The British cryptologists solved the codes without great difficulties, and then decryptment of the letters that were used for the substitution, likewise relatively easy, would give the cryptologists, generally a little past midnight, the plug connections for the entire day. . . . Whoever was first to reconstruct the plug connections, sent them by the teletype line that linked the British and French cryptological centers. The other method [which Welchman calls the "Herivel tip"] exploited a frequently recurring error of German cipher clerks that consisted in the cipher clerk, after past midnight setting [his machine to] the daily keys for the given day, selecting as a telegram [that is, "message"] key the letters which, after their setting, appeared in the windows. Since the basic setting was given in the telegram (the first three letters) it was possible, knowing the plug connections, to reconstruct the remaining elements of the daily key.

In the same enclosure, Lisicki notes: "[On] 17 January 1940. . . in the presence of the British cryptologists D. Knox and A. Turing the keys for 29 November [sic—other sources give 28 October] 1939 were solved [at "Bruno"] and the telegrams read." In a subsequent letter of 19 September 1982, Lisicki gives, as his source for the presence of Knox and Turing, a "conversation with Zygalski." Lisicki, Materials enclosed with letter of 30 August 1982.

About Rejewski's earlier belief that no Enigma had been read at "Cadix," Lisicki writes:

Rejewski either had forgotten or had not known that, e.g., Zygalski and Różycki had read Enigma after the fall of France. In a later letter to me he writes: "Bertrand is doubtless right that we read Enigma."

Bertrand in his book [Enigma, 1973] states: "Le bilan total des décryptements réalisés à Cadix: Armée 673 (Enigma)," page 117.

Langer—report dated 21.1.42, no. 592, writes: "Air force machine ciphers from 3.IV to 20.IX.41, total 17 cipher days, material from the Balkan invasion. . ."

At Cadix Enigma *was* read. . .

Lisicki, Letter of 19 September 1982.—ED.

12. There is a French wine with the trade name "Barsac."—ED.

11.

Vichy France

In mid-1940 the Second World War entered a new phase, and the Third Reich reached the pinnacle of its power. During the summer and fall, the Germans tried to break the resistance of their last adversary in the west, attacking Britain with powerful air forces. The aerial offensive was thrown back, with the conspicuous participation of Polish pilots.[1] Meanwhile, in July 1940, Hitler had begun preparations for the decisive encounter, his assault on the Soviet Union, which would come a year later. A dark night of occupation was settling over most of Europe.

During September 1940, the Poles of Team Z in North Africa received documents issued in false names and, in twos and threes, returned to southern France. Cryptologist Marian Rejewski was now Pierre Ranaud, a "lycée professor from Nantes," Henryk Zygalski was René Sergent, Jerzy Różycki was Julien Rouget, Lt. Col. Gwido Langer was Charles Lange,[2] engineer Antoni Palluth was Jean Lenoir. The Poles had been transformed into businessmen, postal clerks, craftsmen. Those who did not speak fluent French were supplied with credible biographies as naturalized foreigners. In similar fashion the Spanish group and the French personnel of the secret unit were sent back to France.

On October 1, not fully three and a half months after the rout of the French Army and the disbanding of the Bruno center, a reactivated radio-intelligence and decryptment center resumed operations. The new Cadix center consisted of the following units:[3] the Polish Team Z (fifteen persons), the Spanish Team D (seven persons) and the French staff (seven persons plus Bertrand, his wife Mary, and his aide Capt. Honoré Louis), for a total of thirty-two persons.

Thus, the Cadix operation rested on Polish and Spanish professional personnel, with the Spaniards working on Italian and Fascist Spanish ciphers.[4] The most important aspect of the center's work, German military ciphers, was the exclusive domain of the Poles.

The conditions in which the Polish team operated in southern (Vichy) France from 1 October 1940 have been described by Marian Rejewski. The chateau that housed Cadix, he recalls, was set in a modest garden and was smaller than had been Vignolles (the Bruno center) at Gretz. One room of the chateau was reserved for Bertrand, who would go there (sometimes with his wife Mary) to share news of the military and political situation with the Polish team and to inform them of the degree of danger to the clandestine team from German counterintelligence and Vichy police. He would bring them directives and pick up decrypted German signals containing information sought by Allied staffs on the operational plans and intentions of German Army, Air Force, and (less often) Navy commanders.

The channels by which this information reached the Allied staffs through the medium of Bertrand were known to the Poles only in the most general terms. Security dictated that individuals at Cadix should know only what was indispensable to their own work. The officers who enciphered messages for transmittal across the English Channel and the radio operators in the attic did not know what the mathematician-cryptologists did in their rooms on the ground floor, which were always closed and were secured by bars in the double windows.

The bars were associated with an amusing incident. When one of the Poles hit upon the idea of having his picture taken in a barred window, this elicited violent protest from Bertrand, probably resentful of the Pole's wanting to commemorate his stay at Cadix as if it were a place of confinement. He regarded this as a poor joke, or perhaps he was a trifle superstitious. Certainly, the danger of going from Château des Fouzes straight to a Nazi prison was real enough.

An important technical problem was that of reliable radio communications with Allied staffs, not always assured by the available transmitters. In March 1941 Bertrand went to Lisbon, where from Wilfred ("Bill") Dunderdale of Britain's MI-6 he received a new transmitter. A few days later it was installed at Cadix, and after that radiotelegraphic communication proceeded without major disturbances.

The Polish team, though in some ways subordinate to the center's French management, communicated by radio directly with the staff of the Polish commander in chief in London, receiving assignments from the latter and sending in periodic reports.[5] However, regular communication was established only after five months at Cadix, on 7 March 1941. Radiograms in this net were enciphered on a Polish Lacida cipher machine produced before the war for Polish higher commands; two Lacidas had been sent to France prior to September 1939.[6]

Interception of secret German correspondence was, of course, a duty of the French who, despite armistice limitations, possessed the wherewithal to monitor signals of the Wehrmacht and other occupation agencies, including communications between field offices of the German branch of the Armistice Commission, in southern France, Algeria, and Morocco, and its headquarters at Wiesbaden in Germany.

In the armistice agreement signed at Compiègne on 22 June 1940, the Germans had stipulated their total authority over the secret correspondence of the Vichy government and all its civil and military agencies. As with the entire French military intelligence organization (the S.R.), the radio-monitoring services, the R.E.G. and the R.C.R., were officially disbanded. Their military personnel were demobilized, and their civil personnel were sent to other work. However, the Germans permitted the creation of a small new radio-monitoring service called Groupement des Contrôles Radioélectriques de l'Intérieur (G.C.R.) that was supposed to discover clandestine radio stations of the anti-Nazi and anti-Vichy resistance. G.C.R. was to be subordinate to French civil authorities, but the Germans reserved the right to monitor its operations.[7]

The Vichy government also created a secret police, likewise civilian, called the Bureau of Antinational Activities (Bureau Menée Antinationale, or M.A.). In this service, in which the chief role was played by declared Pétainists and collaborationists, the French resistance also placed its own people, including former military intelligence personnel; these sought to use the M.A. as cover for renewed anti-German operations. It was a perilous game of appearances requiring considerable gifts for mimicry and skillful deception.

A circumstance favoring Cadix was the appointment as chief of the Vichy radio-monitoring service, the G.C.R., of Capt. Gabriel Louis Romon, with whom Bertrand shared close ties of friendship dating from before the war. Within a short time, G.C.R. was reorganized for monitoring German transmitters. Working with six monitoring stations, it supplied Cadix with copious material for decryptment. Romon managed to keep the illegal operation secret by placing his most trusted people in the stations organized to intercept Wehrmacht and S.S. signals.[8]

Apart from the civilian G.C.R.'s monitoring net, four receivers manned exclusively by Polish operators were installed at Cadix itself to intercept German short-wave transmissions.[9] The center's stations were basically reserved for detecting and registering signals from Abwehr and S.D. agents operating in southern France. In a pinch, they also monitored German military nets, for example, to collect data on a new communications net and then turn monitoring over to G.C.R.

This well-conceived system for obtaining enemy signals operated to the last day with the same vigor and discipline as it did on the first, "demonstrating [in Bertrand's words] that even with limited resources, given a team of determined people, in this field one can attain such goals as he wishes to set himself."[10]

Decryptment began as soon as Cadix had been organized, and took in the following kinds of monitored materials:

• Signals of Wehrmacht staffs and units stationed in France, Germany, and territories occupied by or dominated by Germany in Belgium, Bulgaria, Crete, Czechoslovakia, Hungary, Libya, Poland, the U.S.S.R., Yugoslavia, and elsewhere;

• Signals of police and S.S. in Austria, Czechoslovakia, France, Holland, Luxembourg, Norway, Poland, and in occupied parts of the U.S.S.R.;

- Correspondence of Abwehr and S.D. agents in France and in North Africa with their intelligence headquarters in Germany;
- Correspondence of the German Armistice Commission headquarters at Wiesbaden with its stations in southern France and North Africa, and among its field stations.[11]

Apart from radio monitoring, another means of penetrating the German communication net was "source K," a bold Resistance operation that regularly intercepted German telegrams going over underground cables, especially between Paris and Metz and between Paris and Strasbourg.[12] Copies of the telegrams were delivered to southern France by Resistance couriers. After decryptment at Cadix, the contents were relayed to Allied staffs in Britain or used in France when they concerned roundups, arrests, or other repressive measures.

The German High Command and Abwehr kept close watch on the internal situation in southern France and were always ready to intervene and occupy the free zone. As early as the end of 1940, Hitler approved an army group for this operation, which was code named Attila.[13] At the end of January 1941, a special plan was framed for Abwehr operational groups which, after the march began, were to occupy key facilities and, together with the Gestapo, arrest French and Allied intelligence personnel.[14]

A sword of Damocles thus hung continually over the heads of the Poles, Spaniards, and Frenchmen at Cadix—as they well knew from Bertrand's intelligence sources, including informants among the Vichy authorities at the German Embassy in Paris and in other occupation agencies.

As in occupied northern and central France, numerous secret organizations arose in the south in the years 1940-42, in which a large role was played by Poles. Their operations found a base among the numerous prewar Polish immigrants and in the Polish labor companies, formed after the dissolution of Polish front-line military units that had evaded capture during the hostilities or internment after crossing the Swiss border. On the orders of General Sikorski the former Polish military attaché in Paris, Gen. Juliusz Kleeberg, assigned officers and noncoms to these companies as "interpreters." Kleeberg himself received from the French authorities the official function of "chief interpreter" (Interprète Général). The numerical strength of the Polish formation that was camouflaged in this way was constantly decreased by secret evacuation to Great Britain. At the same time, it was augmented by escapees from German camps, Swiss internment, and labor companies. In mid-April 1942, the formation numbered about 500 officers and 3,500 enlisted men. Of these, 53 officers and 2,718 enlisted men were in sixteen companies; the rest were in hospitals and hide-outs or were furloughed to institutions of higher education.

After the occupation of southern France by German armed forces in November 1942, General Kleeberg's function was taken over, on December 4, by Col. Józef Jaklicz, who was also in charge of all secret evacuation operations. The practical side was handled by the Section II intelligence network, which had widely ramified field stations and operated independently of Polish underground organizations in France. Earliest to come into existence, in 1940, was the F-2 net that was directed in the fall and winter of 1942-43 by Polish Lt. Col. Marian Romeyko (pseudonym Mak—Poppy).[15]

How could the anti-German Cadix center function in Vichy territory that was penetrated by the Germans? This is one of those paradoxes of World War II that are no doubt more numerous than the official histories indicate. In addition to Bertrand's own security measures, the illegal operations of Cadix and other clandestine centers in southern France were shielded by French Resistance counterintelligence, acting under cover of the Rural Works Enterprise (Enterprise de Travaux Ruraux). This unofficial counterespionage organization in the free zone was headed by the former deputy chief of the military counterintelligence German section, Capt. Paul Paillole, and neutralized German agents as well as overzealous Vichy police officers and collaborators.

In the years 1940-42, probably no area on the face of the earth presented a more complex political and military situation than did the free zone that was dominated, but not occupied, by Germany. The main division was a clear one: the supporters of Pétain and Laval collaborating with the Germans on one side, and the conspirators and soldiers of the Résistance on the other. But between these two sides were groups and individuals who hated the Nazis but were disaffected with the Gaullists and the Allies. The picture was likewise confused with regard to the intelligence organizations that operated in southern France. At least six major anti-Nazi intelligence organizations acted here independently of each other: inter-Allied intelligence, British military intelligence, the British diversion and sabotage organization Special Operations Executive (S.O.E.), Gaullist intelligence, the Polish Section II, and the secret intelligence service of the French armed forces. In addition, some sources name the secret services of the Soviet Union, Switzerland, Belgium, Yugoslavia, the Vatican, and later the United States.[16]

In France, Holland, and Belgium, as had been the case not quite a year earlier in Poland and would later be so in other countries occupied by Germany, the first organized centers of resistance immediately after the entrance of German armies were the secret services. As opposed to the regular armies, these services could not be entirely annihilated by lightning raids with armor and Luftwaffe. The outcome of the secret war, although it was prosecuted under conditions that markedly favored the Germans, was not a foregone conclusion.

The situations in the occupied countries of Europe varied, but everywhere the intelligence units that survived were, as a rule, the most active, the most efficient instruments for continuing the war.

In France, conditions were more favorable than elsewhere because, despite the military collapse and capitulation, the southern free zone enabled a rapid regeneration of the intelligence services. Before the Germans managed to saturate southern France with their secret agents, the old S.R. apparatus had succeeded in "changing its skin," and created a new supersecret organization which, to the end of the war, was never fully penetrated by the Germans.

Due to the special nature of this war of wits, the numbers of personnel and the quantities of material resources thrown into the fray were not always directly translatable into quality. Hence the underground intelligence services in the occupied countries could undertake a successful struggle with the German Abwehr and Gestapo despite the colossal German superiority in personnel and material and technical resources.

In France, it was decided to resurrect the counterintelligence service that had been shattered and scattered in June 1940, creating on the foundations of surviving cadre a new organization that was to act clandestinely under the cover of some legitimate institution. The choice fell upon the Ministry of Agriculture, where one of the heads of the prewar intelligence service, Paul Paillole, found an old friend who was director of the department of rural construction (génie rural).

> How this idea—which I now consider to be a stroke of genius—
> came into being, no one exactly knows. Maybe it was when we were
> speaking ironically about a fifth column of potato bugs that a visionary at
> the General Staff wanted us to help him put over onto Hitler's potato
> patch...[17]

In any case, it was decided to pay a call on the departmental director—his name was Préat—and appeal to his patriotism. Préat agreed to the formation of a fictitious Rural Works Enterprise (Entreprise de Travaux Ruraux) with headquarters in Marseilles and four field offices in Lyon, Limoges, Clermont-Ferrand, and Toulouse. He also promised suitable quarters for five or six people at each field office. Greater difficulties were involved in establishing the head office in Marseilles, where accommodations had to be found for about fifteen people and some thirty tons of files evacuated from Paris in June 1940 and temporarily stored in the underground vaults of a great Roquefort cheese plant in the city of the same name.

In the first days of July 1940, just two weeks after France's collapse, the clandestine counterintelligence organization Travaux Ruraux (T.R.) opened its operations in southern France.

Meanwhile, alarming reports about the Nazi terror had begun to come in from occupied northern France. Wehrmacht courts-martial were passing out ruthless sentences. On just one day, 24 June 1940, they had sentenced to death seventeen patriots who had defied Pétain's decision to capitulate. Such acts of despair could change nothing, however, and more appropriate and effective forms of underground struggle had to be undertaken.

Officers of the outlawed anti-German intelligence who had not reconciled themselves to capitulation constituted the bulk of the new service. There were important questions of finances, material base, and equipment, but it turned out that the secret fund of the late S.R. remained intact and could be used to purchase or rent suitable clandestine quarters in the cities where T.R. counterintelligence stations were to be created. A key matter was the careful selection of housing for the central office. Chosen for this purpose was the Château École on the outskirts of Marseilles, on the Promenade de la Plage, with a spacious garage and a courtyard, enclosed by a high wall. The owner agreed to rent it to a trustworthy enterprise that was recommended by the Ministry of Agriculture.

Maj. Paul Paillole, head of Travaux Ruraux, operated under the alias Philippe Perrier. T.R. headquarters received the cryptonym Cambronne, after Napoleon's general who had commanded the Old Guard at the Battle of Waterloo, and, when called upon to lay down his arms, had replied in the negative with an emphatic "Merde!" The officers who took charge of the T.R. field offices received forged documents and diplomas as agricultural engineers.

The very name of the enterprise was a clever psychological trick that traded on the partiality of Vichy leaders for phrases alluding to the Nazi slogan, "Blut und Boden" (Blood and Soil). The Vichy rendition was "retour à la terre" (return to the soil). Anything whose name contained the words "soil," "agriculture," "rural," and so on, sounded legitimate to Pétainist ears. Philippe Perrier's firm raised no suspicions even when, after a year's time, its personnel had grown from fifty-odd to four hundred agrotechnicians and clerks. In time, eight field offices were established.

After the German invasion of the Soviet Union on 22 June 1941, the main theater of the war shifted away from France. Cadix's monitoring took in the Russian front only at night. But, on the other hand, messages were easily picked up from German territory, and the Poles could not complain of a lack of employment. Often they worked with the same intensity as they had in the hectic days of May and June 1940.

S.S. and Wehrmacht radios in France, especially in the Massif Central, transmitted many reports that gave information on the growing partisan movement. Decryptment of these reports enabled Bertrand to warn resistance organizations of impending punitive expeditions and sweeps. Even individual persons were warned that they were sought by the police. Some messages contained information on Gestapo and military intelligence functionaries; this information was passed at once to Allied intelligence headquarters in London.

In September 1941, a cipher was solved that turned out to serve for communication between a group of German secret agents operating in French Mediterranean ports and Abwehr headquarters in Stuttgart. The cipher was broken by engineer Antoni Palluth who, while maintaining the Enigma machines and radios, renewed his old cryptological specialty. The reconstructed spy reports were sent to Marseilles, where, within a few days, the Rural Works Enterprise discovered the transmitter and neutralized the agents.

Somewhat later, Rejewski, Różycki, and Zygalski broke codes and ciphers used in German telegraphic communications. The encrypted texts had been copied by French postal workers cooperating with the Résistance. They included reports from German radio-location and monitoring stations in southern France that were used to find the clandestine transmitters of underground organizations.

At Uzès the cryptologists did not have the technical facilities that they had enjoyed at Gretz-Armainvillers; nevertheless, decryptment of German messages enabled them in time to considerably broaden their knowledge of the adversary and his methods. Thus, they discovered the newly introduced principles of preliminary preparation of texts and made tables of standard abbreviations, call signals, and so on. In mid-1941 they determined that the Germans were enciphering, unaltered, only certain numbers, those that had varying endings. For numbers that ended in multiple zeros, they were substituting special expressions: for two zeros in succession they used the expression "centa;" for three zeros, "mille;" for four zeros, "myria." This created possibilities of combinations that made decryptment more difficult. The same number 500,000, for instance, could be enciphered as "fuenf centa mille," "fuenf myria null," "fuenf mille centa," or "fuenf null myria."

The Germans also employed other precautions. It was forbidden to transmit the same message a second time after an error had been made; the text had to be reedited, without altering the content, of course. Usually the order of the expressions would be changed.

An unusual episode in the Poles' work was the breaking, in the fall of 1941, of a Swiss cipher. Switzerland was neutral in favor of the Allies, although she would not go so far as to court German invasion. When Swiss messages were first intercepted, the cryptologists, knowing the caution of the Swiss, anticipated difficulties. But it turned out that the Swiss as well had succumbed to the spell of the machine cipher. In their secret diplomatic and military correspondence they used Enigma, but they had not even bothered to modify it.[18] They had, presumably, been satisfied with the assurances of specialists who, before the war, had recommended purchasing a batch of the "unbreakable" devices in Germany.

The hardest part of breaking the Swiss Enigma was realizing that the ciphers *were* Enigma. The reason for the difficulty was that Swiss texts were not always in German, but sometimes in French or Italian, and therefore did not always show certain features usually associated with Enigma. But a flash of imagination sufficed—and eureka! The Swiss machine, recalls Rejewski, proved to be an ordinary Enigma, of course with different wiring than the German machine. In order to continue reading the Swiss, it would have been necessary to recover the keys daily. But why bother? Bertrand's people let it be known in Bern that the Swiss Enigma ciphers were probably being read. In case there was a German agent in the Swiss High Command, this information was passed on in such a way as not to arouse suspicion that the Wehrmacht's Enigma too might be insecure.

In spite of the difficulties, nearly all the Poles at Uzès established a correspondence with their families in Poland. This would have been impossible but for the help of their French comrades, who sought out the unsuspicious addresses of loyal persons in France, North Africa, or Switzerland. The letters made their way by roundabout routes to Poland, sometimes via many countries and continents, such as Turkey and South America.

Contact with Poland and with their nearest and dearest, infrequent though it was, had tremendous importance for men who were cut off for years from the rest of the world. Bruno outside Paris, to say nothing of the supersecret Cadix in southern France, were not places that made for easy contact. Special, ingenious codes had to be used in order to write something more than merely "I am well" or "My best to Aunt Kazia." But even communication like this held great hazards and had to be thought out to the last detail. Occasionally there would be unpleasant lapses.

Letters from Rejewski to his wife in Warsaw came to her from Switzerland, mailed ostensibly by one B. Rosner. Mrs. Rejewska did not even know whether the fictitious sender was a man or woman and, in case of questioning, could not have explained who her correspondent was. One time, in December 1940, she received a letter sent from the United States by an unknown person—supposedly a nun—who, instead of incorporating Rejewski's news into her own letter, inserted into the envelope Rejewski's letter requesting that his wife be discreetly informed that he was in southern France. The nun also enclosed a Christmas wafer, it being shortly before the Christmas season. Fortunately, the Nazi censor, probably due to the press of work, took no interest in the content of the letter; instead, it was streaked with colored lines—reagents for developing invisible ink—and the wafer was confiscated with the remark that samples of merchandise were not permitted in letters ("Warenproben sind nicht erlaubt"). Later, in the spring of 1943, Mrs. Rejewska received a picture postcard from Spain, with only greetings from Señora Maria in Séo de Urgel; she had never heard of the lady, and therefore guessed that her husband Marian was now in Spain.

Relations among the Polish team were not always idyllic; from time to time, ruffled feelings and resentments made themselves evident. There was a considerable distance between the professional officers and the other members, even those without whom solution of Enigma would have been impossible. Before the collapse of France in June 1940, unctuous politicians and senior officers had come to the Gretz-Armainvillers center from the ministry and general staff at the Hotel Regina in Paris. They conferred confidentially with the chiefs, while the latter seldom spoke with the team on matters going beyond their daily work. Prospects for return to Poland and their families were dim; nevertheless, the common wartime vicissitudes and dangers cemented the group together. Both military personnel and civilian specialists showed great psychological stamina. Despite the constant fear that some fine morning they would see a ring of German and Vichy police outside the windows of Les Fouzes, they managed to stay calm. They warded off nostalgia with hard work, self-education, study of languages, and reading of the French books supplied by the invaluable major-domo and quartermaster of the center, Monsieur David. He also made several bicylces available to the Poles and, with permission from the French and Polish chiefs, they could take short rides around the vicinity of Uzès; contacts with the French population, however, were strictly forbidden. Some of the men did not shun alcohol, but apart from a single case of advanced alcoholism,[19] the team maintained temperance and full physical and mental fitness.

Rejewski, Różycki, and Zygalski mostly kept to themselves, but did not shun social gatherings. Polish songs were sung in none too harmonious chorus, and brave solo singers were heard. The specialty number in the program of Major Ciężki, Colonel Langer's second in command, was Nadir's aria from Bizet's *Pearlfishers*, and the mathematicians' entry in these contests was broadly talented Jerzy Różycki.

An attraction for the recluses of Cadix was frog hunting, a pastime in which they were encouraged by their gastronomically self-interested French hosts. These hunts have been described by engineer Tadeusz Suszczewski, a cryptologist who was found in Grenoble and brought to Cadix in the spring of 1942:

> After arriving by car or bicycle at an area of ponds and meadows, we would select a suitable muddy pool where we heard the loudest croaking, and spread a large red cloth on the grass. Evidently this color is very alluring to frogs, because after a few minutes several of them would appear on the cloth, and then more and more would hop aboard. When several dozen frogs had assembled, we would lift the cloth by its corners and sweep them into a carton for transportation home.

Another curiosity was the subtropical vegetation, such as the bamboo shoots, that grew at an incredible speed of twenty or more centimeters a day. In a few days, they attained the height of a man. Yet another "attraction" of these wilds of the Rhone delta, called *garrigues* by the French, were mosquitos and scorpions. One could sleep only under fine-meshed mosquito netting. On hot, sultry nights, this hampered the circulation of air. Scorpions had to be looked out for all the time, especially during walks in the park. Their sting could spell death, for the scorpion venom serums were not always effective. The heat made itself strongly felt. In their constantly closed quarters, the men labored shirtless, dressed only in linen trousers.

The isolation also caused hardship. For relaxation, the men celebrated every available national holiday, Polish, French, or Spanish, their patron saints' feast days, and other personal anniversaries. All the same, homesickness combined with general exhaustion was sometimes hard to stand. "I have allowed myself to be penned up here under a new name," one of the team members jotted down. "I am in strange surroundings, constrained from moving about. Dry-as-dust mathematical and linguistic work, the same company from morning to night." But after a couple of days the depression would pass, and the men would attack the enemy ciphers with renewed vigor.[20]

In early 1941, an overseas branch of Cadix was set up in North Africa to solve German ciphers intercepted by local monitoring stations. This made Cadix's work more efficient by eliminating the transportation of dangerous materials across the Mediterranean. Apart from the time factor, couriers risked being stopped by Vichy police, among whom the Abwehr and Gestapo had many informers.

The new decryptment station was housed in the Château Couba on the outskirts of Algiers. The branch off of Cadix was organized by Major Bertrand and Colonel Langer. It was considerably safer to work there than at Cadix, which was constantly threatened with a surprise raid and where one lived ever on the alert.

For security and personal safety, the Poles seldom participated in courier missions or the like. An exception was departures for two- to three-month stints at the Château Couba. One such expedition across the Mediterranean ended tragically. In circumstances that remain unclear to this day, the French ship *Lamoricière*, on which four Poles were returning from Algeria, suffered catastrophe on 9 January 1942, near the Balearic Islands. It is not clear whether, amid a raging storm, the ship struck a reef or one of the thousands of mines that the belligerents were laying. Killed in the *Lamoricière* catastrophe were Capt. Jan Graliński, Jerzy Różycki, and Piotr Smoleński.[21] The Vichy press did not publish a list of victims, only the names of survivors. The Poles had been traveling under assumed French names which did not appear on that list. Also lost was a French officer accompanying the Poles, Capt. François Lane. The press gave the toll of victims: 222 out of 272 passengers, and 57 of the hundred-man crew.

The crew, to the end, fought heroically to save people and ship. The captain of the *Lamoricière*, Milliasseau, had been accompanied on the voyage by his wife. After losing all hope, he kissed his wife and saw her and a small group of passengers off on the last lifeboat. He himself remained on the sinking ship, which soon went to the bottom. Several ships, including the *General Chanzy* and the *Saint-Louis*, rescued the nearly one hundred survivors.

The activity of the radio intelligence center at the Château Couba is illuminated in a book by Polish Brig. Gen. M.Z. Rygor-Słowikowski, *W tajnej służbie. Polski wkład do zwycięstwa w II wojnie światowej* (In Secret Service: The Polish Contribution to Victory in World War II). Before going to Algiers, then Major Słowikowski had, together with Maj. Wincenty Zarembski (pseudonym Tudor) and Capt. Roman Czerniawski (pseudonyms Wincenty and Armand, who would later become a top star in the Double-Cross deception system described by Masterman[22]), headed a secret evacuation net—set up after the fall of France in June 1940—which ran Polish officers and soldiers across Spain to Great Britain. In time, this net, headquartered in Toulouse, also conducted intelligence operations.

From 1941 to 1944 Słowikowski headed the Allied intelligence net Rygor (Rigor), which covered nearly all of North Africa. When starting out in Algiers in the summer of 1941, and also later, Słowikowski received substantial assistance from Major Ciężki, deputy chief of Cadix, who was in Algiers for a time and was the head of the Couba outpost. (In Africa, Ciężki used documents issued in the name of Miller, and the pseudonym Maciej—Polish for Matthew—which had been formed from the initial syllables of his real first and last names.) Before departing for Algiers, Słowikowski had established with Colonel Langer that, until he had organized his own radio communications, he would correspond with London through radio station Couba.

Słowikowski's first meeting with Major Ciężki, who was lodging in Algiers at the Hotel Arago (on the street of the same name), took place on the evening of 24 July 1941. Ciężki turned over to Słowikowski ciphergrams addressed to him, sent from London to the Algerian outpost by a circuitous route via Uzès. The two officers had not known each other personally, but Słowikowski knew Langer (they had studied together in 1923-24 at the Military Staff College in Warsaw) and this helped them get on a good footing.

Those first ciphers that Ciężki passed on to Słowikowski contained diverse intelligence assignments, such as furnishing detailed information on North Africa's air defenses, on shipments of war materiel to Germany, and a number of others. The next day, Słowikowski gave Ciężki his first report for forwarding by roundabout route to Section II's London headquarters. The messages that came in almost daily via Couba did not always reckon with reality. For example, on July 26, when he had just begun to put together a net of informants, he was instructed to report without delay on the situation in Dakar, thousands of kilometers away (What was the condition of the cruiser *Richelieu*, which lay in that port? What armament did it carry on its turrets? What kind of shore batteries were there, and where were they located? What fortifications were there? Were there tank units in the city? And many other questions). Słowikowski was not in a position to immediately meet these demands since, in addition to recruiting agents, he also had to secure a good cover for a lengthy stay in Algiers. He comments, "For desk officers at Headquarters, distances do not exist; these men do not understand the difficulties, and above all they do not know the dangers, of work in enemy territory." By fairly complex means, he acquired the status of a respected industrialist, co-owner of the Floc-Av firm, which produced (as the sole plant of its kind in Algeria) oat flakes.[23]

Indispensable, too, was some time for becoming familiar with the territory in which the Rygor organization was to operate. Initially, in addition to Słowikowski himself, it was run by two other officers: Lt. H. Łubieński (Banuls) and Lieutenant Gordon (René), who had no experience in intelligence work and had to gradually acquire it. In subsequent months and years, more Polish intelligence officers were sent to Rygor under various covers: Capt. S. Romejko, Naval Captain Jekiel (an engineer), Lt. A. Piotrowski, Naval Lieutenant Żurawski, Artillery Maj. L. Jagodziński, Lt. E. Przemyski, Second Lieutenant Majewicz. During its first weeks, Rygor concentrated its activity in two areas, the cities of Algiers and Oran, then gradually broadened its sphere to include other cities, key air and naval bases, and army garrisons, at first in Algeria itself, then in Tunisia and Morocco, and as far as Casablanca and Dakar. The Polish Rygor intelligence net recruited only non-Poles, chiefly French persons who were in opposition to the Vichy regime, though not always enthusiastic about the Free French movement and de Gaulle. The head of the net also had his people in the Vichy police and counterintelligence, sometimes in high positions. With the latter service he concluded an agreement, pursuant to which material was exchanged concerning German and Italian functionaries of the Armistice Commissions, as well as persons suspected of collaborating with those commissions or with the intelligence services of the Axis states. Considerable funds to finance the ramified Rygor intelligence net, which played a significant role in Allied preparations for the invasion of North Africa, were funneled into Algiers secretly through the local branch of Shell Petroleum, for example, whose French director had a Polish wife, and, after the United States entered the war, through the American consulate general in Algiers. By the same agencies Rygor sent to London numerous intelligence materials—maps, plans, sketches, and longer reports and analyses of the military and political situation in various areas of North Africa—whose transmittal by radio would have been impractical. Just prior to the landings by Allied forces in Algeria and in other sectors of the North African coast, the Rygor intelligence net had several dozen well-situated intelligence outposts. The directors of these outposts were identified not by pseudonyms but by numbers selected from a range (1800 to 1990) designated by headquarters in London.

Thus, Major Ciężki's radio intelligence post at Couba was an irreplaceable channel of communications for Rygor from August 1941 to February 1942. It was only in February 1942 that Słowikowski received his own radio station. Its installation, the finding of a trained, absolutely reliable operator, and technical trials of direct communication with London took several weeks. The former chief of the Rygor net is mistaken when he writes that one of the radio intelligence teams at Couba (called Posterunek Oficerski 1, meaning Officers' Post 1, by the Poles, or P.O. 1 for short) sailed from Algiers to Marseilles aboard the *Lamoricière*, which then sank near the Balearic Islands, "in the first half of March 1942." The *Lamoricière* tragedy, as attested by surviving letters from Rejewski and Zygalski to Maria Barbara Różycka, informing her of her husband's death, occurred on 9 January 1942. However it is likely that Major Ciężki did remain together with part of the P.O. 1 personnel in Algiers, as Słowikowski states, until July 1942.

The Polish Rygor intelligence net was active in North Africa—apart from several weeks' suspension of its activity after the landing of American and British troops—from July 1941 to September 1944. In the first, most important phase of its work, that is, until November 1942, it sent to London, via P.O. 1, Cadix, and its own radio station, 1,244 enciphered, sometimes multipartite intelligence reports. In addition, it sent many priceless intelligence materials by courier's pouch, which, from December 1941, went out regularly each week via the American consulate general in Algiers. For outstanding intelligence services in the North African theater of operations before the landings, Słowikowski received high British and American decorations.

It should be noted that—as Słowikowski's book indicates—overly close horizontal ties between individual intelligence elements and nets were avoided in North Africa. To be sure, the Couba radio intelligence outpost directed by Major Ciężki enabled Rygor to maintain communication with London via France, but friendly relations between the two officers notwithstanding, Słowikowski knew neither the outpost's location nor the details of its operations.

The year 1942 promised momentous events; the world conflict was approaching its culmination. Toward year's end, the German war machine was jolted by the disaster of its crack Sixth Army at Stalingrad and by a series of setbacks in the North African theater. German intelligence received reports on Allied preparations for a landing operation, possibly in North Africa. The mounting nervousness of the German commands and staffs was making itself known in southern France. Hitler and Ribbentrop increased their pressure on the Vichy regime. Pétain was accused of disloyalty and softness toward the increasingly militant resistance, in which the French Communist Party and other leftist groups had begun to play an increasing role. Pierre Laval, despised not only by the Resistance but by moderate Pétainists, returned to power in Vichy. In a radio broadcast on the first anniversary of the German attack on the Soviet Union, Laval declared: "I hope for Germany's victory, because without it communism would tomorrow control all of Europe." Under German pressure and on Hitler's express instructions, Marshal Pétain recalled from North Africa his trusted governor, General Weygand; this was partly a result of the breaking by the Germans of an American diplomatic code.

In the autumn of 1940, after the signing of the armistice, the office of French governor-general in North Africa was set up, Pétain had entrusted this post to Gen. Maxime Weygand. On the day of his appointment, however, Weygand was in an airplane accident; he escaped with his life but suffered serious injuries, and it was only in October 1940 that he arrived in North Africa to take command of the French Army and Air Force. While loudly proclaiming loyalty to Vichy, General Weygand conducted secret talks with the Americans. The U.S. ambassador to Pétain's government was Adm. William Leahy, and, at the end of 1940, a separate minister plenipotentiary, Robert Murphy, was sent to Algiers, accredited to Weygand.

Weygand anticipated that in the long run Germany, whose great aerial offensive against Britain had ended in failure, would lose the war. He worked to preserve, and even covertly to build up, his army in order to throw it into the scales of war at an opportune moment. At the same time, as a conservative and a friend of capital, he opposed de Gaulle and his Free French movement, which he thought excessively radical.

Over many months General Weygand created a modest but well-equipped army in North Africa numbering some one hundred eleven thousand men, including forty-two hundred officers. His air force of twenty-eight squadrons and 450 planes likewise was a respectable force in the region. Thus Weygand was a man with whom it was possible, and worth one's while, to play for high stakes.

But the German High Command and the suspicious foreign minister, Ribbentrop, also joined in the game. After Weygand's secret negotiations with the Americans came to light, the general was kept under surveillance. German radio monitoring, the Horch-Dienst, received orders to intercept all of Murphy's coded correspondence with Washington.

Despite Marshal Pétain's assurances concerning the loyalty of his plenipotentiary Weygand, the Germans suspected Weygand of double-dealing, but could furnish no proof. Meanwhile, Murphy wasn't wasting time. After a few weeks, the clandestine negotiators were already discussing shipments of arms and equipment to form eight new French divisions in North Africa. An agreement had already been signed for deliveries of gasoline, coal, chemicals, textiles, and artificial fertilizers, with the proviso that these not be turned over to the Germans.

The Germans watched the developments in North Africa with anxiety and finally, in the spring of 1941, decided to get rid of Weygand. As a tool they used the ambitious Adm. Jean François Darlan, who was jealous of Weygand's position and who was becoming increasingly vassal to Germany. In May 1941, the Vichy government sent a letter to Weygand announcing still closer collaboration with the Axis, in exchange for which the Germans allegedly were to soften their occupation of northern France. On receipt of this directive, Weygand consulted Murphy and assured him that in Algeria everything would remain as it was. Murphy, for his part, promised to continue the shipments of manufactures and raw materials.

Weygand's position as governor in North Africa seemed as strong as ever. A contributor to his subsequent downfall, and hence to the collapse of his plan, was none other than his American fellow conspirator, Murphy. All of Murphy's secret correspondence with Washington was by radio and, despite the protests of General Eisenhower, who considered the "Diplomaticus" code to be insecure, Murphy insisted on using this code exclusively. As a representative of the State Department, he wanted to be autonomous of the military.

Murphy, of course, did not know that at that very time the German E-Dienst (decryptment service) was only a step away from solving the U.S. diplomatic code. The State Department had been using the same ciphers and codes since before the war. Murphy's obstinacy, and probably that of the secretary of state, who knew about the army's reservations, brought disaster. The Germans discovered the method used for preliminary preparation of texts first, and next, despite superencipherment, broke the American code. The point of entry was the phrase "For Murphy," which was repeated at the beginnings of dispatches and which the Washington code clerks, through sheer laziness, did not prepare in accordance with their instructions. Murphy's operators likewise began their transmissions in a similar way.

In May and June 1941, German E-Dienst headquarters managed to read about half of all the dispatches. To be sure, none of them were reconstructed in their entirety, but individual sentences and expressions permitted the Germans to get an idea of the subject matter of the secret negotiations. Among other things, Murphy informed Washington that Weygand had given him a full list of names of the German military mission in Algiers. Moreover, he mentioned deliveries of arms for eight infantry divisions and a secret mobilization plan. These fragments were enough for Ribbentrop to be able to prove Weygand's disloyalty and demand his recall by Marshal Pétain.

Still the Germans delayed. In mid-August 1941, the German Foreign Office began to receive from radio intelligence headquarters dispatches of Murphy's that had been solved in toto. When Ribbentrop informed Hitler about them, the latter instructed him to act "by whatever means available."

The foreign minister demanded that Vichy remove General Weygand from North Africa, threatening otherwise to send German troops into the free zone. Pétain tried to smooth things over by sending a personal letter to Hitler assuring him that these were only "American intrigues." Hitler would not be convinced and, moreover, accused Weygand of predicting Germany's defeat despite the "auspiciously developing offensive in Russia." A couple of weeks later, Weygand was summoned to Vichy "for consultations." There ensued a clash between him and the increasingly pro-German Admiral Darlan. Finally, the Germans decided to show all their cards. They gave Darlan copies of Murphy's decrypted messages to Washington. A short time later, Weygand was relieved of his post.

In the spring of 1942, relations between Vichy and Germany entered a critical phase. Pressure exerted by Hitler and Ribbentrop restored to power the declared collaborationist Laval, and southern France began swiftly losing even the semblance of autonomy.

The Germans, however, were anxious to exploit the French economy and did their utmost to fan anti-Allied sentiment.

On 3 March 1942 the Poles and French at Cadix learned from radio bulletins that Britain's RAF had bombed the Renault works in southwest Paris and, inevitably, workers' homes in Boulogne-Billancourt. The toll was 623 dead and over 1,500 wounded. Thus, after not quite two years, death had once again rained down upon the residents of this unfortunate district, as it had on 3 June 1940, when the Germans had carried out their massive air raid on Paris (Unternehmen Paula). This time, though, it was Allied bombs that fell.[24]

Seeing an opportunity for propaganda against British "terrorism," the German governor in Paris, Otto Abetz, invited Marshal Pétain and Admiral Darlan to attend the state funeral for the victims. They declined the invitation and sent the ultracollaborationist Adm. Jean Platon to give the eulogy.

In February 1942, Bertrand received a personal radio message from the former British intelligence representative in France, now at Secret Intelligence headquarters, Comdr. Wilfred ("Bill") Dunderdale, who was asking him to undertake a delicate diplomatic mission. Bertrand was to see General Weygand and ask him whether he would agree to take command of an Allied landing in North Africa. If Weygand agreed, he would be assisted in escaping from France.

Weygand, having been recalled from his post as governor-general in Algeria, was now in the town of Grasse, some twenty kilometers from Cannes. Bertrand had no difficulty in reaching the former commander in chief, who remembered him from the Battle of France and who, after the collapse, had supported his organization of Cadix. When Bertrand presented London's proposal, Weygand replied: "I have given my word to the Marshal [Pétain] to do nothing that might make his position difficult, and I cannot break my word. You can carry on, though, and you will always have my encouragement."

Later in the conversation, Weygand's reasons for rejecting the proposal became clearer when he remarked that a North African landing would require at least ten divisions, three of them armored, supported by a thousand planes. In parting, Weygand presented Bertrand with an autographed photograph of himself.[25]

At Cadix, the normal operational rigors were being observed. The various sections were functionally isolated from each other and knew none of the details of each other's work. Thus, Marian Rejewski had not, up to the summer of 1941, ever seen the Polish L.C.D., or Lacida, cipher machine which was used for communication with London. (The machine took its name from the first letters of the names Langer, Ciężki, Danilewicz.)

No one sought the advice of the cryptologists in the prewar German section (B.S.-4) of the Cipher Bureau when the L.C.D. was being designed. The prototype had been adopted and certified for serial production[26] by a commission of Cipher Bureau officers and one or two university mathematics professors. There are no grounds on which to question their scientific competence, but none of the commissioners were as thoroughly initiated into the arcana of cipher machines as were the three mathematician-cryptologists of B.S.-4 who had solved Enigma. The considerations that had prevented their participation, if not in the designing then at least in the final testing of the L.C.D.'s security, are inexplicable. Only in France did the fact come to light that the Polish machine ciphers had never been subjected to rigorous decryptment attempts.

In the first days of July 1941, Rejewski and Zygalski[27] received for testing messages that had been enciphered on Lacida and transmitted a few days earlier to the Polish General Staff in Britain.

The possibility of weaknesses in the Polish cipher machine had been indicated in the spring of 1940 in a document drawn up by a special committee at General Sikorski's behest. The committee had investigated the causes of derelictions by previous Polish governments in preparing the national defense and had also assessed the radio intelligence organization and its decryptment section, as well as the branch of the Cipher Bureau that had been responsible for the Polish armed forces' own codes and ciphers. "It seems," the committee had reported, "that within the Cipher Bureau there was inadequate cooperation between cryptology specialists . . . who were excellent theoreticians of ciphers and codes in general, and the Polish-ciphers branch, which had no such theoreticians."

Still earlier, during the twenties, one of the Polish intelligence chiefs had argued that the various intelligence branches—offensive intelligence, studies and assessment, and counterintelligence—"should be turned against each other." The studies and assessment branch, he wrote, "criticizes the results obtained by offensive intelligence; the methods of the latter are examined by counterintelligence; what has been obtained by one field station is overthrown by the reports of another station, and so on."[28] This sort of feedback system should protect intelligence officers from complacency. The same would hold for the Cipher Bureau. Its offensive instruments are the cryptologists who break enemy codes and ciphers, and they can also test the resistance or strength of their own side's codes and ciphers. Whoever succeeds in breaking a code or cipher of his own side should receive praise and recognition for having preserved his armed forces from the danger that the adversary could do the same.

In practice, the situation has varied. In ancient times, bearers of bad tidings often suffered from the wrath of the mighty. In more civilized societies, customs have changed, but still no emperor likes to be told that he is wearing no clothes. Such reflections may well have passed through the mind of the chief cryptologist at Cadix, Marian Rejewski, when he set to work together with Zygalski on the sample ciphers from the correspondence between Field Office 300 and London.

Solution of the Polish ciphers entailed no great difficulties. After their long duel with Enigma in its ever more complex mutations, breaking the first Lacida message, which was given them on July 3, took the two cryptologists no more than a couple of hours. For a few days they continued working on the Polish cipher, with a similar outcome.

The resultant consternation was enormous. Langer gave instructions to cease transmitting to the staff of the Polish commander in chief in London using L.C.D. If ever anything had been greeted with mixed feelings, this certainly was. The chief of Field Office 300 did not know whether to congratulate his subordinates or to immediately warn London and prepare an extensive report. After this, much must have changed in the system of ciphers used by Polish commands and staffs in the west.

The L.C.D., Rejewski said in 1974, had two serious shortcomings. First, it lacked the commutator that was one of Enigma's strong points. The second matter involved the reflector and wiring. This does not mean that Lacida, somewhat larger than Enigma and also more complicated (for example, it had a special switch for resetting to decipherment), was easy to solve. Quite the contrary. The likelihood of its being broken by the German E-Dienst was virtually nil. Theoretically it did exist, however, and that was enough to necessitate essential changes.

In the summer of 1942, signs of danger to Cadix began to appear. The possibility of German troops entering southern France was becoming ever greater. The chiefs of Cadix were receiving from various sources reports on the concentration of German forces at the demarcation line separating the occupied area from the free zone. This line was only about 250 kilometers—150 miles—from Cadix, a distance that German Schnelle Truppen (rapid troops) could cover in a few hours. The plan of evacuation was thought out once again down to the smallest details, and in early September Bertrand was in Paris to scout the situation.

Unlikely as it may seem, even in countries conquered or dominated by Germany, the intelligence services of the resistance movements fairly often made use of members of the so-called master race. The motives of these few but sometimes highly placed German officials were various: venality, loss of faith in the Fuehrer and in ultimate victory, a desire to hedge their bets.

Bertrand's memoirs do not reveal what induced an official at the German Embassy in Paris to betray secrets to an officer of the French Army that had been defeated by Germany in 1940 and to facilitate his (Bertrand's) trips between southern France and Paris (to bring back, among other things, parts to be assembled into new Enigmas). In any case, on 3 September 1942, Bertrand learned from Max about Wehrmacht preparations for a march south. Occupation of the free zone was to occur automatically in the event of an Allied military landing in North Africa, and the German forces designated for Operation Attila were already in combat readiness. Two motorized divisions concentrated in the Dijon area were to rush down the Rhone valley to Marseilles. The town of Uzès and the nearby Cadix center lay within their path. Also virtually certain was invasion from the southeast by Italian forces.

Bertrand relayed this information to London. It was necessary to determine immediately what help Cadix could expect in evacuating its personnel— "at least the Poles"—to Britain. London advised that they be sent to North Africa or, should that prove impossible, that they wait to be evacuated by sea at one of three points: Napoul, La Ciotat, or between Sète and Agde. The maximum number of evacuees was twenty. If Bertrand waited to the last moment, he and his wife Mary would be airlifted out, preferably after the sea evacuation had been executed. Also given was the code phrase that would warn that the moment, that is, the Allied landing, was close: "The harvest is good."

The message did not reveal where or when exactly the landing was to take place. Hence, reliable radio liaison would now be crucial; its loss could mean surprise.[29]

Much has been written about the uncovering by the Germans of clandestine radio transmitters in the occupied part of France. As far as the free zone is concerned, it was only after the war that Bertrand managed to obtain 142 enciphered telegrams of the German Funkabwehr, the military intelligence section concerned with seeking out and eliminating clandestine enemy transmitters. These documents are part of the secret correspondence between the main Funkabwehr center in the Free Zone, located at Lyon-Charbon-nières, and its four field branches (Abschnitte A, B, C, and D) at Pau (B), Montpellier (C), and Marseilles (D).[30]

Each of these branches had several mobile direction finding teams (Peiltrupps) and detachments of security troops (Sicherungstrupps)[31] that tracked down detected transmitters together with Vichy police. According to German documents captured during the war or found afterwards, the procedures for locating and eliminating clandestine transmitters were as follows:

• The first data on a clandestine transmitter was established by the monitoring system of the Wehrmacht High Command (its main French surveillance post was in Lyons), by police radio monitoring or by the Abwehr. The initial data was passed on to the long-distance direction finding system (Fernpeiler) with posts in Brest, Konstanz, and Oldenburg, and after calculations had been made, the zone (Raum) in which the transmitter was operating was determined.

• The zone was indicated to the appropriate sector (Abschnitt), which checked this result and attempted to find the zone of transmission corresponding to the direct wave (Nahfeld); having gotten this result, it sought to narrow the search zone and to "confirm the pot" (Topf bestätigt).

• Now, mobile close direction finding groups (Nahfunkpeilung-trupps—NFP) entered the small zone and attempted to locate the transmitter as accurately as possible. When the dragnet had tightened (Nächstfeld erreicht) and the distance to the transmitter had decreased, often to within two hundred meters, the transmitter was considered "ripe for taking out" (aushebereif).

• Guided by sound volume (nach Lautstärke fahrend), the mobile units drove up as close as possible to the transmission site, then groups equipped with portable direction finders (Kofferpeiler) jumped out. The direction finders located an operating transmitter to within several meters, for example, down to a specific building or apartment.[32]

The preparations to leave Uzès, Bertrand emphasizes, and the coming Allied landings were kept secret from the French personnel at Cadix. The latter were all dedicated patriots, but, as opposed to the thoroughly isolated Poles and Spaniards, they were in contact with their families and with the local population. Hence there was risk of the information getting out.

On 25 September 1942, Bertrand learned at the prefecture in Nîmes about the arrival to the southern zone of a special German radio counterintelligence (Funkabwehr) unit. This team, stationed at the Château Bionne not far from Montpellier, had obtained from the prefect a dozen French auto license plates, five of which, numbered 1244 FN 5 through 1248 FN 5, were already in use.

Bertrand immediately went to Montpellier to do some scouting. He found twelve vehicles parked on the roadside within the chateau grounds and made mental note of their makes and appearances: three were dark-blue Chevrolet pickups, three were cars of assorted makes, and six were Citroën 11 CV autos, all black except for one that was purple. The purple Citroën became celebrated in the area, because it could not pass unnoticed if it had wanted to. The prefecture had indicated that the car of the Funkabwehr unit's chief was that color. The great hunt for Cadix was on.

The Funkabwehr was just beginning to feel its way around. Cadix's well thought out system of transmission made a precise fix difficult. A couple of weeks later, in mid-October, Bertrand learned at the prefecture that a mobile team from Montpellier was staying at the town of Pont-Saint-Esprit, at the Hotel de l'Europe. Bertrand drove up there and, in the hotel dining room, sitting next to the Germans, watched them talk about the weather.

On his return, Bertrand apprised the Cadix personnel of the recent German moves, gave them the automobile registration numbers, and instructed them to report at once if the vehicles appeared in the vicinity. No hasty steps were taken, however, even when one of the Funkabwehr cars, a dark blue Chevrolet pickup, was seen parked, its doors open, on the road from Uzès to Alès.

Every so often, at all hours of the day and night—more than ten times between October 10 and the beginning of November—electric power was cut off to facilitate a precise fix on the Cadix transmitter. Henceforth all messages were sent "into the air"—after emitting a signal, Cadix did not wait for acknowledgment; it would come later, on a different wavelength.

From 31 October to 4 November 1942, Bertrand, Langer, and Palluth were away at the Côte d'Azur to meet with the head of Reseau F-2, "Mak"—the Polish Lieutenant Colonel Romeyko—and discuss the possibilities should Cadix have to be evacuated. While the Polish and French chiefs were away, Cadix picked up a top-secret signal. No one could read it, since it had been transmitted in Bertrand's personal code. Only upon his return to Uzès next day with the two Poles was the signal read. It contained the phrase, "The harvest is good," meaning that the Allied landings could begin at any moment. At the same time, London asked whether the information on the two German divisions at Dijon was confirmed, and how much time the occupation of southern France would take. Bertrand answered that he would go immediately to Paris to ask Max, but was advised, "the harvest is very good and there is no time for traveling." London added that it thought at least a week would pass between the Allied landings and the southward march by the Germans. Bertrand comments, "this [was] completely inaccurate."[33]

On November 6, as Bertrand recalls, just as day was breaking and he was in his bath, he heard Langer's heavy, rapid steps in the corridor. The Pole was not in the habit of running. He knocked, panting like a marathon runner. "Patron," Bertrand recalls him saying, "the Montpellists are here. As soon as I saw them in the distance, I turned off the radio, but they're coming!"

Indeed, on the horizon—about eight hundred meters away—a dark blue Chevrolet pickup truck, atop it a circular antenna glistening in the light of the rising sun, was advancing toward Cadix, preceded by a black Citroën.

Alert measures were immediately executed. Equipment was cached away, all the doors and windows were closed up, everyone went inside and waited quietly. If necessary, Bertrand would come out alone to the besiegers. "And we waited, watching the horizon from behind the lathes of the shutters [writes Bertrand] more dead than alive."

Arriving at the gate to the chateau, the vehicles stopped. Three men dressed in blue and carrying rubber truncheons in their hands got out of the black Citroën and went over to one of the two neighboring farms, then to the other one, not without—after some discussion—truncheoning the residents, and completely neglected the chateau.

Then they all left, only to return again at 1 p.m., very close to Cadix, then at 10 p.m., and at five in the morning, but they did not show up at Cadix.

How to explain the behavior of the French policemen? Bertrand surmises that either they had received instructions from the prefecture not to act but merely to go through the motions for the benefit of the Germans, and so had been obliged to stage a spectacle; or, after transmission had been broken off, they had lost the bearings and, for want of evidence, had not dared to enter the chateau, with its evil reputation—it was said to be inhabited by dangerous P.D.s or Communists.

After this incident, Bertrand phoned and asked the deputy chief of French intelligence, Delor, to come to Cadix. He arrived at 11 p.m. and, following Bertrand's suggestion, ordered that Cadix be evacuated and the personnel proceed toward the coast between Nice and Cannes for possible embarkation.

Next morning, on 8 November 1942, Cadix learned from the BBC that the Allies had landed in North Africa.

On the morning of November 9, Cadix was evacuated completely. All the equipment had previously been concealed, and now only the transmitter remained to be put away in its hiding place. Team Z[34] set out for the Côte d'Azur, an area that was regarded as the least dangerous.

Bertrand loaded up his car with the most secret files that had not been burned and managed, with his wife, to get through the "German tide" and conceal them in a safe place.

On the morning of November 12, the Germans occupied Cadix.[35]

Cadix—Field Office 300—had operated in southern France for over two years, from October 1940 through the first days of November 1942, supplying Allied staffs with a broad spectrum of valuable intelligence. The decrypted Wehrmacht, S.S., and Gestapo correspondence had originated not only from French territory but from nearly all the countries of Europe, and had made possible the determination of many aspects and details of Germany's military and repressive machinery.

Over their two years at Cadix, the Polish cryptologists had read a total of 4,679 German signals. Most numerous were dispatches of police and S.S. formations (3,097), followed by Wehrmacht staffs (673), Nazi agents (518), and the German Armistice Commission (391). Since nearly all the signals comprised two parts transmitted in separate radio signals, the number of intercepts read should be multiplied by two. Thus the efforts of the Cadix cryptological team had netted over nine thousand secret dispatches of the German armed forces, police, and other agencies of the Third Reich.

As far as the end effects of Cadix intelligence are concerned—its use by Allied commanders—it is hard to assess these due to the inaccessibility of French and British archives. It may, however, be supposed that the decrypts, in combination with other intelligence, helped Allied staffs reconstruct the numbers and dispositions of German troops and their higher commands, as well as of police and S.S. units in France and in many other areas of Europe. Also particularly valuable to Allied commands were, for instance, German Air Force dispatches decrypted in the spring of 1941 during the campaigns in Yugoslavia and Greece. There was, as well, a great deal of information on Nazi atrocities and war crimes, including exterminations of the populace in occupied territories. For example, police and S.S. correspondence showed that on just one day, 27 August 1941, 5,130 Jews were shot to death in occupied Soviet territory: 4,200 by Polizeibataillon 320; 914 by a Regiment Süd; 16 by an S.S. brigade. It may be supposed that information from occupied areas, reported along with other military data to British and Polish higher staffs, was furnished to the political leaders of the Grand Alliance, as well as to leaders of resistance movements in various countries, and was used both in propaganda and in military and political decision making. Of course, it had to be disguised so that, in analyzing Allied radio dispatches, war news, and commentaries, the Germans would not stumble upon evidence that their ciphers were being read.

Many radio intercepts were correspondence of German agents in southern France who had been planted there before the war or during or after the French campaign. A circumstance favoring the Abwehr and S.D. was a mass influx into the south of people from the northern and central regions of the country.[36]

The Cadix monitoring stations intercepted about three thousand encrypted spy reports and instructions to spies transmitted from Germany. Five hundred eighteen of these messages were decrypted completely, permitting counterintelligence to determine their places of transmission and to apprehend many agents. Also exposed were the actual roles of five Abwehr field offices organized under cover of the Armistice Commission, at Toulon (surveillance of naval movements and collection of information on the French admiralty), at Marseilles (gathering of information on the merchant marine and on the activities of Allied and other intelligence organizations in southern France), at Casablanca (transmission to Berlin, via Madrid, of daily reports on ship and aircraft traffic at this port city), at Saint-Jean-de-Luz (daily reports to the Abwehr center in Paris), and at Nantes (daily reports to the Abwehr center in Paris, and meteorological reports for the Luftwaffe).

In early 1942, 150 messages obtained from an agent's radio correspondence with the Abwehr were read. They were drafted in French, were signed "G." or "S.," and dealt exclusively with Russian affairs. Their contents were communicated to the Soviet military representative at Vichy by the S.R., and attempts at radio liaison with Moscow were made at a certain moment from Cadix for more rapid communication.

Analysis of radio intercepts led to the discovery of an espionage "E" Net operating in the Gibraltar area and at various points on the Spanish coast. The net was run by an Abwehr representative in Madrid, Col. Hans Roschmann, and the military attaché, Gen. Walter Bruns. Cadix delegated the interception of this net's reports to a radio monitoring post in Morocco (the Rabat Group) located nearer to the Iberian peninsula.[37]

After the Allied landings in North Africa on 8 November 1942, Hitler extorted from Pétain an order to French armed forces to oppose the invasion. Pétain also radioed a countermessage in a secret naval code to Adm. François Darlan, commander of all Vichy air, sea, and land forces, who happened to be in Algiers. Confusion mounted by the hour. Finally, on November 11 the Wehrmacht divisions concentrated above the demarcation line in northern France began their march south, occupying the hitherto unoccupied free zone. Sporadic resistance by French garrisons was instantly broken. The Germans now ruled all of France.

At news of the breaking of the armistice and the southward march by German forces, General Weygand drove out of Nice, heading toward Gueret. On the way, near Saint-Pourçain, his car was unexpectedly sandwiched by two trucks carrying armed S.S. men. The driver was ordered to stop, and an S.S. officer presented a personal order from Hitler, and arrested the seventy-five-year-old general. He was taken off in a unknown direction. Later, it was learned that Weygand had been interned in Germany, where he remained for the duration of the war. Thus he came to share the fate of General Gamelin, five years his junior, who had earlier been imprisoned by the Vichy authorities.

At the end of 1942, military operations, the clandestine war, and political intrigues created one great tangle. Operation Torch, the Allied landings in North Africa, was beginning, and the popular French general, Henri Giraud, on whom the Allies pinned great hopes, was in Gibraltar. Seven months earlier, he had managed to escape from German captivity to France, where he had been looked after by the intelligence net "Alliance." In early November, a British submarine had taken him to Gibraltar.

The Anglophones saw General Giraud as a future commander for the French armed forces in place of de Gaulle, whose strong personality created many problems for them. Nevertheless, Giraud—popular after his breakneck escape from the fortress of Königstein, perched atop a rocky precipice—was setting conditions. In return for making a radio address to French-African troops loyal to Pétain, calling upon them to switch over to the Allies, he demanded to be given command of all Allied invasion forces. The Americans declined, and treated the general rather shabbily. An "address by General Giraud" was put on the air from a captured broadcasting station in Algiers; without his knowledge or approval it was read by a stage actor in the resistance who did an excellent imitation of the general.

At the time of the Allied landings, Admiral Darlan happened to be in Algiers visiting his son, who was desperately ill with poliomyelitis. He was recognized by young French resisters, who placed him under arrest. The Allies were still fairly far away, however, and Darlan succeeded in convincing the teen-age insurgents that he likewise hated the Nazis. Released, he regained his self-assurance and presented himself to the commander of the Allied troops that were entering the city. He soon met with General Eisenhower and signed an armistice with the Allies on November 10 at 10 a.m. Shortly thereafter, he received a message from Pétain ordering him to resist the Allied invasion, and later the countermessage, "Act for the best. You have all my confidence." The confusion in Darlan's mind as to the marshal's true intentions led to a tragic series of orders, counterorders, armistices, and breaking of agreements. Before it was over, fifteen thousand French troops and as many British and Americans had died in North Africa.

The Americans' contacts with Darlan called forth sharp protests in Britain and in French resistance circles. It was feared that, with the help of Vichy politicians, the Americans would entrench themselves in North Africa (including Tunisia) to the detriment of British interests. The intra-Allied dissension was broken off by Darlan's assassination on 24 December 1942; he died at the hand of a twenty-year-old rightist Algerian resister, Fernand Bonnier de la Chapelle. Whether this was a spontaneous act or whether hidden political forces stood behind it is an unsolved riddle of World War II. As de Gaulle later wrote, Bonnier's

> hasty and abbreviated trial before a military tribunal convened at night and in private session, the immediate and secret execution of Fernand Bonnier de la Chapelle...all these led to the suspicion that someone wanted to conceal at any price the origin of his decision [to kill Darlan].[38]

In any case the disputes ended, and the Allies continued their great African operation. General de Gaulle eventually won out in the contest for leadership of the French forces, although his rival Giraud remained in command until 1944.

As has been mentioned, on 11 November 1942, three days after the Allied landings in North Africa, the Germans abruptly invaded the free zone, thereby putting an end to the collaborationist, but semiautonomous, Vichy regime. In unleashing Plan Attila for the occupation of all France, which had been drawn up back in 1940, Hitler initially attempted to save face. He still needed Pétain as a stabilizing factor to limit the growth of the resistance. On November 11 with German divisions on their way south, he tried in a message to Pétain to justify the step.

> Observation of American military transports as well as other formations [stated Hitler] points to an impending invasion of Corsica and southern France... I would like to assure you, however, that the present action by German forces is not directed against the French Army. I hope that the moment will yet come when, shoulder to shoulder, we shall defend Europe from the coalition of Anglo-Saxon pirates.

Upon entering the free zone, the German forces at first acted with restraint. Then suddenly, on 27 November 1942, shock troops descended upon the barracks of the French armistice army. Scattered attempts at resistance were instantly broken. The German occupation, no longer even disguised with a semblance of French autonomy, now took in southern France as well.

Next, the Germans did away with the French General Staff, converting it into a Board of Liquidation. Its Section I (Operations) was to see to demobilization; Section III (Military Schools), to liquidation of military schools; Section IV (Cartography), to turning cartographic materials over to the Germans. These were humiliating tasks for officers of the army that in 1918 had dictated its terms to a defeated Germany. In vain, however, did the Germans search for the Intelligence Section (Section II); its records and personnel had seemingly vanished into thin air.

From documents captured in the last phase of the war by Allied armies, one may reconstruct what the Germans knew in the years 1940-42 about intelligence operations being conducted against them in France. Reports by S.D. and Abwehr stations in France refer to the growing activity of intelligence organizations and to secret French preparations "to defend the remaining territory," but there is no indication that they ever picked up the trail of Cadix.

After the occupation of southern France, the Abwehr prepared an extensive paper for the Wehrmacht High Command. It contained little verified information but many conjectures and inaccuracies.

> It has not... been definitely determined whether the anti-German intelligence activity was conducted in concert with British, Gaullist or American intelligence. It should nevertheless be noted that certain officers regularly traveled to Portugal in the character of diplomatic couriers.

Mentioned by name was "Capt. Perrier, alias Capt. Paillole," allegedly a courier to Lisbon. Obviously, the man referred to was the Major Paillole who had used the pseudonym Perrier (and not vice versa), head of clandestine counterintelligence (the Rural Works Enterprise). But he had never once been to Portugal, where in fact Bertrand had gone. Ironically, even as the Germans were sending their paper to Berlin, Paillole, on the night of November 28-29, was crossing the Pyrenees. Later he would go to Portugal for the first time in his life.

Prior to their invasion of southern France, the Germans hardly had any conception of the tangled state of affairs in the unoccupied zone. Thus, they failed to distinguish between the general staff's intelligence section, the Second Bureau, which was concerned with studies, and offensive intelligence (the S.R.). They considered all the officers and employees of both intelligence services to be spies and searched feverishly for them.

The great Abwehr and Gestapo roundup of French and Allied intelligence personnel began, however, only on 8 January 1943. It was directed by the ranking S.S. officer in Vichy, Major Geissler, who first arrested several elderly officers in the Army Ministry. On Pétain's protests, the German ambassador to Vichy, Krug von Nidda, requested clarification from Ribbentrop and on the same day received a telegram: "I advise you to maintain a distance from these matters. The operation was ordered personally by the Fuehrer." Ribbentrop's subordinate was no fool and instantly joined the roundup. The next day, he sent in a triumphant report on subsequent arrests—at the Air Force Ministry, an intelligence organization had been uncovered, disguised under the name Secours Familial (Family Assistance); the minister, General d'Harcourt, and two of his officers had been jailed. The German ambassador reported further such successes in subsequent diplomatic dispatches. This was now merely a grim farce.

The German ambassador to Paris, Aschenbach, likewise reported to Berlin on his achievements, including the capture in Lyons of some French Second Bureau files. "These documents," he reported, "were discovered thanks to a Frenchman who betrayed their place of concealment." Only now could the Germans learn how many of their secrets had been penetrated: dispositions, movements, and strengths of German forces in both parts of France, military facilities under construction, data on thousands of Wehrmacht and S.S. officers, and much else. Part of these documents were of the most recent date. The German ambassador also reported the suicide of an arrested French Air Force captain, Billion, who had been one of the heads of intelligence in Lyons.

Although in many cases the Germans were operating in the dark, the losses of French intelligence and of the Resistance, as a result of the mass arrests, were serious. Whoever did not decamp after German forces had entered the unoccupied zone inevitably fell into the hands of the Gestapo. Nearly all the officers of the French underground intelligence Arab department were arrested after that department had moved by mistake into a chateau that had earlier been vacated by another intelligence unit and was under constant S.D. surveillance.

Fortunately, Cadix had been kept secret better than other intelligence units in southern France. Not even ranking intelligence officers had known about it, including the chief of the ciphers department of the postarmistice army.

The great roundup conducted by the Gestapo, S.D., and Abwehr on the territory of all of France lasted until April 1943. Lists of wanted persons still at large were turned over to local Gestapo offices. Arrests of individual intelligence officers continued, but many of those in danger managed to cross the Pyrenees or to reach partisan units in the Massif Central. Some, including Bertrand, remained and continued to act in France.

NOTES

1. Polish airmen formed the largest foreign contingent to fly with the RAF in the Battle of Britain. For most of the Poles, it was the third campaign within a year. In Poland they had shot down 129 German airplanes, themselves losing thirty-four pilots, and in France they had shot down 51 German aircraft and lost eleven pilots. In the Battle of Britain, the Poles were responsible for 203 confirmed enemy aircraft shot down, 12 percent of all German losses from air and ground defenses; the 139 Poles themselves lost thirty-five pilots (another thirty-six died in later years of the war, thus bringing total losses among Polish Battle of Britain veterans to over 50 percent).

From 1940 through 8 May 1945, the Polish Air Force in the west destroyed a total of 745 German planes (confirmed), plus 178 (probable), and damaged 243. When London was attacked for the second time during the war, this time by flying bombs, Poles accounted for 187 (10 percent of the nineteen hundred V-1s that were destroyed by fighters. Up through 8 May 1945, bombers of the Polish Air Force flew nearly twelve thousand sorties against enemy industrial facilities, ports, and U-boats, dropping eighteen thousand tons of bombs, mines, and depth charges. Polish bomber targets after D-Day included Caen and Falaise.

For a survey of the Polish Air Force's role in World War II, and of Poland's flying traditions generally, which are as long and illustrious as those of any other country, see Jordan, *Aviation in Poland: A Brief Historical Outline.*—ED.

2. Colonel Langer's first name was actually Karol (Charles), though he generally went by his middle name, Gwido; hence the alias "Charles Lange."

3. Bertrand, *Enigma*, 120.

4. No more information is available on Team D, regarding either the Bruno or Cadix periods, nor is anything known about these officers' subsequent fates. Only the name of the team's chief is known: Camazone.

5. Radio "Cadix" also played another important role: it acted as intermediary in communications between the Polish Rygor (Rigor) intelligence outpost in Algiers and the Polish intelligence center in London. Rygor's assignment was to collect military and political information in Algeria and Morocco preparatory to the planned Allied landings in North Africa. (On Rygor *see* Woytak, Review of *W tajnej służbie. Also see* Rygor-Słowikowski, *W tajnej służbie.*—ED.)

6. They were probably intended for a Polish intelligence station at Paris (in a war-intelligence net) that, with the cognizance of the French General Staff, was being organized in the final weeks before the war. The station had not been set up by 1 September 1939.

7. Though reduced to a rump "État Français," France in 1940-42 still had an extensive radio net that girdled the entire globe. The overseas communication headquarters (cryptonym FUB) was housed in the Ministry of Marine; in the Far East there were French communication stations at Shanghai (FUZ), Saigon (FUS), and on the flagship of the French Navy in the Pacific (FNEO); a relay station for long-distance communication was located at Beirut.

8. Romon, in the latter years of the war a leading resistance worker, a lieutenant colonel and signals chief of the French partisan army (the A.S., later the F.F.I.), was arrested by the Nazis in June 1943. Imprisoned at first in Vichy and later transported to the Reich, he was murdered on 20

August 1944 in a collective execution at Schwaebisch prison. Shot along with him were twenty-three fellow prisoners, mostly his former subordinates.

9. Two of the receivers also worked in Cadix's foreign net and served for communication with London and North Africa. See Bertrand, *Enigma*, 116.

10. Ibid., 117.

11. Radio traffic was monitored on seventeen lines, including Wiesbaden-Paris-Marseilles, Wiesbaden-Toulon, Paris-Nantes, Tangier-Casablanca, Casablanca-Madrid. Ibid., 119.

12. Tapping of long-distance underground cables (Lignes Souterraines à Grande Distance) in northern France for German ciphers involved great technical difficulties. Details of the operation are given in *Un des Mystères de la dernière Guerre: La Source K,* édité par le Comité Robert Keller, cited by Bertrand, *Enigma*, 129.

13. Compare the wartime diaries of Gen. Franz Halder, chief of the German Army General Staff from the resignation of Gen. Ludwig Beck, in late August 1938, until 24 September 1942, when Hitler fired Halder.

14. "Einsatz von Abwehrtrupps im Fall 'Attila,' 21.1.1947." Series T-311, roll 251. Each operational group comprised 11 Abwehr personnel, supplied with transportation (two automobiles, one motorcycle, one truck).

15. The reports that F-2 sent to Polish intelligence headquarters in London (in 1944, the monthly reports reached a volume of two thousand typed pages) included information on German troop movements, locations of arms depots, naval redeployments, and the first information on the V-1 "buzz bombs" and V-2 rockets. Coordinates provided by F-2 enabled the British and U.S. air forces to bomb the indicated targets. F-2 agents were everywhere: in war-production directorates, in plants that worked for the Germans, in offices, ports, railroad stations. On 18 May 1944, the Allied supreme command praised F-2 for supplying "information of amazing quality" and stated that "your sources are beginning to surpass the superb French sources."

The F-2 net survived to the liberation of France, and attained its greatest development in the period of the Allied landings and the fighting in Normandy. The list of members of the F-2 net included 2,561 French and Polish names. All were recognized by the Free French authorities as resisters. The organization's losses included 85 killed, 151 deported, and 60 interned. Bieganski, *W konspiracji i walce: z kart polskiego ruchu oporu we Francji, 1940-1944*, 120-22.

16. Nord, *Mes Camarades sont mortes*, passim.

17. Paillole, *Services Speciaux 1935-1945*, 214.

18.   The Enigmas used in Italy, Spain and Switzerland were machines of the commercial type, i.e. they had no "plugboard" [commutator], and moreover all the signals on a given day were enciphered from the same starting position, which tremendously facilitated the reading of messages.
Rejewski, "Uwagi do 'Appendix 1,' " 491.

19. A civilian worker, who was sent to dry up in Algeria; afterwards he did not return to Cadix, but was sent to a different unit.

20. Suszczewski, *Wspomnienia z lat II Wojny Światowej.*

21. Lisicki writes, in response to a question from the editor-translator: "The outpost in Algiers did *NOT* specialize in Soviet ciphers. Undoubtedly it was only a coincidence that the three men [all] knew the Russian language; an Enigma double [and files] went down with them." (Graliński and Smoleński had been members of the Cipher Bureau's Russian section, and Różycki, of the German section—B.S.-4—had also known Russian.) Lisicki, Letter of 19 September 1982.—ED.

22. Masterman, John C., *The Double-Cross System in the War of 1939 to 1945*, 140-142.

23. Rygor-Słowikowski, *W tajnej służbie*, 96, 129.

24. Losses sustained by French civilians due to Allied military action, including air raids, in 1940-44 are difficult to estimate. Some sources give at least sixty thousand dead and seventy-five thousand wounded. *See* Dank, *The French against the French: Collaboration and Resistance*, 170.

25. Bertrand, *Enigma*, 127-28.

26. Figures on the number of L.C.D.'s produced before the war show large discrepancies. Sadowski speaks of 125 machines, of which the vast majority were destroyed during the evacuation to Rumania and several were brought to France. Sadowski, *Oddział II Szabu Głownego*. Other sources speak of 40 L.C.D.'s having been produced.

27. Różycki was, by then, at P.C. Couba in Algiers, for which he had sailed from Marseilles on 24 June 1941.

28. Kozaczuk, *Bitwa o tajemnice*, 142.

29. Bertrand, *Enigma*, 134-35.

30. The location of Abschnitt A has not been established.

31. These were troops from Uberw. Komp. 616. Bertrand, *Enigma*, 130.

32. Ibid., 130-31.

33. Ibid., 137.

34. Team D had embarked for North Africa at the time of the earlier alert.

35. Bertrand, *Enigma*, 137-41.

36. For example, the population of Vichy, the capital of Pétainist France, increased in the summer and fall of 1940 from the prewar number of twenty-five thousand to about eighty thousand.

37. Bertrand, *Enigma*, 117-20.

38. Dank, *The French against the French*, 137.

12.

Spanish Interlude

The underground Cadix center had disappeared from the Uzès area just in time, two days before the entry of German forces into the free zone, and three days before their occupation of the Château des Fouzes. The Poles, split up by twos and threes, found themselves in the apartments of trusted resistance workers and next took trains and buses to larger cities, where it would be easier to shake off any pursuers. There began dangerous and tense days of homeless wandering.

Active in southern France since as early as the fall of 1940 were secret centers and networks that evacuated people from France to the British Isles. One of them, located at Marseilles, specialized in transfers by sea. At various places along the coast, small groups of Poles were smuggled aboard fishing boats and taken to Gibraltar or transferred on the high seas to British naval vessels. Evacuated in this way were especially men in various "short" specialties, such as flyers and sailors. Others attempted to cross from France directly into Spain, and from there into Portugal, where it was easier to get aboard Allied naval or merchant ships. Poles who were unlucky enough to get arrested after crossing the Franco-Spanish border and who knew a little English often identified themselves as Canadians, hence as subjects of the British Crown, which prevented their immediate deportation back to France.

The ingenuity of the organizers of escapes from Hitler's Fortress Europe knew no limits. Apart from the evacuation networks of the Resistance and of the intelligence services of countries that were at war with Germany, there were also private firms that operated on a fee-for-service basis. One of these, run by a young man from Marseilles, a waiter by profession who used the pseudonym Coco-La-Boule, took a novel approach: two Spanish gendarmes working for the firm picked up four men on the Franco-Spanish border, snapped handcuffs on them, and took the "prisoners" by train to the Portuguese border, where the Portuguese authorities admitted them as political refugees. This was a fairly safe but expensive way to go, costing about 10,000 francs per person. (Still, the Allies on occasion did not hesitate to pay ten times as much to get back people whom they considered especially important for their war effort.)

On passenger ships bound for North Africa, Lisbon, or ports in the Western Hemisphere, people were stowed away in scuttles, bins, under coal. Such evacuation organizations, with their people among the longshoremen and sailors, operated principally at Marseilles, Nice, Sète, Port Vendres, and Port St. Louis, and also at St. Jean, Cap Ferrat, Hujers, Cassis, La Ciotat, and Adge.[1]

Most extensive were the networks of escape (réseaux d'évasion) by land, across the Franco-Spanish border in the Pyrenees. Usually chosen for the crossings were unpopulated, wild mountain areas that could be reached from towns near the border: Perpignan, Terdets, Osseja, or Andorra. Sometimes a guide, after receiving money from fugitives, turned them in to the Germans for a large reward. The Gestapo set up hotel traps in various localities. The Resistance issued strict warnings. Names and addresses of collaborators and swindlers who preyed upon refugees were registered, and death sentences were executed on a few of them. Some answered for their deeds after the war.

These traps and hazards had to be reckoned with by the Poles, who had left Uzès on the night of November 7-8 for Nîmes, and the next day for Antibes.

Bertrand had sent Rejewski and Zygalski on November 11 into the Italian occupation zone to Nice, where the danger of arrest seemed smaller. But they had to flee the *pension* Petit Paris, after the Italian security police, the OVRA, began taking an interest in these "Frenchmen" who spoke a strange dialect. For many weeks, the Poles played a game of cat and mouse with the OVRA and Gestapo agents who were now ubiquitous throughout southern France.

Various means of camouflage were used. Antoni Palluth and his nephew Sylwester, natives of Poznań but endowed with a Hungarian-sounding surname and dark complexions, could pass as Magyars allied with Germany. But Tadeusz Suszczewski, nearly two meters—well over six feet—tall, stood out prominently among the generally short southerners. Pierre Ranaud (Marian Rejewski) had no such problem, with his cosmopolitan European intellectual's face; he could pass as French, Swiss, or German, for he spoke both French and flawless Hochdeutsch. Colonel Langer and Major Ciężki were also fluent in German. The other Poles of Team Z likewise tried to select the best biographies for themselves, in accordance with their appearance, knowledge of languages, and education. In critical moments, when dealing with Italian police or Gestapo, it could mean the difference between life and death.

After their flight from the Italian occupation zone, Rejewski and Zygalski found themselves in Cannes, at a small, seedy hotel whose owner was in the confidence of the Resistance. When things began to get hot there, they left for Antibes. There they got in touch with another Pole, who was known to his neighbors as a sculptor, but who, in fact, headed an Allied sabotage and intelligence station—the hollowed-out busts and plaster casts in his studio stored explosives. But the sculptor had many matters on his mind and could not tender much help to his compatriots who wanted to cross the Pyrenees.

They returned once more to Nice. Bertrand's people had rented a small house on the city's outskirts in which they had organized a stopping point. Some time later, with the help of a local resistance net, an escape route was set up, but once again obstacles appeared. The cryptologists had to go back to the German occupation zone once more, this time to Marseilles. Their refuge was a dismal corner of an attic on the periphery of the city of a million inhabitants.

After Marseilles, Rejewski and Zygalski spent four days at Toulouse, in a suburban coal dump. They departed on 21 January 1943 for Narbonne, after which they went to Perpignan, a small city located on the Gulf of the Lion, in the Pyrenées Orientales department. On January 27 at 6 p.m., there was a train ride to Aix-les-Thermes, several dozen kilometers to the west and still closer to the Spanish border. The French had seen to good cover, as Rejewski's account testifies:

> When the train stopped at the Aix-les-Thermes station and we were alighting, two young women threw their arms around our necks and kissed us as if we were good friends, in order to make the watching German guards feel sure that we had no intention of crossing the Franco-Spanish border. This was, after all, a border area. The trick worked like a charm, and the two women—they were waitresses—took us to a hotel where we stayed for several days. At Aix-les-Thermes a smuggler got in touch with us, and we set a date and hour for departure to Tour de Carol. He promised that he would board the train together with us. Maybe he did, but in any case he did not enter our compartment. He found us only at dusk, amid the underbrush where we had hidden in accordance with his instructions. He said he had missed the train. More likely, he hadn't wanted to travel in the same compartment with us for fear of the unpleasant consequences if we fell into the hands of the Germans. He took us to a tavern where we had supper, grabbed a few hours' sleep, and began our assault on the Pyrenees.

On the night of 29 January 1943, Rejewski and Zygalski set out with the smuggler for the border. They succeeded in evading the German and Vichy patrols, but faced long, tense hours of march over uninhabited mountain terrain. On the way, they destroyed all their documents and evidence of their stay in France, so that in the event of being stopped by the Spanish they would not be deported and turned over to the Vichy authorities.

It was past midnight when the guide declared in broken French that it was not far to the border. Then he began muttering angrily and, afterwards, cursed and alleged that he had not been paid a franc for the dangerous work. Finally, he made an outright demand for money, and when this produced no effect, he took out a pistol and began fiddling with the trigger. It might have been a couple of kilometers to Spain, but in the night and the unfamiliar terrain the Poles could not tell. Overpowering the hoodlum guide would not have improved their position, so they had to cough up the rest of their money.

At last they reached the longed-for border and, somewhat farther on, down in a valley, the first Spanish settlement, Puigcerda. The quiet Spanish cities and towns—Puigcerda, Séo de Urgel, Ripoli, Figueras—never saw so many Poles as in the years 1940-43.

All fugitives crossing the Pyrenees were advised to try right away to get deep into Spain, preferably to Barcelona or Madrid, where Polish evacuation and intelligence stations were operating under cover of the Polish Red Cross. Nevertheless, most of the refugees were stopped in the border area, whence they landed in prisons and camps. The Spanish side of the Pyrenees—apart from border guard and municipal police—swarmed with agents of Franco's security police (Policia de Seguridad) and patrols of the Guardia Civil. The most dangerous thing for detainees was to be sent back to France, which meant confinement at the concentration camp, Camp Le Vernet.

Rejewski and Zygalski, like most of those fleeing France, were arrested before they had gotten beyond the border area. There was little surprise at the constabulary in Puigcerda when on 30 January 1943, at about 5 a.m., a patrol brought in two foreigners without any papers on them. There were already several Frenchmen in detention who had crossed the Pyrenees illegally and were none too keen on returning to their occupied homeland. The Guardia Civil noncom was only waiting for a round number in order to send the captives to the police station at Belever, about thirty kilometers—eighteen miles—from Puigcerda where they would be investigated. That same day, late in the evening, the two Poles were transported to the district prison at Séo de Urgel, where they were kept until 24 March 1943. Then they were sent to the prison at Lerida, about 130 kilometers (eighty miles) west of Barcelona.

The path of other Polish fugitives from Cadix who were stopped by Spanish police led through Modelo (Model) Prison in Barcelona and other places of confinement.

Modelo, recalls Tadeusz Suszczewski, who was jailed there, resembled a regular six-armed starfish with truncated rays. The rays converged in a central tower that contained the only exit and entrance to the entire complex, which had been planned for a thousand inmates, and where upwards of five thousand were being kept. The food rations were barely subsistence: a cup of grain coffee and a piece of bread for breakfast, bean soup for lunch and supper. Each concrete cell, with a floor area of ten square meters (twelve square yards), held six to eight prisoners. Interrogations usually began about two o'clock at night and lasted until morning. The most stringent prison regimen was reserved for Spaniards—ex-soldiers of the Republican Army, mostly young, some of them fifteen years old.

In April 1943, the Poles and other foreigners were moved from Modelo to a special camp improvised in buildings left over from the Las Misiones International Exposition which the Franco regime had organized at Barcelona in 1939 after strangling the Republic. Several hundred manacled foreign prisoners were paraded down the streets of the city, escorted by armed guards and a crowd of gaping onlookers.

All the prisoners were lodged in a single cavernous exposition hall. The multilingual hullabaloo beggared description. On Sundays, they were all conducted to church, where, entertainingly at odds with the solemnity of the place, was the sight of Moslems, Jews, and other non-Christians squatting during the elevation of the host instead of kneeling as prescribed by Catholic ritual. Thus human tragedies and adversities mingled with unintended farce.

When the Polish Red Cross office in Barcelona obtained permission to supply supplementary food rations to imprisoned Poles, someone struck upon the idea of using the list of recipients to smuggle in secret messages. The Spaniards checked only the number of persons on the list and the number of packages, and paid no attention to the "impossible" Polish names. Thus a list of recipients might look something as follows:

1. Zygmunt Przybylski	
2. Komisja Przyjeżdża	[Commission Arrives]
3. Jutro Zestolicy	[Tomorrowfrom Thecapital]
4. Będzie Uwas	[Itwill Visityou]
5. Przygotujcie Uwagi	[Prepare Remarks]
6. Owarunkach Wobozie	[Onconditions Incamp]
7. Ispis Chorych	[And Sicklist]
8. Trzymaj Ciesię	[Good Luck]
9. Mikołaj Cieślak	
10. Marian Woźniak	

and so on, real names.

This stratagem was used for many months, up to the liquidation of the camp.[2]

The Polish Red Cross office in Barcelona looked after not only the large concentrations of prisoners at Modelo and Las Misiones, but also after inmates at Séo de Urgel, Lerida, Caldos, Gerona, and Figueras. Other places where Poles were imprisoned were Jarama, Tarragona, Pamplona, Irun, and above all the gigantic camp at Miranda de Ebro.

The camp at Miranda had come into being during the Spanish Civil War, when it had served as barracks for foreign units, mostly German and Italian, fighting on the side of General Franco. It had been built for about twelve hundred men, but in the years 1942-43 three to four thousand at a time were interned there. The quadrangular camp was enclosed by a high wall and barbed-wire entanglements three meters—3.3 yards—high. Every hundred meters there stood a sentry box, and over the gates and at the corners of the wall were machine gun emplacements. The camp was floodlit from dusk to dawn. Patrols circled around the wall twenty-four hours a day.

"At night," a Polish former inmate has written about Miranda,[3] "the guards continually shout, 'Alerta! Alerta!' The cry runs down the length of the camp, and this way the commandant is sure that the guards aren't asleep and nobody will escape."

The internees were segregated by nationality and divided into twelve companies. Company 1 comprised mixed officers; 2, Polish officers; 3, "Canadian" officers. Company 7 consisted of Polish soldiers. In privileged circumstances was Company 10, grouping genuine Britons. Concentrated in

Company 11 were persons of assorted nationalities and unclear backgrounds, and in the last, number 12, were the stateless. There were primarily German and Jewish refugees from Germany, as well as Hungarians, Rumanians, and former soldiers of the Spanish Republican Army. The largest group in the camp were the Poles, grouped in Companies 2, 6 (mixed), and 7. On the average, during various periods of the war, there were thirteen to fourteen hundred of them. Some of the Poles were also lodged in Canadian soldiers' companies 4 and 5.

During morning roll call, the camp command sought to obtain something like a demonstration of support by forcing the internees to raise cries in honor of Caudillo Franco, and the like. After receiving the strength reports from his noncoms, the commandant lifted his hand and cried, "España!" (Spain!) and the internees were expected to shout back, "Granda!" (It's great!) The Poles obliged with some relish, inasmuch as in Polish "granda" means "scandal," "racket" or "swindle." But other cries—"Una!" "Libra!"— were supplanted by a murmur of unprintable words in several languages, along with the Spanish "mierda," "puta," and the like. Some of the prisoners, in response to the commandant's salute, lifted their right hands in an Allied V-for-victory sign.

The Spanish camps, of course, cannot be compared with the Nazi concentration camps, but brutal beatings occurred here too, and harassments were the order of the day.

In late 1941 a group of officers, under pretext of choir practice, regularly went to the camp chapel. Over a period of a couple of weeks, they succeeded in digging a tunnel from the chapel to outside the wall. During an escape attempt, one of the Polish officers was shot and killed.

The ingenuity of the Polish soldiers in their efforts to escape and rejoin their fighting units was inexhaustible. In early 1943, even as the group of Poles from Cadix were preparing to cross the Pyrenees, several officers imprisoned at Miranda suddenly felt a calling and expressed the desire to enter a monastery. After protracted negotiations with the authorities and an appeal to the Papal Nuncio in Madrid, they were granted permission to take monastic vows at a Spanish monastery. The monks *manqués* made their way to Portugal, and thence to Polish units in Britain.

When German and Italian forces began suffering reverses in North Africa, Britons and genuine Canadians had a chance for immediate discharge from the camp. Ironically, the sole genuine Canadian—a flyer shot down over southern France—landed in the stateless company. This was due to the Polish interpreter who had been summoned to camp headquarters on the presumption that this Canadian too was another of his compatriots. The conversation went more or less as follows:

INTERPRETER: Z jakiego jesteś pułku? (What's your regiment?)
CANADIAN: I don't understand.
INTERPRETER: Dobra, dobra! Takich "Kanadyjczyków" jak ty mamy tutaj na kopy. (Yes, sure! Listen, we've got "Canadians" like you here by the bushel.)
CANADIAN: I don't understand.

INTERPRETER: No, dosyć tych wygłupów! Mów skąd jesteś i niczego się nie bój. Nasi opiekunowie sami mają już porządnego pietra. Nic ci złego nie zrobią. (Cut the fooling! Tell me what unit you're from, and don't worry about a thing. Our hosts are good and scared themselves now. They won't do you any harm.)

The Canadian kept protesting his incomprehension, until finally the Spanish officer became exasperated.

"No es Canadiense!" ("You're no Canadian!") he shouted. "Todos Canadienses hablan polaco!" ("All Canadians speak Polish!")

The flyer was put in with the stateless prisoners, and it was only a couple of days later that he managed to prove that he really was Canadian. The next day, he was on his way to Madrid.

But the situation of most of the inmates continued to be hard. There was indignation at the fact that, from mid-February to early March 1943, no representative of the Polish authorities in exile had appeared at the camp, even though—after the Allied victories in Africa and at Stalingrad—they could expect a better hearing from the Spanish authorities. The Poles, and the other internees with them, decided to go on a hunger strike. A strike committee was set up, monitors were selected, and food stocks were deposited in sealed bins. The strike began at breakfast. The inmates poured the ersatz coffee down the drains and carried the bread and jam back to the kitchen. The same happened at lunch and supper.

At first the camp authorities rejected all demands. After three days, however, when the first, frailest strikers were carried into the dispensary, panic overwhelmed the Spaniards. The hunger strike at Miranda could bring incalculable consequences, including Allied intervention. The Spanish government, fearing fatalities, was forced to make concessions. A commission came to the camp, comprising—apart from representatives of the Spanish authorities—emissaries of the semiofficial Polish legation, the British Embassy, the Papal Nuncio, and the Red Cross. The negotiations ended in victory for the prisoners: the authorities announced officially that within two months the internees would regain their freedom.

There were casualties, however. Even though a medical commission oversaw the prisoners' recuperation, an interned Frenchman died, and a dozen or so men emaciated by the hunger strike were hospitalized. At the beginning of April 1943, the gradual liquidation of the camp began.[4]

Though Rejewski and Zygalski were not imprisoned at Miranda, they did not fare much better. Prison was as rough in Lerida as it was in Miranda. Moreover, for unknown reasons, they were kept there longer than were most Polish prisoners. It was only on 4 May 1943, upon the reiterated demands of the Polish Red Cross office, which cited the promises that had been tendered to the Allies by the Spanish government, that the two cryptologists emerged from prison. They were permitted to put up temporarily in rented quarters in town, where for another two weeks they waited for transportation to Madrid. Finally, on May 19, they reached the Spanish capital, where the semilegal Polish representatives secured places for them in the Pensión Minguez at Calle Esparteros núm. 6. They had to report every few days to a police station, being foreigners who had entered the land of the Caudillo without passports and visas. But this limited freedom and the meager assistance furnished by the Polish Red Cross seemed to them splendid after months in jail. They could—even if under the watchful eyes of plainclothesmen—freely move about town and talk with compatriots, like them waiting for an opportunity to leave for Polish military units.

Their fate continued to depend on military developments, since these directly influenced the attitude of Franco authorities toward the Polish refugees. The outcome of the war was still not settled, in spite of the now fairly distinct superiority of the anti-Nazi coalition. If pressed by Hitler, Franco's government could turn over to the Germans or to Vichy all those who had clandestinely crossed the border in the Pyrenees and were now in Spain. Also, Spain's entry into the war on the side of the Axis was still possible. The refugees' fears were not groundless.

Immediately after the collapse of France, Hitler ordered preparations made for the occupation of Gibraltar. A special group of intelligence and staff personnel, including Abwehr chief Adm. Wilhelm Canaris and his deputy, Col. Hans Piekenbrock, had gone to Madrid. Comdr. Wilhelm Leissner, the Abwehr chief in Spain, had for many weeks before been conducting talks with the Spanish minister of war, Gen. Juan Vignon. But the Spaniards had not been overly enthusiastic about plans for attacking the British fortress. The German team had also been received by General Franco, who basically approved of the plan but harbored doubts concerning its feasibility; casually he mentioned in conversation that the British had just reinforced the garrison at Gibraltar.

During the years 1940-43 the Germans attempted several times to organize an assault on Gibraltar (Operations Felix and Isabella) but after their disaster at Stalingrad, which coincided with the Allied offensive in North Africa, the chances of an attack steadily declined. When, beginning in the winter of 1942-43, the German armies were in slow but constant retreat, Franco had no intention of betting on a losing hand. He either put off proposals for a joint strike against Gibraltar with vague promises, or demanded such astronomical quantities of tanks, aircraft, and ammunition in return for bringing Spain into the war that the Germans were obliged to refuse.[5]

Following instructions, Rejewski and Zygalski said nothing about their rare military specialty when contacting representatives of the Polish Red Cross and other Polish agencies charged with assisting in evacuations, although mentioning the work they did might have hastened their departure from Spain. It was too risky; any indiscretion might have had incalculable consequences. What assurance could they have that German intelligence, which operated freely in Spain, did not have people in these wartime Polish agencies, which were often quickly organized? There was nothing to do but mix in with the mass of refugees and patiently wait their turn. They had a fairly long wait. They left Madrid after two months, on 21 July 1943.

As it turned out, Rejewski and Zygalski had been the first of the Polish cryptological team to get out of occupied France, and, indeed, were among the few to succeed in doing so. After leaving Cadix, the members of the Polish team had sought to cross the Pyrenees in small groups. Both of the ranking officers, Colonel Langer and Major Ciężki, were arrested by the Germans while attempting to cross the Franco-Spanish border along with Antoni Palluth and Edward Fokczyński.

After a couple of unsuccessful attempts at organizing a crossing, the four Poles were finally to have crossed the border on the night of 10-11 March 1943. In addition to the Poles, the group included two Frenchmen: Humbert, an industrialist from Algiers, and Rosier, a chemist by profession. The guide, Gomez, drove the six men in an automobile belonging to bribed French Garde Mobile (mobile police) to the small border town of Elnes, from where they were to have gone toward the border on foot, led by a second guide. Before parting, Gomez, wishing them good luck, kissed Langer, from whom he had received half of a signed 20-franc bank note. The next day he handed it to Bertrand as evidence that he had safely conducted the fugitives to the border and, as had been agreed, received 600,000 francs (100,000 per man).

By a deserted rocky path Langer and his group, under cover of night, moved on with the second guide. The colonel did not know that they had been betrayed by the effusive Gomez, and that his had been a Judas's kiss.

> About three kilometers out of Elnes [Langer wrote after the war] out of a
> grove of young trees there suddenly jumped out military [that is, uni-
> formed] Gestapo men, and almost simultaneously others drove up on
> motorcycles from behind and in front. They began firing, surrounded us,
> and arrested us, letting the guide go free.... Next they drove us to
> Argeles sur Mer... to the Gestapo [for] the first interrogation.

Thus began the two years' Gehenna of the arrested men. After interrogation, the two officers were sent by the Nazis to Stalag 122 in Compiègne, France, and next, on 9 September 1943, to the S.S. concentration camp Sonderkommando Schloss Eisenberg in Czechoslovakia. They were freed on 10 May 1945 by American forces. Palluth and Fokczyński were sent to the concentration camp at Sachsenhausen-Oranienburg near Berlin, where both died before the war's end. The circumstances of their deaths are unclear. According to the most reliable version, Palluth was killed during an Allied air raid and Fokczyński died from emaciation and exhaustion.

NOTES

1. Szumowski, *Account.*

2. Suszczewski, *Wspomnienia.*

3. Jabłoński, *Żołnierze polskich sił zbrojnych w obozie koncentracyjnym Miranda de Ebro 1940-1943 (relacja byłego więźnia).*

4. Ibid.

5. The last plan of the German staff involving Spain, dating from the end of 1943 and code named "Nürnberg," provided only for the defense of Fortress Europe at the Pyrenees in the event of Allied occupation of the Iberian Peninsula. Characteristically, Hitler kept returning obsessively to the matter of Spain up to the last days of April 1945. He regarded errors that had been made in this region to be the key to explaining Germany's loss of the war. Hermann Goering, during his Nuremberg trial, took a similar assessment of the importance of Gibraltar and the Iberian Peninsula.

13.

Enigma Abroad

As has been noted earlier, in the spring of 1939 Britain's Government Code and Cypher School (G.C.C.S.) had moved from London to Bletchley Park, where a small team of cryptologists had been at work since the previous fall, at the time of the Czechoslovak crisis. Initially the entire Foreign Office facility at Bletchley had numbered no more than thirty persons and had been accommodated in a single large, two-story, red-brick Tudor-Gothic Victorian house set in the midst of a park with lawns, cedars, croquet lawn, and sunken boundary fence that was invisible from the house and gave an impression of unbroken space. With time, as the number of personnel grew, numerous huts would be put up in the park to accommodate the burgeoning staff.

Bletchley Park's location, almost midway between Cambridge and Oxford, facilitated recruitment of personnel from those two most ancient of English universities, principally from Cambridge, with its strong mathematics program. Thus, the beginning of September 1939 had seen the arrival of the Cambridge mathematical tutor Gordon Welchman, until then a dean at Sidney Sussex College who, back in the fall of 1938, had gone through a cryptology course conducted by Oliver Strachey of World War I's Room 40, among others.

Upon arrival, Welchman found that the team that had been directly concerned with Enigma in peacetime was unprepared to cope with the cryptological-intelligence tasks of wartime. Comdr. Alastair Denniston, as Bletchley's head, was preoccupied with administrative duties. In any case, no one in Britain had personal experience in using for military-intelligence purposes information that had been obtained by decryptment of enemy machine ciphers. Denniston needed help from a specialist who also had a practical bent. The brightest star at his side, Alfred D. Knox, was a scholar par excellence; his sharp mind moved freely about the labyrinth of cryptology. But he was remote from the practical requirements of the approaching war.

The daily routine at Bletchley was one of tedious, unexciting, thankless labor. Knox's disposition and mind did not lend themselves to such routine. Intuitive, original, erratic, his mind moved like the flight of a kingfisher over the waters. Whether in Room 40, or on Broadway between the world wars, he was more a visionary dreamer than a dogged conformist.[1] Knox eventually died of cancer, on 27 February 1943; Denniston was replaced as Bletchley's head in late 1942 by Comdr. Edward Travis, during the thirties head of the G.C.C.S.'s Naval Section and number two to its chief, Commander Denniston.

Recruits for Bletchley had to pass a rigorous security clearance; this was especially important in regard to the large numbers of intellectuals selected for their knowledge of Germany and its language, of Italy and Italian, and so on. After Bletchley had grown to number hundreds, later thousands, of workers, considerably more personnel would be drawn from the armed forces; in particular, there were many Wren and WAAF women who operated communications and other technical equipment.[2] Whoever had been hired at Bletchley had to remain for the duration. The grounds were surrounded by barbed wire and guarded day and night by an RAF detachment.

Recruitment of top mathematicians and other specialists to work at Bletchley was no easy matter because of competition from other supersecret projects, such as radar and the atom bomb, which sought to obtain top-priority status from Churchill. The prime minister, by all accounts, never stinted resources for scientific and technical intelligence, especially for Ultra.

Like the Enigma operations in Poland and France before it, Ultra[3] involved three basic functions: interception; decryptment; and translation, assessment, and distribution of the information gleaned in such form and manner as to protect the Ultra secret.

Interception was the function of the stations that had operated before the war in the British Isles, Gibraltar, Malta, Cyprus, and Egypt. Later, after Japan's entry into the war, additional stations were created in India, Singapore, Burma, and Australia.

The mainstream of German Army intercepts flowed in to Bletchley from a station at Chatham, about thirty miles east of London, near the mouth of the Thames. The Chatham station had a direct teletype link with Bletchley, by which it sent in the opening of every Enigma intercept so that the cryptologists could begin retrieving the keys without delay; the main texts followed in a dispatch rider's pouch. German Air Force signals were intercepted mainly by stations at Cheadle and Chicksands Priory in Bedfordshire. German Navy intercepts came in from Flowerdown and Scarborough, on the east coast.

In addition to intercepting signals, these stations conducted radio intelligence in a broad sense, including identification of enemy transmitters and networks, their operating procedures, technical features of apparatus, and personnel.

The most crucial of Bletchley's functions was, of course, decryptment. The breaking of German Army and Air Force ciphers was handled by cryptologists at Hut 6 under Gordon Welchman, and later under Stuart Milner-Barry, another Cambridge mathematician. Naval ciphers were broken by a team at Hut 8 that was headed by Alan Turing, later by C.H. Alexander. Both teams made use of the same apparatus: the Zygalski sheets, cryptological bombs, and so on.

Peter Calvocoressi, who eventually became head of air intelligence at Bletchley Park, states that throughout the war Enigma ciphers were broken in only three ways: by decryptment of twice-enciphered message keys; by the discovery of cribs, such as stock phrases or addresses; and by the identification of reencipherments into an Enigma key that could *not* be read from a key that *could* be read, or vice versa. (We shall say more about these methods later.) If the cryptologists thought that they had a crib, they fed the suspected expressions along with the cipher text into a bomb (these devices, derived from the Polish bomb, were scattered about the surrounding countryside so that they could not all be destroyed at one fell swoop), which rapidly permuted cribs against cipher text, in search of a match. At the beginning of the war, the number of Enigma ciphers in daily use was not much more than half a dozen; before war's end, it had grown to several dozen—at one point, the German Navy alone was reportedly using some forty different settings of the Enigma machine at one time.[4]

Two special teams dealt with hand-enciphered messages (ISOS— Intelligence Services Oliver Strachey) and with ciphers that had not yet been broken, but were thought to have originated on some kind of Enigma (ISK—Intelligence Services Knox). The latter broke an Italian naval cipher that was based on a commercial-model Enigma, and an Abwehr system which used an Enigma that lacked a commutator. ISK also read Enigma messages from the Spanish Blue Division at the eastern front. Decrypts of Abwehr manual ciphers furnished invaluable information on Germany's foreign intelligence operations, thereby enabling the British to turn German agents against their masters and to conduct deception operations against the Axis (the Double-Cross System described by Sir John Masterman); Abwehr and S.D. traffic was processed by an intelligence unit that included the future professors of Greek and comparative philology Denys Page and Leonard Palmer.

An Italian section, headed by Prof. E.R. Vincent, handled much Italian naval traffic, based at first on a variant of commercial Enigma, later on Swedish Hagelin machines (which were also used by the U.S. Army). The female employees in Professor Vincent's section accordingly became known as "The Hags."

A Japanese section was staffed largely with able young men from Cambridge who had been put through a six-month crash course in Japanese. Presumably, they worked with Japanese machine ciphers after the British obtained reconstructed "Purple" machines from the U.S. in 1941.

The third of the functions comprising the Ultra operation was the domain of Hut 3 (which handled army and air force materials decrypted by Hut 6) and Hut 4 (which handled naval decrypts sent over from Hut 8). At Hut 3, processing included precise translation of signals into English and entry of information that might prove useful in processing subsequent messages into special card files. The Hut 3 files were maintained in duplicate, one set being held for safekeeping at the Bodleian Library at Oxford University. At Hut 4, the procedure was simpler. Decrypts were not translated, but were merely checked and forwarded in the original German to the Admiralty's Operational Intelligence Centre.

Ultra materials were graded by priority on a five-degree scale from "Z" (lowest priority) to "ZZZZZ" (deliver immediately) and reached their ultimate recipients in Britain by secure teletype. Initially, the recipients were the chiefs of staff (three), the directors of intelligence of the services (three),[5] the commander in chief Fighter Command (one) and the commander in chief Home Forces (one)—eight persons altogether. The most important decrypts were delivered to Churchill in a red box to Number 10 Downing Street or, as the Battle of Britain developed, to the underground war rooms below Storey's Gate.

All armed forces commands outside the British Isles received Ultra through the Special Liaison Units (SLUs) that have already been described. In the spring of 1940, before the German general offensive in the west, SLUs had already been active there, attached to Lord Gort's British Expeditionary Force (B.E.F.) in France, and to the Advanced Air Striking Force, to pass on such Ultra as might be available from Bletchley and Bruno.

In subsequent months and years of the war, further SLUs were established—

In 1941-42:

Middle East Headquarters (Cairo);

the Desert Army;

the Desert Air Force;

the Royal Navy at Alexandria;

British and Allied commands on Malta, in Beirut, on Gibraltar, and in Algiers.

In 1943:

General Alexander's Fifteenth Army Group Headquarters in Italy (first at Bari, later at Caserta), with feeds to the Fifteenth U.S. Air Force, the Balkan Air Force, the U.S. Fifth Army and the British Eighth Army.

In 1944:

Eisenhower's Supreme Headquarters Allied Expeditionary Force (SHAEF);

Spaatz's Strategic Air Force;

the tactical air commands (both British and U.S.);

Bradley's Twelfth U.S. Army Group;

Montgomery's Twenty-First Army Group;

British Second Army;

U.S. First, Third, Seventh, Ninth and Fifteenth Armies.

In addition, by 1944, British and American SLUs in Southeast Asia were serving Mountbatten, Slim, Stilwell, and the U.S. bomber commands in India and China, drawing on a worldwide informational loop that linked Bletchley, SEAC (the Southeast Asia Command), Washington, D.C., and Brisbane, Australia. By mid-1945, as the Pacific war moved on, SLUs had been established at Morotai Island, at Lae in New Guinea, at Labuen, and elsewhere. An SLU was about to be set up at Manila, but was pre-empted by the dropping of the atom bomb on Hiroshima.

All British SLU members were RAF personnel and wore RAF uniforms. Each SLU comprised an officer and a small section of cipher sergeants and signallers.

After enemy signals had been decrypted at Bletchley (Hut 6) and translated (Hut 3), the substance of some was sent to the appropriate government departments and to the commands of the armed forces in Britain. Others, destined for overseas commands and staffs, were encrypted using a one-time pad or, later, the new Typex cipher machine and sent to the intelligence radio-communication center at Whaddon Hall. From there, powerful transmitters beamed the signals to SLUs in all the theaters of operations, from Europe and North Africa to the Far East and Australia.

After an Ultra signal had been received and deciphered, the SLU officer showed it to the authorized commander or to a member of his staff designated to receive it; then the signal was immediately destroyed. The SLUs, like Bletchley, worked around the clock.

Some commanders liked to have their SLUs physically as close as possible, sometimes within fifty yards of their tents (for example, Gen. Miles Dempsey of the British Second Army). Others, such as Gen. Bernard Montgomery, would banish them to a solitary spot half a mile away, allegedly for fear of the enemy getting a bearing on their radio transmissions. Winterbotham concluded that it was the presence of RAF personnel concerned with intelligence that Montgomery for some reason disliked. SLU chiefs were authorized to intervene if they felt that a planned operation might give away the Ultra secret, and could notify headquarters in Britain by radio about such a situation.

The work of the SLU organization was facilitated by the support given it by Churchill, who himself often took an SLU along on his frequent wartime travels.

In the fall of 1975, after thirty-two years of silence, the British government permitted the Public Record Office to release photographs of an early, wartime computer—perhaps the first modern electronic computer—named Colossus. These photographs confirmed that "a series of programmable electronic computers were built in Britain during World War II, the first being operational in 1943." The computers had been designed by Prof. M.H.A. Newman (responsible for formulating the requirement for Colossus) and T.H. Flowers (leader of the team that developed the machine). The design was influenced by the theoretical work of Alan Turing, who in 1937 had demonstrated the feasibility of a universal automaton capable of carrying out any calculation that any special automation could.[6]

In September 1939, Turing had begun work at Bletchley. The British, by then, had the Polish Enigma and the Polish design plans of the cryptological bomb, the perforated sheets, and other equipment that facilitated recovery of Enigma keys. Turing obtained assistance from the Post Office Research Station at Dollis Hill in building a device called, like its Polish prototype, a bomb.

The first, still very imperfect Heath Robinson electronic computer (so named after a British equivalent of Rube Goldberg) came into being only later and never produced much output that was of value in itself. Exploitation of the Heath Robinson was entrusted to a team that included Professor Newman, D. Michie, Dr. I.J. Good and Dr. S. Wylie. The early computers had many reliability problems, including difficulties with accurate physical synchronization of two fast-moving perforated tapes, which probably replaced the perforated Zygalski sheets.[7]

At the beginning of 1943, work began on a new device that was to use one thousand five hundred tubes, "approximately twice the number. . .that were used in some of the early post-war computers!" Flowers, having failed to get official support from skeptical administrators at Bletchley, had gotten the project authorized by the director of the Dollis Hill Research Station. In the incredibly short period of eleven months, the machine, which came to be known as the Colossus, was built at Dollis Hill and then commissioned at Bletchley, where it became operational in late 1943. Colossus was more reliable and much faster than the Robinsons.

In March 1944, Flowers and his team, which by then had been joined by Dr. A.W.M. Coombs, were informed that more machines were needed by June 1. Production of an initial set of three was begun, and the first machine became operational at Bletchley Park on 1 June 1944, just in time for D-Day. These Mark II machines were effectively five times faster than the original Colossus and incorporated two thousand four hundred tubes. A number of the Colossi were built and gave reliable and effective service until war's end; what happened to them later has not been revealed. Design work continued up to the end of World War II, and no two Colossi were exactly alike. In addition, a series of smaller special-purpose machines and attachments were built at Dollis Hill for Bletchley.

After the war, official rewards were given to a number of the persons who had been involved in the Bletchley work. "However," observes Randell, "the great originality and importance of their work remained. . .unappreciated by the general public." Professor Newman and two of his staff went to Manchester University, Turing to the National Physical Laboratory, and Coombs and Chandler, while still at Dollis Hill, designed and built the MOSAIC computer.

As early as 1945, Turing drew up one of the earliest complete designs for a stored-program computer. His report marked the real beginning of the ACE computer project. The original plan was for Turing's machine to be built for the National Physical Laboratory by Chandler and Coombs at Dollis Hill, but this fell through, and they went on to design and build the MOSAIC, which was largely based on an early version of the ACE design.[8]

As of late 1978, the British government's Public Record Office held German Army and Air Force signals only for the period from 18 November

1943 to 25 March 1945. These signals, totalling forty-eight thousand, were just the ones in that period that had been selected and worked up from among a considerably greater number by Bletchley Park and sent to various Allied higher commands. Many documents are not available in the Public Record Office, including intelligence summaries and papers specially prepared on selected topics.[9] But even within those limitations, the German signals were sent out by Bletchley at an average rate of four to five per hour throughout that period of sixteen and one-half months.

The intelligence analysts who worked around the clock at Bletchley's Hut 3 did not limit themselves to selecting, translating, and annotating signals. In collaboration with the cryptologists at Hut 6, they also set priorities for solving the cipher keys of the various German signals nets. In some situations, the cryptologists at Hut 6 would tell the analysts at Hut 3: "In one month we can solve key A or key B. Which is the more important?" The analysts, of course, could answer such questions only when they had been apprised of their high commands' operational plans. Hence, there was continuous contact and exchange of views between the operational commands and the intelligence service, including its representatives at Bletchley's Hut 3. Hut 3 eventually had about two hundred experts on the German Army and Air Force, who worked around the clock in four shifts, and a teletype facility for constant communication with London.

Although only part of the wartime Ultra documents have been made public, enough is already known to give a general idea of the role of Enigma decrypts in various periods and theaters of the war.

The Battle of France

In March and April 1940, during the German invasion of Norway and Denmark, many German signals were read, referring chiefly to logistics: pedantic reporting on unit strengths, airplanes, tanks, artillery, ammunition, and spare parts. These data made possible the accurate determination of German Army and Air Force orders of battle.

During this period, two SLUs were created in France, one to pass Enigma intelligence to the British Expeditionary Force's commander in chief, Lord Gort, and the commander of the B.E.F.'s air component, and another posted to the British Advanced Air Striking Force.

In the first days of May 1940, as in April, a great deal of information came in over Enigma on German preparations for a general offensive in the west.

During the first three weeks of ensuing war, between 10 and 31 May 1940, a number of Enigma signals were read between the commander in chief of the German Army, Gen. Walther von Brauchitsch, and the commanders of the army groups. On the morning of May 23, an order was decrypted from von Brauchitsch for the two Army Groups A and B "to continue the encircling movement [that would trap the British forces at Dunkirk] with the utmost vigor." Winterbotham believes that it was this message that made Gort and Churchill decide to evacuate British forces from France.[10]

The Battle of Britain

Churchill was impressed with the results of Enigma decryptment and requested that any important dispatches be sent to him. If something important turned up while Churchill was weekending at Chequers, Winterbotham read it to the prime minister over a scrambler phone. Churchill was especially intrigued by the long political dispatches that Hitler occasionally sent to governors of his new empire.[11] Winterbotham's team at Hut 3 that translated and annotated the Enigma messages quickly grew from six to sixty.

On 16 July 1940, Hitler issued "Directive No. 16 on the Preparation of a Landing Operation against England." The goal was to eliminate England as a base against Germany and, if necessary, to occupy it completely. Success of Operation Seelöwe (Sea Lion) depended—as Hitler's directive emphasized—on the Luftwaffe's total control of the air; the Royal Air Force had to be swept from the skies.

The invasion was scheduled for 15 September 1940, and was to be carried out by twenty-five divisions grouped in two armies under Field Marshal Gerd von Rundstedt. Landing of the first units on the English coast was to be supported by airborne landings.

In mid-July a signal was read, from Reich Marshal Hermann Goering, commander in chief of the Luftwaffe, summarizing Hitler's directive to the commanders in chief of the army, navy, and air force. This was the first time that the expression "Sea Lion" had been used on the air, and made it much easier now to identify activities connected with the invasion plan.

Commencement of Operation Sea Lion was conditional on the results of the air battle, whose objectives were stated in another directive (Number 17) from Hitler issued on 1 August 1940, for "Conduct of Air and Sea Warfare against England." It provided for the opening on 5 August 1940 of "intensified aerial warfare," whose forms and detailed objectives were to be set out by the Luftwaffe High Command and by Reich Marshal Goering personally.

By the latter half of July 1940, Bletchley had been decrypting a prolific radio correspondence from the Luftwaffe High Command, giving detailed information on the deployment and strength of German Air Fleets (Luftflotten) Two, Three, and Five, which were preparing for massed raids against Britain. In late July, Enigma signals had revealed disagreements among army, navy, and air force commanders as to the chances for a landing on the English coast. Ultra disclosed an order from Goering for his troop carriers to practice landing on narrow runways simulating roads. The British Air Ministry got to work constructing barriers that were kept ready along all the long, straight roads in southern England.

On 1 August 1940, in a message to the commanders of his air fleets, Goering ordered the Luftwaffe to overcome the Royal Air Force with all the means at its disposal as soon as possible. Thanks to Ultra, Britain's Fighter Command learned the general outlines of the coming air offensive. Goering had assigned zones to his several air fleets, which were to concentrate their bombing raids principally on British airfields.

In these early days of August, writes Winterbotham, "the number of German signals began to boil over," and Bletchley got two or three hundred a day to read.

On 8 August 1940, Goering issued his order for Operation Adler (Eagle), declaring: "Within a short period you will wipe the British Air Force from the sky." In less than an hour, the decrypted order was in the hands of the prime minister, the chiefs of staff, and Air Marshal Hugh Dowding, commander in chief of Fighter Command.

On August 12 a new order from Goering reset Eagle Day, which had been expected on August 11, for August 13. Early on the thirteenth, however, Goering ordered postponement of the attack until the afternoon. The result was chaotic. Although the British got his signal, apparently some of his units did not, and the morning attack "went off at half-cock."

On August 15, the German raids continued. Intercepts again provided precise warning of their timing and objectives. The attacks were carefully timed to keep the British defenses busy all day long. The day's massive effort was part of Goering's strategy, intended to bomb British airfields in the south in order to make them unoperational, while at the same time drawing as many RAF fighters as possible into battle, where the Germans hoped to destroy them quickly. Dowding, who recognized Goering's strategy from his Enigma orders, avoided this trap and used the minimum of fighters to disrupt the German bomber squadrons.

Early on August 18, Enigma intercepts gave advance warning of a repetition of the immense raids of Adlertag (Eagle Day). In the ensuing battle, the Luftwaffe took one of its heaviest day's losses to that point. Once again there followed a lull, and then the weather turned sour.

Goering now issued orders in Enigma that "the attacks were to go much farther inland in order to bring the RAF up to battle." The attacks on the inland airfields began on August 24 and lasted, with extreme intensity, for a fortnight. Ultra gave no set pattern, but when units from two different Luftflotten were employed, occasional signals coordinating their efforts gave an idea as to the size and timing of larger raids. Aside from bombing airfields, the Luftwaffe had also turned its attention to aircraft factories in southern England.

On 30 and 31 August 1940, writes Winterbotham, Goering must have been getting very impatient, for "once again he took personal control of his air fleets and luckily for us on those two days gave us prior warning of the giant raids."

The RAF's position was now desperate, but Ultra showed that the Luftwaffe, too, was having difficulties with repairs and aircraft replacement. Goering had expected the Battle of Britain to be over in two weeks with few losses to the Luftwaffe, and now only 50 percent of his aircraft were serviceable.

At 11 a.m. on 5 September 1940, Goering sent an Enigma order for a three-hundred-bomber raid on the London docks late in the afternoon. Within minutes, Goering's order was in the hands of Churchill and Dowding. All the fire-fighting units in the vicinity were alerted. Despite the scrambled RAF fighters, the sheer weight of the enemy force allowed it to inflict serious bomb damage. Nevertheless, the dock raid was a strategic mistake. Had Goering kept up his blows at the airfields in southern England for another week or two, he might have eliminated the RAF.

At 11 a.m. on September 9, orders were intercepted from Goering for an early evening raid by over two hundred bombers against London. RAF fighters met the Luftwaffe force before it could reach the target.

On 15 September 1940, after several days of rain and clouds, the weather improved. By noon, Goering was sending wave upon wave of bombers against London.

> [Dowding,] correctly judging his moment, the low morale of the German bomber crews, the lack of adequate fighter protection due to the size of their fuel tanks, the desperate state of the RAF and the knowledge that it was now or never for Operation Sea Lion, threw in everything [the British] had.

The Luftwaffe crews had been told that the RAF had no fighters left. Consequently, the unexpected RAF strength came as a shock, and the Germans fled. Goering promptly ordered a second raid. "This was an occasion when the speed of the Ultra operation and the direct line to Dowding made history." The RAF fighters were refueled, rearmed, and ready again to meet the second wave, and once again the raiders dropped their bombs wherever they could and fled.

On the morning of 17 September 1940, the German General Staff sent a signal to appropriate units in Holland that Hitler had authorized dismantling of the air-loading equipment at the Dutch airfields. One of the main features of the German plans for invading Britain had been the vast preparations that had been made on the Belgian and Dutch airfields for loading and quick turnaround of supply and troop-carrying aircraft. If the loading equipment was being dismantled, the invasion could not take place. The signal was sent to the underground war room at Storey's Gate, and at a chiefs of staff meeting that evening Churchill read out the message, "his face beaming."

Night after night throughout the rest of September and October 1940, London was subjected to the blitz, designed to reduce Britain to submission. There was, however, no reference in Ultra to the nightly bombing. In November, since the London raids did not seem to be having the desired effect, Goering decided to start on some of the other large cities. Sometimes the British got warning of a coming raid, but the exact target was hidden by a code name. Winterbotham claims, however (while others, including Lewin, question), that about 3 p.m. on November 14 someone made a mistake, and an Enigma intercept identified Coventry by name. There were four or five hours before the attack would arrive. Still, according to Winterbotham, in order not to give away the Ultra secret to the Germans, Churchill decided not to evacuate Coventry (which would have been difficult anyway, on such short notice) but only to alert fire, ambulance, and police units and get everything ready to light decoy fires.

There would be, according to Winterbotham, one other raid of which Ultra gave prior notice: the second great fire of London in late December 1941 (the first great fire had been in 1666), when Goering ordered the incineration of the city. Here there was no need to evacuate, since offices would be empty anyway. Once again, fire-fighting units were secretly alerted.[12]

North Africa

At the beginning of 1941, the British read a directive from Hitler to the commander of German forces in southern Rumania, telling him to prepare to move south through Bulgaria—like Rumania, already client to Germany—for an attack on Greece. Apparently Hitler, no longer able to rely on the Italians in the Mediterranean, meant to secure his southern flank against the British in the Middle East for an invasion of the Soviet Union.

By mid-February, an Enigma signal to Berlin informed the British that Gen. Erwin Rommel had arrived in Tripoli, in Italian-held Libya. Churchill received further Enigma information that the Germans would soon send units to Tripoli that were to constitute Rommel's Afrika Korps.

In March, Ultra informed British Adm. Andrew Cunningham of an Italian operation against British convoys to Greece that was planned for March 27. At the battle of Matapan, the British fleet, informed of the whole plan, caught up with the Italians and crippled their force; this kept the Italian fleet off the Mediterranean for the duration of the war.

Ultra information on the Afrika Korps enabled Gen. Archibald Wavell, chief of the Middle East Command, and Lt. Gen. Richard O'Connor, commanding the Western Desert Force, to withdraw British and Imperial forces without complete disaster.

At the beginning of April 1941, Bletchley read a signal from Field Marshal Wilhelm List, informing Hitler that he was ready to invade Greece, then further correspondence pertaining to the actual course of the operation.

After their rapid conquest of Greece, the Germans decided to take Crete as well. With the airfields of both Greece and Crete in their hands, they could dispose of any threat to the flank of their planned invasion of the Soviet Union. Thanks to Ultra, British Gen. Sir Bernard Freyberg, commanding the defense of Crete, "was in possession of the most detailed plans of an enemy's proposed operation that were ever likely to be available to any commander." The assault on Crete opened on 20 May 1941. Thanks to their Ultra information, the British prevented the Germans from capturing any of the airfields except for one at Maleme. Unfortunately, Freyberg did not counterattack, and this permitted Gen. Kurt Student to consolidate his hold on the airfield, fly in reinforcements, and master the island.

In April 1941, the Libyan port of Tobruk, seventy miles west of Egypt, had been isolated by the German advance. "The gallantry of the Australian, Polish and British forces that held on to this fortress," writes Winterbotham, "posed a constant threat to Rommel's supply lines." About mid-May, however, OKW (the Wehrmacht High Command) sent Rommel an Enigma order to leave the siege of Tobruk to the Italians and to press east to Sollum and the Egyptian border. Wavell, though warned, was unable to stop the Afrika Korps, and a week later Rommel had recaptured the Halfaya Pass, the gateway to Cairo. By mid-June 1941, Wavell failed to relieve Tobruk as Churchill ordered, and he was replaced in command by Gen. Claude Auchinleck.

Before Hitler's launching of Operation Barbarossa, his invasion of the Soviet Union on 22 June 1941, a number of German Army and Air Force movement orders were read by the British. Churchill wondered how much information to give the Soviets, consulted military intelligence chief Stewart Menzies and, according to Winterbotham, wrote Stalin about the German build-up but received no reply. Evidently Stalin considered this and other similar warnings to be attempts at undermining the Soviet-German Nonaggression (Molotov-Ribbentrop) Pact of 23 August 1939.

In an Enigma signal to Berlin, Rommel outlined his plans to attack the British in order to open the way to Cairo, and Auchinleck made good use of the intercepted information. In July 1942, a premature OKW announcement claiming Rommel's victory at Alamein, on the Mediterranean coast sixty miles west of Alexandria, apparently angered Rommel, for in a dispatch he stated that Auchinleck was holding him, and reinforcements were reaching the enemy, whereas he was being starved of supplies and troops.

On his way to see Stalin in Moscow in July 1942, Churchill stopped in Egypt for a conference with his chiefs of staff in the Middle East. Auchinleck was relieved of his post, Gen. Harold Alexander was made commander in chief in the Middle East, and Gen. Bernard Montgomery was brought from England to take command of the British Eighth Army.

On his way back from Moscow in mid-August 1942, Churchill again stopped in Egypt to meet his new generals. The British commanders had the complete order of battle of Rommel's forces and an estimate of his desperate situation with fuel and other supplies, virtually all based on Enigma intercepts. Alexander also produced a long, detailed dispatch from Rommel to Hitler describing his proposed final assault on the Eighth Army on 31 August 1942. Rommel intended to make a strong surprise attack across the Qattara depression on the southern end of Montgomery's left flank and then, with a great northward sweep of his tanks, roll up the Eighth Army and drive them into the sea. All the units for the attack were designated; so was the date. It was to be Rommel's final attempt to reach Alexandria, Cairo, and the Suez Canal. This, writes Winterbotham, was "the biggest 'plum' since the Battle of Britain."

With Rommel's plan before him, Montgomery called a conference of his commanders and told them of his "intuition" that Rommel would try to attack around the British southern flank before the British attack at Alamein was mounted. Thanks to Ultra, Montgomery had ample time to prepare his defense in depth, centering it on the high ridge at Alam Halfa. Despite the warning, it was still a tough battle. Eventually Rommel's attack was halted, and he was forced to withdraw, leaving behind some tanks for lack of fuel.

By 2 September 1942, Rommel had to admit failure and withdraw to his old position. His Enigma message to Hitler giving the reasons showed his disappointment with the way he had been starved of supplies. Hitler, however, was preoccupied with his eastern front, where the German offensive had bogged down at Stalingrad.

Churchill urged Montgomery to open his own attack on Rommel by mid-September. Montgomery, who had seen both Wavell and Auchinleck pushed into offensive operations before being fully prepared, told Churchill that he was not ready. Eventually his attack was postponed until late October, giving Rommel six weeks to put down minefields and dig in his fuel-starved tanks. Nevertheless, Rommel's message to Hitler summing up his chances was not optimistic. The second battle of Alamein began on 23 October 1942. It was "the first real German defeat of the war," says Winterbotham.

On 2 November 1942, Rommel asked Hitler for permission to retreat. In reply, Hitler sent his now famous order that "there could be no other course but that of holding out to the last man and that for the German troops there was only the choice, victory or death." There would be more such do-or-die messages over the next few years. On the night of 3-4 November 1942, Montgomery's breakthrough attack was launched. Enigma information had indicated Rommel's center to be his weakest point; hence, Montgomery made his main thrust there, between the German and Italian armies. By November 4, the British decrypted a message from Rommel to Hitler admitting defeat. This was the first news that Churchill had of the victory, for the cautious Montgomery had not been willing to claim it so soon.

Rommel's retreat must finally have made an impression on Hitler, because Ultra indicated that Hitler had decided to take personal strategic command in North Africa. His direction of the war from remote East Prussia provided the Allies with the supreme German decisions and directives.

To weaken Rommel's tired, supply-starved army, the Allies proceeded to sink the convoys that were desperately trying to bring him supplies. Every time that ships were loaded in Naples or Taranto and sent to North Africa, Rommel was informed by Enigma what supplies were loaded and when the ships would sail, as well as about their course. The British observed the Ultra security rules: they made sure each convoy had seen the aircraft that was sent up and was supposed to have spotted it, before the Royal Navy turned up and sank it. After about the third of the convoys had been sunk, a dense fog came down shortly after the next one had sailed from Naples. The British left the operation as late as possible in the hope that the fog would clear, but as the convoy was nearing the African coast action had to be taken, and Malta-based Royal Air Force units and the Royal Navy turned up in a dense fog in exactly the right spot at the same moment and sank the ships. The Germans became suspicious about a possible leak of information on the convoys. The Abwehr could not account for the leak. Nevertheless, the British took the precaution of sending a message to a mythical agent in Naples in a cipher that the Germans would be able to read, congratulating him on his excellent information and raising his pay.

A final convoy was ordered to sail as near as possible to a spot on the North African coast where Rommel's retreating army was now concentrated, and there throw its barrels of fuel overboard to be retrieved by the Afrika Korps. Despite patchy fog and an evident change in course by the convoy, it was found by an RAF spotter plane and sunk by the British Navy. Rommel's sense of humor rose above his anger and frustration, and he signaled receipt of two or three barrels that had floated ashore from the wrecks.[13]

The Allied breaking of German codes and ciphers should be viewed in context with similar German undertakings with regard to Allied communications.

A number of accounts describe the reading by the Germans, from the fall of 1941 to July 1942, of reports to Washington from the U.S. military attaché in Cairo, Col. Frank Bonner Fellers, who was later to become a brigadier general and military secretary to Gen. Douglas MacArthur. Fellers encoded his messages in a new, top-secret code called Black. The code was broken by German cryptologists, who received unwitting assistance from Fellers, who always began his messages with "Milid Wash" (Military Intelligence Division, Washington) or "Agwar Wash" (Adjutant General, War Office, Washington). The code was already in the possession of the Italians, who had "borrowed" a copy from the safe at the U.S. Embassy in Rome, photographed it, and returned it so that no one suspected anything. The head of Italian Military Intelligence, Gen. Cesare Amé, had decided to keep the Black code to himself and to give the Germans only the decrypts.[14]

The Germans used their own knowledge of the Black code, obtained the hard way, to read the dispatches of Colonel Fellers, who wandered about the desert among the British units and reported back to Washington on the situation. It would take the cryptologists in Germany two hours to strip off the reencipherment number from Fellers's code groups and decode and translate his message. Then it was put into a German code and radioed to Rommel's intelligence unit in North Africa, where Rommel each day at lunch knew exactly where the Allied troops had been the previous evening.

After their advance eastward in the autumn of 1941, the Germans had been slowly driven back again to Mersa Brega. On 21 January 1942, with the help of intercepted information including Fellers's, they went on the offensive and advanced three hundred miles in seventeen days. Fellers cabled to Washington his belief that Rommel would reach Cairo. To stop him, the British, from their air base on Malta, raided Rommel's African fuel supplies. Consequently Malta became a prime German target, and by late May 1942 was so short of food and fuel that it was on the verge of surrender.

Malta was the key to Allied victory in Africa and had to be relieved by convoy. To lessen the effect of Axis air power, the convoy was split in two: one half would sail from Gibraltar, the other from Alexandria in Egypt. As the seventy-eight ships set sail, the Italians in Rome and the German radio-intercept station in Lauf, near Nuremberg, picked up Fellers's report to Washington announcing a coming attack against nine Axis airfields by British sabotage units. The British intended to safeguard the Allied convoys by destroying the enemy planes on the ground. On the night of 13 June 1942, when British paratroops went into action, they were picked up as soon as they landed, while British bombers bombed airfields from which the enemy planes had been moved to safety. At dawn, both arms of the Allied convoy came under attack by enemy aircraft, submarines, and destroyers. Ultimately, only two convoy ships reached Malta, with food for only a month, and no fuel.

That same month, Bletchley Park discovered the leak. The code was changed, and Fellers was recalled. The Germans did not succeed in solving the new code.

In addition to information from decryptment units in Germany, Rommel's staff used intelligence gathered by its own monitoring unit. During operations in Libya in early 1941, the Afrika Korps employed a radio intelligence platoon (Horch-Zug) that was soon expanded to a company (Horch-Kompanie). British, especially Imperial, forces in North Africa were plagued by lax radio discipline. The Afrika Korps radio-intelligence unit eagerly exploited this weakness.[15]

In the summer of 1942, the Germans got a windfall when one of their U-boats on the Mediterranean stopped an Allied supply ship. A part of the booty was code tables that, for two weeks, enabled the Germans to read secret messages of the entire British military supply system from Gibraltar to Egypt.

An interesting episode in the North African campaign was Nazi interception of radio signals from a battalion of German anti-Nazis who, along with other Allied troops, were surrounded in the desert stronghold of Bir Hacheim, southwest of Tobruk. The unit was commanded by the well-known German writer Ludwig Renn. Despite fierce attacks by the Nazis, the battalion managed to break out of its encirclement and join the main Allied forces.

In the final phase of the battle of Alamein, when Rommel had to throw in his last reserves, the Horch-Kompanie, along with other staff units, was used to stiffen the Italian sector. When the Allies broke through there, the Kompanie was shattered. The British captured Axis cipher documents and other materials that furnished information on German field radio intelligence.[16]

Operation Torch

In early October 1942, there had been messages between Field Marshal Albert Kesselring and Berlin concerning intelligence reports of a coming Allied landing in the western Mediterranean. Kesselring admitted he did not know where it would take place, but in early November he said he expected it to be in North Africa, Sicily, or Sardinia. This was important information, because had Kesselring had firm information on Allied intentions, he might have used the French in Algeria to resist the invasion, with disastrous results. Gen. Dwight Eisenhower, at Gibraltar waiting to go over to Algiers, was elated at the prospect of the Allies being able to achieve suprise.

During this same period, Rommel sent a message to Kesselring proposing to retreat west to El Agheila, on the Gulf of Sidra in Libya, in view of the possible Allied landings in North Africa. If Kesselring could hold Tunisia, to the west of Libya, his forces might then join up with the retreating Afrika Korps. In an Enigma message to the German Commission in Tunis, Kesselring demanded immediate agreement by the French for the Germans to take over airfields and ports at Tunis and Bizerta in Tunisia. Shortly afterwards, a message arrived from Hitler giving Kesselring permission "to seize these areas and prepare forces to despatch to Tunisia."

Ultra had informed the Allies of the forces that Kesselring had at his disposal, but had given no hint as to how quickly they could be airlifted to North Africa. Immediately after the Allied Operation Torch landings to the west of Tunisia (at Casablanca in Morocco, and at Oran and Algiers in Algeria) on 8 November 1942, Kesselring sent messages to the Luftwaffe and to army formations ordering an immediate airlift of German troops from southern Italy to Tunis and the transfer of fighter squadrons to Tunis and Bizerta airfields. He was able to report to Berlin that Luftwaffe aircraft, together with an airlift of troops to guard them, had landed at Tunis the day after the Allied landings. On the evening of November 9, Hitler sent orders to the German Army Command in Paris for the commencement of Operation Attila, the occupation of southern France.

Due to Enigma news of Kesselring's rapid moves into Tunis, Maj. Gen. Sir Kenneth Anderson, commanding the British First Army and U.S. forces, did his best to get the Allied armies moving east before the Germans could seize too much ground.

On the evening of 11 November 1942, Kesselring ordered via Enigma the air command at Tunis to send a parachute battalion to seize the coastal airfield at Bône, thirty miles west of Tunisia and in the path of the advancing Allies. The operation was ordered for the next day. Since airfields were few and far between, the Allies decided to forestall the Germans. A small British paratroop battalion was transported to Bône in American Dakota airplanes, just beating the Germans to it. The German aircraft arrived as the last British paratrooper landed, and the Germans had to return to base. The incident was convincing demonstration that Ultra could be of tactical as well as strategic use.

Ultra had also gotten the U-boat situation in the Mediterranean under control. The German submarines gave the Allies no trouble at Algiers or during the later amphibious operations in the area.

Enigma messages now showed that the OKW had promised Kesselring massive reinforcements. By the end of November 1942, Kesselring was able to report to Berlin that he had landed fifteen thousand troops with a hundred tanks at Tunis and that eight thousand Italian troops had been brought into the area.

From the end of November on, Enigma intercepts provided information not only on the German forces in Tunisia commanded by Lt. Gen. Walter Nehring, but also on Rommel's Afrika Korps retreating westward from the province of Cyrenaica in eastern Libya. Hitler ordered Rommel to make a stand at El Agheila. This information prompted Montgomery to send the Second New Zealand Division to try to cut off his retreat. Eventually Rommel had to abandon his stand. He informed Rome and Berlin of this and announced his intention of withdrawing to the Homs Line in Tunisia. But since Hitler had ordered him to make a stand as far to the east as possible, Rommel decided, probably against his own better judgment, to dig in at Buerat. His message to Hitler to this effect prompted Montgomery to send the Seventh Armoured Division through the desert to attack from the western flank.

Rommel had given his strength time to return after the El Agheila stand, and, despite his difficulties with fuel and supplies, he still had a formidable tank force.

Maj. Gen. George S. Patton, who had sailed directly from the U.S. with his landing force to Casablanca, was briefed by Winterbotham in Algiers about Ultra and was delighted with the idea of reading enemy messages. He refused, however, to abide by the security rule concerning users' personal safety.

In January 1943, Churchill took an SLU with him to the Casablanca Conference. While he was there, a dispatch from Rommel to OKW again reported that he had been forced to abandon the Buerat Line and was retreating to Homs. This time the Eighth Army did not give him time to dig in, and almost immediately another message from Rommel told Hitler that he was withdrawing to the Mareth Line in Tunisian territory.

In February 1943, General Alexander, who had come from Egypt, was given overall command of the British First Army and the U.S. forces, together with the Eighth Army on the other side—to the east—of Tunisia, to form the Eighteenth Army Group. Enigma information confirmed that the two German armies, the Afrika Korps and the army commanded by Gen. Jürgen von Arnim, had joined with the First Italian Army under Gen. Giovanni Messe to form Army Group Africa, commanded by Rommel. Enigma dispatches indicated some discord among Rommel, Kesselring, von Arnim, and the Italians.

The degree to which Allied commanders had come to rely on Enigma intercepts, sometimes to the neglect of adequate air reconnaissance, was demonstrated when Enigma correspondence failed to warn of Rommel's attack on the advancing U.S. forces at Kasserine Pass in central Tunisia on 20 February 1943. The first Enigma reference to the action came in a message from Rommel to OKW stating that, owing to the pressure of a French division to the southwest, he was withdrawing back to the Mareth Line.

Almost at the same time, Kesselring passed on to Rommel Hitler's order that the Mareth Line was to be held. There was to be no withdrawal. Rommel sent one of his most detailed reports ever, giving the complete layout of the Mareth Line with the positions of every unit in its defense. Montgomery now knew exactly what he was up against. Hitler ordered that Rommel mount a delaying attack against the Eighth Army. Rommel signaled back to Kesselring that an attack on the Eighth Army could only have a slight delaying effect and that, since an Allied attack on the Mareth Line was expected anyway, he suggested a further withdrawal from Mareth to unite the army group on a shorter perimeter. Kesselring replied that Rommel's proposals were overruled. Accordingly, Rommel proceeded to carry out Hitler's orders. Enigma messages warned Montgomery of the precise Axis forces to be used for the holding attack on the British Eighth Army at Medenine, fifteen miles southwest of the Mareth Line, and gave details of where the Axis armored thrusts would come from. Rommel's attack of February 20 failed. The Eighth Army beat back the panzers with concentrated antitank fire. The Allies shortly learned that Rommel had given up and returned to Germany; General von Arnim was appointed to replace him. Montgomery now proceeded with his main attack on the Mareth Line, fully aware of its weakest points.

Since the Torch landings in Morocco and Algeria in November 1942, Allied forces had been more or less steadily pushing toward and into Tunisia. Over those six months, the Axis troops had been compressed into a diminishing pocket in Tunisia between Eisenhower's forces on the west, the British Eighth Army on the east, Free French forces on the south, and Allied air and naval forces in the Mediterranean to the north. The end for the German forces came quickly after the final Allied assault on 6 May 1943. Ultra gave the Allied air forces the movement orders for the fleet of transport aircraft and gliders that were to be used in the evacuation of German troops from Tunisia. The Allied air forces had to be restrained from taking too quick action, but ultimately most of the German aircraft were shot down. The same fate met the last German destroyer in the Mediterranean and the Belino evacuation convoy. The Axis forces capitulated on 12 May 1943. On May 13, Kesselring reported briefly to Berlin, by Enigma, the total loss of Tunisia and Army Group Afrika.[17]

Sicily

According to Winterbotham, Allied operations beginning with Operation Husky, the invasion of Sicily, were based very largely on Enigma information. Before the start of Husky, SLU 5 at La Marsa, near Carthage, where the principal Allied commanders for the operation had assembled, was handling two hundred signals every twenty-four hours, many of them very long ones, keeping all three watches fully occupied.

In June 1943, Enigma messages disclosed that Kesselring's forward headquarters in Sicily were in the San Dominico Hotel at Taormina, high on the cliffs overlooking the sea. The RAF accordingly dropped a bomb in the center of the former monastery. Kesselring was away in Rome, but the bomb struck the officers' mess and caused considerable loss of life.

Kesselring informed OKW by Enigma of the complete disposition of Italian and German forces in Sicily. From Enigma dispatches it appeared that he feared a landing at Palermo because he stationed part of the German Fifteenth Panzer Division with two Italian field divisions in that area. However, he was obviously uncertain, since he then split the rest of the Fifteenth Panzer Division, together with the Hermann Goering Panzer Division, into three groups in the center of the island, ready to move in any direction.

It was evident from Kesselring's Enigma messages that, although the German units were officially under Italian command, they were, in fact, ordered to operate on their own initiative and that Kesselring was in direct contact with them through the German liaison officer at the headquarters of the Italian General Guzzoni. From the disposition of Axis forces in Sicily, it was clear that the Allied landing areas were only lightly guarded by Italian coast brigades and that, in view of the mountainous terrain, if the few roads to the coast could be denied to the German panzers, the landing operations should meet with little resistance. It was also evident that Kesselring and Guzzoni were unsure where the attack would come and when. Thus Enigma information not only gave the full strength and disposition of the Axis forces, but showed that the Allies could achieve tactical surprise, and, in the event, allowed Allied paratroops to block a number of the German panzers in their race for the beaches.

It was only when the armada of Allied ships sailing from Alexandria, Egypt, had been spotted by the Germans on 9 July 1943 that Enigma messages showed that Axis troops on Sicily and elsewhere were on alert. But the Axis uncertainty as to the precise objectives continued, and the Allies attained a strategic advantage when they landed in Sicily on July 10.

On July 12, Kesselring received an Enigma message from OKW advising him that reinforcements would be arriving in Sicily, but it was too late. Patton, taking advantage of the move of the panzers to hold Montgomery, and knowing from Ultra that there was nothing to stop him, was soon making his famous high-speed left hook toward Palermo and Messina on Sicily's northern coast.

Kesselring had reported to OKW on July 15 that he had checked the British south of Catania on the island's east coast, but by August 8 he was reporting his withdrawal from there. This was followed shortly thereafter by his decision to remove all units to the Italian mainland. The Allied conquest of Sicily ended on 17 August 1943.[18]

Mainland Italy

The invasion of Sicily triggered the collapse of Mussolini's government. At the end of July 1943, he was arrested by the king of Italy. Marshal Pietro Badoglio, the conqueror of Ethiopia, succeeded Mussolini as premier and gave Kesselring assurances, which Kesselring passed on to Hitler in Enigma, that Italy would remain in the war. Hitler, quite rightly, did not believe Badoglio. Within a week, the Italians had started secret negotiations for an armistice with the Allies. Hitler had anticipated this and was already preparing to send German troops into northern Italy should the Italians defect. The first definite news that the Allies had of this, however, was in a message from Hitler to Kesselring in Rome telling him to expect German divisions in northern Italy and to tell the Italians that the troops were to form a strategic reserve for the whole Balkan area, in order not to upset them too much. This northern force, Army Group B, was to be commanded by Field Marshal Rommel.

During August 1943, an Enigma message duly reported Rommel's divisions to be moving into northern Italy, and Kesselring reported the position of his own divisions in southern Italy. More detailed messages gave the route of the reinforcements and the times that they would be passing through Grenoble. As a result, the Fifteenth U.S. Air Force had a field day and apparently inflicted great damage.

At the end of August, Kesselring informed OKW that he had ordered the Tenth Army to start a northward withdrawal of the units in the extreme south of Italy. In a signal to Hitler, he expressed his belief that the Allies would land north of Naples in order to have the shortest march on Rome. In the same message, he reported that the withdrawal north of the panzer divisions from the extreme south was in progress. Montgomery's Eighth Army was thus able to cross from Messina to mainland Italy without serious opposition. Kesselring signaled Berlin that he did not consider this to be the main Allied effort, which he still expected nearer Rome, and that he would continue to withdraw north in accordance with Hitler's instructions.

Winterbotham observes,

> If one analyses the amount of knowledge about the enemy's strength, disposition and intentions available to the Allied command at that time, one cannot help feeling that had the Allied plans been more flexible and had we been able to keep the Italians on the hook a little longer, Kesselring might have been given time to withdraw northward and the misfortunes of Cassino and Anzio might have been avoided.

As it was, on the day the Allied invasion fleet was spotted off the Gulf of Salerno, Gen. Heinrich von Vietinghoff had not yet started to withdraw his troops from the area. Nevertheless, U.S. Gen. Mark Clark's Fifth Army obtained strategic surprise for the actual landing. Vietinghoff quickly moved his panzer corps to the landing area, and after four days of bitter fighting, sent Kesselring an Enigma message that Allied resistance was collapsing and the German Tenth Army was driving the Allies back on a wide front. However, the Fifth Army just managed to hold on, and the threat of the Eighth Army's advance under Montgomery was probably partly responsible for a message from Vietinghoff on 16 September 1943, asking Kesselring's permission to withdraw due to the intense naval and air bombardment. Kesselring gave permission, but ordered Vietinghoff to delay the enemy and deploy his retiring army right across Italy. Kesselring stated that he would do his best to prepare a defensive position on the Volturno and Bifurno Rivers. Hitler had apparently been impressed by Kesselring's ability and strategy, for he now changed his own original orders to move north and sent Kesselring orders to hold the line running eastward, north of Naples, for as long as possible.

At the end of November 1943, Churchill went to the Teheran Conference, taking along an SLU to keep him up to date on Enigma signals and to transmit his own urgent messages.

In an effort to force Kesselring to abandon his Gustav Line and put an end to the bloody battles around Monte Cassino—which towers above the Liri Valley and, together with Monte Cairo, formed a key defensive position in the Gustav Line, dominating the road from Naples to Rome—the Allies decided upon a landing at Anzio, on the coast about thirty miles south of Rome. Nothing in the enemy's Enigma correspondence suggested that the Germans suspected what was to happen, and up to the very moment of landing Gen. Mark Clark was assured of strategic surprise and the probability that no new opposition could be brought to bear before forty-eight hours. In fact, the beachhead was successfully secured. But indecision by Clark, until it was too late to make the drive inland to cut the German Tenth Army's supply lines, nearly proved fatal.

During the fighting around Monte Cassino, Ultra informed the Allies about the German defensive lines in Italy: the Cassino Line, the Adolf Hitler Line across the Liri Valley, and a final one, the Caesar Line, twenty miles south of Rome.

At midnight on 12 May 1944, General Alexander's offensive at Cassino began. Kesselring reported that the main attack on Monte Cassino had been repulsed, but that some ground had been lost south of the town of Cassino. On May 13 he told OKW that available German reserves had been committed.

About noon the same day, Churchill asked to see all the Enigma messages dealing with the Cassino front. As a morale booster he desperately wanted to capture Rome before the beginning of Operation Overlord.

On 14 May 1944, Kesselring reported to Hitler that French Moroccan troops had scaled the mountains south of Cassino and that "the whole Cassino line was now in danger." The next day, Kesselring reported to Hitler a breakthrough by another strong French force over the massive Aurunci Mountains, which dominated the whole Liri Valley and the supply routes to the Cassino Line.

On 16 May 1944 came reports from Kesselring of the successes of the British and Polish forces around Cassino. On May 17 Kesselring ordered the evacuation of the entire Cassino front since the French had penetrated twenty-five miles behind the German lines. On May 18, after extremely heavy and difficult fighting, the Polish Second Corps, a component of the British Eighth Army, captured Monte Cassino, thus opening the road to Rome.[19]

By May 19 it was hard to tell what was going on, even from the Enigma signals. The German Tenth Army signaled desperately for reinforcements, having lost most of two divisions. Kesselring ordered withdrawal from the Liri Valley on May 22, and the next day the Allies began their breakout attack from Anzio. Kesselring reported to Berlin that his Tenth and Fourteenth Armies had been divided by the Allies, and asked Hitler's permission to abandon the Adolf Hitler Line, ten miles behind the abandoned Cassino Line, and to withdraw to the Caesar Line. In another signal, he ordered his last reserve divisions from northern Italy into the battle. On 24 May 1944, Hitler signaled permission to withdraw to the Caesar Line.

On June 2, Kesselring asked Hitler for permission to evacuate Rome without fighting. The next day Hitler agreed. General Alexander's plan, supported by Churchill, to trap and destroy the German armies south of Rome rather than drive them north had failed due to General Clark's not following instructions. Knowing from Kesselring's Enigma signals that Rome was undefended, Clark organized two flying columns and realized his ambition to make a triumphal personal entry into the Eternal City ahead of anyone else. Rome was occupied two days before the opening of Operation Overlord.[20]

Overlord

After the Casablanca Conference in January 1943, Lt. Gen. Sir Frederick Morgan had been chosen by the Allied political and military leaders to be COSSAC—Chief of Staff to the Supreme Allied Commander—to set up planning for Operation Overlord, the Allied invasion of France. By prior arrangement, he was supplied Enigma information already digested and coordinated at the British War Office and Air Ministry, while urgent items were furnished him specially as the occasion arose.

Since 1942, when von Rundstedt left the Russian front and reappeared as commander in chief in the west, there had been a fair stability of the Enigma traffic in that area. The usual strength reports of the more than sixty divisions in the Western Command changed little. The Allies obtained a

17. An Enigma double constructed by the Poles in France. Since at Bruno, outside Paris, the Poles had only three doubles to work with, and they were wearing out from round-the-clock use, in November 1939 Bertrand had ordered parts for 40 copies from a French precision-mechanics firm. Engineer Antoni Palluth and Edward Fokczyński had stripped down one of the Polish machines and prepared detailed drawings of all the parts in a scale of 1:1. Unfortunately, manufacture had proceeded sluggishly, and it was only after the fall of France and the opening of underground work in the Free Zone of the south in October 1940 that *four* machines were finally assembled from parts produced in occupied France. (Bertrand went to Paris under false papers to pick up the parts.) The machine pictured—now in the Sikorski Institute in London—was brought to England in May 1945 by Rejewski and Zygalski, whom Lisicki had sent to France to tie up some loose ends.

    1. "Typing" keys (arranged in *alphabetical* order—in German Enigmas, they were in standard typewriter sequence). 2. Glowlamps. 3. Two rotors for exchange. 4. Entry ring. 5. Three rotors in operational position (with *letters* about their circumferences—German military Enigmas had numbers instead). 6. Reflector. 7. Plugboard (at opposite end from its usual location in German military Enigmas). (From Rejewski's files.)

18. Henryk Zygalski in Algeria, August 1940. On 22 June, France's Marshal Henri Phillippe Pétain had signed an armistice with the invading Germans, and on 24 June Bertrand had evacuated Bruno's international personnel—15 Poles and 7 Spaniards—in three airplanes to Algeria. (Originally appeared in "The Key to the Secrets of the Third Reich," by the author, in *Poland* magazine in 1975. Photo from the author's files.)

19. Henryk Zygalski, Jerzy Różycki, and Marian Rejewski in the gardens at Cadix (Château des Fouzes) before 24 June 1941 (when Różycki sailed for Algiers, never to return). This photo was pasted on the title page of General Gustave Bertrand's copy of his book, which Bertrand sent to Marian Rejewski with a dedication in 1974. (From Rejewski's files.)

20. Polish and Spanish cryptologists at Cadix, in southern France before 24 June 1941. From left: 1. Marian Rejewski, 2. Edward Fokczyński, 4. Henryk Zygalski, 6. Jerzy Różycki, 8. Antoni Palluth. (From the author's files.)

21. Cadix, before 24 June 1941. From left: Captain Jan Graliński (before the war, head of the Cipher Bureau's Russian-decryptment section), Jerzy Różycki, Piotr Smoleński (formerly a civilian employee in Graliński's Russian-decryptment section). All three Poles were to perish on 9 January 1942, in the *Lamoricière* catastrophe. Behind them is, possibly, the very barred window in which a member of the Polish team wanted to photograph himself, thereby incurring Bertrand's anger. (From the author's files.)

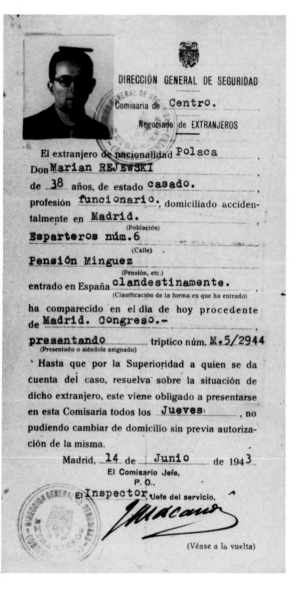

DIRECCIÓN GENERAL DE SEGURIDAD

Comisaría de **Centro.**

Negociado de EXTRANJEROS

El extranjero de nacionalidad **Polaca**
Don**Marian REJEWSKI**
de **38** años, de estado **casado.**
profesión **funcionario.**, domiciliado acciden-
talmente en **Madrid.**
(Población)
Esparteros núm.6
(Calle)
Pensión Minguez
(Pensión, etc.)
entrado en España **clandestinamente.**
(Clasificación de la forma en que ha entrado)
ha comparecido en el día de hoy procedente
de **Madrid. Congreso.-**

presentando tríptico núm. **M.5/2944**
(Presentado o siéndole asignado)
Hasta que por la Superioridad a quien se da
cuenta del caso, resuelva sobre la situación de
dicho extranjero, este viene obligado a presentarse
en esta Comisaría todos los **Jueves**, no
pudiendo cambiar de domicilio sin previa autoriza-
ción de la misma.

Madrid, **14** de **Junio** de 194**3**
El Comisario Jefe,
P. O.,
El **Inspector** Jefe del servicio,

(Véase a la vuelta)

22. Spanish General Directorate of Security registration card issued on 14 June 1943, to "the
foreigner of Polish nationality, Don Marian Rejewski, aged 38 years ... civil servant by
profession, residing *accidentalmente* in Madrid at Calle Esparteros no. 6, in the Pensión
Minguez, having entered Spain *clandestinamente*." Pending resolution of "said foreigner's
situation, he shall be obliged to present himself at this office every Thursday, and may not
change his residence without previous authorization of same."
Rejewski and Zygalski had, on 4 May been released following three months in Spanish
prisons, and it would only be on 3 August 1943 that they would reach Britain. (From
Rejewski's files.)

23. Marian Rejewski (1905-80) as a second lieutenant (signals) of the Polish Army in Britain, in late 1943 or in 1944. (Courtesy Richard Woytak.)

REF. CX/MSG/T531/3

KO 1444 IN TWO
~~NORTHN~~PART ONE.
PART 1

ZZZ

KO 1444 C 1444

KC HS OB 47 C 47 RJ 32 C 32 JY 10 C 10 PK 89 C 89

CR CNA ON CXA CX YKA YK UC ZSA ZS FZ OU 77 C 77 TOA

TO 68 C 68 WM 36 C 36 NX 44 C 44 LF 30 C 30 DL 72 C 72

STR 30 C 30 STA 59 C 59 ST 54 C 54 MI 72 C 72 XF 91 C 91

SHR 55 C 55 FOR WILD SH 23 C 23
IN TWO PARTS, PART ONE %

WA 472 C 472

HITLER C HITLER AT NOUGHT FIVE HOURS TWENTYFIFTH COLON
(ONE) OKW C OKW RESPONSIBLE TO HITLER C HITLER FOR FURTHER
CONDUCT OF OPERATIONS AS A WHOLE. (TWO) THE FOLLOWING TO
DIRECT OPERATIONS IN ACCORDANCE WITH INSTRUCTIONS TO BE
ISSUED THROUGH ARMY CHIEF OF STAFF GENERAL KREBSC KREBS
WHO IS WITH HITLER C HITLER. (ABLE) IN SOUTHERN AREA WITH
HELP OF OPERATIONS STAFF BAKER (GENERAL-LEUTNANT WINTER
C WINTER) COLON ARMY GROUPS SOUTH AND CENTRE, CHARLIES IN
CHARLIE SOUTHWEST C SOUTHWEST, SOUTHEAST C SOUTHEAST, AND
WEST C WEST. (BAKER) IN NORTHERN AREA, DIRECTLY COLON
CHARLIES IN CHARLIE ARMED FORCES NORWAY C NORWAY AND

JB/CAZ/KH   261452Z/4/45

Tel.: Hayes 3831.
Ext.113 & 120

THE WAR OFFICE RECORDS CENTRE (Polish),
Bourne Avenue,
Hayes,
Middlesex.

CONFIDENTIAL   *November*, 1957*

Ref.: Z/PIF/1-1/1905/*UC*

Dear Sir,

In reply to your recent letter, the following are the particulars of the military service of:

No. 32145 Lieutenant (Sig) Marian R.JEWSKI

born on 16th August, 1905 **at** Bydgoszcz, Poland

parents: Jozef and Matylda nee THOMS

Marital status (while serving): Married to Irena neé LEWANDOWSKA

Nationality: Polish   **Religion:** Roman Catholic

Civil occupation (prior to Army Service): Civil Servant

Service with the Polish Forces under British Command:-

from 16th August, 1943 (U.K.) **to** 15th November, 1946, when
discharged on repatriation to Poland.

Service with the Polish Resettlement Corps: ~~Enlisted~~ on
~~Commissioned~~ None

~~enlargement box~~
~~Class W. Reserve~~
~~Unemployed list~~   ~~finally discharged on~~
~~relinquished commission~~
~~(honourably discharged)~~

Former Service and History:-
On 1.9.1939 called up but immediately exempt as
civil servant (War Department). On 17.9.1939, evacuated and proceeded to France
where with Col. Langner's Polish Group was attached to French Military authorities
until 20.6.1940. Then served with Polish Military Underground organisation in
France 21.6.1940 - 30.1.1943. Evacuated to the United Kingdom on 30.1.1943 via
Spain (imprisoned for 3 months), Portugal, Gibraltar, arrived in the U.K. on
3.8.1943 and served there with Polish Forces as above.

Medals and Awards:-
Polish Gold Cross of Merit, Silver Cross of Merit with
Swords, Army Medal.

Remarks: (1, He was commissioned in rank 2/Lt. on 10.10.1943 and
promoted Lieutenant 1.1.1945.
(2, His record and services were satisfactory.

(POLISH)
HAYES
MIDDX.

Yours faithfully,

Mr. Marian Rejewski,
Ulica Dworcowa, 10, M.3,
Bydgoszcz,
POLAND.

14648 (M) 6/56

25. Marian Rejewski's military service record: transcript issued by the War Office Records
Centre (Polish) in England on 8 November 1957, and sent to him in Bydgoszcz, Poland,
where he lived from November 1946 to 1969. (From Rejewski's files.)

26. German armored vehicles on the Saxon (Piłsudski) Square, before the Polish General Staff building and the statue of Prince Józef Poniatowski, during the Warsaw Uprising, 1 August through 2 October 1944. (Reprinted from *Stolica* magazine.)

27. Major Maksymilian Ciężki after his liberation together with Lieutenant Colonel Gwido Langer on 10 May 1945, by American forces from a German camp and their arrival in Britain. Colonel Mayer notes that when Lieutenant Colonel Langer and Major Ciężki arrived in London in mid-1945, "they were received in a[n] unfriendly manner by Col. Gano [chief of the Polish Section II, or Intelligence, in Britain], who believed [a] biased and distorted [account by] Lt. Col. Bertrand ... that the [failure to] evacuat[e] Langer's group [had been] due to the latter's hesitation, lack of iniciative [sic] and almost cowardice.... Langer, bitter, disappointed, convinced that he [had been] betrayed by [the] French [after] they had no more use [for] him, died on 30 [March] 1948. Ciężki died on 9 [November] 1951 after living on subsidies from the Assistance Board for the last three years." In his book, Bertrand would later blame General Louis Rivet, his chief at least from May 1940 until November 1942, for leaving him and the Polish and Spanish teams behind when Rivet fled the November 1942 Nazi occupation of the Vichy Zone. (From Rejewski's files.)

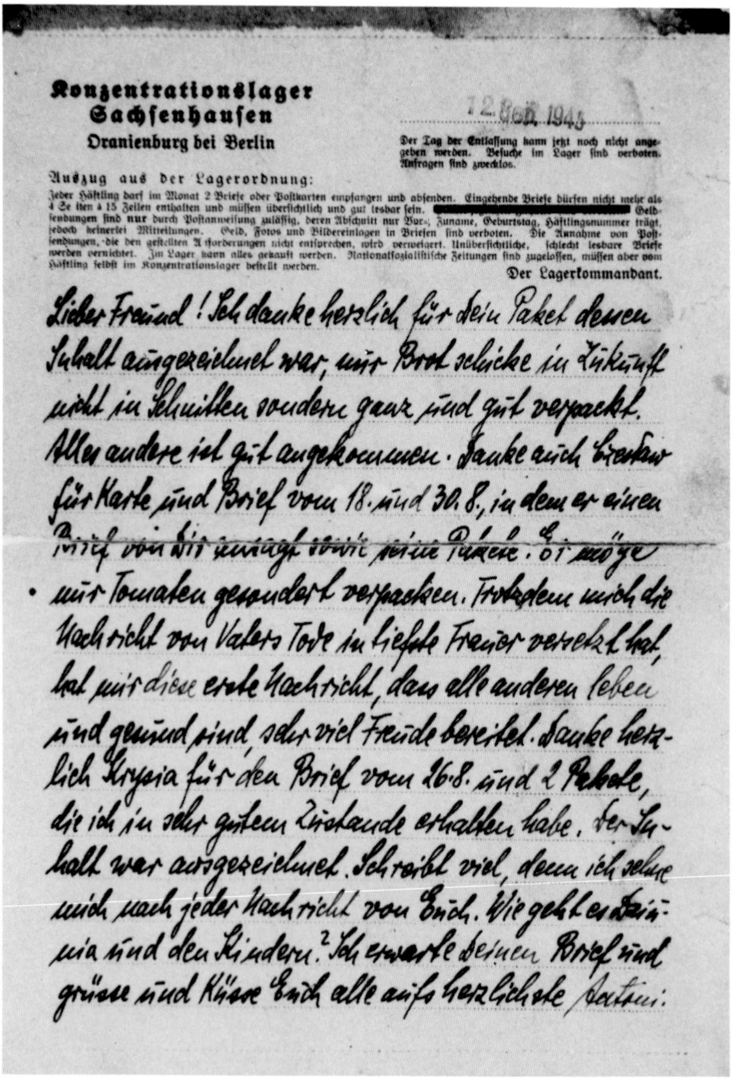

Konzentrationslager Sachsenhausen
Oranienburg bei Berlin

12 Sep 1943

Der Tag der Entlassung kann jetzt noch nicht angegeben werden. Besuche im Lager sind verboten. Anfragen sind zwecklos.

Auszug aus der Lagerordnung:

Jeder Häftling darf im Monat 2 Briefe oder Postkarten empfangen und absenden. Eingehende Briefe dürfen nicht mehr als 4 Seiten à 15 Zeilen enthalten und müssen übersichtlich und gut lesbar sein. [redacted] Geldsendungen sind nur durch Postanweisung zulässig, deren Abschnitt nur Vor-, Zuname, Geburtstag, Häftlingsnummer trägt, jedoch keinerlei Mitteilungen. Geld, Fotos und Bildereinlagen in Briefen sind verboten. Die Annahme von Postsendungen, die den gestellten Anforderungen nicht entsprechen, wird verweigert. Unübersichtliche, schlecht lesbare Briefe werden vernichtet. Im Lager kann alles gekauft werden. Nationalsozialistische Zeitungen sind zugelassen, müssen aber vom Häftling selbst im Konzentrationslager bestellt werden.

Der Lagerkommandant.

Lieber Freund! Ich danke herzlich für dein Paket dessen Inhalt ausgezeichnet war; nur Brot schicke in Zukunft nicht in Schnitten sondern ganz und gut verpackt. Alles andere ist gut angekommen. Danke auch [illegible] für Karte und Brief vom 18. und 30.8., in dem er einen Brief von Dir ansagt sowie seine Pakete. Er möge nur Tomaten gesondert verpacken. Trotzdem mich die Nachricht von Vaters Tode in tiefste Trauer versetzt hat, hat mir diese erste Nachricht, dass alle anderen leben und gesund sind, sehr viel Freude bereitet. Danke herzlich Krysia für den Brief vom 26.8. und 2 Pakete, die ich in sehr gutem Zustande erhalten habe. Der Inhalt war ausgezeichnet. Schreibt viel, denn ich sehne mich nach jeder Nachricht von Euch. Wie geht es Daninia und den Kindern? Ich erwarte deinen Brief und grüsse und Küsse Euch alle aufs herzlichste Antoni.

28. Letter to his family from engineer Antoni Palluth, confined at Sachsenhausen Concentration Camp in Oranienburg, near Berlin, date-stamped 12 September 1943. The letter is written "in German on special Sachsenhausen Concentration Camp stationery, imprinted with an Extract from the Camp Regulations," and is addressed to engineer Stanisław Guzicki in Warsaw. Guzicki, like Palluth, had been associated with the AVA Radio Company before the war; for security, Palluth did not write to his family directly. As Col. Mayer wrote in 1974, Palluth, like his four Polish colleagues arrested with him by the Germans on 13 March 1943, was "acquainted to the last detail with the ... breaking [of] Enigma. [They] did not reveal [the Enigma secret] to the Germans, thus [making it possible to continue] exploiting this source of information till the end of the war." Palluth was killed during an Allied air raid. His colleague Fokczyński died of emaciation and exhaustion. (From the author's files.)

29. Tomb of the Unknown Soldier today. Once more, two soldiers with shouldered arms stand guard around the clock. Visible behind the tomb are the Saxon Gardens. (Reprinted from *Stolica* magazine.)

30. Marian Rejewski as doting grandfather with grandson Wojtek, in his Warsaw apartment in 1976, three of four years before his death on 13 February 1980. At about this time, Rejewski broke ciphered correspondence of the future Marshal Józef Piłsudski dating from 1904. (Courtesy Mrs. Irena Rejewska.)

31. Henryk Zygalski after the war in Britain, where he remained and died in 1978. (From the author's files.)

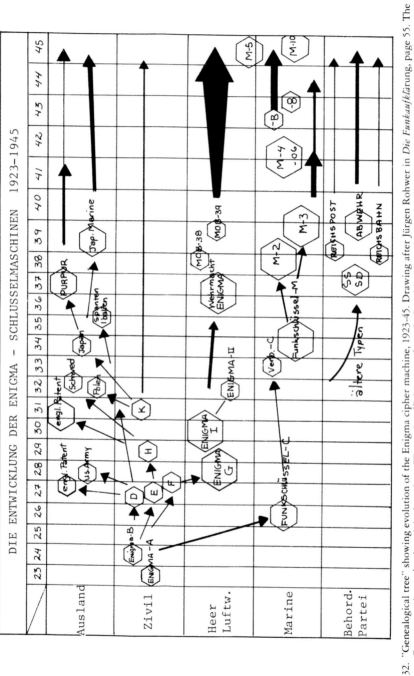

DIE ENTWICKLUNG DER ENIGMA – SCHLUSSELMASCHINEN 1923-1945

32. "Genealogical tree" showing evolution of the Enigma cipher machine, 1923-45. Drawing after Jürgen Rohwer in *Die Funkaufklärung*, page 55. The German caption under the original cautions: "Due to insufficient records on the [machine's] evolution, this diagram can lay no claim to completeness and absolute correctness. Supplementary material and corrections are desired." Note that, according to the chart, the German civil (zivil) model K Enigma of 1931 begat the Japanese machine of 1934, which begat the famous "Purple" (Purpur) of 1937, which was broken by the U.S. in 1941. This would lend support to Marian Rejewski's hypothesis concerning a possible connection between the Polish breaking of the German Enigma at the end of 1932 and the

rough picture of the manpower, equipment, and other shortages, as well as the difficulties experienced over the policy of introducing prisoner of war contingents into the German units. They learned, too, that the actual strength of the new divisions did not amount to more than 50 percent of the total previously thought available. Von Rundstedt complained to OKW about the inadequacies in manpower and in the general condition of defenses. All this information was vital to Allied planners.

Of extreme importance to planning for Overlord in late 1943 was von Rundstedt's own appreciation of where he considered the Allied invasion would take place. He felt the Allies would surely take the shortest sea route and attack in the Pas de Calais area. It was probably this message that sowed the seed of the elaborate deception plan to install a phantom army (the First United States Army Group, supposedly commanded by Patton) in Kent, opposite the Pas de Calais, in order to bolster von Rundstedt's views.

General Morgan had presented his initial plan for Overlord to the Quebec Conference in August 1943. But it was until November that Roosevelt and Churchill, stopping in Cairo on their way to the Teheran Conference, finally agreed on the command structure. General Eisenhower was named supreme commander, and the RAF commander, Arthur William Tedder, his deputy. In February 1944, Eisenhower set up SHAEF—Supreme Headquarters Allied Expeditionary Force. Winterbotham saw to preparing a new network of SLUs for the commanders and their staffs.

By April 1944, the Allies learned from an OKW signal that Rommel had been given command of Army Group B, responsible for the defense of the coast from Holland to Normandy and Brittany as far south as Nantes. Rommel proceeded to send impassioned requests for materials and labor to strengthen the Atlantic wall. His messages, together with Allied aerial photography, gave a good timetable for the construction of the beach and coastal defenses that the Allies would later meet. Despite Rommel's incessant bullying of Berlin for more of everything, he had done a good job with what he had at his disposal.

During the spring of 1944, the Germans made their most important decision affecting the Overlord plans. It arose from a clash of views among Hitler, von Rundstedt, Rommel, Gen. Heinz Guderian, and Gen. Geyr von Schweppenburg, who commanded four panzer divisions that made up the panzer reserve stationed near Paris. The discussions were mostly conducted personally with Hitler in Berlin, but at times he was away at his eastern headquarters at Rastenburg in East Prussia, and the exchange of one or two messages on those occasions gave the Allies the vital clues they needed. Von Rundstedt believed that the Allied invasion would come across the Pas de Calais. Hitler and Rommel firmly believed it would occur on the Normandy beaches. Rommel was convinced that the only way to repel an invasion was on the beaches themselves, and early in 1944 had made plans to deploy the powerful reserve panzer divisions, which were normally stationed not far from Paris, in positions behind the Normandy defenses, where he could quickly get them to the landing areas. He knew that, with the completely inadequate German air defense over Normandy, these divisions could not be moved along the roads by day and that time would be the vital factor if he were to get his tanks to the water's edge. Guderian, who in 1943 had been made inspector general of armor, argued that to commit the precious panzers to the beaches was far too dangerous. In the event of a landing elsewhere, they could not be withdrawn to meet any new threat that might come across the English Channel.

When, at Hitler's suggestion, Guderian went to talk the matter over with Rommel, he took along von Schweppenburg to back him up. Rommel apparently refused to budge from his proposed dispositions and sent a message to Hitler at Rastenburg, reinforcing his previous views that the panzer divisions should be deployed behind the Normandy beaches.

The result was a compromise. In May 1944, Hitler confirmed to von Rundstedt that the four reserve panzer divisions would be held where they were under the direct control of OKW. Had the final decision gone the other way, it would have seriously jeopardized Operation Overlord as it then stood.

About 2 a.m. on D-Day, 6 June 1944, the first signal came through from the German naval headquarters in Paris. It was addressed both to the commander in chief west and to Hitler at his headquarters at Rastenburg, and stated simply that the invasion had commenced. After the war, it was learned that both von Rundstedt and OKW had refused to believe the story. Von Rundstedt is supposed to have told the navy that they had seen a flock of seagulls on their radar. Nevertheless, still believing in a short sea-route invasion, he alerted the Fifteenth Army in the Pas de Calais. His message was a godsend to the Allies, especially as he evidently did not think it worthwhile alerting the Seventh Army in Normandy. He seemed determined to believe that the Allied paratroops being reported to him by the Seventh Army were a bluff. It was dawn before von Rundstedt's chief of staff, Gen. Guenther Blumentritt, sent a message directly to OKW, advising of the urgency of the situation and asking Hitler's permission to employ the OKW panzer reserve. There were no messages from Rommel until later in the morning, when he ordered his chief of staff, Gen. Hans Speidel, to use the Twenty-First Panzer Division against the Allied landings west of Caen. The order came from Germany and showed that Rommel was not on the spot in Normandy.

On the evening of June 6, Hitler released to von Rundstedt the Twelfth Panzer Division from the OKW reserve. But it was too late. By evening the Allies were well ashore, and, in any case, the Twelfth Panzer Division did not dare move until dusk, the sky being full of Allied aircraft.

Late that night, Rommel dispatched his situation report to OKW, stating that "the British advance on Caen had been halted and that the Twenty-First and Twelfth S.S. Panzer Divisions were in position west of the town from the north round to a point some seven miles to the southwest." The Twelfth S.S. Division made remarkable speed as soon as dusk fell.

On June 7, Rommel advised OKW that he had ordered the withdrawal from Brittany of a motorized and an infantry division, together with the XI Parachute Corps, to try to hold the Americans on the Cotentin Peninsula. Von Rundstedt ordered another of the reserve panzer divisions—the Panzer Lehr—to move to the Caen area in addition to the Twelfth S.S. Division.

On June 9, von Rundstedt instructed Rommel to counterattack. Rommel replied to von Rundstedt and OKW: "The Twelfth S.S. Panzer Division has arrived short of fuel and the Panzer Lehr Division is quite unready for action. Under the circumstances no immediate dislodgement of the enemy is possible and a return to the defensive on the Vire-Orne front is necessary until preparations for a counterattack are complete." This message gave Gen. Miles Dempsey and his British Second Army a short breather.

On June 10, Montgomery went over to Normandy. Knowing from Enigma correspondence about the mounting German tank forces and enemy intentions, he changed the original plan, which had provided for the capture of Caen by British and Canadian forces. He decided to pin down as many of the main enemy armored forces as possible, in order to give Gen. Omar Bradley's First Army a chance to try to break out to the south against less heavily armed resistance. A British thrust by the Seventh Armoured Division toward Caen on June 10 drew the German panzers into the open, and the Panzer Lehr Division was reported by Rommel on the night of June 13 as having "lost 100 tanks and as now being unable to thrust towards the sea."

The same night, Bradley's forces secured the important little town of Casteau at the eastern base of the Cherbourg Peninsula, with its main road and railway connections. On June 14 Rommel signaled the loss to OKW, at the same time reporting: "I am satisfied at the moment that the American landing at the east of Vierville [Omaha beach] is only making slow progress and the Caen front is now held."

On June 18, Hitler signaled orders to von Rundstedt to attack Bayeux and also signaled the garrison commander at Cherbourg that "the port must be held at all costs." But the U.S. VIII Corps pushed across the peninsula to the western coast, cutting off Cherbourg and the northern half of the Cotentin. On June 18, Rommel had to signal to OKW the almost total loss of his Ninety-First and Seventy-Seventh Divisions.

As the Americans started closing in on Cherbourg, Hitler sent a personal message to Gen. Karl Wilhelm von Schlieben, commander of the garrison:

> Even if the worst comes to the worst, it is your duty to defend the last bunker and leave the enemy not a harbour but a heap of ruins. The German people and the whole world are watching your fight; on it depends the conduct and result of operations to smash the Allied beachhead and the honour of the German Army and of your own name.

Von Schlieben signaled to Hitler: "In view of the great superiority of the enemy in aircraft, tanks and artillery, and now finally the naval bombardment, I must state in the line of duty that further sacrifices can alter nothing." Rommel's reply was short: "You will continue to fight to the last cartridge in accordance with the orders of the Fuehrer."

Further Enigma dispatches informed the Allies that around Caen the three German armored divisions were now in full working order, even if a bit short of tanks, and that the Ninth and Tenth Armored Divisions were on their way from the Russian front to the Caen area. This was soon followed by another message from OKW to von Rundstedt and Rommel, that the First S.S. Panzer Division was coming across from Belgium and the Second S.S.

Panzer Division was coming up from Toulouse to the Saint Lô area on the U.S. sector. This and other Enigma information caused major changes in Allied operational plans.

In late June 1944, von Rundstedt and Rommel saw Hitler at Berchtesgaden, proposed a phased withdrawal from Caen in order to put their divisions out of range of Allied naval guns, and asked for reinforcements to be sent from the Fifteenth Army, which was still sitting in the Pas de Calais area waiting for Patton's phantom attack. Hitler refused, apparently still fearing another landing in the Pas de Calais. This was not known to the Allies at the time, but the day after von Rundstedt got back from Berchtesgaden with Rommel, Hitler—as was his custom—sent a mesage to von Rundstedt confirming his decision and stating, "Present positions are to be held." That was the first indication from Enigma that von Rundstedt and Rommel wanted to withdraw. Eventually, as was learned after the war, von Rundstedt phoned Keitel, telling him that it would be impossible to carry out Hitler's orders to attack Bayeux. When Keitel asked what they should do, von Rundstedt replied, "Make peace, you fools . . . !" Next day von Rundstedt was relieved of command, to be replaced as commander in chief west by Field Marshal Günther von Kluge.

Probably warned by Rommel that Hitler was wont to order attacks by nonexistent or nonoperational units, von Kluge sent to OKW and OKH a careful inventory of the formations under his command. This brought the Allies up to date on the strengths and losses of the German units. Especially valuable was information that the Fifth Panzer Army had even fewer serviceable tanks than Allied intelligence had estimated.

On 10 July 1944, Gen. Omar Bradley renewed his attack on Saint Lô. The capture of the strategically important town was finally accomplished on July 17. As Bradley was moving into Saint Lô, Montgomery was bringing pressure on Caen to keep the panzers away from the Americans, who could now prepare the planned breakout by the U.S. First Army. By July 18 the British and Canadians had cleared the whole of Caen of the enemy.

On 25 July 1944, Bradley's breakout Operation Cobra began, and that evening von Kluge sent a message to OKW that "from this moment the front has burst." Over the next couple of days, Cobra turned into a rout. As the Americans advanced, a large pocket of German troops on the left of the German line were cut off and surrounded. Gen. Paul Hausser, in command of the German Seventh Army, ordered them to break out to the southeast. His dispatch, which the Allies did not get, was apparently picked up by von Kluge who, fearing for his disintegrating left flank, sent orders countermanding Hausser's order for the breakout. This signal showed that von Kluge was out of touch with the situation. On the strength of that Enigma message, U.S. Maj. Gen. Elwood R. Quesada's fighter-bombers had a field day. Only a few of the enemy who escaped the pocket got back to their comrades, with all their transport and equipment destroyed.

As the rout gathered momentum, von Kluge was unable to find out what was going on. His messages to Hausser's Seventh Army, demanding information, remained unanswered, and it was only on 31 July 1944 that von Kluge was finally able to signal Hitler at OKW that the Americans had already occupied Avranches (they had arrived the day before). Von Kluge went on to admit that, apart from Avranches, the situation was completely unclear, that the Allied air activities were unprecedented, and that the Americans had ripped open the western front.

Hitler signaled von Kluge that he had taken over command of the whole western theater. Among his orders was one to all units in the west that "if withdrawal was ordered, all railways, locomotives, bridges and workshops were to be destroyed and that the commanders of the fortress ports were to fight to the last man to deny the ports to the Allies."

On 2 August 1944, in a long message, Hitler told von Kluge "not to pay any attention to the American breakout, which would be dealt with later," and gave detailed instructions to collect four of the armored divisions from the Caen front with sufficient infantry divisions and make a decisive counterattack to retake Avranches and thus divide the U.S. forces at the base of the Cherbourg Peninsula. He was then to roll the U.S. forces to the north of the armored thrust back to the sea, in a repeat of the successful strategy in the 1940 Battle of France. This highly important Enigma message was immediately sent to Churchill and the Allied Supreme Command.

The following day, von Kluge replied to Hitler in an equally long signal, setting out all the possible consequences of such a move. "Apart from withdrawing the essential defensive armoured divisions from Caen, such an attack, if not immediately successful, would lay open the whole attacking force to be cut off in the west."

Next day, in another long message, Hitler acknowledged von Kluge's argument, but said "the situation demands bold action. The attack to split the American forces must be carried out."

Thanks to Enigma, the Allies had been given three days' warning. Eisenhower prepared to change the whole plan of the broad frontal advance eastward across France and seize the chance to encircle and destroy the bulk of the German armies in the west. It was, comments Winterbotham, "a bizarre situation with Eisenhower and Ultra deciding the fate of the German armies with the help of Hitler." Churchill was getting Hitler's messages within an hour of their dispatch.

On 5 August 1944, von Kluge made one more attempt to dissuade Hitler and boldly stated that the attack could only end in disaster. Hitler replied without further comment, ordering the execution of his orders.

On August 6, Montgomery duly issued the order swinging three Allied armies, the British Second, the Canadian II Corps, and the U.S. First Army into the flanks of the German forces, and for the U.S. Third Army to pass them on the southern flank. That same day, von Kluge faithfully carried out Hitler's orders. The Allies' ability to read his Enigma correspondence with Hitler had given them four vital days to prepare for the German onslaught.

In the afternoon of August 7, von Kluge radioed his situation report to OKW: "The attack has been brought to a standstill with the loss of over half the tanks." He proposed to disengage his remaining forces at Mortain to cover the British strike toward Falaise. But Hitler replied: "I command the attack to be prosecuted daringly and recklessly to the sea, regardless of the risk." He went on to instruct von Kluge that, far from reinforcing Gen. Heinrich Eberbach's remaining panzer group at Falaise, he was to "remove forces from Eberbach and commit them to the Avranches attack in order to bring about the collapse of the enemy's Normandy front by a thrust into the deep flank and rear of the enemy facing the Seventh Army." The Fuehrer, unaware that the Allies were reading his Enigma correspondence, continued with his rather hysterical rhetoric: "The greatest daring, determination and imagination must give wings to all echelons of command. Each and every man must believe in victory. Cleaning up in rear areas and in Brittany can wait until later."

Accordingly, von Kluge sent a message to Eberbach early that evening, telling him to send three of his precious panzer divisions, with which he was desperately defending Falaise, to Mortain to comply with Hitler's orders. He told Eberbach that continuation of the attacks on Avranches, if they failed, could lead to collapse of the entire Normandy front, but "the order from Hitler was so unequivocal, it must be obeyed." In the event, a massive Allied armor and bomber counterattack toward Falaise aborted the German move to reinforce Mortain.

Although SHAEF was not due to move from Portsmouth to Granville, on the west coast of the Cherbourg Peninsula, until August 9, as a result of the Enigma correspondence Eisenhower was already at Bradley's headquarters and set in motion the operation to surround the three German armies.

After the thwarting of the German attempt to move armor from Falaise to Mortain, von Kluge had sent Hitler an Enigma message in the middle of the night, stating that the attack could not now take place. Hitler replied: "The front attack has been launched too early and was too weak, a new attack must be launched on August the eleventh." He ordered "a massive attack by several corps to be commanded by Eberbach himself." The latter replied that there could be no attack before August 20.

On 10 August 1944, von Kluge signaled OKW that the Americans were moving north to Argentan, and, for the first time, he warned OKW that he was threatened with envelopment. The Allies had known what was happening for the past four days. Now von Kluge learned that his worst fears were becoming reality.

By August 11 Hausser signaled von Kluge that he had lost a hundred tanks, and Eberbach, who had orders from von Kluge to drive off the threat from the U.S. XV Corps from the south, informed von Kluge, "my ammunition and fuel supplies are already short. Due to Allied aircraft, I cannot move in the daytime and some of my divisions exist in name only." There was now a gap of only thirty miles between the Canadian and U.S. forces, and in the bag to the west, which was slowly shrinking under the pressure of the First U.S. and Second British Armies, were the German Seventh Army and Fifth Panzer Army. Their commanders warned von Kluge that if the front was not withdrawn immediately, the Army Group would have to write off both armies. This Enigma message was repeated to OKW.

Just as Maj. Gen. Wade H. Haislip was preparing his U.S. XV Corps to attack north to capture Argentan, he received instructions from Bradley to stop offensive operations and await further orders. In the plans for Overlord, a line of demarcation had been drawn dividing the operational zones of the British and U.S. forces, and that line passed through Argentan. This meant that Montgomery would have to give Bradley permission to cross the line from the south. For twenty-four vital hours Bradley waited. The delay ultimately allowed a large part of the German forces to escape the bag.

On August 16, von Kluge signalled OKW recommending immediate withdrawal of all forces through the Argentan-Falaise gap, adding that "hesitation in accepting this recommendation would result in unforeseeable developments."

On the same day the Canadians finally took Falaise, now only a pile of rubble. Only then did Montgomery propose to Bradley that they should close the pocket, meeting halfway between Falaise and Argentan. The gap was still fifteen miles wide, and after dark the German escape from the pocket began. Not until midnight on August 20 was the exit from the bag finally sealed by the Polish First Armored Division, commanded by Gen. Stanisław Maczek.[21] By then, between twenty and thirty thousand German troops had escaped east, many of them veteran panzer men.

A signal on August 16 had informed von Kluge that Marshal Walther Model would take over the German armies in the west. On the night of 18 August 1944, Field Marshal von Kluge, who had dared to question the Fuehrer's orders, set off for Germany. On the way, he committed suicide.

Winterbotham remarks that the Allied reading of Enigma messages between Hitler and von Kluge that led to the Battle of Falaise and the destruction of a large part of the German Army in the west was "probably Ultra's greatest triumph."[22] Until the ultimate German collapse in May 1945, many more Enigma messages would be read, but none as crucial. When there were no Enigma signals available to guide the Allies, the extent to which the Allies had come to rely on Enigma information was made plain.[23]

Germany's V weapons

Several years before World War II, intensive German work had begun on flying bomb and rocket propelled missiles. The embryo of the largest testing range came into being in 1932, before Hitler's rise to power, at the Reichswehr artillery range in Kummersdorf, where experiments were conducted on the application of various types of liquid fuel in missles. During the years 1937-39 the Germans built at Peenemünde, at a cost of ten million marks, the world's largest center for missile experimentation. During the war, this center was further expanded. Work on the V (Vergeltungswaffe— retaliation weapon) missiles was accelerated, especially beginning in early 1943, when Hitler declared total war following the reverses suffered by Rommel's armies, the Allied landings in North Africa, and the surrender of Paulus's Sixth Army at Stalingrad.

According to Winterbotham,[24] the reading of Enigma correspondence played an important role in the investigation of the Germans' V-1 flying bomb. Early in 1943, agents had reported on a secret flying bomb.[25] The V-1 first appeared on Enigma in a message ordering special antiaircraft protection for the "FZG76" site on the Baltic Sea. A British scientific intelligence expert, Dr. R.V. Jones, surmised that the Germans might try to use radar to plot the missiles they were developing. If so, they might call on their most experienced radar plotters. Believing that the latter were in the Fourteenth and Fifteenth Companies of the Luft Nachrichten Versuchs Regiment, Jones briefed his contact at Bletchley to look out for anything concerning these two companies and to inform him if one of them moved up the Baltic coast. A month or two later, an Enigma message showed that the Fourteenth Company had moved there and had begun plotting the flights of the flying bombs. From the broadcast plots, Jones worked out the disposition of all the plotting stations and obtained detailed performance figures on most of the flying bomb trials. According to Winterbotham, when Jones had worked out the coordinates of the launching point at Peenemünde by backtracking from the radar plots, he asked for a spy plane sortie over that point and over the other launching point, which he had similarly identified a few miles farther along the coast at Zempin. The photographs showed the two launching sites, with a V-1 on the ramp at Peenemünde. Peenemünde was bombed in August 1943, and the damage was so great that production of the V-1 was put back six months. Both the radar plots and Enigma signals ceased for a while. Enigma returned when the launching site was transferred to Blizna in south-central Poland and signals again had to be put on the air.

As the time for Overlord approached, many reports came in from agents of the construction of launching sites on the French coast. These sites were photographed and bombed as they appeared, forcing the Germans to make prefabricated mobile ramps in order to avoid their destruction.

In April 1944, Ultra produced Hitler's orders to establish a special headquarters near Amiens, France, to control the V-1 operation. The new headquarters was to be commanded by Col. Max Wachtel and was called the 155th Flak Regiment. Since the message was also addressed to Gen. Erich Heinemann, commanding the LXVI Corps, the new regiment would evidently come under his administrative command.

At the end of May 1944, an Enigma message from Wachtel to Heinemann reported that fifty sites were ready to launch the missiles. This, according to Winterbotham, finally convinced Churchill to press for the start of Overlord in June, at all costs. On D-Day, Wachtel received orders to prepare for an immediate all-out offensive to start June 12. The first V-1 landed on June 13.

Electronic warfare

On 9 June 1940, while the evacuation of British troops from Dunkirk was under way and two weeks before the final collapse of France, an Enigma message was decrypted at Bletchley which gave exceptionally important information concerning German trials of two powerful radio transmitters equipped with directional antennas. These transmitters, which broadcast directional beams intended to guide Luftwaffe raids to target, were located at

Cleves, near the French border, and at Bredstedt in Schleswig-Holstein. Soon it was discovered that the two beams intersected in the vicinity of the town of Retford, in central England. Over the next several months, through the autumn of 1940, as the British instituted successive electronic counter-measures, Enigma decrypts supplied clues to further German attempts to surmount these countermeasures and regain the initiative in the electronic war.[26] The first of these, Lorentz, was instituted by the Germans in July 1940, and was followed in August by Knickebein, and finally in the autumn of the same year by a system that the British christened Ruffian.

Until recently, the standard explanation for the Royal Air Force's capacity to anticipate German air raids and to meet the Germans, often before they had even crossed the English Channel, was Britain's use of radar. Now it has become clear that the decisive factor in Germany's loss of the Battle of Britain may well have been Allied mastery of Enigma.

Psychological warfare

The least known aspect of Bletchley's work involves its role in British psychological warfare, including the black propaganda campaigns waged by radio stations such as Gustav Siegfried Eins, Radio Calais, Atlantiksender, and others. These radio stations simulated the transmitters of ostensible resistance groups within the Wehrmacht and other instrumentalities of the Third Reich, and voiced both nationalistic slogans and opposition to a Hitler, a Nazi party, and an S.S. that were leading Germany to inevitable disaster. This Allied propaganda, which was meant to spread defeatism among the German populace and military, exploited all available information on the internal situation of Germany and her armed forces, drawing it equally from monitoring of official German radio stations, from captured documents and prisoner-of-war interrogation, and from secret-agent and radio intelligence. The enormous masses of Enigma decrypts during the years 1940-45 clearly supplied much material that, after suitable editing, was used in Allied psychological warfare.

NOTES

1. Lewin, *Ultra Goes to War*, 51ff.

2. Ibid., 56.

3. About the origin of the name "Ultra," Winterbotham writes:

> I felt it was necessary...to distinguish our particular Enigma Intelligence completely from other types which came under the headings of Secret or Most Secret (the American category of Top Secret had not yet arrived on the scene), so I had a talk with each of the directors to see if we could decide on a name by which it would be known to all those persons on the list I kept of authorized recipients. The title of Ultra Secret was suggested, but the final agreement was just to call it Ultra.

Winterbotham, *The Ultra Secret*, Chap. 3.

4. Calvocoressi, *Top Secret Ultra*, 49-53.

5. Later, the Joint Intelligence Committee, comprising the directors of intelligence of the armed services and representatives of the Foreign Office and the Ministry of Economic Warfare, also received Ultra materials.

Winterbotham notes that in the course of the war he lost his personal control of Hut 3 and its "Shadow OKW", and that, while Menzies never told him the real reason, he

> gradually pieced together the facts that the Foreign Office and the directors of Intelligence of the armed services became alarmed at the power that Ultra had placed in Menzies' hands, so that the Foreign Office decided to place control of this vital source of information in the hands of the Joint Intelligence Committee, which was given a Foreign Office chairman (Cavendish-Bentinck). It had been considered advisable to put all the departments at Bletchley under one director, Commander Travis, who was put in to replace Commander Denniston, the real founder of Ultra, now posted back to London on other cryptographic duties.

Winterbotham, *The Ultra Secret*, Chap. 10.

6. Randell, *"The COLOSSI."*

7. According to Rejewski's comment cited in chapter 9, the perforated sheets that the Poles had been using since 1938 were ideally suited to computerization.

8. Randell, *"The COLOSSI."*

9. Peter Calvocoressi in Rohwer and Jäckel, *Die Funkaufklärung*, 88ff.

10. Winterbotham, *The Ultra Secret*, 28-29, 34-35.

11. Ibid., 37-39.

12. Ibid., 41-61.

13. Ibid., 64-82.

14. Norman, *Secret Warfare*, 123ff. Active in Italian intelligence in the years 1939-43 was a special *Penetrazione Squada* that similarly penetrated all the other diplomatic posts in Rome, except for the Soviet and Japanese Embassies.

15. Schramm, *Der Geheimdienst in Europa 1935-1945*, 183ff.

16. Ibid., 187. According to Erich Hüttenhain ("The Successes and Failures of the German Cryptological Services during World War II," in Rohwer and Jäckel, *Die Funkaufklärung*), in 1939 there were seven different German institutions working on the decryptment of foreign secret communications. They are summarized in the following table:

Institution	No. of decryptment personnel	Seat	Nature of foreign communications
Foreign Office	200	Berlin	Diplomatic
OKW (Armed Forces High Command)	500	Berlin	Diplomatic, agents
Navy	700	Berlin, naval bases	Navies
Army	600	Berlin, field staffs	Armies, agents
Air Force	1,000	Berlin, air fleets	Air forces
Research Office (Forschungsamt)	1,500	Berlin	Diplomatic
Chief Reich Security Office	?	Berlin	Agents

Thus, according to incomplete data (no figure is given for the Reichsicherheitshauptamt, or RSHA), already, in 1939, the Germans employed a total of at least forty-five hundred people in their foreign-decryptment services. Compared to the corresponding numbers for Britain (about two hundred), France (about one hundred thirty) and especially Poland (about sixty), this was a staggering number and invalidates the view that Germany attached little importance to having a large intelligence establishment (the argument is that the aggressor chooses the time and place of attack and therefore does not need so much information). Indeed, the reverse was true.

There was, however, great diffusion and duplication in German decryptment efforts. Also, there was inadequate coordination among agencies charged with developing German codes and ciphers; the latter were six: the first five in the table above, plus the Abwehr (military intelligence). Finally, there was inadequate liaison between cipher- and code-breakers on the one hand and -makers on the other: some degree of contact existed only within the first three institutions.

This state of affairs lasted into the first years of the war. Some thought began to be given to the situation only in 1943, when higher commands and staffs started wondering about the causes of the growing numbers of defeats being suffered by the German military machine. But even in 1943, OKW was unable to convince Ribbentrop, Goering, and Himmler of the need for centralized control of the various German codes and ciphers, especially those that were being newly introduced; it was only in October 1943 that approval of crypto-systems was centralized for the armed forces. Only in November 1944, when Allied armies were approaching Germany's borders from both the east and the west and total defeat loomed for the Thousand Year Reich, did Hitler issue from his bunker under the Reich Chancellery an order entitled "Procedures for Encryption in the Wehrmacht, Waffen-SS, Party and Reich Authorities," making the Signals and Cryptographic Agency of the Wehrmacht High Command (Ag WNV/Chi) responsible for the cryptological security of all encrypting systems (ciphers, codes, and equipment for secret conversation) that had been or might be introduced in the Wehrmacht, S.S. formations, the NSDAP (Nazi party) and administrative agencies.

In 1942 a special office had been created within the Cryptographic Agency of the OKW Signals Department to study the security of German ciphers and codes; into it had been transferred, from various cryptological agencies, twelve cryptologists and numerous auxiliary personnel, including statisticians. However, it was early 1944 before this office established contact with other cryptological agencies. A special interagency committee to study the security of ciphers and codes was formed, and, at five sessions from August to October 1944, it successively studied all the encrypting procedures then in use. Looked into at the first of these sessions was Enigma, which was beginning to cause uneasiness; the anxiety apparently was not serious, however, since the result was merely recommendation of three minor amendments to procedures for operating the machine.

17. Winterbotham, *The Ultra Secret*, 93-103.

18. Ibid., 105-8.

19. Cassino was the location the Germans had chosen to establish their main defense of Rome; hence, the battle of Cassino was the battle for Rome. The fourth battle of Cassino, 11-18 May 1944, which culminated in the Poles' capture of Monte Cassino, cost the Polish Second Corps 4,199 men (924 killed; 2,930 wounded; 345 missing). Corresponding German losses totalled 1,100 men. A Polish military cemetery now stands on the slopes of Monte Cassino. *See also* Majdalany, *The Battle of Cassino*.

During World War II, Polish units fought on land, sea, and in the air from the very first day of the European war to the last, on virtually every front, from Narvik in Norway to Tobruk in Libya, from the Atlantic and Britain to Lenino in Byelorussia, and were among the first to raise an Allied flag over Berlin. The Polish armed forces and government never made a general surrender to the Germans, but went underground or into exile, and Poland was the only Nazi-occupied country in which the Germans were unable to put together even the beginnings of a Quisling-type collaborationist government (no Pole would have participated in one, or would long have survived the anger of his countrymen had he done so). Poland and the German-occupied parts of the Soviet Union were the only territories where the Germans implemented a systematic "policy of eradication" (Ausrottungspolitik) of the nation's potential leaders, chiefly the educated, and a policy of "collective responsibility"—of mass reprisals for the killing of German military or civilian occupation personnel; in no other countries besides those two did the Germans kill so many people (between 10 and 20 percent of the population) or pursue such a systematic and ruthless program of destroying their cultural heritage. (This was in keeping with German Drang nach Osten—Drive to the East—traditions reaching back to prehistoric times: much of eastern Germany, including Berlin and all the area to the River Elbe, had once been Slavic territoiry, and as late as the Franco-Prussian War of 1870 the mass of Prussian enlisted men and noncommissioned officers spoke a Slavic language; even today, in East Germany there live three hundred fifty thousand Lusatians who speak a language closely related to Polish.)

In September 1939, nearly one hundred thousand Polish soldiers and airmen evacuated from Poland to the West via Hungary, Rumania, Lithuania, and the other Baltic countries. (The Polish Navy had been sent to Scotland in August 1939.) A further one hundred thousand men joined them after the German invasion of the Soviet Union in 1941, when the Soviets permitted the Polish government in exile, in London, to form Polish Army units of its citizens on Soviet soil, under Gen. Władysław Anders, and to evacuate them to the Middle East in 1942. By war's end, there would be two hundred fifty thousand Polish soldiers, sailors, and airmen in the west, with most of the balance comprising Poles who had been inducted into the German armed forces and who had availed themselves of opportunities to surrender to the Allies.

In 1943, further Polish units were formed in the U.S.S.R. under Gen. Zygmunt Berling, and subsequently accompanied the Soviet armies through Byelorussia, the Ukraine, and Poland, on to Germany and Czechoslovakia. At war's end, the Polish First and Second Armies in the East would number 385,000 men and women (185,000 in front-line, and 200,000 in second-line and reserve units). *See Polski czyn zbrojny w II wojnie światowej*; also, Kozaczuk, "The System of Command of the Polish Army Higher Formations in the East in the Final Period of the Second World War."

By the time of the Battle of Lenino in Byelorussia (12-13 October 1943), and certainly by the Battle of Monte Cassino in Italy in 1944, the approximately 80 percent of the Polish soldiers in both west and east who hailed from east of the Bug River and the Curzon Line (the postwar eastern border of Poland) already knew that they would never return home: it had been settled that the eastern third of prewar Poland—73 percent of whose population were Ukrainians, Byelorussians, and other non-Poles—would remain in the Soviet Union. After the war, only 10 percent of the two hundred fifty thousand Polish soldiers, sailors, and airmen in the West returned to Poland.—ED.

20. Winterbotham, *The Ultra Secret*, 109-18.

21. On August 7, even before encountering the Germans, the Polish First Armored Division had

sustained losses when American planes bombed artillery positions backing the Fifty-first High-land Division and Polish rear units that were just setting out to attack.

On August 17, Lt. Gen. Guy Simonds, an enthusiastic Ultra user and commander of the Canadian Second Corps, into which the Polish First Armored Division had been incorporated, had visited Polish headquarters with orders from Montgomery for the Poles to take Chambois. They had done so, thereby sealing off the gigantic "Argentan pocket"—an action that was to become decisive for the battle of Normandy and for the entire French campaign. This brought against the Poles all the fury of the trapped German First and Second Corps. At the same time, from outside the pocket, German armies to the east, especially the Twenty-first S.S. Infantry Division, concentrated ceaseless artillery fire upon the Poles. On August 20, due to the desperate, concentrated German attacks, the Polish division found itself practically alone: the Polish division was up against two German armies. When, that same day, the Polish Tenth Armored Cavalry Regiment captured the German General Elpelt and his staff as they tried to break through to the east with several Panther tanks, his first words to General Maczek were: "Sir, I do not know whether you are my prisoner or I am yours." In fact, the Polish division was all but surrounded by the Germans; all day, the Poles withstood constant attacks from all sides, eventually to be cut off from the Canadians. Finally, after two days, on August 22, the Fourth Canadian Armored Division broke through to contact the Polish units, which, in turn, contacted elements of a U.S. division and a French armored regiment. The Falaise gap had been closed, the Battle of Normandy had been won. On visiting the battlefield, General Simonds' superior and fellow Ultra user, Lt. Gen. Henry Crerar, commanding the First Canadian Army, stated he had "never before seen devastation on a scale, and it was evident that the whole fury of the two S.S. Corps attempting to break out of the ring was unleashed against the Poles." The Polish First Armored Division had sustained the loss of 325 dead, 1,200 wounded, 114 missing; the Germans—5,063 men and much equipment. The Germans never really recovered from the shock that they suffered at the Argentan pocket.

The subsequent route of the Polish First Armored Divison took it to Belgium: Ypres, then Roulers, Ruisselede, Thielt, and Ghent. After liberating Ghent on 16 September 1944, the division proceeded on through Holland—Axel, Zaamslaag, and, finally, Terneuzen on the sea. Next, the divison took an airfield near Gilze and liberated Breda on 30 October 1944. After four days of brutal fighting and heavy losses, the division crossed the Mark Canal on November 3 and, after fierce fighting, took Moerdijk. The first sizable town encountered in Germany was Haren. Finally, on 6 May 1945, the Polish colors flew over Wilhelmshaven, Germany's largest naval base; the same day, at Sillenstede, an enemy parachute division surrendered formally to the Poles. Lorentz, *Caen to Wilhelmshaven with the Polish First Armoured Division.*—ED.

22. Winterbotham, *The Ultra Secret*, 119-58.

23. For example, Winterbotham writes of "the apparent failure of Ultra to warn either Eisenhower, Bradley or Montgomery of Hitler's offensive through the Ardennes" (the Battle of the Bulge) in December 1944. Winterbotham, *The Ultra Secret*, Chapter 19. However, Calvocoressi states that Bletchley had sufficient grounds to believe there were strong German armored forces in the Ardennes, and so informed the Allied High Command. He also maintains that Ultra gave a fairly full and disquieting picture of German forces available to move against the Allied parachute operation at Arnhem in September 1944. Calvocoressi, *Top Secret Ultra.*

24. Winterbotham, *The Ultra Secret*, 119-21.

25. In fact, as early as 1939, in an anonymous "Oslo report" that had been dropped one night at the British Embassy in Norway, the British had been warned about German weapon development, including missiles, but the British either had paid scant attention to the warning, considering it propaganda aimed at demoralizing them, or had lost themselves in vain speculations. In the summer of 1941, Polish underground intelligence, having obtained fragmentary and vague information, began their efforts to penetrate the secret of Hitler's miracle weapons. In the summer of 1942 they supplied the first information to the British, supplemented with more details in 1943. This information included the site of the secret V-1 (flying, or buzz, bomb) and V-2 (rocket) works at Peenemünde, which were duly bombed on the night of 17-18 August, 1943, by over six hundred R.A.F. bombers. Subsequently, the Germans moved their missile production into underground tunnels in the Harz Mountains, and their flight tests to occupied Polish territory (Blizna, near the town of Kolbuszowa). The British kept up unremitting pressure on

the Polish underground to supply data on the V-2s, even suggesting that the Poles steal an entire missile. The Poles forwarded, to the British, information—obtained from analysis of missile fragments—on the fuel used in the rockets and on their radio guidance (the latter determined by Professor Janusz Groszkowski—see chapter 4, note 4). In the early summer of 1944, they succeeded in spiriting away an unexploded, virtually intact V-2 from where it had fallen into the Bug River, near Sarnaki, before the Germans arrived to retrieve it. The Poles concealed the missile, stripped it down, and, on the night of 25-26 July 1944, forwarded the key parts to London in a Douglas DC-3 Dakota that had been specially sent to Poland; over a hundred members of the Polish underground participated in secretly landing the plane and sending it off—the third such Operation Most (Bridge)—in difficult circumstances and practically in full view of the Germans.

The Polish underground army (Armia Krajowa—A.K.) officer and ex-inmate of Auschwitz who took the V-2 parts to England aboard the Dakota, Jerzy Chmielewski (pseudonym "Rafał"—Raphael) had been warned by the A.K. chief of intelligence, Kazimierz Iranek-Osmecki:

> There are [British] tendencies to depreciate our [Polish] contribution to the war effort. . . . If [the V-2 parts] that you are taking should deprive [the Germans of the victory that they believe the V-2 will bring them], there will be forces that will want to prevent the Poles being given credit for it. Your premature and unauthorized dispossession of the "shards" [V-2 parts] might facilitate the creation of appearances that they were worthless.

The warning proved apt. Already during the flight to Italy, the Dakota's British crew asked to be given the V-2 parts; later, the pilots announced that it might be necessary to bail out and again requested that the Polish payload be turned over to them. Chmielewski replied that if he jumped, it would be together with the knapsack containing the V-2 parts. Upon arrival in London, Chmielewski was taken from the airfield straight to a villa outside the city, and attempts were made to separate the knapsack from him by force. Only when Chmielewski told the Britons that the V-2 parts would be of no use to them without certain explanations from him (which was not true) did they drive him back to London and put him in touch with Polish officers authorized to take delivery of the V-2 parts. Subsequently, Chmielewski was given a sizable monetary reward, the use of a small house in a London suburb, and, finally, an audience with Churchill. The prime minister later, in his *Second World War*, mentioned Chmielewski (though not by name), confusing and combining his story with that of another A.K. officer, the engineer Antoni Kocjan, who had been involved in the discovery of Peenemünde and the securing of the V-2 parts, and who was murdered by the Germans on 13 August 1944. Chmielewski himself emigrated from Britain to Brazil in April 1945, after he had been shot at in his bathroom shortly following a visit by a mysterious man who had proposed that Chmielewski engage professionally in intelligence work (the Pole had declined). Chmielewski died in Rio de Janeiro on 1 August 1966. Wojewódzki, *Akcja V-1, V-2*, especially 405-10.

26. Lewin, *Ultra Goes to War*, 75ff.

14.

Enigma at Sea

As of late 1978, Britain's Public Record Office held 324,000 decrypted German signals dealing with the war at sea from 15 June 1941 to 15 January 1945. Day and night throughout this period, Bletchley Park sent to the Royal Navy's Operational Intelligence Centre an average of eleven decrypts an hour.[1]

When the war broke out in September 1939, the Operational Intelligence Centre had thirty-six workers and was headed by retired Vice Adm. Jock Clayton. At first it was housed beneath the Admiralty, later in specially constructed underground facilities.[2]

The Operational Intelligence Centre drew information not only from Enigma intercepts but from radar, direction finding, and reports by agents active at German bases and ports and in occupied territories. Nevertheless, information from the decrypted radio correspondence of the German Navy played a unique role among all these sources since it came straight from the sea horse's mouth, was timely, and was absolutely reliable. As opposed to radar and direction finding, which could locate only an occasional cruiser or submarine, Enigma delivered to the British the German Navy's plans, tactics, and concrete moves on the chessboard of naval warfare.

The latter expression was more than a mere metaphor. One of the Operational Intelligence Centre's key sections, the Submarine Tracking Room, featured a great world map whose coordinates formed chessboardlike squares on which the naval struggles were waged.

The work of British naval intelligence in 1939-45 was presented a dozen years ago in an extensive book abounding in previously unknown facts by Donald McLachlan.[3] The book appeared to be the last word in matters not previously discussed, due to the inaccessibility of British records. Yet, according to Patrick Beesly,[4] a lieutenant commander in the Operational Intelligence Centre during the war, McLachlan's account—due to restrictions still in effect in 1968—was necessarily incomplete and, in many instances, misleading.[5]

In 1974, six years after McLachlan's book and after restrictions had been eased, Winterbotham still treated naval Enigma marginally. Beesly's subsequent publications take account of both earlier authors, but also disclose some previously unknown facts. We are told, for example, that in the hierarchy of intelligence sources, German decrypts held top place at the Operational Intelligence Centre, and that this hierarchy was as follows:

1. Decrypts of radio signals;
2. Direction finding of enemy ships;
3. Aerial reconnaissance;
4. Sightings by Allied naval vessels;
5. Sightings by Allied merchantmen;
6. Agents;
7. Analysis of enemy naval radio traffic;
8. Observers in friendly and neutral countries;
9. Other services, for example, Coastal Command, that could supply intelligence on enemy naval movements.

Whatever may have been the case with German diplomatic, Army, and Air Force ciphers, maintains Beesly, the British were unable to read Kriegsmarine ciphers until mid-1941, since the cryptologists lacked sufficient material to break the German Navy's cipher system.[6] The material was finally obtained in May 1941, when, in carefully planned operations, the British managed to capture two German meteorological ships and a submarine from which they obtained intact Enigma machines together with key tables and other materials.[7]

Although the actual decryptment of Enigma signals from all sources was strictly centralized at Bletchley, distribution of the product followed two separate paths. Material on the German Army and Air Force was processed together, was translated into English and annotated at Bletchley's Hut 3, and then was sent to the appropriate authorities and commands, as previously described. Kriegsmarine decrypts, on the other hand, went by teletype straight from Hut 4 to the Operational Intelligence Centre in London, in the original German.[8]

The Admiralty, like the army and air force high commands, used various means to safeguard the security of Enigma intelligence. In addition to restriction of distribution to a minimal number of users, Enigma data were attributed to false sources such as aerial reconnaissance, direction finding, or agents, or it was simply asserted that data on enemy positions were based on projections by the Admiralty, which possessed diverse sources of intelligence. Additionally, Enigma intelligence was edited so as to omit any characteristic expressions peculiar to the German text.

The Operational Intelligence Centre included two basic units: Section 8.E, concerned with the surface forces of the German Navy (headed by Comdr. Norman Denning), and Section 8.S, which tracked submarines (headed by Commander Thring, later Comdr. Rodger Winn).

The great German battleships posed a serious threat, writes Beesly, but they were not always on the high seas, spending as they did part of their time in port and in training cruises on the Baltic. The great surface ships used radio sparingly so as to elude Allied direction finding, and so Enigma supplied relatively little information on them. A hitherto unclear matter is Enigma's role in the sinking on 27 May 1941 of the great German battleship, the *Bismarck*. British authors express diametrically different views.

Many accounts of the Battle of the Atlantic have been written [says F.W. Winterbotham] but up until now none of them have been able to reveal the role of Ultra. One of the most dramatic examples occurred in the *Bismarck* affair .... Early on 25 May Admiral Lutyens, thinking that he was still being shadowed by a British warship, sent a long signal to his Naval Headquarters in Germany. It listed all his difficulties but mainly the loss of fuel from his earlier battle and he asked what he was to do now. It was this signal, picked up by us, which gave away once more his position. I remember the thrill that went through the office as the next signal came over the telephone from Hut 3 that *Bismarck* had been ordered to Brest where all available air and submarine protection was to be given to her. Later we were to know that the Admiralty had already made plans to cope with either her return northwards to Germany or southwards to France, but now her position was certain. On 26 May at 10:30 a.m. the *Bismarck* was again sighted. The rest of the story is well known.[9]

However, Beesly maintains that the sinking of the *Bismarck* had nothing to do with Ultra, since at that time—in late May 1941—the German naval cipher had not yet been broken. He ascribes the information regarding the battleship having put to sea and its whereabouts at the critical moment on the morning of 25 May 1941 to British agents, to Swedish intelligence,[10] to aerial reconnaissance, and to direction finding.[11] Calvocoressi (*Top Secret Ultra*, 89-90) and others add Bletchley's reading of Luftwaffe Enigma correspondence.

An interesting episode in propaganda warfare involved the breakout in February 1942 of the three great German naval ships, the *Scharnhorst*, the *Gneisenau*, and the *Prinz Eugen*, through the English Channel into the North Sea, an event that was hailed in Germany as a great triumph. From Enigma signals the British knew that, while running the English Channel, the *Scharnhorst* had been severely damaged by two mines and the *Gneisenau* by one. Both ships were later hit by aerial bombs while in port at Kiel. Yet, the British press and radio reported only the escape of the three German ships. Publishing the fact of their having run into mines would have disclosed the source of Britain's information. The discretion shortly paid off when the same source provided the sailing time of the *Scharnhorst* from the Alta fjord, thus leading to the destruction of the great German battleship.

Another chapter in the surface naval war concerns German auxiliary cruisers—merchantmen armed with artillery and torpedoes. Capitalizing on deception and surprise, and widely employed in the First World War, auxiliary cruisers were also used in World War II, particularly from the beginning of 1941. The first German auxiliary cruiser, the *Pinguin*, was intercepted and sunk in May 1941 in the Indian Ocean by the British cruiser *Cornwall*, which had picked up the SOS of a sinking tanker. In November 1941, Enigma supplied information on the rendezvous point of a German submarine with the auxiliary cruiser *Atlantis*. The British cruiser *Devonshire*, operating in the south Atlantic, found the *Atlantis* precisely on target at the Tropic of Capricorn and sank it after a brief fight. The German auxiliary cruisers operated at sea only slightly over a year. Their discovery, chiefly with the help of Enigma, was so effective that, at the beginning of 1943, Kriegsmarine headquarters was forced to stop sending them out.

The beginnings of Britain's Submarine Tracking Room went back to 1936-37, when, after the outbreak of the Spanish Civil War, the British began to systematically track the submarine fleets of Germany and Italy, due to those countries' interventions on the side of General Franco.

In 1938, the commander in chief of the German submarine fleet in a memorandum estimated wartime requirements for submarines at a minimum of 300, one-third to be in operational zones, one-third outbound or homebound, and one-third in port or dry dock. "There is no upper limit," he added.[12]

In September 1939, the Kriegsmarine had 57 submarines fit for active duty: 9 heavy, 18 medium, and 30 smaller ones. Of this total number, 18 heavy and medium U-boats operated in the Atlantic west of the British Isles, and the rest were in the North Sea and the Baltic.

In mid-August 1939, two weeks before the German attack on Poland, the personnel of the Submarine Tracking Room had been brought up to full wartime strength, and operations proceeded around the clock. During the "phony war," from September 1939 to May 1940, when the other armed forces were practically idle, the struggle against the U-boats was, alongside intelligence operations, virtually the only form of Allied military activity.

After the intensive U-boat operations during the first months of war, the German Supreme Command stepped down its submarine warfare during 1940, as reflected in the decreased number of U-boats operating in the Atlantic, North Sea, and other waters (41 in April 1940, 27 in June 1940, 22 in January 1941). Following his victory in June 1940 over France, Hitler probably still counted on concluding a peace with Britain on his own terms, and on keeping the United States neutral in the European conflict. At the same time, he wanted to preserve his naval forces intact, so as to be able, in the event of continued resistance, to use them in support of Operation Sea Lion, his planned invasion of Great Britain. Another cause of the relative lull in U-boat operations in 1940 and early 1941 was the intensive training of submarine commands and crews in a new tactic later called the wolf pack.[13] Occupation of western Europe, especially of France and Holland, enabled the Germans to develop a vast network of fixed radio facilities to direct the naval war in the Atlantic.

Beginning in the spring of 1941, the number of U-boats operating at sea rose again: 32 in April 1941; 57 in July; 78 in October; 100 in January 1942; 164 in January 1943; and 196 in May 1943.[14]

Adoption of the wolf pack technique had important bearings for Allied radio intelligence. The direction finding and intercept stations were more frequently able to locate the U-boat packs and to catch their enciphered orders and reports. The farther the German submarines put out into the Atlantic—from mid-1940 operating also out of French ports—the greater were the opportunities for accurate direction finding and for reading the necessarily more numerous radio signals.

Enigma was heavily used for tracking U-boats from July 1941 to the beginning of 1942. Then, at the end of January 1942, Adm. Karl Doenitz, commander of U-boat operations in the Atlantic, ordered a change in Enigma enciphering procedures. On 1 February 1942, a new Enigma key, "Triton," was adopted for the U-boats. Overnight the flow of information from Bletchley stopped. The Submarine Tracking Room was forced, for the next ten months, to rely on direction finding, aerial reconnaissance, and sporadic agent reports. Only in the first days of December 1942 would the British succeed in breaking the new Enigma procedures used by the U-boat wolf packs and their higher commands in the great battle for the convoys. Nevertheless, the enormous mass of Enigma information that came in before Doenitz's changes made possible the establishment of a priceless bank of information of long-lived usefulness. This information bank contained the exact number of German submarines fit or being fitted for duty, their home ports, the speeds of different types of submarines on their outbound and return voyages, and various types of radio signals used upon sighting convoys, in guiding submarines to target, and in operating in the immediate vicinity of convoys. All this continued to yield large dividends until the reading of signals from U-boats in the Atlantic suddenly stopped.[15] To be sure, Bletchley could still decrypt Enigma from Kriegsmarine surface units and from submarines in the Baltic, which had not changed their cipher procedures. But the situation was clearly becoming unfavorable to the Allies on the main front of the naval war.

The Germans also had their positive cryptological successes. Already during the Norwegian campaign (April-May 1940), Kriegsmarine radio intelligence had read enough of the Royal Navy's signals to reconstruct a fairly detailed picture of its strengths and movements in operational areas. In August 1940, the British Admiralty had introduced changes in its administrative and operational cryptography thereby preventing the Germans from reading British naval correspondence for a time. But beginning in the spring of 1942, as a result of the Germans reading British naval signals, U-boats again began attacking in force and sinking Allied convoys, whose losses mounted by the month. After Commander Denning, who worked with Enigma material in the Naval Intelligence Division, smelled a rat and changed the code book in 1943, the Royal Navy once again got the upper hand. Only after the war did the diaries of Admiral Doenitz reveal that the Germans read British naval codes during that critical period. The Germans had used the old cryptological trick of concentrating on recurring addresses in hundreds of signals. Once they had part of the code groups worked out, they could begin decrypting.[16]

Thus, the situation in radio intelligence and decryptment favored the Germans through most of 1942. Although the Allies were unable to read the Atlantic U-boats' Enigma, the cryptologists of the B-Dienst (Beobachter

Dienst, the German naval interception unit) were able, beginning in the spring of 1942, to read Allied signals to convoys on the safest routes and on course changes. For example, during just three weeks in March, the Germans intercepted Admiralty orders to thirty convoys out of a total of thirty-five then at sea. However, the time factor was of tremendous importance. On the basis of German sources, Beesly states that of 175 British signals then read, only 10 were of current usefulness to U-boat attacks on Allied convoys and individual ships. Beesly does not explain whether the delays were in decryptment or in the passage between intercept stations and the decryptment center.[17]

Other sources indicate that, while the B-Dienst and other German decryptment agencies employed leading specialists, the Germans never succeeded in automating cryptological work—a field in which Britain's Bletchley had a clear advantage.[18]

As already mentioned, it was not until December 1942 that the British managed to break the "Triton" Enigma key and that the Admiralty was again able to read signals concerning U-boats—often at the same time as their addressees (though, on occasion, decryptment took as long as a week). By the end of 1943, Bletchley had sufficiently perfected the technique of solving Kriegsmarine signals that throughout 1944 they were reconstructed and sent to the Royal Navy's Operational Intelligence Centre immediately, or nearly so.

This increase in the effectiveness of Allied decryptment coincided with the perfection of antisubmarine warfare techniques: shipboard and airborne radar, depth charges, and so on. Meanwhile, in 1943, German naval intelligence had lost its capacity to decrypt Allied naval signals.[19] From mid-1943 on, when close collaboration between the naval and air escorts of Allied convoys made it impossible for U-boats to use their greater surface speed (since they had to remain constantly submerged), the German submarines were practically beaten. Grand Admiral Doenitz began construction of high speed U-boats, but he did not succeed in bringing this program to a conclusion before the end of the war.[20]

Enigma's greatest contribution to the struggle against the submarines came in 1943, when renewed British decryptment made possible Allied location and sinking of numerous U-boats and of the tankers—milk cows— that supplied them at sea. The most hazardous parts of U-boat operations were the outbound voyage into the Atlantic and the return to home ports. While negotiating the English Channel, U-boats were within range of British destroyers and Coastal Command aircraft. They were again vulnerable during rendezvous with the milk cows. Increasingly frequent captures and sinkings of U-boats during rendezvous aroused the suspicions of the Abwehr, which on several occasions conducted investigations, looking for Allied agents within Kriegsmarine staffs and units.

When the U.S. entered the war in December 1941 and U-boats began to play havoc with the inadequately protected U.S. merchant fleet, the U.S. Navy at first refused to make use of British experience in combatting U-boats, relying instead on its own fleets and intelligence capabilities. According to

Ladislas Farago, the incompetence and inexperience of U.S. Navy staffs in this phase of the war were frightful. British naval intelligence sent a representative to Washington to convince the Americans that close working relations and exchange of intelligence were crucial to success in the naval war.

Subsequent British-U.S. cooperation included Enigma intelligence, which the Americans often used in excessively hazardous fashion. A flagrant example was U.S. operations against German milk cows and submarines from June to October 1943 in the vicinity of the Azores. As a result of those operations, conducted almost entirely on the basis of Enigma data, at least 19 U-boats and all but one of the supply ships were sunk. The German Submarine Command (Befehlshaber der U-Boote) ordered detailed investigations. However, the possibility of enemy cryptologists having cracked Enigma was once again discarded.

The German Navy regarded as absolutely secure its type M Enigma, especially after the introduction of the four-rotor version equipped with two additional, "Greek" rotors, alpha and beta, which were exchanged at irregular time intervals. Allied operational prescience was ascribed to radar, to intensified aerial reconnaissance—to just about anything but German cryptographic shortcomings.[21]

The last phase of the battle in the Atlantic, from the standpoint of intelligence operations, began after the Allied landings in Normandy and the German Navy's loss of its French bases. As a consequence of massive U-boat losses, the Germans were obliged to give up the wolf pack technique. This, in turn, greatly cut down on the numbers of intercepted U-boat signals, hence making it difficult for Allied aircraft to track down the now individual, lone wolf submarines. According to Beesly, "If the Germans had succeeded in bringing into action, as planned, their new long-range type XXI and XXIII U-boats, they could still have inflicted on Allied merchant marines losses not smaller than those of 1942 and early 1943."

The outcome of the war depended to a great extent on Britain's survival during the early years of the war, and Britain's survival depended on the results of the battle for the Atlantic. Hence, no Allied convoy, lone merchantman, single naval ship, or squadron was allowed to plot a course before it had cleared it with the Submarine Tracking Room. This held as well for the allocation to convoys of naval escorts and Coastal Command air patrols, the planning of attacks on German convoys, and mine laying.

Charges of dereliction have been leveled at Britain's Naval Intelligence Division, headed by Adm. John Godfrey, for periodically failing to assure the security of the Royal Navy's codes and ciphers against the German Navy's decryptment service, the B-Dienst. Already before 1939, the B-Dienst had solved some administrative and operational ciphers resulting, as previously mentioned, in the reading of Royal Navy signals by Germany during Britain's Norwegian campaign in 1940. At the end of 1940, the B-Dienst had managed to break British Naval Cipher No. 3, used for signals about convoy routes, which later became a common British-American cipher. This helped the Germans plan U-boat attacks on Allied convoys, especially in the second half of 1942 and the first months of 1943.

Who was responsible for these Allied security failings? According to Beesly, it was none other than Bletchley Park, which not only broke Enigma ciphers but also elaborated ciphers for use by all British government institutions, including the navy.

The Admiralty was also culpable to the extent that it failed before the war to heed Adm. (later Earl) Louis Mountbatten's recommendations that the Royal Navy adopt cipher machines. Also, others had warned that Cipher No. 3 might be broken due to the enormous volume of signals that were being sent in it by ships operating on all the seas. Partly to blame for the protracted use of Cipher No. 3 as an inter-Allied cipher were the Americans, who had enthusiastically adopted the cipher without revealing or proposing to their ally their own superior navy machine cipher. It took Allied reading of Enigma to demonstrate that the British cipher had been compromised. But even with that knowledge, it still took twelve months, beginning in mid-1942, before a new cipher was fully introduced. It was only in May-June 1943 that the B-Dienst, the U-boat command, and the entire German Navy found themselves in the dark. (A year later, in May 1944, when Hitler asked the B-Dienst which British ciphers it could read, the answer was: neither of the two most important ones.) Meanwhile, the Allies had begun reading naval Enigma freely once more.[22]

Marian Rejewski observes:

> We know that the British solved their first messages from the Wehrmacht's land forces, using "Zygalski sheets," in January 1940, and their first air force messages in April 1940 (Winterbotham). Now we learn that it was only in the middle of 1941 that they began reading naval messages, and this only because they managed to sink or to capture some German naval ships and thereby to obtain cipher materials. It may be supposed that those materials included rotors VI and VII to the naval Enigma and that it was only possession of those rotors that enabled the British to recover keys to the main Kriegsmarine cipher nets.

Rejewski further observes that it is interesting that Bletchley commonly announced half an hour or an hour in advance that there would shortly be more information. This may be interpreted to mean that the main obstacle (for example, the commutator connections) to the key's recovery had been removed and that the rest was now merely a matter of a short time.

NOTES

1. Calvocoressi, in Rohwer and Jäckel, *Die Funkaufklärung*.
2. Patrick Beesly, in Rohwer and Jäckel, *Die Funkaufklärung*, 133.
3. McLachlan, *Room 39: Naval Intelligence in Action, 1939-1945*.
4. Beesly, "The Operational Intelligence Centre in the Second World War."
5. Some of McLachlan's statements are simply untrue, as when he says that, in general, the higher grade German machine ciphers could not be read.
6. It should be emphasized that the German Navy's Enigma system actually embraced a number of discrete nets, each with its own keys. The most important nets were as follows:

- Hydra: used by surface ships in the Baltic and North Seas and off the shores of occupied countries; initially, also by U-boats.
- Triton: used by U-boats, operating in the Atlantic, commanded directly by U-boat Command.
- Thetis: used by U-boats in training on the Baltic.
- Medusa: used by U-boats in the Mediterranean.
- Aegir: used by surface ships outside the Baltic and North Seas, for example, on operations against Allied convoys.
- Neptun: used by battleships and great cruisers, for example, the *Bismarck*, *Gneisenau*, *Scharnhorst*, and so on.
- Tibet: used by tankers and other supply ships that had taken refuge after the outbreak of war in neutral ports (they had Enigmas of an earlier type).
- Freya: used by OKM (Navy High Command) in corresponding with naval commands and bases on the seacoast.
- Bertok: used between OKM and the German naval attaché in Tokyo.
- Sleipner: used by vessels in training (for example, torpedo exercises) on the Baltic.
- Potsdam: used in operations against the Soviet Navy in the Baltic.
- Süd: used by surface ships on the Mediterranean and Black Seas.

Additionally, the German Navy used a Sonderschlüssel (special key) 100 for communication with individual ships on special operations, and with auxiliary cruisers; an M-Front U-Boote, a cipher net for submarines operating in distant seas; an M-Heimische Gewässer, a net for ships operating in offshore waters; and others. Rohwer, "Vorläufige Bemerkungen zur Frage der Sicherheit der deutschen Schlüsselmittel."

7. On 7 May 1941, the meteorological ship *München* was taken, on May 9 the submarine U-110, and on May 29 the meteorological ship *August Wriedl*. The lucky streak continued into June; further cipher machines were obtained from two supply ships, the *Gedania* and *Lothringen*, sunk in German coastal waters, and from a third meteorological ship, the *Lauenburg*.

8. In *The Ultra Secret*, Winterbotham and the author of the foreword, Marshal of the Royal Air Force Sir John Slessor, write critically of the Admiralty's reserving, exclusively to itself, the

assessment and distribution of materials from German naval decrypts. Slessor writes: "(characteristically and not always with happy results) the Admiralty were allowed to keep these Signal Intelligence matters in their own hands." Beesly, however, points out that, by contrast with the War Office and Air Ministry, the Admiralty was also, by its very nature, an institution that directly planned naval operations, and with respect to British coastal waters, was, in fact, the supreme command. Beesly remarks that he shudders to think what would have happened had raw Enigma information gone out to the various Royal Navy shore commands, to Coastal Command posts, and to ships at sea. The experiences of the U.S. Navy—which followed exactly that procedure until June 1942, when it created its own counterpart of the Royal Navy's Operational Intelligence Centre (F 21, later Op 20 G)—according to Beesly, indicate the consequences for the Royal Navy might have been disastrous. Beesly, in Rohwer and Jäckel, *Die Funkaufklärung*, 133ff.

9. Winterbotham, *The Ultra Secret*, 83-84. Should Winterbotham's claim about the role of Ultra in the sinking of the *Bismarck* prove true, then the demise of this, the most formidable warship then anywhere afloat, will have been doubly a Polish victory. First, it was thanks to the Poles that the British were able to read Enigma. Secondly, the *Bismarck* was finally located and pinned down by a Polish destroyer, the *O.R.P. Piorun* (Ship of the Polish Republic *Thunderbolt*), captained by Comdr. Eugeniusz Pławski, who purposely, for an hour, from 10:45 p.m. on May 26, drew upon his small ship the fire of the world's most powerful battleship, in order that the Royal Navy might catch up. A Polish historian recounts the scene:

> From a distance of nearly 12,000 meters [about seven miles] the *Bismarck* opened fire with its 150 mm. guns. The *Piorun* immediately replied. [The *Bismarck* next opened up with its eight 380 mm. guns. When German shells came uncomfortably close, the Polish ship put up smoke screens and made radical course changes.] The small Polish destroyer fought the world's most powerful battleship. The disproportion in forces between the two vessels was so great as to defy conception. Any comparison of the oft-used David-Goliath kind is absolutely inadequate. Little is conveyed by a comparison of the displacements of the two ships: the *Piorun* weighed in at 1,760 tons, the *Bismarck* at over 42,000, or 25 times as much; nor is a precise picture obtained by comparing the crews of the two ships: the *Piorun*'s 220 men, with the *Bismarck*'s nearly 2,200! Finally, perhaps the most telling comparison: a broadside from the *Piorun* weighed 132 kg. [290 pounds], a broadside form the *Bismarck*'s heaviest and medium guns, upwards of 8,000 kg. [17,600 pounds, or about 9 tons]—over 60 times as much.
>
> There was never the slightest doubt as to the outcome of the battle, should the *Piorun* be hit just once; whereas the *Piorun*'s guns could not do the slightest damage to the *Bismarck* [which] had armor plate about 400 mm. [16 inches] thick, against which a 120 mm. shell was utterly ineffective. . . .
>
> For about an hour the *Piorun* was under fire from the *Bismarck*'s guns. For 60 minutes the heavy and medium artillery of the powerful floating fortress was concentrated on the small destroyer. A whole 60 minutes, any one of which might have spelled inescapable doom [for the *Piorun*]. For 60 minutes the *Piorun* concentrated on itself the fire of the colossal German battleship and diverted its attention from what was happening around it. These several score minutes decided the fate of the *Bismarck*. During that time the [British] destroyers [in the task force] managed to steam up to the place of battle and slip about the *Bismarck* a net out of which it would never extricate itself. To a certain extent, this was made possible by the selfless action of the Polish ship, which had enabled the commander of the destroyer task force to surround the *Bismarck* and take up suitable positions for nighttime torpedo attacks.

Jerzy Pertek, *Wielkie dni małej floty*, 286-310.—ED.

10. Recently, it has been stated that at least some of the information came from German Geheimschreiber (cipher teletype) messages obtained from Sweden. The cables carrying Geheimschreiber messages from occupied Norway to Germany ran partly across Swedish territory, and Swedish intelligence clandestinely tapped them. Swedish intelligence officers who sympathized with the Allies turned these materials over to the Norwegian military attaché in

Stockholm, who gave them to his British opposite number, who then sent them to London. It was in this way that the British are alleged to have gotten their first information on the *Bismarck*'s putting to sea, as well as the German Navy's orders for operations against the PQ-17 convoy. Employed in solving Geheimschreiber ciphers were the Colossus computers which were introduced at Bletchley Park beginning in late 1943.

The Geheimschreiber was one of the important means of communication between Hitler's headquarters (the Wolfsschanze, or Wolf's Lair) near Rastenburg, in East Prussia, and the Wehrmacht operational commands at army and army-group levels. In the east, according to a West German author, that communication was often interrupted by partisans destroying the teletype cables; the same sometimes happened in France. Though the partisans did not know it, such operations not only disrupted German communications but increased the flow of radio intercepts to Allied decryptment stations: to the Polish-French Cadix in southern France, and to Bletchley. High-level secret orders and reports that could not be sent by Geheimschreiber had to be put on the air, thereby making them liable to Allied interception. This aspect of sabotage against German communications was unknown even to ranking resistance leaders, who were directed by the Allied commands or by de Gaulle's Free French organization to conduct ever more intensive sabotage.

Calvocoressi states that a special cryptological section was set up at Bletchley to deal exclusively with Geheimschreiber ciphers. The generally high-level decrypts were never sent to Hut 3 for processing. From a discussion in Rohwer and Jäckel, *Die Funkaufklärung*, 110.

11. During the first months of war, from September 1939 to June 1940, the British direction-finding net included installations in France which facilitated tracking of Kriegsmarine movements in the North Sea. After the collapse of France, when these stations had been withdrawn, and in the face of increased activity by German surface and submarine fleets in the Atlantic, the direction-finding net was quickly expanded; new stations were established at sites around the globe, including Iceland, Bermuda, Freetown, and Ascension Island. Enemy vessels were located with none too great accuracy (within a radius of about 45-80 km. of the vessel).

12. Hans Meckel, in Rohwer and Jäckel, *Die Funkaufklärung*, 121. In the years 1935-45, according to Rear Adm. Eberhardt Godt, chief of operations of the U-boat command (in *Die Funkaufklärung*), the German Navy commissioned a total of 1,170 submarines. Of that number, 860 took part in combat operations in the years 1939-45 (the average number of operations per U-boat was five to six, lasting from one day to two hundred days at sea). U-boat losses were high. In combat at sea the German Navy lost 630 U-boats, at bases from enemy bomber and torpedo-plane raids a further 81, and as a result of various kinds of accidents during training cruises, and so on, 42. Thus, the German Navy lost a total of 753 submarines. The personnel losses of the U-boat fleet in World War II came to twenty-eight thousand officers and men out of the forty-two thousand who took part in combat cruises, or 67 percent.

13. The first trials of this tactic under battle conditions were conducted on 10-19 October 1939, in actions against the British HG-3 convoy, and, subsequently, in November 1939 and February 1940 against French convoys.

14. The numbers for January and May 1943 pertain to U-boats operating in the Atlantic alone. The grand total at that time was greater by some 50 boats.

15. Beesly, "The Operational Intelligence Centre," 374.

16. Winterbotham, *The Ultra Secret*, 84-85.

17. In many places, in writing of the great importance of information obtained through decryptment (by the Germans as well as the British), Beesly nevertheless argues that the most important source of information was, after all, the analytical work of the Operational Intelligence Centre, which collected intelligence on the enemy derived from all available sources. Still, Enigma intelligence, with respect to its reliability, range, and the speed with which it was obtained, clearly comes to the fore.

18. It was only in 1943 that Germany's E-Dienst (Entzifferungs-Dienst, or Decryptment Service) began using Hollerith calculating machines; no details are available as to the uses they were put to. Bonatz, *Funkaufklärung*, 105.

19. Beesly, in Rohwer and Jäckel, *Die Funkaufklärung*, 133ff.

20. Brian B. Schofield, "The Role of the Admiralty's Trade Division and the Causes of the

Breakthrough in the Battle of the Atlantic in the Spring of 1943," in Rohwer and Jäckel, *Die Funkaufklärung.*

21. Jürgen Rohwer, "The Influence of German and British Radio Intelligence on Convoy Operations in the North Atlantic," in Rohwer and Jäckel, *Die Funkaufklärung*, 167 ff.

22. Beesly, in Rohwer and Jäckel, *Die Funkaufklärung*, 133 ff.

15.

War Ends

In the final third of July 1943 Marian Rejewski and Henryk Zygalski, along with a large group of other Poles, had managed to get out of Spain and into Portugal. Unlike most refugees, they did not go to Lisbon. On reaching the Portuguese town of Marvao, near the Spanish border, they followed the border due south about 400 kilometers to a designated point near Villa Real de San Antonio, on the Gulf of Cadiz. From a dilapidated fishing port on Portugal's south coast, under cover of night, a boat slipped out to sea. At the appointed hour, naval vessels loomed out of the dark. The HMS *Scottish* came alongside the boat and threw across a narrow, swaying gangplank.

"Go on—jump!" cried a British boatswain, supplementing the words with an inviting gesture.

The sailors gave a warm welcome to the ship's unusual guests. The captain had several bottles of whiskey brought on deck and personally poured equal shots into mess tins, cups, and glasses of diverse shapes and sizes. Toasts were raised to victory and to a safe return home. There was no space in the cramped sailors' quarters, but it was a clear, warm night. The fugitives from Hitler's Festung Europa got a good rest after their hazardous journey on several dozen mattresses brought up on deck. When they were awakened at dawn by a sharp breeze blowing out from land, they saw a tall rock looming on the horizon.

Gibraltar, where they had arrived on the morning of 24 July 1943, had the ambience of a stronghold under siege. Daily just before nightfall, a tattoo was sounded, and strong patrols of British Tommies in tin hats ran through the town, Sten guns at the ready. The Spanish laborers who, in wartime, still worked the port's docks, immediately departed the fortress, returning through designated gates to Algeciras and other Spanish border towns.

Less than three weeks earlier, on July 4, the Polish premier and commander in chief, Gen. Władysław Sikorski, had died in unclear circumstances when his Liberator dove into the Mediterranean shortly after takeoff from Gibraltar on a return trip to England following an inspection of Polish troops in the Middle East. Of the dozen persons aboard, only the pilot survived.

After registering with the local Polish military authorities in barracks on Church Lane, Rejewski and Zygalski, quartered in an officers' hotel on Main Street, waited for a chance to fly to the British Isles. They had spent nearly three years fighting on the secret front in western Europe—at Bruno outside Paris, and at underground Cadix in southern France—and now they also had behind them three months of Spanish prison. Two and a half months' rest in Lerida and Madrid, however, had been enough to prepare them for their illegal border crossing into Portugal, and to give them a fresh pool of energy with which to rejoin the Polish armed forces and to continue the struggle.

The war was entering its decisive phase. One blow after another was raining down upon the war machine of the Third Reich, badly jarred by its disaster at the Volga. However, the Germans still ruled in Warsaw, in Rejewski's Bygdoszcz and in Zygalski's Poznań. Horror stories were coming out of Poland about death camps, removal and extermination of the populace, and mounting resistance operations. For many months, ever since leaving Cadix in the fall of 1942, the two men had known nothing about their loved ones. They had sent letters from Spain, and some of these had reached their families, but they would know this only after the war.

On 30 July 1943, the two Poles were driven to the Gibraltar airfield and boarded an old Dakota, but after a couple of hours' wait the flight was canceled. Only at 10 p.m. on August 2 did they finally take off. Planes flying out of Gibraltar first made a course for the northwest, then flew over the Atlantic south of Ireland, turned sharply eastward and slipped down the Bristol Channel. From there they flew on under cover of British fighters and antiaircraft batteries. The Poles' twin-engine craft traced a broad arc over the Atlantic to evade Messerschmitts operating from advanced bases on France's Breton Peninsula, and several hours later landed safely at the Hendon RAF station in southeast England.

Upon disembarking, all who were arriving on the Isles for the first time were subjected to lengthy interrogation by British counterintelligence, MI-5. They had to answer countless tricky, if ostensibly naive, questions. Those who knew no English were questioned through interpreters, who seemed to speak all the languages of the world. The danger of infiltration by Nazi agents still existed, and arrivals submitted to these tests without a murmur. This was the Patriotic School outside London. (Only the British could have called a counterintelligence operation a school.) Already in Gibraltar, Rejewski and Zygalski had learned from old hands who had frequently been to the British Isles as couriers or on other missions that it was best not to let on that one knew English. That way, the procedure was considerably shorter. However, the two Polish cryptologists did not go through the interrogations.[1] Apparently, some ranking officer had seen to it that they not reveal, even to counterintelligence, any details of their war work.

After a couple of days' stay in London and conversations at the Polish supreme command, they departed by train for the Scottish town of King

Horn. At the barracks of a Polish signals unit, they were issued uniforms and documents stating their new assignment to the Signals Battalion of the Staff of the (Polish) Commander in Chief (Batalion Łączności Sztabu Naczelnego Wodza) at Stanmore, outside London. Privates Rejewski and Zygalski went through more administrative procedures before they could depart King Horn for their new unit.

The subordinate Polish intercept and decryptment center at Boxmoor, to which they were detailed, was located on a side street of this small town, much like dozens of others that surrounded London. Besides a spacious villa called The Arches where the command was housed and the cryptologists worked, the grounds—enclosed by a tall iron fence—contained two corrugated metal huts and, next to these, a tangle of tall antennae. Another hut housed a unit of security troops and the radio operators and technicians who, in three shifts, manned the receivers that intercepted German signals. For security against enemy intelligence, the Polish decryptment center bore the uncommunicative name Service Platoon (Pluton Eksploatacyjny).

The commander of this small, super-secret unit, Maj. Kazimierz Zieliński (commander of Radio Intelligence Station no. 4 at Poznań up to the outbreak of the war), was pleased at the arrival from the continent of the two mathematician-cryptologists, and later of other members of Field Station 300. They had been preceded, within a narrow circle of initiates, by the opinion that no code or cipher could withstand their scrutiny. Zieliński would find that their reputation was justified over the next days and weeks.

It might have seemed logical that the British, who, on the eve of war, had received from the Poles an Enigma double and methods for solving the ciphers, and who had worked together with their Polish and French allies at Bruno and Cadix, would now reestablish the interrupted contact. "Quelle aubaine pour les Anglais!" ("What a windfall for the English!") exclaimed General Bertrand in describing the final moments in France of his Polish comrades in arms, who were preparing to make their way across the Pyrenees on their way to the British Isles.

Everything connected with the German machine cipher had become a British monopoly. Of the British cryptologists who had visited B.S.-4 at Warsaw and Pyry in July 1939 and who were identifiable, Comdr. Alastair Denniston had been relieved of his directorship at Bletchley in late 1942, and Alfred Dillwyn Knox had died in February 1943. It might have seemed that no one else in Britain remembered about that historic visit to Warsaw in 1939, about the British using the Polish techniques for solving Enigma, about Britain having received, gratis, a five-rotor Enigma double built in Poland before the war, or, finally, about day-by-day British cooperation with the Polish-French Bruno center at Gretz-Armainvillers outside Paris and—if on a smaller scale—with clandestine Cadix in southern France. If, in December 1939, Britain's cryptological authorities had requested Colonel Langer to bring his organization to England and turn it over to them (chapter 9), now the British seemed to feel no need for expert Polish reinforcements or for acknowledgment of their debt to the Poles. If the behavior of the British can be explained by the imperatives of wartime secrecy, then certainly the passing over of the Poles' contributions until recently in contemporary publications is, to say the least, incomprehensible.

Great changes in the war situation had taken place over the months since the German invasion of southern France had interrupted the active cryptological work of the two Poles. Increasingly, large operational S.S. units were appearing at the fronts. This fanatical guard of the Nazi regime was growing stronger by the month. Hitler, in proclaiming total war, rested his hopes for improving the military situation in the east and in the Appenine Peninsula on the S.S. formations. Despite the Wehrmacht's reverses at the fronts and the massive Allied bombing of Germany, the production of tanks, guns, and aircraft continued to rise until the summer of 1944. Meanwhile, in German-occupied Europe, and especially in Poland, the terror intensified with every week. The threads of the vast German police machine ran together in Berlin, in the hands of S.S. Reichsfuehrer Heinrich Himmler, supreme head of the S.D. (Security Service); since 1936 head of the Gestapo (Secret State Police) that had been founded in 1933 under Goering; and head of front-line S.S. units, whose numbers approached one million men.

The Polish cryptologists in the British Isles, unable to work with Enigma, occupied themselves more energetically with breaking S.S. ciphers. These contained information both on front-line S.S. forces and on units stationed in the occupied countries. Hence, solution of the ciphers was important also to the European resistance movements.

Certain S.S. and S.D. ciphers had been solved before the war at Poland's B.S.-4 center at Pyry. Since then, much had changed. The S.S. and S.D. cryptological services, which were in their infancy during the mid-thirties, had now matured into experienced organizations. The quality of secret communications in Himmler's police and military empire had improved markedly. Leading German mathematicians and cryptologists had been recruited into the work. Following the annexation of Austria in March 1938, future S.D. intelligence chief Walter Schellenberg had discovered cryptological files in the Austrian intelligence archives, and specialists had determined that some of the ideas found there were unknown in Berlin and should be exploited. The Gestapo had imprisoned the head of Austria's interception and decryptment unit, the leading theoretician of cryptology, Gen. Andreas Figl. In time, he was persuaded to work for the Greater German Reich. At Wansee outside Berlin, where Figl was detained, the S.D. in 1939 established a cryptological unit independent of the Foreign Office and the Wehrmacht. A separate department of S.S. and S.D. secret communications came into being, and its specialists elaborated their own cipher systems, including the complicated digraphic cipher that was used by S.S. units during the years 1943-45.

"In these altered conditions," recalls Rejewski, "we took up once more our work so suddenly interrupted in France." Rejewski and Zygalski had to make quick work of the newest system of S.S. codes and ciphers. The war was entering its decisive phase, and every early reading of a directive or order from S.S. headquarters could save the lives of Allied soldiers. Resistance movements in various countries could also be forewarned of arrests, mass roundups, and operations against partisan units. The Poles at Boxmoor almost never found out how their information was used, and archives of higher Allied staffs that might establish this remain largely inaccessible.

The S.S. and S.D. ciphers solved by the Poles were usually based on the Double Casket (Doppelkassetenverfahren) system.[2] The Poles had begun work on these ciphers already in France. At Boxmoor, they were able to concentrate all their attention on them, and results were soon forthcoming. The basic difficulty, according to Rejewski, was caused by the method of preparing the texts. These were first divided into bigrams (groups of two letters) and shuffled. Only then was the text enciphered. But even in this complicated system the Poles managed to find weak points. As in the thirties, the Nazis continued to believe in the absolute security of their ciphers. Yet, improper use of the cipher sometimes left the Germans vulnerable. Stereotyped expressions recurred. There was a predilection for certain abbreviations and epithets. Even before the war, a favorite expression in S.S. radiograms had been, ironically, the adjective "einwandfrei"—faultless, impeccable (chapter 5, note 14). The breaking of a certain cipher was markedly speeded by an S.S. operator's careless use, in a practice signal, of the German proverb: "Wie die Alten sungen, so zwitschern jetzt die Jungen" (As once the old sang, so chirp now the young).

The Double Casket was the last cipher system that the Polish cryptologists worked on at Boxmoor. To the war's end, they decrypted many hundreds of S.S. radiograms—messages more and more foreshadowing the collapse of Hitler's barbaric Thousand Year Reich.

The lives of the two mathematicians at Boxmoor, not far from London, were fairly monotonous. They lived in a bungalow on Bargrove Avenue rented for them by the army. The similar adjoining house was occupied by a professor who often worked in his garden, pushing a wheelbarrow filled with compost. Having struck up an acquaintance with their industrious neighbor, one day the Poles asked him why he did not collect the beautiful saffron milk cups, wild mushrooms that grew bountifully in his garden. The Englishman was amazed to learn that they were edible, and was only too glad to let the Poles have them. The next day, he could not get over his surprise at finding the men alive and well.

In the evening of 10 October 1943, Rejewski and Zygalski invited colleagues from their unit to the only restaurant in Boxmoor, the White Horse Inn, to celebrate their commissions as second lieutenants.[3] Their promotions had no bearing on their work, but would protect them from the intrusions of self-important men (of whom there is never a shortage, even in wartime).

As officers, Rejewski and Zygalski could also go to London and attend the theater. During the final period of the war, it was easy to get tickets even to the most attractive premieres, thanks to the V-1s and V-2s that were falling upon London. Many theatergoers preferred not to risk several hours inside a theater. It was safer to be somewhere near a concrete shelter, an underground metro station, or one's cellar. Hence, during the first few weeks of London's bombardment, the theaters stood nearly empty.

In February 1944, the Luftwaffe conducted a series of brief but powerful nighttime bombing raids on London and the vicinity, including Boxmoor. In contrast with earlier terror raids, the German pilots tried to hit preselected targets, using aerial flares dropped on parachutes (a technique earlier employed by the British). Destroyed buildings included a number near Allied Headquarters, which was housed in St. Paul's School. In June, July, and August 1944, the Nazis showered England with V-1 flying bombs.

The first V-1 fell on London during the night of 12-13 June 1944. Although the British High Command had known since 1943 about German preparations to use the V-1s, the civilian population was taken completely unaware. The official government bulletin stated that on that night an enemy bomber had been shot down over London and had exploded upon striking the ground. Only in the next bulletin was the explanation added that it had been a pilotless aircraft.

If such gradual dosing of information was appropriate on account of the population's psychological unpreparedness, it was certainly an error to have disclosed that the first flying bomb to be fired at London had been on target, even if the latter was as broad as London. The V-1 was still a very unreliable weapon. Many missiles impacted far from London, and some did not even reach England, dropping into the sea. The Germans should not have been informed about their effectiveness. The British soon stopped giving details as to the V-1s' sites of impact. Barrage balloons were deployed to the southeast of London, and antiaircraft batteries were concentrated there. Antiaircraft guns near London ceased firing at the V-1s, since a struck V-1 would fall upon London. Most effective in combatting the V-1s were fighter aircraft (including the new Tempest jets), piloted by Poles, among others. Meanwhile, British bombers ceaselessly attacked V-1 launching sites on the French coast. On one occasion, a V-1 exploded half a kilometer (a quarter of a mile) from The Arches, where Rejewski and Zygalski worked.

Within three months, the situation had been brought under control. Between June and August 1944, the Germans fired about eight thousand V-1s at England—about one hundred a day. About 75 percent of the flying bombs were destroyed in flight, and only about 9 percent reached London (the remainder falling outside the limits of Greater London). In spite of this, losses in people and property were substantial.

In the next several months, V-2 rockets made their appearance over Britain. About a thousand were fired from launching sites in Holland. Despite the V-2's bigger payload, the new weapon's destructiveness was not much greater than that of the V-1. Dropping from a higher altitude, the V-2 rocket plowed deep into the ground, dampening the force and destructiveness of the explosion.

As more and more flying bombs and rockets exploded and could not be completely passed over in silence, a general formula was adopted for news bulletins, stating that enemy flying bombs had exploded in southern England—no distinction was made between V-1 and V-2 rockets. The Germans were thus deprived of information that might have improved their aim.

One afternoon a few weeks after D-Day, as the two Polish mathematicians were looking at a fresh batch of S.S. signals from Germany, the telephone rang. At first Rejewski could not believe his ears—it was Lieutenant Colonel Bertrand. A few days later, they met. It was a moving experience for the Poles and for the newcomer from France. Over supper at the White Horse in honor of their guest, they reminisced about Gretz-Armainvillers and the tragic war of 1940, about Algiers and the underground P.C. Cadix, and about the tension filled weeks in the winter of 1942-43 when, eluding the S.D. and Gestapo, they had made ready to cross the Pyrenees.

On instructions from his Resistance superiors, Gustave Bertrand remained in France, organizing the new intelligence stations and nets (réseaux) indispensable to Allied staffs which were planning Operation Overlord after the successful landings in Africa. Bertrand's new assignment was a particularly dangerous one. He was again forced to change his name, from Barsac to Monsieur B. Gustave. The Germans, now freely operating throughout all of France, had thrown thousands of experienced operatives into the struggle against the Resistance. One of Bertrand's intelligence missions ended dramatically. On 5 January 1944, he arrived in Paris from the south and had waited at the Church of Sacré Cœur in Montmartre for a courier from London. There he was suddenly surrounded by Nazi thugs and dragged into the street. A waiting police car drove him to prison. The Abwehr suggested that he work for them, turning his underground radio communications with London against the Allies. Bertrand pretended to agree, and was allowed to return with his wife Mary to Vichy to contact British intelligence. There he sent his underground colleagues into hiding and went underground himself. Later, on 2 June 1944 at 10:30 p.m. at an improvised airstrip in the Massif Central, Bertrand and his wife, together with a Jesuit priest who was a courier of the Polish Resistance, climbed into a small, unarmed Lysander III aircraft that took them to the British Isles. Bertrand had now received a new assignment, in General de Gaulle's Free French forces.

From Bertrand, the Boxmoor Poles learned the fates of their Cadix colleagues who, in the spring of 1943, had also attempted to cross the Pyrenees. Of Team Z's fifteen men, there remained at their posts only the two cryptologists Rejewski and Zygalski and three radio-telegraphers.[4]

Some of the B.S.-4 personnel who had worked with Enigma, and most of the technical personnel of the AVA Radio Company, which had employed over two hundred people, had remained in occupied Poland. The great majority of them fought in various underground organizations against the Germans. Among them was engineer Stanisław Guzicki, a pioneer in the scientific organization of work who, during the German occupation and after the war, was a leading activist of the Polish Workers' Party (Polska Partia Robotnicza, or P.P.R.). Before the war, working at AVA facilities involved in Poland's defense effort, Guzicki had introduced a number of innovations (chapter 4). Now to his address came letters, mutilated by German censors, from Engineer Antoni Palluth, who was imprisoned at Oranienburg concentration camp in eastern Germany (one of the first concentration camps to have been set up by the Nazi regime). Writing directly to his family might have put the Germans on the scent of Enigma.

Throughout the war, the Abwehr painstakingly studied captured documents belonging to Poland's military intelligence unit, Section II. During the hectic evacuation there had not been time to destroy all the archives, and many documents stored at Warsaw's Fort Legionów (Fort of the Legions) had fallen into the hands of the Germans[5] (most were moved to the German military archives branch at Oliva, a district of Danzig). But they included no Cipher Bureau material, none concerning B.S.-4 or Enigma. Thanks to this, the secret of Enigma's solution was never discovered by the Germans. Decisive in this regard were carefully thought out security measures and the exemplary posture of the people concerned.

At the Cipher Bureau there had been two supreme and most strictly guarded secrets: first, the breaking of the German Enigma; second, the construction both of a Polish Enigma and of a Polish cipher machine, the Lacida or L.C.D., reserved for wartime use. Assembly of the devices used in decrypting Enigma—the cyclometers and cryptographic bombs—as well as the most important work on the Polish cipher machines took place not at AVA facilities but in a special room at the Cipher Bureau itself, in the general staff building (and at the new B.S.-4 center at Pyry beginning in 1937). This was Room 13, which bureau workers called the Clock Room (pokój pod zegarem) because of a clock located over the door. The entrance to this room—as to the cryptologists' office—was shrouded by a black curtain. No one had access to this room except the head of the Cipher Bureau, Colonel Langer, and the persons employed there: engineer Antoni Palluth, engineer Ludomir Danilewicz, his younger brother Leonard Stanisław Danilewicz, Edward Fokczyński, and the specialist in precision mechanics, Czesław Betlewski, who was directly responsible for final assembly. Here they had at their disposal measuring instruments, precision lathes, and milling and grinding machines. Only separate parts and certain subsystems were produced at the AVA facilities. Other electrical, mechanical, engraving, and similar firms and shops were also commissioned to execute various details of the cipher machines, but these were exclusively details whose purpose could not be guessed from their appearance. The final shape and function of the devices that emerged from Room 13 were known only to a few persons.

The war years showed how justified such drastic security precautions had been. One day at the beginning of 1941, as Betlewski was walking across the Poniatowski Bridge over the Wisła (Vistula) River in Warsaw, he encountered, going in the opposite direction, a man in S.A. uniform whose face seemed familiar. Before Betlewski could recall where he might have seen him, the S.A. man distinctly slowed his pace. Yes, it was the same man he used to see in civilian clothes before the war and had known as the owner of a mechanical shop on Puławska Street (ulica Puławska) that had executed certain Enigma parts on commission from AVA (in fact, from the Cipher Bureau). Anticipating that the Volksdeutsch[6] might ask questions, Betlewski sought for evasive answers. Unexpectedly, the man took a defensive stance and proceeded to explain that he had been threatened with loss of his shop if he did not sign the Volksliste. The man, fortunately, was one of those fledgling members of the Herrenvolk, the Master Race, whose fear of reprisals by the Polish underground was stronger than their zeal in serving the Greater Reich. But who knows how the man might have behaved had he known something about the purpose of the details that had been manufactured in his shop?[7]

There were also other, more dangerous, incidents. A former long-time worker at the Cipher Bureau—from 1924 to September 1939—was Zofia Pawłowicz, director of the B.S.-4 secretariat and Major Ciężki's right hand. She had not had time to evacuate to Rumania and, until the summer of 1941, stayed in Lwów, later in the Tarnopol area, southeast of Lwów, where she found temporary employment within the administration of a hospital. Following the German invasion of the Soviet Union and the Nazi occupation of Tarnopol, she made her way back to Warsaw. She supported herself by working in a café belonging to Mrs. Mróz-Długoszewska, an old friend, with whom she took lodgings. A few weeks after her return to the capital, however, betrayed by some informer, she was arrested and taken to the infamous Warsaw headquarters of the Gestapo on Aleja Szucha (Szuch Avenue, now Aleja Pierwszej Armii Wojska Polskiego—Avenue of the First Polish Army). She was kept, at first, with hundreds of fellow prisoners, in the "streetcar" (tramwaj), where the Gestapo sought to soften prisoners physically and psychologically prior to interrogation. [The "streetcar" is preserved as a memorial on the ground floor of the building. The elongated room, which communicates directly with the hallway, takes its name from the streetcar-like arrangement of the rows of wooden seats. Prisoners were forbidden to move, to look about, or to communicate in any way. A breach of the rules brought brutal physical punishments. Loud martial music was played on a radio to drown out the cries of interrogated prisoners.—ED.]

The interrogations to which Zofia Pawłowicz was shortly subjected were conducted on the second floor of the Gestapo headquarters, but in a strikingly different setting than usual.

> I found myself in a large, elegantly furnished room, and behind a long table covered with documents sat three officers in Wehrmacht uniforms: army, air force, and navy. In a flash I realized that I was probably standing before an Abwehr commission and not before police authorities—which made me feel a little better. The officers, or at least two of them, if I remember correctly, spoke fluent Polish. Already from the first questions I saw that they had a fairly good knowledge of the structure of the Polish General Staff, and that they wanted to surprise me with their supposed omniscience, mentioning the names of the chiefs of various sections and of other officers known to me. At first they were very courteous and assured me that they wanted only to confirm known facts [and] to elucidate some less important details. They knew that for many years I had been a civilian employee at the [General] Staff, and surely I would not be so unreasonable as to deny obvious facts, otherwise they would be forced to leave me for some time under arrest by the Gestapo. . . Apparently I was fairly good at playing the role of a none too intelligent, but also not excessively dull, ordinary military clerk, like the

hundred or more that had been employed by the prewar Polish General Staff and Ministry of Military Affairs.

Although the Wehrmacht-uniformed inquisitors wanted to impress her with their omniscience, Zofia Pawłowicz quickly realized that their knowledge of the Polish General Staff was superficial and that they were not specialists in cryptology or, more generally, in secret communications. Therefore, she sought to answer them in such a way as to expatiate on unimportant, partly fabricated, details of her "clerk's" job, for as long as possible absorbing, therewith, the attention of the investigators and diverting them from fundamental matters: decryptment and radio intelligence. With the whole strength of her will she strove to master her anxiety and the thoughts that were being obsessively prompted by her imagination concerning the solved Enigma and other most secret matters of B.S.-4, for whose extraction the complaisant Abwehr officers and Gestapo men would not have shrunk—of this she could be sure—from the most brutal methods, including the most sophisticated tortures. The fact that she succeeded completely in leading her persecutors astray must be ascribed principally to the enormous courage and skill of the long-time Polish intelligence worker. But the success of the deception may also have been favored by the blind faith of the Nazi authorities, persisting, as well, through the war years, in the insolubility of Enigma.

The interrogation of Zofia Pawłowicz ended with threats that "severe punishment" awaited her in the event of false testimony and pending "verification [of her statements] in Berlin" she was to remain under arrest and investigation. Taken to the Pawiak prison in Warsaw's Muranów district and placed in a solitary cell, Zofia Pawłowicz was beset by the blackest thoughts and premonitions. [Named for its proximity to ulica Pawia—Peacock Street—the old czarist prison, built in 1829-35, would be blown up by the Nazis in August 1944, after they had processed one hundred thousand Poles—20 percent of them women—through it, murdering 37 percent of them outright and sending nearly all the rest to concentration camps. The building's basement now houses a memorial to the Nazis' victims.—ED.] But the Abwehr apparently decided that she was, in fact, not a person who had had access to matters that could, after two years of war, still interest German intelligence.[8]

Similarly released following a rather cursory interrogation was another civilian worker of the prewar Cipher Bureau, a man named Pański (who was encountered by Zofia Pawłowicz in a corridor during investigation at the Gestapo). He was likewise treated as inconsequential. It should be noted that all this was happening in the autumn of 1941 when, intoxicated by their initial, stunning successes, the Nazis expected any day to occupy Moscow and to achieve ultimate victory in the east. When the way to world dominion for the Third Reich seemed to lie open, the affairs of the defunct Polish General Staff—the affairs of a state that had been erased by the Fuehrer from the map of Europe—might well have seemed to the Nazis of little account.

At the beginning of 1943, while the Polish cryptological team was striving to get out of occupied southern France, there unexpectedly turned up in Warsaw a technical worker of the prewar Cipher Bureau, Konstanty P., who had also sometimes served as a courier and, just before the war, had been sent abroad. The war caught him in France, and there he had remained. Despite his radiotelegrapher's qualifications, he was not included when the Polish intercept organization was being formed in October 1939 to work at Gretz-Armainvillers, outside Paris. For Konstanty P. was known to have a penchant for smuggling and assorted shady dealings—not very serious ones, perhaps, but nevertheless bespeaking a rather unsavory character. Konstanty P. did not join the Polish Army that was being organized in France, but decided to set himself up on his own. Then he dropped out of sight, and gradually everyone forgot about him.

Reappearing in Warsaw in early 1943, Konstanty P. proceeded energetically to renew acquaintances with AVA employees, and after obtaining several addresses he began asking about various details of the company's prewar work. His intuitions were good. He was especially persistent in questioning Czesław Betlewski, one of the employees in the Clock Room. Konstanty P. also attempted to get close to a veteran worker at AVA's technical laboratory, Edward Bonczak, formerly the right hand of the company's chief technologist. Apart from the past, he was also interested in current work. Both men were employed at radio firms in occupied Warsaw and, as he could guess, had contacts with Polish underground organizations. When he found that he was not going to learn anything concrete and that persistence could unmask him, Konstanty P. decided to go all the way. He confided that he was working for Allied intelligence and had been sent to Poland on a special mission. For starters he requested, on behalf of his superiors, the secret manufacture and delivery of fifty mechanisms to be used in time bomb detonators. Naturally, this was not to be done gratis. He backed up the proposal with what he considered to be the strongest possible argument, displaying a wallet stuffed with bank notes—not only occupation currency, but also a wad of dollars. And here he overplayed his hand. He was told that some time would be needed to check on the feasibility of filling the order. That same day the resistance movement's counterintelligence organization was informed.

Surveillance of a person suspected of collaborating with the Germans was very difficult under occupation conditions. Usually it was conducted in sporadic fashion, but this matter was of sufficient seriousness that it was decided to clear it up fully. As chance would have it, at this time Konstanty P. apparently had many matters to take care of with his actual principals—the Gestapo. On four separate occasions over a short span of time he entered—by a secret back entrance, after first dodging through the streets—the infamous Gestapo headquarters on Szuch Avenue (Aleja Szucha). Those were the last days of his treachery. During his next trip, in the vicinity of Lublin Union Square (Plac Unii Lubelskiej) not far from the headquarters of the Geheime Staatspolizei in Warschau, two shots rang out, fired in execution of an underground court sentence. They concluded the career of a traitor who, after his unsuccessful provocation involving the time bomb mechanisms, had begun openly blackmailing some of his acquaintances who were initiated into the affairs of the AVA Company and Enigma. The secret of its solution, and of its decryptment over many years running, was never uncovered by the Nazis.

In the summer of 1944, when the fighting in France had entered the decisive phase, the German High Command was still considering the introduction of changes in the Enigma system.[9] The German Supreme Command in the West (Ober-West) on 8 August 1944 issued a directive concerning new rotors (Walzeneinstellungen) intended to make decryptment as difficult as possible for the enemy. But the introduction of these innovations encountered great difficulties, as the German armies, hard pressed by superior Allied forces in east and west, slowly but continually retreated. The changes in the cipher system ordered on August 8 were never effected.[10]

Almost up to the final weeks of the war, Germany's Chi-Dienst attempted to improve techniques of secret communications and painstakingly analyzed anything that suggested that the enemy's cryptological services might be breaking German ciphers. These matters were discussed at conferences of ranking commanders and signals chiefs. However, conclusions drawn from investigation of suspect signals continued to be optimistic. The high functionaries still believed in the security of their secret signals, assured by the newest generation of improved Enigma machines which were equipped with ten exchangeable rotors each in the final months of the war.[11]

This conviction remained unshaken even by evidence that enemy radio intelligence had read one or another German signal. This was still believed to involve sporadic incidents rather than an entire system.[12] In investigating the cause of various difficult-to-explain facts regarding the opponent's behavior and operations that indicated an excellent knowledge of the dispositions of German field staffs, signals centers, artillery positions, armor concentrations, and so on, German specialists seemed to discount in advance the possibility of this information being acquired from decryptment of radio correspondence. Usually they were of the opinion that the source was some unknown new device, based on radar, that had the capability of locating, with enormous precision, these sensitive units and concentrations of German combat forces.[13]

Still—to the amazement of the German staff officers—precise massed artillery bombardments and air raids occurred, as well, in conditions when radiolocation was simply impossible. In an effort to find some rational explanation, such causes were mentioned as derelictions and errors in camouflage, enemy air or ground reconnaissance, breaches of discipline in German radio correspondence (for example, giving place names in clear), and so on.[14]

Beginning in August 1944, OKW made preparations for a decisive counteroffensive in the west that was meant to repeat the victory of 1940, when the Allied armies were routed and pushed into the sea. If successful, this campaign would make it possible to shift the bulk of German forces to the east, where the front was sagging. In view of the shrinking possibilities for accurate reconnaissance of the enemy, who now had clear superiority in the air, the German High Command decided to shift some radio-intelligence units from the eastern to the western front. At the beginning of December 1944, just before the opening of the great offensive through the Ardennes, two long-range radio intelligence companies (Nachrichten-Fernaufklärung) and a short-range radio intelligence company (Nachrichten-Nahaufklärung) arrived and were placed at the disposal of the western armies. This more than doubled the resources of German radio intelligence in the west. Neverthless, most of the Reich's radio intelligence still remained in the eastern theater. In addition to the radio intelligence companies and platoons at the fronts, the Germans had established eight stationary long-range radio intelligence and direction finding centers and seventeen medium- and close-range units in the occupied territories of Poland, the U.S.S.R., and other central and southeast European countries.

Five months before the final throes of the enormous German war machine, still numbering some ten million men under arms, the supreme command was staking all on a single card. It wanted to compensate, at least partly, for the loss or shrinkage of other kinds of intelligence by means of stepped-up radio intelligence and decryptment, so as not to be operating completely in the dark, and to make up for the acute shortages in cadres and armaments of the front-line divisions by means of operations conducted with numerous diversionary groups. The latter were formed deep in the hinter-land by the celebrated Otto Skorzeny.

On 4 September 1944 at Berlin's Plötzensee prison, after the abortive attempt on Hitler's life of July 20 at the Wolf's Lair (Wolfsschanze) near Rastenburg in East Prussia, the head of Wehrmacht signals, Gen. Erich Fellgiebel, and his deputy, Gen. Fritz Thiele, and the chief of staff, Colonel Hahn, were executed. The head of OKW signals intelligence (Leitstelle für Nachrichtenaufklärung), Colonel von der Osten, shot himself when the Gestapo summoned him for interrogation.

Designated Fellgiebel's successor was Gen. Albert Praun, who had been in command of the 277th Infantry Division in the west. In view of the growing role of radio intelligence, the OKW signals intelligence center had been elevated to Generalstelle rank, and a Colonel Bötzel had been put in charge. At this time (the autumn of 1944) information from radio intelligence constituted about 80 percent of all information on the enemy.[15] A staff report of the German Supreme Command in the West for the third quarter of 1944 states:

> Due to the nearly total lack of P.O.W. statements and of captured enemy orders, the absence of aerial reconnaissance capability, as well as frequent difficulties in transmitting to the rear reports from front-line units, radio intelligence has become virtually the sole means of supplying our com-mand with information on the enemy.[16]

German military preparations in these final months of the war resembled the movements of a man who is trying to cover both his head and his feet with a much too short blanket. This was equally so in operations at the front and in the secret war that was being conducted on the airwaves. At the end of 1944 and the beginning of 1945, German radio counterintelligence, though numbering six thousand military and civilian specialists, was able to locate barely every fourth radio station of the various resistance and foreign intelligence organizations. The total number of clandestine radio transmitters in the last phase of the war operating on territories occupied or dominated by Germany is estimated by historians to be fifteen hundred to two thousand.

This number represents a vast effort—paid for with many human lives—by thousands of people in various European countries who fought the Nazi war machine on the invisible front (in Poland, from the first weeks after the aggression that opened World War II). A special role, attacking the enemy's most sensitive system, was played by a group of radio intelligence and decryptment specialists. The results of their work were exploited not only in planning Allied military operations, but in anti-Nazi propaganda and psychological warfare. General Paun asked the following in his memoirs:

> How could secret, privileged information from the Führer's Headquarters reach the Allied Sender [Radio] Calais or Luxemburg within a few hours? I deployed a monitoring company around the Führer's Headquarters in order to discover the clandestine transmitter. In vain! Then again it was suggested that the operators servicing the Führer's secure telephone lines might be listening in on Hitler's conversations, or that unauthorized persons may be plugging into these lines. So we made surprise inspections of the switchboard at the Führer's Headquarters, but discovered nothing.[17]

After the war, speculation arose about astonishing leaks to the Allies of secret information from the highest levels of German command—almost instantaneous leaks, for, within hours, they were reflected in Allied official and "black" radio broadcasts. There was speculation concerning Nazi party secretary Martin Bormann's order in 1944 to establish a special radio net for him in addition to the teletypes that he already had for direct communication with Nazi party *gauleiters* (administrators of provinces or districts) throughout the Reich. The Wehrmacht signals command had begged off, pleading a shortage of personnel and equipment, but the Kriegsmarine had obligingly offered to build him such a net. Used in it were surplus radio stations that had been intended for use in submarines.

Today it would be difficult to establish whether or not supposed leaks from Hitler's headquarters had any connection with this communications net of Reichsleiter Bormann's. It may be supposed that they did not, since the information sent over it pertained to organizational and political, rather than to military, matters. It is worth noting, however, that these deliberations never considered another possibility: decryptment of Enigma signals from Hitler's headquarters. Although Allied use of decrypts in propaganda would have been risky, since it could give away the source of the information, by the final year of the war the British could afford to take such a risk. Exchange of the some hundred thousand Enigmas that were sounding off in all the theaters of the war, on land, sea, and in the air—even had the Germans determined that the enemy was reading their correspondence—would by then have been simply impracticable.

On 25 May 1945, at the request of Prime Minister Churchill, F.W. Winterbotham sent a signal to all the Allied commanders and their staffs in the European theater of war who had been in receipt of intelligence from what Churchill called "my most secret source." Winterbotham asked them not to divulge the nature of the source or the information they had received from it, "in order that there might be neither damage to the future operations of the Secret Service nor any cause for our enemies to blame it for their defeat."[18] The intention, it would seem, was to prevent a recurrence of the "stab-in-the-back" theory of German defeat that had appeared after the previous world war and that may have contributed to the rise of German fascism between the wars. But does that explain why the Ultra operation had to be kept secret for as long as thirty years after the close of the Second World War, or why it could suddenly be made public after those thirty years had elapsed?

David Kahn has offered a very down-to-earth explanation for those thirty years of secrecy:

> It seems that after World War II, Britain gathered up as many of the tens of thousands of Enigmas as she could find and later sold them to some of the emerging nations. Presumably if she could read Enigma messages in 1940, she could do so in 1950. Only recently have these countries replaced their Enigmas with new cryptosystems.[19]

NOTES

1. Account given by Marian Rejewski. Rejewski, Virtually continuous interviews given to the author.

2. Generally known as the "double Playfair." See Bertrand, *Enigma*, 130.—ED.

3. According to a transcript of Rejewski's confidential military service record issued on 8 November 1957 by the War Office Records Centre (Polish) in Britain, "He was commissioned in rank 2/Lt. on 10.10.1943 and promoted Lieutenant 1.1.1945." Rejewski, Transcript.

4. Mayer writes that, due to Bertrand's incompetent preparations for their evacuation, Lt. Col. Langer, Major Ciężki, Lt. A. Palluth [and] civilian employees Fokczyński and Gaca were arrested near Perpignan by the Gestapo on 13 [March] 1943. They [had been] betrayed by the unreliable local guide provided by the French. Langer and Ciężki were kept initially [at] Frontstalag [No.] 122 in Compiegne, whence they were sent to . . . SS [concentration camp] Sonder-Kommando Schloss Eisenberg in Czechoslovakia on 9.9.1943. On 10 [May] 1945 they were freed by [the] Americans. Palluth, Fokczyński and Gaca were taken to Germany to be used . . . as slave labourers. Palluth was killed there during [an A]llied air raid. Fokczyński died from exhaustion. Gaca returned but his present whereabouts [are] unknown.

It [should be] emphasize[d] that all these five members of . . . Station . . . 300, when they fell into the hands of [the] Germans, were acquainted to the last detail with the . . . breaking [of] "Enigma." They were kept by [the] Germans in most awful conditions [at a time] when [the] "Enigma" secret was still of great importance for the Western Allies. Langer and his four comrades did not reveal this to the Germans, thus [making it possible to continue] exploiting this source of information till the end of the war.

The remaining members of . . . Station . . . 300 escaped . . . to England. Major Michałowski died in 1973. The whereabouts of Lt. Paszkowski and civilian employees Krajewski and S. Palluth are unknown. Lt. Szachno, promoted to . . . captain, died in London in 1973. Civilian employee H. Zygalski, [whose last wartime rank was that of] lieutenant . . . was for [a] time [a] lecturer at the Battersea Technical College. Now [May 1974], partly paralysed, [he] lives near Plymouth. [He died on 31 August 1978.] Civilian employee M. Rejewski, [who] also last [held the wartime rank of] lieutenant . . . the best of all [the] Polish cryptologists, returned to Poland with the intention to have nothing more to do with . . . cryptological work and to start dentistry [studies. He died in Warsaw of a heart attack on 13 February 1980.]

Lt. Col. Langer and Major Ciężki arrived in London in the middle of 1945. They were received in a[n] unfriendly manner by Col. Gano [chief of the Polish Section II in Britain; before the war, head of the Section II Technical Department], who believed [a] biased and distorted [account by] Lt. Col. Bertrand (Bolek) that the [failure to] evacuat[e] Langer's group [had been] due to the latter's hesitation, lack of iniciative [*sic*] and almost cowardice. . . . Langer and Ciężki were sent to the Polish signal troops camp [at] Kinross (Scotland). Here Langer, bitter, disappointed, convinced that he [had been] betrayed by [the] French [after] they had no more use [for] him, died on 30.3.1948.

Ciężki died on 9 [November] 1951 after living on subsidies from the Assistance Board for the last three years.

Mayer, "The breaking up of the German ciphering machine 'ENIGMA,' " 8-9.—ED.

5. In 1976, Colonel Mayer gave Richard Woytak some details of the matter. According to Mayer, in September 1939 Major Waligóra, chief of the Central Military Archives, either did not succeed or did not have the heart to destroy the collections in his charge. This failure was to be costly in human lives. For example, decapitated by the Germans were two Polish railway officials who without recompense had run "Wózek" (Car, Wagon, Cart, or Buggy), an operation that had been one of Poland's best sources of intelligence: the clandestine inspection of mail transported by exterritorial railroad between West and East Prussia. For three or four hours a train would be in Polish territory, and the mail car would move untended, and then the Polish railway workers would get aboard, open the mail sacks, take out the correspondence, open it, and photograph it. From this source, Polish intelligence would get superb information, including a German annual counterintelligence report that described exactly what the Germans knew about Polish espionage operations. Recommendations filed by Major Żychoń (chapter 5, note 24) that the two railway employees be given decorations for their selfless and valuable work, stating their names and routinely deposited, as well, in the Central Military Archives, became their death warrants when the documents fell into the hands of the Germans. Major Żychoń also caused other embarrassments to Polish intelligence, through the personality clashes that he provoked: a brilliant officer who was solicitous for the people who worked under him, he was also insolent, pushy, uncouth, often brutal, and some of the fellow intelligence officers whom he rubbed the wrong way happened to be in the Soviet section of Polish intelligence; consequently, when the debacle of September 1939 unleashed a tide of internal recriminations, Żychoń was unjustly accused by some of them of having been a German agent—and such incidents later fueled speculation, which, according to Mayer, was wholly unfounded, about the existence of political struggles between the Soviet and German sections in prewar Polish intelligence.—ED.

6. Volksdeutsche were citizens of various European countries, of German extraction, who, during the German occupation in World War II, officially declared themselves to be of German nationality and served the German authorities. In Polish Silesia and Pomerania, the Germans also used terror to force populace of Polish descent to sign the Volksliste.

7. Account given to the author by Czesław Betlewski. Betlewski, Interview.

8. Pawłowicz. Interviews granted to the author.

9. The Germans had, for years, been introducing successive new variants of the machine, in order to prevent the development of a "critical mass" of cipher material that might facilitate the breaking of their messages. As noted in earlier chapters, changes had been introduced both into the machine's construction and into procedures for its use, especially regarding the formation of keys. Changes tended to come at moments of unusual political or military significance.

The German Navy had raised the number of exchangeable rotors in its machines to eight, and, in 1942, had put into service a completely new model of Enigma with four rotors.

Not long in use was a model designated Enigma III, with an automatic printing device, which could be operated by one person. Retained, instead, was the standard model operated by two persons, which, among other things, had the advantage of assuring continuous cipher communication even in the event of one of the cipher operators being incapacitated by illness or the effects of military action.

In the summer of 1942, changes of daily key began to be made every eight hours instead of every twenty-four as theretofore. Inexplicably, however, the selection and ordering of rotors (three from among the eight available for the purpose) continued to be changed once every twenty-four hours.

A document of the German commander in chief west (Oberbefehlshaber West) lists the following Enigma nets:

- Command nets:

    Wehrmacht-Schlüssel West

    OKH-Schlüssel

Rundfunk-Schlüssel
Sonder-Schlüssel Inseln
- Supply nets: O. Qu Schlüssel
- Transport nets: Eisenbahntruppen-Schlüssel
- Reconnaissance-intelligence nets:
  Luftwaffen-Sonderschlüssel
  Wehrmacht-Schlüssel
  Rundspruch-Schlüssel
- Special nets: AA - ZZ
- Net of the commander in chief west.

In addition, separate systems for operating Enigma were used by Waffen-S.S., S.S.-Totenkopf, and S.D. units. Thus, simultaneously, about twenty separate communication nets used Enigma, but in different ways.

In the month of June 1944 alone, a dozen cases of compromise of Enigma keys were reported. Waldemar Werther, in Rohwer and Jäckel, *Die Funkaufklärung*, 50-65.

10. German Army signals chiefs reported that, with personnel overtaxed, changes in the cipher system would cause "intolerable embarrassment to cipher operations and occasion time-consuming errors" (nicht tragbare Erschwerung der Schlüsselei und Quelle zu zeitraubenden Fehlern). Report of German Army Signals Chiefs, *Records of German Field Commands*, series T-311, roll 18.

11. See minutes of signals commanders' conference at OKW (late 1943), particularly the statement by Gen. Fritz Thiele: "The improvement of Enigma and of the automatic cipher teletype is concluded. The improved equipment will soon be put into use." (Die Verbesserung der Enigma und der Schlüsselfernschreibmaschine ist abgeschlossen. Verbesserte Geräte werden in absichtbaren Zeit herauskommen.") Higher formations, down to and including divisions, were to have been equipped with cipher teletype by the spring of 1944. *See* OKW Signal Commanders' Conference, late 1943.

12. The head of the OKW cryptographic service, Colonel Kempf, gave it as his opinion that "the adversary has excellent personnel in his decryption units as well as every kind of ancillary equipment. He is partly able—as our information shows—to solve some signals within two hours." From a German document of 1944 in Rejewski's files. Kempf also stated that captured British and American signal corpsmen were interrogated at the Diez an der Lahn POW camp, where they were grouped.

13. A report by the signals chief of the German Supreme Command in the West (Ober-West) of 20 February 1945. The German U-Boat Command evidently succumbed to the same delusion. When thirty thousand pages of secret U.S. World War II cryptological documents were turned over to the National Archives at Washington in September 1978, it was discovered that

the decisive secret weapon of the Allies in the struggle against the German U-boats was not, despite the opinions of the Oberkommando der Wehrmacht, advanced radar equipment. The German submarines operating in the Atlantic were located and destroyed by Allied aircraft and ships as a result of the interception and decryptment of radio messages from the commander in chief of the U-Boat Command, Admiral Karl Doenitz . . . . Such a possibility was not considered either by Hitler's Headquarters or by O.K.W. Meanwhile Doenitz was calling in experts from all over Germany to find effective measures to counter the radar, and ordering his U-boat commanders, invariably, to attack!

Hamburger Abendblatt, 12 September 1978.

According to these U.S. documents, between January 1943 and V-E Day (9 May 1945), a total of 489 German submarines were sunk in the Atlantic. Of these, the Americans alone, thanks to Enigma information, sank 93.

14. Report by the signals chief of the German Supreme Command in the West, of 20 February 1945. Cf. the following fragments:

Mit ziemlicher Sicherheit hatte das Feuer auf die Stäbe und einzelne Funkstellen andere Gründe, entweder das Sichten aus der Luft bzw. auf der Erde (durch schlechte Tarnung, starken Meldeverkehr usw.) oder das Erkennen aus dem Inhalt des Funkverkehrs (Verstösse gegen Funkdisziplin, ungetarnte Ortsangaben usw.). . . . Vorläufig bleibt die Behauptung, dass der Feind ein fabelhaftes Funkmessverfahren besitzt, immer noch eine Vermutung.

According to Waldemar Werther, the Germans fell victim to their own illusion of security. The high command was completely convinced that decryptment of Enigma was impossible, even in the event of the capture of any of the machines, on account of the enormous number of possible settings. Likewise, after the war, West German specialists who studied the Wehrmacht's cryptographic methods concluded that the Enigma ciphers had not been read by the other side. A study in 1958 by a former OKL specialist concluded, "Enigma had a satisfactory degree of security when relatively few of the machines were employed. Following their large-scale introduction into the armed forces, the degree of security decreased substantially." However, a leading OKW specialist took issue: "The matter isn't that simple, because the enemy never did succeed in reading Enigma ciphergrams, although he possessed many of the machines! More problems were caused by the slow operation of the machines than by their security."

Nevertheless, during the war, as indicated by surviving documents, German staffs and units were becoming increasingly nervous. Some specialists and commanders, doubtless noting enemy moves that suggested foreknowledge of their most secret plans, had growing doubts as to the security of their ciphers. Werther cites examples of high- and middle-level commands and staffs that introduced their own measures, such as additional coding or double encryptment (for example, Army Group North and the Sixteenth Army in February 1942, the Sixteenth Army in June 1942).

In January 1943, at a conference of cipher specialists, it was stated, "It has been determined beyond any doubt that in individual cases the Russians have been able to solve Enigma ciphergrams." Causes postulated for such a state of affairs included incorrect use of the Enigmas by operators and an excessive volume of cipher correspondence using the same starting position (setting) of the machines. For the latter reason, an eight-hour cycle of key changes had been introduced, as well as a new special key for transmittal of top secret messages (Chefsache). Werther in Rohwer and Jäckel, *Die Funkaufklärung*, 50-65.

15. Von Schramm, *Der Geheimdienst in Europa*, 173ff.

16. "Tatigkeitsbericht für die Zeit von 1.7.-30.9.44—III Funk." *Records of German Field Commands*, series T-311, roll 18.

17. Quoted after von Schramm, *Der Geheimdienst in Europa*, 225-26.

18. Winterbotham, *The Ultra Secret*, Introduction.

19. Kahn, "Enigma Unwrapped."

Appendix A

Epilogue
by Christopher Kasparek and Richard Woytak

On 15 November 1946, according to his military service record, "No. 32145 Lieutenant (Sig[nals]) Marian REJEWSKI [was] discharged on repatriation to Poland." With the blessing of Col. Stefan Mayer of Polish military intelligence, Rejewski became one of the approximately twenty-five thousand Polish soldiers, sailors, and airmen in the west to return to Poland at war's end.[1]

In Poland, for reasons of a practical and family nature, it proved difficult for Rejewski to find employment as a mathematician at an institution of higher learning, and, in the early postwar period, he felt it imprudent to apply for a job in cryptology. An obituary published in Poland[2] states, somewhat cryptically, that "on November 21, 1946, he returned to Poland, then for 20 years worked in the administrations of various concerns in Bydgoszcz, and in February 1967 retired."

What had Rejewski and his colleagues personally gained from their unique cryptological work?

Not money. To be sure, Colonel Mayer has stated that before the war they had received a sizable cash reward for having given their country the mastery of Enigma. Rejewski later confirmed to Richard Woytak that they had indeed received a bonus, but denied that it had been a princely sum.

Certainly their rewards did not include rank. Rejewski and Zygalski were commissioned second lieutenants on 10 October 1943, after two months' military service in uniform, and Rejewski (and probably also Zygalski) was promoted to lieutenant on 1 January 1945. In subsequent civilian life, both ended their careers humbly, Zygalski, according to Mayer, as a lecturer at the Battersea Technical College in England. He died near Plymouth in 1978.

As for distinctions, Rejewski's service record lists only the Gold Cross of Merit, the Silver Cross of Merit with Swords, and the Army Medal, all Polish and all relatively lackluster. Considering the uniquely valuable nature of their contributions, all three mathematicians would not have been excessively honored had they been given Poland's Order of Polonia Restituta, France's Légion d'honneur, and Britain's Distinguished Service Order. (Rejewski finally received the Officer's Cross of the Order of Polonia Restituta on 12 August 1978, a year and a half before his death.)

Rejewski, however, did not seem unduly concerned with the trappings of success. When proposals were advanced around 1978 to bestow on him the degree of doctor honoris causa, he expressed no interest in attending such a ceremony. He was a rather private person, and, moreover, he was not in the best of health. In any case, he did not live to take receipt of an honorary degree. (Henryk Zygalski received an honorary doctorate in 1977.)

What satisfaction Rejewski and Zygalski derived from their prewar and wartime work doubtless stemmed from the knowledge that they had contributed to the winning of the war and the survival of their country, a state foredoomed by the Nazis to extinction, and from that peculiar feeling that is enjoyed by those who have made unique discoveries or inventions (they and Jerzy Różycki, but Rejewski especially, had made both).

Rejewski hypothesized about a possible connection between the Polish solution of Enigma in 1932-33 and the U.S. solution of the Japanese Purple machine in 1941 (by some accounts, the Purple machine was, in fact, a modified Enigma).

When public recognition finally came—over thirty years after the war, in the wake of the revelations by Gustave Bertrand (1973) and F.W. Winterbotham (1974)—Rejewski gave unstintingly of his time to all who wished to know, through interviews or correspondence, about his achievements and those of his colleagues. In his last years, he was interviewed by scholars, journalists, and television crews from Poland, East Germany, Britain, Sweden, Belgium, the Soviet Union, Yugoslavia, and Brazil. A master of the German language and fluent in French and English (he also knew Greek and Latin from high school), he managed to keep abreast of most of the polyglot nonsense being written about Enigma. A few years before his death, at the request of the Piłsudski Institute of America, Rejewski broke ciphered correspondence of a conspiratorial Józef Piłsudski dating from 1904, the year before Rejewski's birth. Earlier, at Gustave Bertrand's request, he began translating the general's book *Enigma* into Polish (no Polish translation has yet been published). In 1980 he and his colleagues became heroes of a Polish movie, *Sekret Enigmy* (The Enigma Secret—screenplay by Stanisław Strumph Wojtkiewicz), that used Enigma as what Hitchcock called a McGuffin—a more or less plausible business that serves as pretext for a plot—for a Polish-cryptologists-and-German-spies thriller, complete with a spurious love story foisted upon Maj. Maksymilian Ciężki, the head of B.S.-4, who died in Britain on public relief in 1951. Late 1980 also saw a Polish television serial based on the Enigma story.[3]

At the time of his demise at the age of seventy-four, Marian Rejewski was living with his wife Irena on Gdańsk Street (ulica Gdańska) in northern Warsaw's Żoliborz district, in a spacious, comfortably furnished second-floor apartment in a prewar building that was part of the less than 20 percent of the city that the Germans had not managed to destroy during World War II.

Rejewski had been suffering for some years from ischemic heart disease. Death came on 13 February 1980 at his home, apparently of a heart attack. He had just returned home from a shopping trip. As he was removing his shoes, he uttered a cry, fell back into an armchair, and was dead. He was given a funeral with military honors at Warsaw's historic Powązki Cemetery, one of the pantheons of Poland's great and valiant.

In a letter of 6 October 1982 to the editor-translator, Władysław Kozaczuk supplied further details of Rejewski's postwar life.

> Rejewski...could after the war have worked academically and was urged to do so by Prof. Krygowski, who proposed a position at the institute of mathematics at Poznań or at Szczecin. He was, however, exhausted psychically, in ill health (in the Spanish prisons he had contracted, among other things, rheumatism, and after his return to Poland for three years slept in a woolen shirt). A grievous blow to him also was, not long after his return, in the summer of 1947, the almost sudden, after five days' illness (poliomyelitis), death of his 11-year-old son Andrzej [Andrew]. After that he did not want to part from his wife and daughter, as would have been necessary if he had accepted Krygowski's offer, which might I think have promised him a rapid academic career in view of the postwar shortages in personnel, decimated by the enemy. In Bydgoszcz they lived with their fairly well-to-do in-laws (Mrs. Rejewska's father was a dentist). Rejewski at first worked in an electrotechnical-materials factory as director of the sales department, later in a union of cooperatives as director of the Inspectorate of Costs and Prices until his retirement on a disability pension in 1967. In 1969 he moved together with his family to Warsaw, to his own former apartment (he had acquired it just before the war, in May 1939, with substantial financial help from his father-in-law). [After the Germans had suppressed the Warsaw Uprising of 1 August through 2 October 1944, they had evacuated Mrs. Rejewska and her two children, Andrzej, then eight, and Janeczka, then five, along with the other surviving population of the city, and had sent them west, where Mrs. Rejewska and her children eventually found refuge with her parents in Bydgoszcz—ED.] It is, of course, an apartment in a prewar building, by Warsaw standards rather large...comprising several rooms, with a spacious kitchen, servant's cubicle, etc. The move was fairly costly, since the apartment was, of course, occupied by tenants. Rejewski wrote to me not long after the publication of my first book, *Bitwa o tajemnice* [Secret Battle, 1967] and it is from then that our acquaintance dates. He began writing his memoirs just before retiring, although before that he had already corresponded in the matter with the Military Historical Institute, which purchased them as an account by a participant in World War II.

Mention has been made in this book of the fates of other members of Rejewski's cryptological unit—including its administrative chiefs, Lt. Col. Gwido Langer and Maj. Maksymilian Ciężki—partly on the basis of papers written by Col. Stefan Mayer, prewar chief of the intelligence department in the Polish General Staff. Mayer, the source of much of the information incorporated into this book (as well as into other publications, often in distorted form), and who relied on "papers left to [him] by Lt. Col. Langer and Major Ciężki and on [his own] personal recollections," died in London on 23 March 1981. Col. Tadeusz Lisicki, a graduate of the Warsaw Polytechnic who, during the war, commanded a Polish signals unit stationed outside London and who now lives in England, employed his knowledge of wartime Polish signals and decryptment, his special technical expertise,[4] and information supplied by Marian Rejewski to correct the early, distorted British accounts of the Enigma-Ultra epic.

The recent publication of the official history of *British Intelligence in the Second World War*, edited by F.H. Hinsley, has borne out Eisenhower's assessment of Ultra (cited in the introduction to Winterbotham's *The Ultra Secret*) as a "decisive contribution to the Allied war effort." During World War II, signal intelligence was, indeed, of decisive importance, for the first and perhaps the last time in the history of strategy. It was the Allied reading of Enigma ciphers that made possible Britain's preservation as a vital base for operations in Europe, North Africa, and the Atlantic, and Enigma decryptment decisively facilitated the prosecution of those operations. The role that was manifestly played by Enigma decryptment in World War II will require a wholesale rewriting of the history of that war.

Before such a revision can be undertaken, however, historians will need to obtain direct access to all the Enigma materials that are extant. Calvocoressi pointed out in 1980 (*Top Secret Ultra*) that Britain's Public Record Office did not have the bulk of the most important cryptological materials, including: decrypts; verbatim translations; Ultra intelligence appreciations, forecasts, and postmortems; the card indexes that held the essential radio intelligence gleanings; internal memoranda; diplomatic Enigma.

Of equal importance to history are precise details of how the British actually decrypted Enigma messages. A valuable contribution in this regard has been made by Gordon Welchman's 1982 book, *The Hut Six Story* (see Appendix F: Polish and British Methods of Solving Enigma). However, as Welchman himself acknowledges, there are many matters still to be elucidated. What is already clear, from Welchman's account, is that virtually all the major techniques that the British used to solve Enigma had been obtained by them from the Poles.

Another major question concerns what intelligence the Soviets obtained from Enigma intercepts—by their own efforts, or by courtesy of their western allies.

NOTES

1. Colonel Mayer told Richard Woytak that, shortly before, he had conducted an intelligence course that had been attended by Rejewski and Zygalski, and that, consequently, Mayer had been the last person to see Rejewski off at the railroad station when he departed for Poland.

A year and a half earlier, in May 1945, Tadeusz Lisicki, chief of the larger unit to which Rejewski and Zygalski were attached, had sent them to France to tie up some loose ends. From southern France they brought to England, "along with other things," the Enigma machine that had been produced in France during the war and was ultimately deposited in the Sikorski Institute, in London—after being kept for a time by Lisicki in his home—following the disbanding of their unit. Lisicki, Letter of 10 August 1982.

A number of documents connected with Enigma decryptment, including reports by Colonel Langer and a paper by Rejewski, had reached Britain several years earlier. "Reports from unoccupied France had come [to Britain] in the diplomatic mail of neutral countries which had representatives in Vichy and which were friendly toward Poland. Some were sent in abbreviated form by radio." Lisicki, Letter of 30 August 1982.

2. *Wiadomości matematyczne* (Mathematical News).

3. In 1983, a street and a school in Rejewski's home city of Bydogoszcz were named after him, and a memorial tablet was placed on the building where Rejewski was born. A Polish postage stamp commemorating the breaking of Enigma just over fifty years earlier—apparently the first stamp ever to honor a cryptological achievement—was scheduled for first issue on 16 August 1983, and a special envelope bearing images of the three mathematician-cyptologists and a special cancellation, associated with an international mathematical congress to be held in Poland, was scheduled for release on 18 August 1983. Letter of 22 May 1983 from the author to the translator-editor.

4. Lisicki designed the "Polish Mine Detector," which saw its first large-scale application (five hundred units) at the second battle of Alamein, in October-November 1942. The Germans had put down half a million land mines, and the Polish Mine Detector, in Lisicki's words, "certainly contributed to Rommel's defeat on a par with Enigma [decryptment]." In the introduction to a paper on Enigma, Lisicki lists as examples twelve major Polish technical contributions, including Enigma decryptment, to Allied victory in World War II.

Appendix B

A Conversation with Marian Rejewski
by Richard A. Woytak

On 24 July 1978, the thirty-ninth anniversary of the historic Polish-French-British cryptological conference that opened in Warsaw, Poland, on 24 July 1939, and a year and a half before Marian Rejewski's death, Richard Woytak tape-recorded a conversation with the former Polish cryptologist at his home in Warsaw. Below are some highlights of this, possibly the only such extensive interview to have been recorded with the foremost—and last surviving—of the Polish cryptologists who broke Enigma.

WOYTAK: [H]ow [did your involvement with Enigma] begin, back in Poznań?

REJEWSKI: Well, it was like this: At the time [in early 1929] I had, actually, stopped being a student [of mathematics at Poznań University]. I was writing my master's dissertation and was no longer attending lectures. But the other, younger mathematics students were still attending lectures. Well, one day or one evening, I don't exactly remember which, one of the younger mathematics students came up to me and said that on such-and-such a day, at such-and-such an hour, Professor [Zdzisław] Krygowski [director of Poznań University's Mathematics Institute] wanted me to come to the Institute. This student had some sort of list, and he would go and tell each of the persons on the list about this. Not everybody was invited, only a certain number [of] selected students. What the criteria were, I can only guess.... I expect it wasn't Professor Krygowski who selected the students, but rather Section II [the Intelligence Section of the Polish General Staff] that had made the selection. Probably there had been correspondence between Section II and Professor Krygowski, and on the basis of this correspondence Professor Krygowski had given them a list of all the third- and fourth-year students... who were close to graduating, and then Section II had by its own methods conducted some kind of selection. In any case, not all the students were selected—so much so, that even Professor Krygowski's *teaching assistant* wasn't informed. That was because she was, actually, of German extraction.

Transcribed and translated from the Polish by Christopher Kasparek.

[On the appointed day and hour] we all met at the Institute [in a large] mathematics seminar room. We assembled there, and there were three men.... Later we found out [who they were], or maybe Professor Krygowski introduced them.... They were [Maj. Franciszek] Pokorny...Capt. [Maksymilian] Ciężki...and a certain Antoni Palluth.... All were dressed in civilian clothes. At that time Major Pokorny headed the Cipher Bureau [of Section II of the Polish General Staff], Captain Ciężki headed the German section of the Cipher Bureau [B.S.-4], and Antoni Palluth was a civilian employee at the Cipher Bureau....

[Palluth] was...a graduate in engineering of the Warsaw Polytechnic. [He was] a civil engineer, and so he was...from a completely different field. But he was also interested in short-wave radio. He was what was called a radio ham. And it was probably on account of his being a ham and also being interested in ciphers that he had found himself at the Cipher Bureau and was one of the oldest workers of the Cipher Bureau.

But to get back to that meeting in Poznań: Major Pokorny explained what it was all about—he said a course was going to be organized in Poznań, and he was inviting all those present to participate. It met once or twice a week for several months, a couple of hours each time. I don't recall exactly where it met, it was somewhere else, at some military institution, some fort.[1] It was always that way. Pretty far from downtown [and the university]. [There were] twenty-odd [students enrolled].

The three men lectured in turn. The first was Antoni Palluth, about whom I've told you, who talked about the basics, the elements of ciphers. [I]t was only many years later [in France, during World War II] that I discovered that they [had] quite literally—indeed, even uncritically...—repeated what was written in a French book by Gen. [Marcel] Givièrge, *Cours de [cryptographie*, published in 1925]. [W]hen [Palluth] had finished, Captain Ciężki lectured. [He] spoke only about a certain period...about just one cipher... which at the time was not [?][2] used...by the Germans. This was the so-called double transposition. Just how the double transposition was solved was also spelled out in detail in Givièrge's book. [T]his book was the basis of the course. [W]hen Captain Ciężki had finished, the third lecturer was Major Pokorny, but I didn't attend his lectures.... I had finished my studies at Poznań [receiving a master's degree in mathematics from Poznań University on 1 March 1929] but I intended to become an insurance mathematician ...an actuary.... Göttingen, in Germany, had a very good ...institute of insurance mathematics [which was] Mecca [to persons interested in actuarial mathematics]. So I went there [but] I didn't complete the course.... The [actuarial] course at Göttingen...basically took two years. But after a year I came home [to Bydgoszcz] for the [summer of 1930] because...I didn't want to spend the vacation [in Germany]. [In Bydgoszcz] I found a letter waiting for me, from my [old] professor, Krygowski, offering me a teaching assistantship. A position had opened up, you see, and he was offering me an assistantship. So now I had a choice to make. Either to take over the assistantship and give up finishing...the insurance course there, or vice versa. Well, I decided to become a teaching assistant. So I didn't go back to Germany, but was an assistant [at Poznań] for several years. During that time, I began wondering what had ever become of the [cryptology] course. I began asking [around] and I found out that two [of the students, Jerzy] Różycki and [Henryk] Zygalski, were—[A]fter the conclusion of the course. . . the Cipher Bureau had set up a branch office in Poznań. Right next to the university, in the vaults of the local military command post. . . on St. Martin's Street [ulica Świętego Marcina]. [The office was housed] in one room. . . actually, it was a cellar. [W]hen I found out, I said: "Well, I wouldn't mind doing some work there too." Accordingly, [the student] who ran this [operation], Zygalski. . . contacted, wrote Warsaw, and [some] days later. . . the new [head of the Cipher Bureau, Lt.] Col. [Gwido] Langer. . . came down. . . to see me and agreed that I could work there too. . . .

I don't know [how it was that Różycki and Zygalski happened to have been chosen to work at the branch office upon completion of the cipher course]. Those who completed [the course] might be able to say. There . . . may have been some kind of final examination. . . . I imagine that there weren't very many persons who *wanted* to go into this. [P]eople had various plans. . . . [Anyway, it was] Zygalski and Różycki [who] happened to be there. Later I worked with them, too, but only for a very short time. [T]hey were younger than me:. . . I was born in 1905, Zygalski in 1907, Różycki in 1909. They had started their university studies a little later, and finished later, than me. When they graduated, the Cipher Bureau in Warsaw decided. . . to close this branch office. From the very beginning it had been thought of as a temporary thing, you see. . . .

[The Cipher Bureau had apparently not set as a recruiting requirement that the mathematicians be single males, though all three of those finally selected were.] Several female students had also taken part [in the cryptology course] but none of them. . . later [worked] in the branch office. . . . Then. . . in 1931, the Cipher Bureau informed us that the branch office was going to be closed. And I was once again. . . in. . . the same kind of dilemma as two years earlier: either [I could] stay on. . . as a teaching assistant, or move to Warsaw and break with the university. Well, I decided to break with the university. . . . I took leave of my professor by letter, because this was all [happening] during the vacation [and] the professor was away, he'd gone off somewhere, to—I don't know, to Majorca, or wherever it was he used to go. [By] September 1, 1932, all three of us were in Warsaw [at the general staff]. . . .

[I]n Warsaw. . . we didn't know [the nature of the work that we would eventually be doing; all we knew was] that we would be solving German codes and ciphers. And we got our first independent job. Because, you see, what we had been doing in Poznań was, as I have said. . . the double transposition. We knew well, thanks to General Givièrge's book, how this was solved. We did improve on a few things there. . . , especially. . . Zygalski, [and] I also [contributed] a little. . . that was new to [the solution of] that cipher. But when we moved to Warsaw, we got an entirely new, an independent job: to solve a German naval code. That was [our] first independent assignment. [T]he material was a bit old, as it were; that is to say, what we got. . . was complete.... In German (do you know German?)... in philately this is called an "abgeschlossene Sammlungserie" [a closed series]. And there wasn't too much of this material; besides that, we had no experience, we hadn't solved any codes. So it didn't go easily, but somehow we did succeed [in breaking] it. [A] characteristic feature of a code is that it is never really completely solved. You just... keep manipulating the material over and over again, you see, and you look [at it] and make guesses—it's a little like... crossword puzzles, like riddles, you have to figure out what this [code] group could mean....

But when the greater part had been solved... it was somewhere around the end of October, maybe the beginning of November—my boss Ciężki called me in [and] asked whether I had some time in the afternoons. I said I did. He said: "In that case, I would like you to come [in] in the afternoons as well. Only don't tell your colleagues anything about this—Two hours a day, in the afternoons." Well, I came in and then I found out what sort of material he had given me, that it was—that I was now to work with this cipher. My colleagues kept on [with the naval code]—it was just a matter of finishing up—and I got the new cipher. Well, it soon turned out... to be... a machine cipher—it was Enigma. I can't even say whether I figured that out for myself or whether somebody told me, because there had already been some work done on it.... In a staff, and particularly in a cipher bureau, it's not customary to ask [questions. I] didn't ask who had worked [on this]. It's only just now, only recently, that I've learned that it had been worked on by Mr. Palluth and by Ciężki... the head of the German section. [B]ut they hadn't come up with anything. In any case, I got this material, and now my own work began. Shall [*laughing*]—shall I go on about this, shall I tell you how things went on from there?

WOYTAK: When did Zygalski and [Różycki] become involved?

REJEWSKI: A couple of months later. Well, it very soon... turned out—and this was no cryptological discovery—that... the first six letters of any message held a special meaning. [Y]ou could see that by inspection.... As it turned out, this was a doubly enciphered key. Maybe they told me, I can't say. Anyway, when I began thinking about this, I very quickly got results, and I succeeded in solving... these keys... these first six letters which constituted the key (every message had its own individual key which was doubly enciphered). [A]nd thanks to my having decrypted these keys, I also had... as a bonus some additional material that later served me in solving the whole machine. So if the Germans... hadn't enciphered these keys but had given them plain at the head [of the message] they would have come out better in the end. Because I managed to solve the keys anyway, and in addition [I got] this material on which I was able to work and solve the Enigma [machine] itself. [This work] went quickly—it may have [taken me] a couple of weeks....

WOYTAK: That quickly?

REJEWSKI: Very quickly. No—that part of it, just the beginning—the beginning. Then, having this—this—

WOYTAK: How many drums were [the Germans] using at the time?...

REJEWSKI: ... There were three—It depends how you count them—Four. Three rotors and a fourth—a reversing drum [or "reflector"] and you could even say a fifth [drum], if you want to count the so-called entry [ring]. But, basically, the ones that revolved...were three....And the fourth was as in the commercial machine. Oh, something I forgot to say:...one day Major Ciężki brought me a commercial machine, when I already had the first results, so that I could get a better feel for the thing....

And now, having...all this...additional material that...I had gotten thanks to the Germans' enciphering the individual keys twice....Oh...∴. I must tell you one more thing. When I had these results, Major Ciężki made another decision. "You won't work in the afternoons any more; you'll work before noon, but you'll continue working in isolation. As before, don't tell your colleagues anything." Now I didn't come in in the afternoons any more.... I got a separate little room, and there I...now worked [on Enigma] seven hours a day, instead of two hours [as before]. The idea was to speed [things] up. [T]he subsequent work consisted in manipulating certain equations in order to solve them. Here...I ran into problems. [I] hadn't expected [the work] to go quickly, but in any event there was a snag here. This may have been in the first...days of December [1932]. And then...one fine day, it may have been the ninth or the tenth of December, Major Ciężki brought some intelligence material. I didn't know it came from the French. It might equally well have been furnished by a Polish agent.... But, anyway, this material included...tables of keys for two months. September and October 1932, so far as I recall. And this was a great help to me, because thanks to my having these keys...the number of unknowns in the equations was reduced, and I was able to solve these equations, and one fine day, as I was sitting there writing, the internal connections just came out in the form...of letters or numbers. I don't recall [which]—the internal connections ["wiring"] for the first drum [rotor], the one...on the far right, which always ...revolved at every depression of a key.

WOYTAK: Those were the materials from "Asche" [pseudonym of an agent of French intelligence who worked in the German Army's cryptographic service] which [Capt. Gustave] Bertrand [chief of French radio intelligence and decryptment] supplied to [Poland's] Cipher Bureau?

REJEWSKI: Yes.... I later...learned that—I believe it was on December 8 [1932]—Bertrand had come to Warsaw and delivered this material. I didn't meet him, I didn't know about it. All this took place at a higher level—he describes it in his book [Bertrand, *Enigma*. T]here is a mistake [in the book] and he gives the year [as] 1931. But later I corresponded with him, and it turned out that it had been...1932. It was the eighth of December, 1932.

Well, once I had that, the work went forward very quickly. I don't know [for sure], I can't swear to it, but I think that by the end of that year, 1932, the machine was solved. Solved, that is, in the sense that the internal connections [wirings] in the three drums [rotors] and the fourth drum were known. Now all that had to be done was to build the machine, in order to be able—But that took a while longer. So we did it a different way. An ordinary commercial machine was altered—Mr. Palluth simply stepped in here. I doubt whether this was [done] at AVA [the AVA Radio Manufacturing Company, of Warsaw, Poland, founded in 1929-30 by persons who, in subsequent years, would be associated with B.S.-4, and which did work for the Cipher Bureau on a cost-plus basis]; it probably took place in one of the rooms [at] the Cipher Bureau. There was a special room where various such technical matters were handled [the Clock Room, so called because of the clock over the black-curtained door leading into the employees-only room] so it was probably there that the commercial machine was disassembled [and] the drums removed; [then] they had to be opened, the connections [wiring] removed and reconnected differently. Then there still remained—it was also necessary to make other changes, various small changes. I don't want to talk about all of that, because it's too—fairly complicated. In any case, you could write on it [the machine] just as... if it were an original [military Enigma] machine. A little harder:...you had to hunt for the ["typing"] keys. The keys would change their order.... When a typist gets used to one keyboard, later it's hard for her to type if the keyboard is altered. Well, the keyboard was changed every day, so the typing was rather tedious. But in any event it was possible to read...messages to which Bertrand had supplied the keys, for those two months, September and October 1932. Here, if this will interest you, I would add that it was very important that the months happened to be September and October, in other words, periods that belonged to two different quarters. [This is] because... the key consisted of several elements [and] one element of the key was changed only once a quarter. Namely, the order of the drums [rotors]. The drums were numbered: Roman numeral one, Roman numeral two, Roman numeral three. One could insert them [into the machine] in any order that he pleased. Now, at that time they were changed once a quarter. [S]ince September and October belonged to two different quarters, in September and October the orders of the drums [rotors] were different. [With] the method that I had been using to find the connections in a drum... I could only solve the [far] right-hand drum, the one that revolved one place every time [a key was depressed]. The point is that, thanks to the keys for September, I could solve the drum that was in the far right-hand position in September. And since I also had the keys for October, using the same method I was later able to find the internal connections in the drum that was at the [far] right in October.... So, in this way, I already had two drums [rotors].... And the third drum [rotor] and... the reversing drum [reflector] now weren't so difficult...I managed to find them by other methods. So in this way, thanks to the fact that [we had] the keys for those two months ...September and October [1932, it proved possible] to reconstruct the whole machine. [T]hen, as I recall, Ciężki said: "...We can't have you ...solving [all] these messages yourself. Now...you'll work together with your colleagues again. [They]'ll solve this material for the two months, and I want you to think about how to go on from here." Because [now] we had the machine, but... we didn't have the keys [and] we couldn't very well require ...Bertrand to keep on supplying us with the keys every month. Supposedly he *did* supply [further keys] but I never got any more.... [T]he situation had reversed itself: before, we'd had the keys but we hadn't had the machine—we solved the machine; now we had the machine [but] we didn't have the keys. We had to work out methods to find the daily keys. And this, also, we managed to do.... Within a short time we had found...several methods [particularly] the grill [and] the cyclometer.... The cyclometer method especially was very important;...it required a lot of preparation, but after that finding the keys would take ten to twenty minutes: it would go very quickly.

WOYTAK: Did you ever have visits from Col. [Stefan] Mayer [chief of the intelligence department in Section II of the General Staff] or any of the other higher-ups?...

REJEWSKI: Basically...once a day Ciężki [the head of the Cipher Bureau's German section] would come by.... Langer [the overall head of the Cipher Bureau], very seldom. And as for still higher [officers], maybe once, maybe twice during the entire period from 1932 to 1939—once for sure, but...at that time I didn't know Mayer well, so I couldn't even say [whether he was one of them]. I don't know who it was; they didn't tell us.... They just came in for a moment, then left. [Yes, they were] in uniform...I think it was twice.

WOYTAK: Did you explain your methods to them?

REJEWSKI: Well, it's pretty hard to explain [these things]. All I could do was tell them...superficially. I could say: this is this, that is that....

[The Germans made] changes [of] various kinds [in their ciphering procedures. It's] hard to describe [them] all here. For example, in the first period, only in the first period, that is, at the end of 1932 and the beginning of 1933—how things were before that, I don't know—...the cipher operators made certain mistakes.... As you know, for every message they selected an individual key...consisting of [three] letters. Well, they would make the mistake [of] favoring [message] keys such as "aaa," or "bbb," or "ccc," and so on. This made things easier [for us]. But after a few months they were forbidden [to do this]. Hm! it's funny that after a few months [they stopped]—But then they started choosing other [cipher] keys.... Do you have a typewriter? Do you type?...On a [German] typewriter...the keys go in a certain order: Q W E R T Z U I O A S D and so on. After a while, I knew by heart how they go. [T]hey would pick three letters...three [typing] keys that stand next to each other. Or...diagonally [from each other] or like this—excuse me—But by then we already had them [the Germans] in our hands. So—it *availed them nothing [laughing]—that they forbade them*—to use [combinations like] "aaa," or successive letters "abc"—*pft!*—now they were using letters [picked] from the keyboard! Six of one to half a dozen of the other! That helped us too. To be sure, they had forbidden [certain combinations], but they hadn't forbidden using these letters—[And] when [eventually] they were forbidden [to use] three letters according to [the lay of] the keyboard,...we found another characteristic again.... There's no avoiding it—[W]henever there is arbitrariness, there is also a certain regularity. There's no avoiding it. For example,...they didn't use letters with the same frequency...some letters were used oftener; the Germans didn't like certain letters, I don't know which they were, "x" or something, and on the basis of that—[*End of tape.*]

WOYTAK: Were you present [at the working meetings of Polish, French, and British cryptologists that took place at Pyry, outside Warsaw, on 25 July 1939]?

REJEWSKI: . . . At the working meetings, my colleagues [Jerzy Różycki and Henryk Zygalski] and I talked with the specialists, the cryptologists. We split things up so that . . . Zygalski and Różycki talked and explained things in English, as well as they could: they didn't speak English well—in fact, hardly at all—but somehow they managed to make themselves understood. They talked with Knox [Alfred Dillwyn Knox, the chief British cryptologist] and I spoke in French with Braquenié [Capt. Henri Braquenié of the French Air Force staff]. Since I knew some French, it was only natural . . . that I would take Braquenié. And—[laughing] and since my colleagues knew neither French nor English, it was absolutely all the same whom they took, you see. . . . Just how much Braquenié understood, I don't know; but there is no question that Knox grasped everything very quickly, almost quick as lightning. It was evident that [the British] really had been working on . . . Enigma. . . . So they didn't require many explanations. They were specialists of a different kind—of a different class. Knox. Later Denniston [Comdr. Alastair Denniston, then chief of Britain's Government Code and Cypher School, during World War II located at Bletchley Park, fifty miles north of London] also came by briefly—but as the chief [of the British cryptological organization]. And Bertrand would also come by.

WOYTAK: Colonel Mayer told me that there was another person present.

REJEWSKI: Yes, there was . . . that's true. . . . But it isn't clear just who he was. There is a suspicion it was Menzies [then-Col. Stewart Menzies, deputy chief of Britain's Secret Intelligence Service, from the end of 1939 the chief of SIS]. Well, it's possible. [At Pyry] they said . . . his name was Sandwich. . . . But he only came in for a moment—made as if he wasn't even looking, just talked with Denniston [who] happened to be there. No doubt it had been set up in advance that way, that he would go into that room when Denniston was there, you see; he exchanged a few words with him, I don't know what [about]. That . . . Frenchman Braquenié nudged me with his elbow and said: "Sandwich—his name is Sandwich." [Laughing:] And the man left—a moment later he left. It's one of those mysteries. But—Mayer claims it was most certainly Menzies. . . . Mayer met him [again, after the war]. It's hard [to imagine Mayer] making this up. But, then again, Bertrand claims that it wasn't [Menzies], that he knew this Sandwich well, [that] he was a radio expert, or something like that. It's hard to know what to make of this. . . . [3]

Some letters from Marian Rejewski to Richard Woytak

Warsaw, 26 October 1978

Dear and Esteemed Sir,

. . . As for the changes [introduced into] Enigma in 1938, the matter presents itself as follows: In short order, three changes occurred:

1) The first change, of September 15, 1938. There was a change in the system of enciphering message keys. Whereas until then all message keys had been enciphered from the same position (the so-called "Grundstellung"), now every message key had its own "Grundstellung," given in the heading. Consequently, our earlier methods of reconstructing keys became useless, with one exception. That exception was the S.D. net, which had not introduced the change in encipherment of the message key (the S.D. net introduced it only later, probably in July 1939). Thus we could still read S.D. messages, but for the remaining nets we were forced to create other methods. Those methods were the bomb and the perforated sheets.

2) The second change, of December 15, 1938. Drums [rotors] IV and V were added. This change was introduced also by the S.D. net. But since the S.D. net had not changed its manner of enciphering the message key, we were able to reconstruct drums IV and V, using the old methods. Thus we were still able to solve the S.D. net as before, since in this case drums IV and V constituted only a slight added difficulty. For the remaining nets, however, drums IV and V [entailed] a tenfold increase in the work necessary to overcome the difficulties that had arisen, or, what amounts to the same thing, a tenfold decrease in our output.

3) The third change: As of 1.I.1939 [1 January 1939] there was a sharp increase in [the number of] plug connections [in the commutator], making still more difficult the work, especially the use of the bombs.

... In order to present all this more precisely, I would have to expound all of permutation theory and the operation of our methods and devices....

1 March 1979

... I have in hand the two books that you mention, "The Secret War" [Brian Johnson, *The Secret War*] and "Ultra goes to War" [Ronald Lewin, *Ultra Goes to War*]. They show the role of the Poles in the breaking of Enigma to a considerably more faithful degree than did earlier publications, nevertheless the authors have not managed to avoid mistakes. I would point out just one:

The Enigma machine that workers of Section II [Intelligence] of the [Polish] General Staff had the opportunity, in 1928, of examining and analyzing at the Customs Office in Warsaw, was not a military but a commercial Enigma. The mistake stemmed from misinterpretation of the words of Col. [Tadeusz] Lisicki, which both authors make reference to [Johnson, *The Secret War*, 311-12; Lewin, *Ultra*, footnote on 30].

Whether the British or the Americans passed on to the Russians information obtained from the reading of messages enciphered on Enigma, I do not know. Directly, I would think not; indirectly, perhaps through the "Red Orchestra" or the "Dora" net in Switzerland. But that is nothing definite....

15 April 1979

... About [Maj. Maksymilian] Ciężki, although he was my superior, I can say little.... What I write about him below, are largely my conjectures.

He came from the Poznań area. When World War I broke out, he was mobilized and mustered into the German army. When the war ended, no doubt he decided to become a regular army officer. In this character he took part in the Polish-Soviet War of 1920. Later, presumably, he received directorship of the German section [B.S.-4] of the Cipher Bureau [Biuro Szyfrów—hence B.S.] in Section II of the General Staff.

Since Poland had [in 1918, upon the collapse of Russia, Germany, and Austro-Hungary] regained her independence after about 150 years of bondage, there were no people with cryptologic experience. Those who worked in the just created cipher unit, were all completely self-taught, and so therefore was Ciężki. So much the greater was their achievement, for they carried out pioneering work. I imagine that, when Gen. Givièrge's book Cours de cryptographie appeared in France in 1925, it became a catechism for the workers of the German section. In any case, when a few years later, in 1929, the cryptology course was set up in Poznań, it was entirely and literally based on this very book, as I had occasion to discover when, in France in 1939, this book fell into my hands.

But before that, in 1928, when the first messages enciphered by machine had appeared on the airways, Ciężki and engineer Palluth had tried to solve the messages, and it may well have been their fruitless efforts that prompted the organization of the Poznań cryptology course.

Ciężki had a family in Warsaw, I believe a wife and two sons. . . .

Since Ciężki was not only the director of the Cipher Bureau's German section but also deputy to the Chief of the entire Cipher Bureau [Langer], he had a great deal of organizing work [on his hands, including supervision of the monitoring stations at Starogard in the Polish Corridor, at Poznań, and at Krzesławice outside of Kraków] and probably by the thirties he was no longer directly working at solving ciphers. As a superior he was very pleasant and very tactful, as indeed was also his chief, Col. Langer.

Were I to characterize Ciężki in a few words, I would say that he was a pioneer in the field of German ciphers and an excellent and tireless organizer of the Bureau's German section. . . .

25 November 1979

. . . About my colleague Jerzy Różycki, I do not have too much to say. He was the youngest of our trio; he was 4 years younger than me, having been born on 24.VII.1909 [24 July 1909]. He hailed from the Kiev area [in the Ukraine]. His father was a pharmacist. He went to school, so far as I know, in Wyszków, not far from Warsaw, but he studied in Poznań—simultaneously both mathematics and geography. All three of us began work at the Cipher Bureau on 1.IX.1932 [1 September 1932] and we always worked together, indeed in one room, with the exception of several months in 1932 when I worked completely alone. As a cryptologist he had several nice ideas, [with regard] not only [to] the Enigma cipher but also [to] other ciphers. As a person, he was a very good friend, cheerful, sociable. He died on 9.I.1942 [9 January 1942] when, while returning from Algiers to France, the ship on which he was sailing, the Lamoricière, sank after hitting submerged reefs or perhaps [a] mine. He had married shortly before the war in Poland, and when he left Poland [in September 1939] he left behind his wife and a child of several months. His son is presently living in England....

To my letter of April 15 of this year I would like to add a few bits of information about Major Maksymilian Ciężki, as in the interim I have met his son, the only one of [his] three [sons] who survives. What did I learn from him? His father was born in 1899 and died on 9.XI.1951.... He came from Szamotuły [fifteen miles northwest of Poznań] in Wielkopolska [western Poland]. [Ciężki's hometown—15,200 population in 1975—had, in the second half of the nineteenth century, been a strong center of Polish nationalism, and later an important center of the Western Polish Uprising of 1918-19 against German occupation.] He married a woman from Wilno [now Vilnius, capital of Soviet Lithuania]. He took part in the Western Polish Uprising of 1918/19....

With best regards
[Signed] M. Rejewski

NOTES

1. Richard Woytak believes that this may have been the fort, built by Bismarck's Germany, that stood on Królowej Jadwigi Wały (now ul. Dzierżyńskiego—Dzierżyński Street), across from a brewery. The fort has, since World War II, been replaced by the Hotel Poznań; the brewery survives.—ED.

2. Rejewski says further on that, in Poznań, he and his colleagues had, "as I have said," worked on the double transposition. Hence, it is possible that here he had meant to say "Niemcy" (Polish for "the Germans") but did not complete the word, breaking off after saying "nie" (Polish for "no" or "not").—ED.

3. Another case of possibly mistaken identity of a Briton occurs in Winterbotham's *The Ultra Secret*, when the author describes the middle-aged Dilly Knox in the Ultra period as having been "quite young." Winterbotham may have confused Knox with Turing, Welchman, or another of the younger staff. This error may shed light on why it was possible to keep Ultra a secret for thirty years after the war. As the incident shows, every few people, even at the top, had a clear overview of the totality of the operation, from interception of ciphered German messages, through their breaking, translation, editing and annotation, to the distribution of decrypts and intelligence summaries. The operation was so compartmentalized that hardly anything that any one person could have divulged about it would have given the secret away.

Similarly, when Marian Rejewski was asked by Richard Woytak whether he had known Capt. Jan Graliński, chief of the Russian cryptology section at the Polish General Staff's Cipher Bureau in Warsaw, Rejewski replied that he had but that, for reasons of security, they had never discussed their cryptological work. Rejewski added that Graliński "was supposed to have been very talented."—ED.

Appendix C

Summary of Our Methods for Reconstructing ENIGMA and Reconstructing Daily Keys, and of German Efforts to Frustrate Those Methods
by Marian Rejewski

This paper, written in 1977, is presented by courtesy of Tadeusz Lisicki, whose several years' correspondence with Marian Rejewski helped to jog the Polish mathematician-cryptologist's memory concerning important aspects of Polish work at breaking and reading Enigma. Note: Despite Rejewski's statement in this appendix (section 12.b) that the Poles "probably after 1940...ceased to work with Enigma," evidence indicates that some Enigma was read at "Cadix," in southern France.

The Enigma machine, in its final form, was used by the German Army from 1 June 1930. What the procedure for operating it was in the initial period, I do not know. But, in all likelihood, it was the same as in late 1932 [when Rejewski reconstructed the Enigma machine]. Thus it may be supposed that throughout this two-and-a-half-year period the German cipher clerks had had a predilection for selecting [message] keys such as AAA, ABC, and the like.

1.a. After, however, in late 1932, these kinds of keys had made considerably easier the reconstruction of daily keys as well as the reconstruction of the internal connections in the drums, and thus the reconstruction of Enigma itself.

b. The German military authorities (sometime in 1933, maybe even early 1933, I do not remember exactly when) prohibited the use of such [message] keys.

2.a. In order to reconstruct the daily keys, we then began relying on such keys as PYX [and] ASD, which formed a horizontal or diagonal line on the Enigma keyboard.

b. But after several months such keys too were prohibited.

Translated from the Polish by Christopher Kasparek.

3.a. The oldest of the methods for reconstructing daily keys was the so-called grill method. This was based on the fact that the plug connections [in the commutator] exchanged only six pairs of letters, thus leaving fourteen letters unchanged.

b. But from 1 October 1936 the number of plug connections was variable, ranging between five and eight. This ostensibly small change constituted, in reality, a considerable limitation on the usefulness of the grill method. For that method required unchanged *pairs* of letters, and the number of such pairs, given eight plug connections, was on the average two times smaller than given six connections. One may estimate that, after this change in number of plug connections, the number of solved days declined by about 40 percent.

4.a. Fortunately, however, before the increase in number of plug connections, that is, before 1 October 1936, probably in 1934 or 1935, we had hit upon the idea for another method, the method of the cyclometer and card catalog, whose utility was independent of the number of plug connections (and of the reconstruction of message keys). Preparing this method was laborious and took over a year, but when it was ready, the obtaining of daily keys was a question of between twelve and twenty minutes.

b. However, on 1 November 1937, the Germans changed the so-called reversing drum [or reflector], and the entire job had to be started over again.

5.a. Another aid in reconstructing daily keys was the circumstance that the sequence of the drums [rotors] at first was changed once a quarter.

b. But from 1 January 1936 the sequence of drums was changed once a month, from 1 October 1936, daily, and in a later period, during the war, as often as every eight hours.

6.a. As mentioned above, we were forced after 1 November 1937 to make a new card catalog, a task which consumed, on account of our greater experience, probably somewhat less than a year's time.

b. But then, on 15 September 1938, the Germans changed entirely the procedure for enciphering message keys, and as a result our card-catalog method became completely useless.

7.a. We had to think of new methods. One of these, the method of the bombs, consisted in a mechanization of the process of reconstructing daily keys and was based, like the grill method, on the fact that the plug connections did not change all the letters. But while the grill method required unchanged *pairs* of letters, the method of the bombs required only unchanged letters. Hence, it could be applied even though the number of plug connections in this period was five to eight. In mid-November the bombs were ready, and the reconstructing of message keys now took about two hours.

b. But, from 1 January 1939, the number of plug connections was increased to seven to ten, which, to a great degree, decreased the usefulness of the bombs, to say nothing of the fact that two weeks earlier, as I will state in the next point, the number of drums had been increased from three to five, thus increasing the work of the bombs tenfold.

8.a. More or less at the same time as the bombs [were invented, our] colleague [Henryk] Zygalski invented another, manual method, the method of so-called perforated sheets, which, like the card-catalog method, was independent of the number of plug connections. But the manufacture of these sheets, at least in our Polish circumstances, was very time consuming, so that by 15 December 1938, only one-third of the whole job had been done.

b. But then the Germans introduced drums [rotors] IV and V, which increased the labor of making the sheets tenfold [since ten times as many sheets were now needed], considerably exceeding our Polish capacities.

9.a. However, the British undertook to manufacture the perforated sheets and, toward the end of 1939 or maybe at the beginning of 1940, delivered a complete set (60 × 26 sheets) to us Poles in France (where we had found ourselves after war broke out), and with their help we continued solving Enigma daily keys.

b. But after the defeat of France, sometime in 1940 or 1941,[1] the Germans once again completely changed the procedure for enciphering message keys, and, as a result, Zygalski's sheets, too, became completely useless.

10.a. During the final phase in the reconstruction of Enigma in 1932, the task had been made somewhat easier by the inclusion in German service instructions of a genuine plain text and the genuine cipher text, together with a precise statement of the genuine message key.

b. In one of the later service instructions, the genuine example was replaced with a fictitious example. Unfortunately, it is not known when this change in the instructions was introduced for the first time. In any case, the change was of no importance to us Poles, since we already had Enigma reconstructed anyway, but it does attest to the ceaseless vigilance of the Germans.

The subsequent items refer to changes introduced by the Germans after we Poles had ceased to be involved in solving Enigma.

11.a. Reconstruction of daily keys required, at least with the methods used by the Poles, a certain minimum number of messages, about seventy to one hundred.

b. Avoiding this minimum number had been an objective of the Germans even before the war, but was so above all in later years, and was pursued in two ways. One way was through ever more frequent change of daily keys. I have already mentioned ever more frequent change of drum sequence. But the remaining components of the [daily] key were also changed in the later period of the war years (maybe from 1942?) every eight hours. The second way consisted in creating an ever greater number of nets (with their own keys). This process, too, began in the prewar period. For example, the German Navy then had at least three nets: officers', staff, admirals'. However, in the subsequent phase of hostilities, the number of all the nets approached sixty.

12.a. The last phase in reconstructing daily keys was finding the settings of the rings [on the rotors]. In that phase, we relied on the fact that the greater number of messages began with the letters ANX [German for "To," followed by "x" as a spacer].

b. But the Germans frustrated this method too, to be sure, only later, probably after 1940, when we had ceased to work with Enigma.[2] For they introduced a rule that, at the beginning of a message, one should place some word that has no meaning in connection with the content of the message, so that the message would not open with the letters ANX.

13.a. When, on 15 September 1938, the Germans had completely changed their system for enciphering message keys, and before we had invented either the method of the bombs or the method of the sheets, we had been wondering whether it would not be possible to base a new method for reconstructing daily keys on the circumstance that in the German language the letter Y basically does not occur. We never thought the matter through completely, because we found other methods.

b. However, the Germans, in one of their subsequent instructions, introduced a rule that the period mark was to be represented by the letters YY, and as a result a method that had existed only in our musings was also eliminated.

It would be immensely interesting if, by obtaining a complete set of all the German service instructions, it were possible to establish the precise dates when all the changes described here were introduced.

NOTES

1. Lisicki writes: "Rejewski is mistaken [about] 'sometime in 1940 [or 1941].' The Germans changed the system on 14 May—in some nets, on 10 and 12 May—as a result of which at Vignolles there was a hiatus until 20 May in reading Enigma. . . ." Lisicki, Letter of 19 September 1982.—ED.

2. Rejewski was apparently mistaken about this. Evidence, including the recollections of Colonel Lisicki and Rejewski's own later testimony (chapter 10, note 11), indicates that the Poles *did* read some Enigma at Cadix.—ED.

Appendix D

How the Polish Mathematicians Broke Enigma
by Marian Rejewski

Introduction

In late 1927 or perhaps early 1928, there arrived at the Warsaw Customs Office from the German Reich a package that, according to the accompanying declaration, was supposed to contain radio equipment. The German firm's representative demanded very strenuously that the package be returned to the Reich even before going through customs, since it had been shipped, by mistake, with other equipment. He was so insistent that his demands alerted the customs officials, who notified the Cipher Bureau of Section II [Intelligence] of the General Staff, an institution that was interested in anything new in the field of radio equipment. And since it happened to be a Saturday afternoon, the employees sent over by the bureau had time to examine the matter at leisure. They carefully opened the box and found that it did not, in fact, contain radio equipment, but, instead, a cipher machine. They examined the machine minutely, then carefully closed the box again.

It may readily be surmised that the cipher machine was an Enigma, of the commercial model of course, since, at that time, the military model had not yet been put into use. Hence, this trivial episode was of no practical importance, though it does fix the date at which the Cipher Bureau's interest in the Enigma machine began—manifested, initially, in the acquisition by entirely legal means of one copy of the commercial model machine. When, on 15 July 1928, the first machine enciphered messages to be broadcast by German military stations appeared on the airwaves, Polish radiotelegraphers manning monitoring stations began to intercept them, and Polish cryptologists employed in the Cipher Bureau's German section were instructed to try to read them. The effort was fruitless, however, and after a time was abandoned. There remained very slight evidence of this effort, in the form of several densely written-over sheets of paper, and there remained, also, the commercial model Enigma machine.

This article, translated by Christopher Kasparek from the Polish, originally was published posthumously and in a slightly different form in the Polish *Wiadomości matematyczne* 23 (1980) 1-28.

Nevertheless, the Cipher Bureau, which was headed at that time by Maj. F. Pokorny (a relative of the outstanding Austrian Army cryptologist during World War I, Capt. Herman Pokorny) did not give up. At the turn of 1928-29, a cryptology course was organized in Poznań for students who were finishing their mathematics studies and were fluent in German. When the course had ended, a temporary field office of the Cipher Bureau was set up in Poznań for several participants of the course, and, finally, as of 1 September 1932, three mathematics graduates employed in the field office, Jerzy Różycki, Henryk Zygalski, and I, were hired to work permanently at the Cipher Bureau in Warsaw, located in the now nonexistent general staff building on the Saxon Square.

There the first independent assignment that we received was to solve a German naval code, a task in which a knowledge of German was very helpful. In our subsequent work, however, as I shall try to show, it was knowledge not so much of language as of mathematics that was of use, and it is to the great credit of the earlier mentioned Major Pokorny, as well as his successor, Lt. Col. Karol G. Langer, and his deputy, Capt. Maksymilian Ciężki, that they realized considerably earlier than other cipher bureaus the utility of requiring of cryptologists, in addition to knowledge of languages, a higher education in mathematics.

At this point I shall make mention of another person, whom I will mention again later, who played an exceptional role in the breaking of the Enigma cipher. I have in mind Gen. Gustave Bertrand of the French Army, deceased in 1976, who, in 1932 (in the rank of captain), as director of Section D of French intelligence, obtained and delivered to the Polish Cipher Bureau intelligence material of enormous importance. Moreover, on several occasions he materially influenced the fates of the Polish cryptologists and finally revealed to the world their decisive part in breaking Enigma.[1]

It is not my intent to give a detailed description of the commercial or the military machine. I shall merely outline that which is indispensable to an understanding of what follows. The military machine (fig. D-1) was of the dimensions and appearance of a portable typewriter and had twenty-six keys bearing the letters of the Latin alphabet, but, in lieu of type, it had a board that held twenty-six bulbs of the kind used in flashlights, and designated by the same letters as the keys. The machine also contained a source of current in the form of a small battery.

The most essential parts of the machine, however, were, mounted on a single axle, three rotatable and mutually transposable cipher drums [also called rotors] I, II, III (in the positions marked by the letters L, M, N in figs. D-1 and D-4) and a fourth drum (stationary in the military machine), the so-called reversing drum [also called reflector] R. Each of the cipher drums was equipped with a ring that had engraved on its circumference the twenty-six letters of the alphabet, visible in figures D-2 and D-3. The letter found at the top was visible in a small window located in a metal lid of the machine. The ring could change its position with respect to the rest of the drum.

The central part of the drums comprised an ebonite disk with twenty-six fixed contacts arranged concentrically on one side (visible on the right in figure D-3) that were connected by insulated wires in irregular fashion with twenty-six spring-loaded contacts (visible on the left in figure D-3), likewise concentrically arranged on the other side. The reversing drum had only, on one side, twenty-six spring-loaded contacts, connected in irregular fashion among themselves.

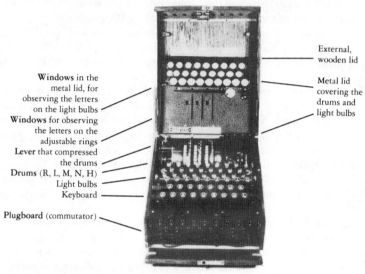

Windows in the metal lid, for observing the letters on the light bulbs
Windows for observing the letters on the adjustable rings
Lever that compressed the drums
Drums (R, L, M, N, H)
Light bulbs
Keyboard

Plugboard (commutator)

External, wooden lid

Metal lid covering the drums and light bulbs

FIGURE D-1. General view of a military-model Enigma.

FIGURE D-2. The cipher drums (cf. figs. 1 and 4).

FIGURE D-3. The two sides of a cipher drum.

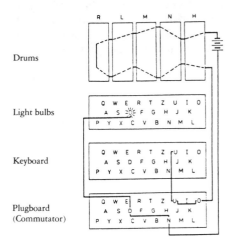

FIGURE D-4. Diagram of the path of electric current through the military Enigma.

When a key was depressed, cipher drum N (the drum in the N position, at the far right) executed one twenty-sixth of a revolution, and current flowed from the depressed key through the three cipher drums, the reversing drum, and back through the cipher drums, and lit one of the bulbs (fig. D-4). When at a given moment one depressed a key, for example, that with the letter "u," a lamp with another letter lit (always different from the one that had been depressed—in fig. D-4, it is the letter "d"). Upon the next depression of the same "u" key, one obtained—as a result of the drums' revolution in the meantime—this letter now enciphered differently. That is, a different lamp would now light.

When, in this manner, one tapped out the successive letters of an open or plain text, the letters of the bulbs that successively lit formed a cipher text or ciphergram, or simply, a cipher. Conversely, when one tapped out the successive letters of the cipher, the letters of the bulbs that successively lit would recreate the plain text (in other words, at every setting of the drums the enciphering permutation at that moment was an involution that was a product of thirteen transpositions). This was due to the reversing drum.

It is known that the number of cipher drums with different connections that could be made is

$$26! = 403,291,461,126,605,635,584,000,000,$$

and the number of different reversing drums,

$$\frac{26!}{2^{13} \cdot 13!} = 7,905,853,580,025;$$

thus, the factory that produced the Enigmas could have furnished every customer a batch of machines with different connections in the drums. This applied particularly to the drums of military machines, which, of course, had to have different connections than the drums of any commercial machine. However, all the sets of drums in the military machines, whose number during the war is estimated at between one hundred and two hundred thousand, had the same connections, so that cipher clerks in any military units could communicate among themselves using these machines, on condition that they had their machines set to the same key.

Next to the connections in the drums, the key was the second secret of the military Enigma cipher. Each cipher drum could be set twenty-six ways, and so three drums could be set $26^3 = 17,576$ ways, and, since the sequence of the three drums on the axle could be changed six ways, the setting and sequence of the drums together permitted

$$6 \cdot 26 = 105,456$$

possibilities. Still, this number seemed to the specialists of the German cipher bureau too low, and, therefore, something that resembled a telephone switchboard [known as a plugboard or commutator] was added to the military model machines, where any six pairs of letters could be exchanged, thereby creating a further

$$\frac{26!}{2^6 \cdot 6! \cdot 14!} = 100,391,791,500$$

possibilities. Now, the Germans reasoned, even if the opponent got his hands on one of the military machines, for example, as a result of military action, not knowing the key, he still would be unable to read any message. I will try to show, however, that in this regard the Germans were mistaken.

The system of settings imposed on cipher clerks—the setting of the drums, their sequence, the connections in the plugboard, and certain additional settings that I will not mention now—was called the daily key (although some elements of that key changed more than once daily, especially in the last phase of the war, and others less often, at least in the initial period of the machines' use). Cipher clerks received the daily keys in the form of printed tables for an entire month.

But that was not the last of the secrets of the military Enigma cipher. Encipherment of all the messages for a given day from the same position of the drums would have left the messages vulnerable to decryptment. For the first letters of all the messages would then have constituted an ordinary substitution cipher, a very primitive cipher easily soluble given sufficient material, and all the second letters of the messages would have constituted another substitution cipher, and so on. These are not merely theoretical deliberations. It was in that very way that in France in 1940 we solved the Swiss Enigma cipher machine. Consequently, it was necessary to leave to the German encipherer the choice of the drum positions from which he would begin the encipherment of a given message. And he had to pass these drum positions to his decipherer colleague so that the latter too would know how to set the drums in order to be able to read the message. This required giving three letters—in the conviction of the Germans, necessarily enciphered—and since radio transmittal did not always ensure good reception, these letters were enciphered twice, and the six letters so obtained were placed at the beginning of the message. These three letters, selected freely by the encipherer, were called—in contradistinction to the daily keys—the message key, and they constituted the third secret of the military Enigma cipher.

Message Keys

Today, after nearly half a century, I no longer remember whether I was aware of the difference in construction between the military Enigma and the commercial Enigma when, in the fall of 1932, I was separated from my colleagues Różycki and Zygalski, given a separate small room in the [general] staff building, and instructed to renew the studies of Enigma abandoned by my predecessors. It is conceivable that I received this information somewhat later. Anyway, I did not need it in the initial phase of my work. The commercial machine mentioned earlier was placed at my disposal, as well as several dozen messages daily, enciphered on the military Enigma.

That the first six letters of each message constituted its three-letter key, twice enciphered, was readily apparent, and I shall not dwell upon this. But where to go from there? First I shall describe how I proceeded at the time, and then I will try to justify my procedure.

I wrote out separately the six first letters of all the messages from a given day, that is, their twice-enciphered keys. All the keys that had the same first letter also had, of course, the same fourth letter. The same may also be said of the second and fifth, and of the third and sixth, letters. I arbitrarily chose a key and wrote down the first letter, and next to it the fourth. Then I sought out a key that had as its first letter the fourth letter of the previous key, and I wrote the fourth letter of the second key next to the fourth letter of the previous key. Continuing in this way, after a number of steps I arrived back at the first letter that I had written down. I did not write down this same letter a second time, but put in parentheses the letters written down so far. A small example will make my procedure clearer. Let

$$dmq \quad vbn$$
$$von \quad puy$$
$$puc \quad fmq$$

constitute three, somewhat artificially selected, enciphered keys of messages from a given day. For greater clarity, I have divided the keys in two, so that the first three letters constitute the key after the first encipherment, and the next three letters constitute the key after the second encipherment. Thus, I take the letter "d" from the first message and write next to it the fourth letter, "v"; next to "v" I write "p," then next to "p" the letter "f." In this way, I obtain the fragment

$$dvpf \cdot$$

From the keys of further messages it would transpire that there would arise a whole cycle of letters,

$$(dvpfkxgzyo),$$

and from the remaining keys there would arise further cycles, so that the totality of the cycles formed from the first and fourth letters would appear, for example, as follows:

$$AD = (dvpfkxgzyo) \ (eijmunqlht) \ (bc) \ (rw) \ (a) \ (s),$$

where I have designated the totality of the cycles by the letters "AD" to indicate that it arose from the first and fourth letters of the keys of messages from a given day. I proceeded in similar fashion with the second and fifth, and with the third and sixth, letters of the keys, thus obtaining a picture that appears, for example, as follows:

$$AD = (dvpfkxgzyo) \ (eijmunqlht) \ (bc) \ (rw) \ (a) \ (s),$$
(1) $$\quad BE = (blfqveoum) \ (hjpswizrn) \ (axt) \ (cgy) \ (d) \ (k),$$
$$CF = (abviktjgfcqny) \ (duzrehlxwpsmo).$$

This set is immensely characteristic and, while the picture of such a set was different each day, one feature was always the same, namely that cycles of the same lengths occurred in every line always in even numbers. In view of the role that this set will continue to play, I have named it the characteristic set, or, for short, the characteristic, of a given day.

How may one explain the origin of the characteristic set? If I depress all the keys in turn in such a way that the setting of the cipher drums does not change, for example by holding down one key [drum?], then different bulbs will light each time. In this way, a certain permutation of letters will come into being. With a different setting of the drums the permutation will, of course, be different, but the reversing drum causes all the permutations to comprise solely transpositions, for if striking the "t" key, for example, causes the "z" bulb to light, then striking the "z" key, given the same setting of the drums, causes the "t" bulb to light.

It may easily be verified that if I designate the six successive permutations that arise during the double encipherment of message keys by the letters A through F, then the products AD, BE, CF of those permutations will be identical with expressions forming the characteristic of a given day, and thus the manner of designating those expressions finds justification.

Yes, but why, in these expressions, do cycles of the same lengths occur always in even numbers? This too may easily be explained. For we may derive the following theorem:

If two permutations X *and* Y *of the same degree comprise solely disjunctive transpositions, then their product* XY *will include disjunctive cycles of the same lengths in even numbers.*

We may also prove the converse theorem:

If a permutation (of even-numbered degree) includes disjunctive cycles of the same lengths in even numbers, then the permutation may be regarded as a product XY *of two permutations* X *and* Y, *each comprising solely disjunctive transpositions.*

It may also be shown that:

1) *Letters entering into one and the same transposition of permutation* X *or* Y, *enter always into two different cycles of the same permutation* XY.

2) *If two letters found in two different cycles, of the same length, of permutation* XY *belong to the same transposition, then the letters adjacent to them (one to the right, the other to the left) also belong to the same transposition.*

A proper interpretation of the foregoing determinations implies that it will suffice to know also the habits of encipherers in order to completely reconstruct all the message keys. Suppose, for example, that cipher clerks like to select as message keys three identical letters, such as "aaa," "bbb," and the like. Let us consider characteristic (1). Since in product AD the letters "a" and "s" form single-letter cycles, then if the message keys include key "aaa," upon encipherment the first letter should be "s." Let us suppose that the enciphered message keys from a given day include three keys beginning with the letter "s":

sug   smf

sjm   spo

syx   scw.

The enciphered key "sug smf" could not have arisen from the letters "aaa," because the second letter, "u," is found in a nine-letter cycle of the product BE, whereas "a" is found in a three-letter cycle in the same product. Likewise, the enciphered key "sjm spo" could not have arisen from the letters "aaa," since the letter "j" also is found in a nine-letter cycle. However, the enciphered key "syx scw" could have arisen from the letters "aaa," since "s" and "a" appear in two single-letter cycles of product AD, "y" and "a" appear in two different three-letter cycles of product BE, and "x" and "a" appear in two different thirteen-letter cycles of product CF.

That the enciphered key "syx scw" indeed designated the letters "aaa" prior to encipherment, seemed to be confirmed by the fact that, on that assumption, very many other enciphered keys could be deciphered as sequences "bbb," "ccc," and so on.

And so one of the secrets of the Enigma cipher, that of the message keys, had been solved. It is interesting that attainment of this result had not required a knowledge either of the drum connections or of the daily keys, of neither of the remaining secrets of the Enigma cipher. What was needed was a sufficient number of messages from the same day, about sixty, to make possible the formation of the characteristic set AD, BE, CF.

Also required was a good knowledge of the habits of encipherers regarding the selection of message keys. The first time, when I assumed that there would be many keys such as "aaa," "bbb," and so on, it was only a hypothesis that, luckily, panned out. Later, we followed very closely the evolution in the encipherers' fancies, and when before long they were forbidden to use as keys three identical letters, we always managed to discover other habits of theirs, if only that, since they were not allowed to use three identical letters, they avoided repeating any letter even once, and this trait also sufficed for us to determine what were the message keys prior to their encipherment.

We succeeded in working out several more methods of a similar nature. For it is a well-known phenomenon that man, as a being endowed with consciousness and memory, cannot imitate chance perfectly, and it is the cryptologist's task, among other things, to discover and make proper use of these deviations from chance.

The Connections in the Drums

It would have been better for the Germans had they not enciphered the message keys at all. Enciphering, as we have seen, did not save the keys from being solved anyway, and, moreover, it provided a bonus in the form of the six successive permutations A through F. Knowledge of these brought me closer to discovering the connections in the drums of the military Enigma. For this purpose I must express what happens inside the machine by the aid of operations on permutations. Therefore, let us designate the permutation caused by the commutator with the letter S [for the German Steckerverbindugen], that by the three cipher drums with the letters L, M, N, counting from left to right, and that by the reversing drum with the letter R. I must also make mention of another drum that I have not alluded to up to now: the entry drum, a stationary drum that constitutes the passage between the commutator and drum N. I designate this drum with the letter H. The path of the current may now be expressed as follows:

$$SHNMLRL^{-1}M^{-1}H^{-1}S^{-1}.$$

However, since at every depression of a key, drum N will execute one-twenty-sixth of a revolution, in order to take account of this movement, I had to introduce a special permutation, which I shall always designate with the letter P, that changes each letter into the next letter in the alphabet: "a" to "b," "b" to "c," . . . "z" to "a." So now I can represent permutations A through F in the form of the following equations:

$$A = SHPNP^{-1}MLRL^{-1}M^{-1}PN^{-1}P^{-1}H^{-1}S^{-1},$$
$$B = SHP^2NP^{-2}MLRL^{-1}M^{-1}P^2N^{-1}P^{-2}H^{-1}S^{-1},$$
$$\cdots\cdots\cdots\cdots\cdots\cdots\cdots\cdots\cdots\cdots$$
$$F = SHP^6NP^{-6}MLRL^{-1}M^{-1}P^6N^{-1}P^{-6}H^{-1}S^{-1}.$$

In writing these equations, I tacitly assumed that only the right, the N, drum revolved, while drums L and M executed no revolutions during six successive depressions of [keyboard] keys. This assumption holds for an average of twenty-one cases out of twenty-six, hence, sufficiently often to justify it. In that case, in all the above equations there is repetition of the expression $MLRL^{-1}M^{-1}$, which I can temporarily replace by the single letter Q, designating a fictitious reversing drum:

(2) $$Q = MLRL^{-1}M^{-1}.$$

This permits us to simplify considerably our set of equations:

$$A = SHPNP^{-1}QPN^{-1}P^{-1}H^{-1}S^{-1},$$
$$B = SHP^2NP^{-2}QP^2N^{-1}P^{-2}H^{-1}S^{-1},$$
(3) $$\cdots\cdots\cdots\cdots\cdots\cdots\cdots\cdots\cdots$$
$$F = SHP^6NP^{-6}QP^6N^{-1}P^{-6}H^{-1}S^{-1}.$$

The task was to solve the above set of six equations with four unknown permutations S, H, N, and Q. Aware of the difficulty of this task, I sought, in the first place, to decrease the number of unknowns. Since, in the commercial machine, the connections in the entry drum had the form

$$H = \begin{pmatrix} qwertzuioasdfghjkpyxcybnml \\ abcdefghijklmnopqrstuvwxyz \end{pmatrix}$$

—that is, the upper line of permutation H represented the alphabet in the sequence that the letters followed on the machine's keyboard—I assumed that in the military machine permutation H had the same configuration, since on both commercial and military machines, the keyboards followed the same sequence. I later found that this hypothesis was mistaken, and its adoption caused much unnecessary work and considerable loss of time, so that we nearly broke off the studies of Enigma again. Thus, a rather unusual thing had happened: the Cipher Bureau's purchase of a commercial machine to facilitate breaking the military Enigma cipher had, in fact, greatly impeded that outcome.

But for the moment I had assumed that permutation H was known to me. Thus I had a set of six equations with three unknowns—S, N, and Q. And just as I was wondering how to solve this set, quite unexpectedly on 9 December 1932, at just the right moment, I was given a photocopy of two tables of daily keys for September and October 1932.

Now the situation had changed radically. Since the key tables also contained the daily changes in the commutator connections, I could now regard permutation S as known and transfer it, like permutation H which I had assumed to be known, to the left side of the set, which now took the following form:

$$H^{-1}S^{-1}ASH = PNP^{-1}QPN^{-1}P^{-1},$$
$$H^{-1}S^{-1}BSH = P^{2}NP^{-2}QP^{2}N^{-1}P^{-2},$$
$$\dots\dots\dots\dots\dots\dots\dots\dots\dots$$
$$H^{-1}S^{-1}FSH = P^{6}NP^{-6}QP^{6}N^{-1}P^{-6}.$$

In the set of equations so written, all the permutations on the left side are completely known, and on the right side only permutations N and Q are unknown. Let us further transform both sides of the first equation by the internal automorphism designated by P, both sides of the second equation by P^2, and so on, and for brevity let us designate the left sides by the letters U through Z:

$$U = P^{-1}H^{-1}S^{-1}ASHP = NP^{-1}QPN^{-1},$$
$$V = P^{-2}H^{-1}S^{-1}BSHP^{2} = NP^{-2}QP^{2}N^{-1},$$
$$\dots\dots\dots\dots\dots\dots\dots\dots\dots$$
$$Z = P^{-6}H^{-1}S^{-1}FSHP^{6} = NP^{-6}QP^{6}N^{-1}.$$

Next let us form products, multiplying these expressions successively by twos:

$$UV = NP^{-1}(QP^{-1}QP)PN^{-1},$$
$$VW = NP^{-2}(QP^{-1}QP)P^{2}N^{-1},$$
$$\dots\dots\dots\dots\dots\dots\dots$$
$$YZ = NP^{-5}(QP^{-1}QP)P^{5}N^{-1},$$

from which, by eliminating the common expression $QP^{-1}QP$, we obtain a set of four equations with only one unknown NPN^{-1}:

$$VW = NP^{-1}N^{-1}(UV)NPN^{-1},$$
$$WX = NP^{-1}N^{-1}(VW)NPN^{-1},$$
$$XY = NP^{-1}N^{-1}(WX)NPN^{-1},$$
$$YZ = NP^{-1}N^{-1}(XY)NPN^{-1}.$$

We see that the expression VW is transformed from the expression UV by the action of permutation NPN^{-1}. Subscribing VW beneath UV in all possible ways—and there are several dozen ways—we obtain dozens of possible solutions for the expression NPN^{-1}. Similarly, WX is transformed from VW by the action of the same expression NPN^{-1}. Thus, subscribing WX beneath VW, we will again obtain dozens of possible solutions for the expression NPN^{-1}. One of these solutions should be identical with one of those previously obtained. That is the NPN^{-1} that we are seeking. The last two equations for XY and YZ are now superfluous.

The rest is simple. It suffices to subscribe beneath the expression obtained for NPN^{-1} the permutation P, known to us, in all the twenty-six ways possible, in order to obtain twenty-six variants for the connections in drum N. Which of these variants we select is not of great importance for the moment, since the choice of one or another variant signifies merely a greater or lesser torsion in the N drum of the side with the fixed contacts with respect to the side with the spring-loaded contacts. Final determination of the correct torsion will only be possible later.

That is how the matter appeared in theory. In practice, unfortunately, it was otherwise. As the formulae indicate, products UV, VW, WX, XY, YZ should all be similar. But they weren't, and, as a result, it was impossible to subscribe these products one beneath another. And although I carried out the same operation several times on materials from different days, since I took into account the possibility that the middle drum had turned, the result was always negative. The trials took me a great deal of time, and consideration was being given to a new interruption of work on Enigma, when it finally occurred to me that the cause of my failure may have been merely a mistaken assumption as to the connections in the entry drum.

Here, a small digression: I have the fullest grounds to believe that the British cryptologists were unable to overcome the difficulties caused by the connections in the entry drum. When the meeting of Polish, French, and British cipher bureau representatives took place in Poland in July 1939, the first question that the British cryptologist Dillwyn Knox asked was: What are the connections in the entry drum? And second, Knox's niece, Penelope Fitzgerald, states in her book *The Knox Brothers*, published in 1978,[2] that Knox was furious when he learned how simple it was.

What, then, were the connections in the entry drum? It turned out later that they can be found by deduction, but in December 1932, or perhaps in the first days of 1933, I obtained those connections by guessing. I assumed that, since the keyboard keys were not connected with the successive contacts in the entry drum in the order of the letters on the keyboard, then maybe they were connected up in alphabetical order; that is, that the permutation caused by the entry drum was an identity and need not be taken into account at all. This time, luck smiled upon me. The hypothesis proved correct, and the very first trial yielded a positive result. From my pencil, as by magic, began to issue numbers designating the connections in drum N. Thus the connections in one drum, the right-hand drum, were finally known.

How were the connections in the remaining drums found? It should be recalled that I had been given photocopies of the daily keys for two months, September and October 1932. In that period, the change of sequence of drums on the axle took place quarterly, and since September and October belong to two different quarters, they had a different sequence of drums, and different drums appeared on the right-hand side. Thus, in both quarters, I was able to apply exactly the same method in order to find their connections. Finding the connections in the third drum, and especially the connections in the reversing drum, now presented no great difficulties. Likewise, there were no difficulties with determining the correct torsion of the drums' side walls with respect to each other, or the moments when the left and middle drums turned.

The operations necessary in order to establish these details consisted, basically, of attempts at reading several messages from that period and making such adjustments in the drums as to finally obtain the messages perfectly. An aid in this work, supplied with the monthly tables of daily keys, were German instructions for using the Enigma machine, including a sample plain text and its authentic ciphergram at a stated daily key and message key. In later editions of the same instructions, the example given was always fictitious.

Since, as I have stated, it turned out that the connections in the entry drum could have been found by deduction and not only by guessing, the question forced itself, whether one could not solve also the set of equations (3), and thereby obtain the connections in the drums by deduction, that is, without assistance from intelligence material. To this day, it is not known whether equation set (3) is soluble. To be sure, another way was found, at least in theory, to reconstruct the connections in the drums. Still, this approach is imperfect and tedious. Even its cursory description would cause a further lengthening of this article. Therefore, I shall mention only that it requires possession of messages from two days with the same or close settings of the drums, and hence it conditions the discovery of the drum connections on chance, and then it also requires many trials, so that it is not clear that the Cipher Bureau's directors would have had the patience to employ several personnel for a long period without certainty of getting results, or whether instead they would have recommended abandoning work on Enigma once more. Hence, the conclusion is that the intelligence material furnished to us should be regarded as having been decisive to solution of the machine. A number of years later, I learned that the material had been supplied by the aforementioned Captain (later General) Bertrand.

Daily Keys

Since the connections in the drums were now known, we proceeded to seek a way of finding the third and final secret of Enigma, the daily keys. Earlier, the commercial machine had been suitably modified in the Cipher Bureau's technical section, and I had been instructed—it was probably at the beginning of January 1933—to initiate my two colleagues Henryk Zygalski and Jerzy Różycki into the secret so that, using the daily keys furnished by French intelligence for the two months September and October 1932, they might read the cipher material for that period. I myself was to continue in isolation until the completion of the job.

Nevertheless, its completion was hardly easy, nor could it be, since the Germans were convinced that, even if one possessed the machine, it was impossible to solve the cipher without a knowledge of the daily keys. I concentrated my attention on the fact that permutation S exchanged only six pairs of letters, and thus left fourteen letters unchanged. Let us take another look at equation set (3). We already know that permutation H is an identity, and so may be left out. For a moment let us suppose that permutation S also is identical. If now we transfer all the permutations, except for the unknown permutation Q, to the left side, we shall obtain the following set:

$$PN^{-1}P^{-1}APNP^{-1} = Q,$$
$$P^2N^{-1}P^{-2}BP^2NP^{-2} = Q,$$
$$\dots\dots\dots\dots\dots$$
$$P^6N^{-1}P^{-6}FP^6NP^{-6} = Q.$$

Although the connections in drum N are known, its setting is not. In order to take account of this, it is more correct to write:

$$P^xN^{-1}P^{-x}AP^xNP^{-x} = Q,$$
$$P^{x+1}N^{-1}P^{-x-1}BP^{x+1}NP^{-x-1} = Q,$$
$$\dots\dots\dots\dots\dots\dots$$
$$P^{x+5}N^{-1}P^{-x-5}FP^{x+5}NP^{-x-5} = Q.$$

If permutation S were indeed identical, then by substituting for the unknown "x," in turn, the numbers from one to twenty-six, and each time calculating the left sides of the above set of equations, at a certain "x" we would obtain the same thing for all the expressions Q in the set, and in this way we would find the setting of drum N. Permutation S does exist, however, so for no "x" will the expressions Q be the same, but at a certain stated "x" there will be certain similarities among them, since permutation S does not change all the letters. Carrying out these operations would, however, have been excessively toilsome. I sought for a more practical method, and I found it in what I dubbed the grill method.

For each of the three drums, one writes, permanently, on a sheet of paper of suitable size, thirty-one permutations N, PNP^{-1}, P^2NP^{-2}, ...,

$P^{25}NP^{-25}$, N, PNP^{-1}, ..., P^4NP^{-4}, with the connections in the three drums, in the following form:

N	kjpzydtiohxcsgubrnwfmveqla
PNP^{-1}	ioyxcshngwbrftaqmveludpkzj
P^2NP^{-2}	nxwbrgmfvaqeszpludktcojyih
....	....
P^4NP^{-4}	uzpekdtyocqxnjsbiramhwgflv,

and on another piece of paper with six openings, named by me a grill, one writes out permutations A through F—determined earlier—in the following form:

$$A \quad \begin{pmatrix} \text{abcdefghijklmnopqrstuvwxyz} \\ \text{srwivhnfdolkygjtxbapzecqmu} \end{pmatrix}$$

....

$$F \quad \begin{pmatrix} \text{abcdefghijklmnopqrstuvwxyz} \\ \text{wxofkduihzevqscymtnrglabpj} \end{pmatrix}$$

Next, one moves the grill over the piece of paper with the connections in drum N until he strikes upon a position in which he finds certain similarities among individual expressions Q. At that position, he must rearrange the upper and lower letters in all the permutations A through F so that all the permutations Q become the same. In this way, he will, at the same time, find the setting of drum N and the changes caused by permutation S. This work requires considerable concentration, since the similarities that I have mentioned do not always show up clearly and may very easily be overlooked.

However, the task still is not completed. There remains the unknown Q. But Q, as we recall, is merely the condensed expression (2) designating a fictitious reversing drum. At present we know the connections in drums M, L, R. Nevertheless, we still do not know the positions of drums M and L, since only drum R is stationary. Therefore it would be more correct to write

$$Q = P^y MP^{-y} P^z LP^{-z} RP^z L^{-1} P^{-z} P^y MP^{-y},$$

where the unknowns "y" and "z," like the previously unknown "x," can assume all the values from one to twenty-six. The only procedure that I could apply at that time (the beginning of 1933) to find "y" and "z" was each day to go through all the $26^2 = 676$ possible positions of drums M and L on the machine itself until I hit on their correct position. This was tedious, mechanical work, but that was not the end of the job.

We must recall one more detail of the Enigma machine's construction that I have already mentioned in describing the machine. Placed on the circumferences of cipher drums L, M, N were adjustable rings with the letters of the alphabet engraved on them. How these rings should be set daily was given to the cipher clerks on the monthly tables supplied to them, along with the other components of the daily keys. We still had to find the settings of the rings.

From messages of September and October 1932 that had meanwhile been read, I learned that as a rule all messages, of course leaving aside the subsequent parts of messages comprising two or more parts, began with the letters ANX, from the word "an" (German for "to") and "x" to separate the words. One needed to select a suitable message, beginning, for example, with the letters "tuv," and depressing the "t" key all the time, rotate the drums, observing when the A lamp lit. Then he depressed the "u" key and, when the N lamp lit, depressed the "v" key. If the X lamp lit, there was a large probability that we had found the right case, and then one needed to set the rings appropriately. If not, he had to keep on looking until he succeeded.

This method was a very primitive one and far more tedious than that for finding the positions of drums L and M, since, in an extremely unfavorable case, one had to go through all the possible positions of the drums, of which, as we know, there were $26^3 = 17,576$. But it was an effective method.

Thus, the result achieved during barely a few months' work may be summarized as follows:

1) the German military Enigma machine had been reconstructed,
2) a method had been found for reconstructing the message keys daily,
3) a method had been found for reconstructing the daily keys.

Period of Relative Quiet (1933-1935)

The first decision made by my superiors, when I had communicated my results to them, was to order from the AVA plant, which was under Cipher Bureau control and produced radio transmitter-receiver stations, a series of doubles of the German military Enigmas, built in accordance with the commercial model, with the drum connections supplied by me and with due consideration to other differences in construction between the two types of machines, principally through the addition of a commutator. Next, five or six young persons were hired and put into a separate room, with the sole assignment of deciphering the stream of messages, the daily keys to which we soon began supplying. And, finally, it was again directed that my two colleagues, Zygalski and Różycki, work permanently with me.

So now there were three of us instead of one. By the methods just described, day by day we found the daily keys and supplied them to the decipherers. Since, for three years, until the end of 1935, the Germans introduced no essential changes into the Enigma cipher, we could also devote some time to improving our methods of decryptment.

Thus, for example, we set up for the six possible arrangements of drums—I, II; I, III; II, I; II, III; III, I; III, II—a catalog of all the possible permutations Q in accordance with formula (4). It embraced a total of $6 \cdot 26^2 = 4,056$ items. When the catalog was ready, it sufficed—if, using the grill method, we had found the setting of drum N—to locate permutation Q, which had been obtained at the same time, in the catalog, in order to have at once the setting of drums L and M.

When we were turning all the 26^3 = 17,576 possible positions of the drums on the machine in succession in order to find the settings of the rings by the ANX method, we soon noticed that, if the substance of a message was to open with ANX, several positions of drum N could immediately be excluded as impossible. And since there were between ten and twenty messages daily at whose beginning one could expect the letters ANX, more often than not one could, by pure calculation, discard as impossible all but one or two positions of drum N. At present, though, I no longer remember what the calculations were that had to be done or the theoretical foundations on which they rested.

It was also during this period that Różycki worked out a method which he named the clock method, and which, in many cases, allowed determination of which of the three drums—I, II, III—was that day drum N; that is, was located on the far right in the machine. To be sure, to the end of 1935 the sequence of drums changed once a quarter, so that determination of drum N was not yet an overly important matter, but as of 1 February 1936, the change of drum sequence took place monthly, and as of 1 October 1936, daily. How did this method work?

If we subscribe beneath each other, letter beneath letter, two texts in German, for example,

WEMGOTTWILLRECHTEGUNSTERWE
UEB IMMERTREUUNDREDLICHKEIT,

then, within the compass of twenty-six letters, there will be, on an average, two columns with identical letters, and this feature will be preserved, as well, when we encipher both texts with the same key. However, if we encipher each text using a different key to the machine cipher, then the twenty-six letters will include, on an average, only one column with identical letters. The cause of this phenomenon is, of course, the unequal frequency of occurrence of letters in the German language (as is the case also in other languages). Within the compass of twenty-six letters, this phenomenon does not occur in a perceptible way, but when we have two messages of, say, two hundred sixty letters each, then in general we can tell by this procedure whether they were enciphered using the same key or different keys. We make use of this in the following way:

If we have a sufficient quantity of cipher material, we usually find between ten and twenty pairs of messages such that in each pair the first two letters of the keys are the same and only the third letters of the keys differ. We now subscribe the two messages of a pair beneath each other in such a way that the letters enciphered using the same setting of the drums will appear beneath each other. A priori, though, there are two possible ways of subscribing the messages beneath each other, depending on the position of drum N at which the rotation of the middle, the M, drum takes place. These positions are known and are different for each of the three drums. For example, when drum I is in the N place, the rotation of drum M will occur when in drum N's window the letter "q" shifts to "r." If drum II is in the N place, the rotation will occur as the letter "e" changes to "f," and if drum III is the N drum, the rotation will occur with the letter's change from "v" to "w." It suffices, with each of the two possible ways of subscribing the messages beneath each other, to count the number of columns with identical letters, in order to find out which of the ways of subscribing the messages is the right one, and thereby to determine which of the three drums is at the right-hand side.

Różycki's clock method, which in many cases facilitated our work, also had the interesting property that, of the methods discovered by us, it was the only one that was based on linguistic features, on the frequency of occurrence of the letters in the German language, rather than on mathematical principles.

Period of Increased Changes (1936-August 1938)

Germany's growing military power broadened the sphere of users of the Enigma machines. The German Air Force had already, as of 1 August 1935, created its own radio communications net with its own daily keys, but, of course, using the same Enigma. Gradually other military and paramilitary formations joined in, and since they also formed separate nets, we had to reconstruct more and more daily keys. I have already mentioned the increasingly frequent changes of drum sequence. As of 1 October 1936, the number of pairs of letters changed on the commutator was increased and modified, from six to between five and eight, making it difficult to use the grill method. Hence, we sought other methods.

We turned our attention to the characteristics, whose configurations seldom repeated and, therefore, to a certain degree, defined a given day. The formula

$$AD = SPNP^{-1}QPN^{-1}P^3NP^{-4}QP^4N^{-1}P^{-4}S^{-1}$$

and the two analogous formulas for BE and CF implied that permutation S, as a transforming permutation, did not affect the lengths of the cycles in a characteristic, but only the letters within the cycles. Thus, if an instrument could be devised to furnish the lengths of the cycles for each of the expressions of type AD (and there were not all that many such expressions—for each of the six possible drum sequences, only $26^3 = 17,576$), we could set up a card catalog of the lengths of the cycles of expressions of type AD and, by comparison with the characteristic for a given day, determine the setting of the drums. We in fact succeeded in devising such an instrument, an extremely simple one (fig. D-5). We named it a cyclometer, and it was built by the AVA factory, the same one that had earlier built the military Enigma doubles.

The cyclometer comprised essentially two sets of drums (with the N drum of the second set displacing three letters with respect to the N drum of the first set), an ebonite plate bearing twenty-six flashlight bulbs and a switch at each bulb, and a source of current. When the current was turned on at any of the bulbs by throwing the switch, not only the given bulb lit but so did all the bulbs that belonged to the same cycle and to the other cycle of the same pair. One had to note on a card the position of the drums and the number of bulbs that lit, and to order the cards themselves in a specified way, for example, by the lengths of the cycles.

This job took a long time, over a year, since we carried it out along with our normal work at reconstructing daily keys using the grill. Once all six card catalogs were ready, though, obtaining a daily key was usually a matter of ten to twenty minutes. The card told the drum positions, the box from which the card had been taken told the drum sequence, and permutation S was obtained by comparing the letters in the cycles of the characteristic with the letters in the cycles of permutations AD, BE, CF, which were obtained by tapping on the machine's keyboard.

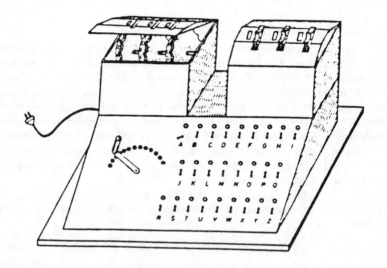

FIGURE D-5. Cyclometer.

Unfortunately, on 2 November 1937, when the card catalog was ready, the Germans exchanged the reversing drum that they had been using, which they designated by the letter A, for another drum, a B drum, and, consequently, we had to do the whole job over again, after first reconstructing the connections in drum B, of course.

In September 1937, a couple of months before the change of reversing drums, a new net had appeared on the airwaves. As it soon turned out, this was a net of the [Nazi] party's security service, the Sicherheitsdienst or S.D., for short. In view of the role that our reading of this net played over a year later in the subsequent work on Enigma, I wish to devote a few words to it.

The S.D.'s enciphering procedure differed little from that used in other nets. When for the first time a day's characteristic in this net was formed, it was located without any trouble in our card catalog. Thus the sequence and position of the drums and permutation S were found, but when an attempt was made to determine the setting of the rings by the ANX method, it ran into difficulties. Apparently none of the messages considered had begun with ANX. Therefore, a fragment was chosen from the middle of one of the messages, and a start was made at tapping it out on the machine in all the possible positions of the drums, in the hope of thereby obtaining a fragment of the plain text. And indeed, fortuitously, after a relatively short time the letters "ein" were obtained. This might be a fragment of the text, but, on the other hand, it might be a quite accidental occurrence of just those letters. When the whole message was tapped out with that position of the drums, no more fragments in German were found.

However, after closer analysis of this ostensibly senseless collection of letters, it turned out that certain repetitions of letters could be extracted from it, that these repetitions formed four-letter groups, and that the intervals between them were multiples of four; the entire message could be divided (neglecting the word "ein") into four-letter code groups. Thus, what we had was a so-called superencipherment. First the sender of the message, doubtless an officer, encoded the text of the message, using a code book, into four-letter code groups—he had used the word "ein" only because he did not find that word in the code book—and it was only then that he gave the text, so prepared, to the cipher clerk for encipherment on the machine.

It was thanks to this slip-up—to the mixing of plain text with code—and to an ounce of luck, that we were able to reconstruct the entire daily key, complete with the settings of the rings.[3] The code, fortunately, did not prove difficult to solve, though of course in such cases one can never reconstruct 100 percent of the code book, since it is never the situation that all the code groups appear in the messages.

At the beginning of 1938 [in January, according to Mayer], the chief of our intelligence department, Col. Stefan Mayer, directed that statistics be compiled for a two-week [test] period, comparing the [quantities of Enigma message] material solved, with the [quantities of] Enigma enciphered material intercepted by the radiotelegraphers. The ratio came to 75 percent. Peter Calvocoressi, a former worker at the British cipher bureau [at Bletchley Park], in a talk broadcast by British radio on 18 January 1977,[4] stated that no one else in the world had achieved such results. He was, of course, thinking of later times, because in 1938, outside of the Poles, no one else was yet reading messages enciphered on the German military Enigma. Nor were those 75 percent of messages read the limit of our possibilities. With slightly augmented personnel, we might have attained about 90 percent of messages read. But a certain amount of cipher material, whether due to faulty transmission or faulty reception, or to various other causes, always remains unread in such cases.

The Greatest Changes (September 1938-September 1939)

As of 15 September 1938, the Germans changed the procedure for giving message keys without changing anything in or adding anything to the machine itself. Commencing from that date, the encipherer was obliged to select three letters at will, which he placed, unenciphered, at the head of the message. Then he set the drums to those letters, chose three other letters as his message key and, as before, after enciphering these twice, placed them at the beginning of the message. Then he set the drums to the message key and began the actual encipherment of the message itself.

The change in procedure for giving message keys was introduced in all the military formations, but not in the S.D. net. All our accomplishments up to that time in the reconstruction of daily keys and message keys—the card catalog method and the grill method—with respect to military formations failed, since there were no longer any characteristics. The only net that we could solve and read as theretofore was the S.D. net.

Yet, within a very short time—maybe a week, maybe two—we had two ideas, or rather, what was more important, we found ways to realize those ideas.

Just as with the previous manner of transmitting the key, we had given it in the form of two three-letter groups. Now we had to give it in the form of three groups, for example

SHP, CHV PZT,

in which the first group, separated from the others by a comma, is unenciphered, and the two subsequent ones constitute the message key, twice enciphered. Given sufficiently ample cipher material, it may happen that, on a given day, there will be three messages with keys such as

RTJ   WAH   WIK
HPL   RAW   KTW
DQX   DWJ   MWR

in which the first and the fourth, or the second and the fifth, or the third and the sixth letters in the keys of all three messages are the same. In this example it is the letter "w," but it may be a completely different letter, just so it is the same one in all three messages. Let us assume, for a moment, that permutation S is identical. If, as well, there were no setting of the rings, and we also knew the sequence of the drums on the axle, it would suffice to set the drums to position RTJ, and a depression of key "w" would cause one and the same lamp to light within the interval of three strokes. The same would happen in position HPN and position DQY of the drums. The setting of the rings causes the positions of the drums at which this will occur to be unknown to us. However, the differences in the positions will be preserved, and are therefore known to us.

Thus, it would be enough to construct a device that basically comprised the sets of drums from six Enigmas and that—preserving the mutual difference in positions of the drums, which is known to us—synchronously revolved the drums and (after, in this manner, over a period of about two hours, running through all the possible $26^3 = 17,576$ positions) signaled when the condition for lighting three pairs of lamps (in each pair the same) was fulfilled.

However, the sequence of the drums was not known, and so it would be best to build at once six such devices, one for each possible sequence. This was true, but there was still permutation S. However, during that period, permutation S comprised five to eight transpositions, and so, on the average, exchanged half the letters. Therefore, one could expect that a letter recurring in three messages six times (in the example given, the letter "w") would not be altered by permutation S about every other time.

I then provided the operating principle, and the AVA factory that has been mentioned completed, within an incredibly short time—already in November 1938—six such devices, which, for lack of a better idea, we named bombs [in Polish, singular "bomba," plural "bomby"]. This was undoubtedly thanks to the plant's director, engineer Antoni Palluth, who, although not a regular employee of the Cipher Bureau, collaborated closely with it and—himself a cryptologist—had great understanding of the bureau's needs.

The second idea, which arose almost simultaneously with that of the bomb, rested on seemingly similar but actually quite different foundations. As with the bomb, we had to have sufficiently ample cipher material. We could then expect to find in that material about ten messages with keys such as

KTL,	WOC	DRC	GRA,	FDR	YDP
SVW,	DKR	IKC	MDO,	CTW	YZW
BWK,	TCL	TSD	AGH,	SLM	PZM
EDV,	PRS	ZRT	JBR,	LPS	TOS
GRN,	UTS	UQA	ITY,	APO	ZPD

that is, keys in which either the first letters are the same as the fourth, or the second are the same as the fifth, or the third are the same as the sixth, but in which the pairs of identical letters in each key might be different. If we recall characteristic (1), we will also remember that identical letters in corresponding places in the key designate single-letter cycles in the characteristic. But permutation S does not, after all, affect the lengths of the cycles in the characteristic, and so it likewise does not affect the fact of the occurrence or nonoccurrence of single cycles.

Therefore what was needed—instead of a card catalog of the lengths of cycles in all the products of type AD—was a card catalog of the positions of all those products of type AD in which single-letter cycles occur, and then to compare these with single-letter cycles occurring in the message keys of given days. But how to carry out the comparison? Here, too, as in the previous idea, the only things known were the relative distances of the single-letter cycles appearing in the message keys of a given day. And here our colleague Zygalski showed a way to carry out the comparison.

For each of the twenty-six possible positions of drum L, there was drawn—on fairly large sheets of paper, about 60 by 60 centimeters, designated with the successive letters of the alphabet—a large square divided into 51 by 51 smaller squares. Down both sides and across the top and bottom of each large square were placed the letters from "a" through "z" and once again from "a" through "y." This was, as it were, a system of coordinates, in which the abscissas and ordinates designated successive possible positions of drums M and N, and each small square designated permutations, with or without single-letter cycles, corresponding to those positions. The cases with single-letter cycles were perforated.

It was an enormous job, the more so as the cases with single-letter cycles had to be perforated four times. When these sheets were superposed—according to a strictly defined program, in the proper sequence, and displaced in the proper way with respect to each other—the number of apertures that shone through gradually decreased, and if one had a sufficient number of keys with single-letter cycles, in the end there remained a single aperture that shone through all the sheets and that corresponded probably to the right case.

From the series to which the sheets belonged, one could tell the sequence of the drums. From the position of the aperture and the letter of the sheet, he could calculate the settings of the rings, and by comparing the letters of the keys with the letters in the machine, he could, likewise, calculate permutation S, thus, the entire daily key. But, as I have said, this was an enormous job. It was necessary to cut about a thousand apertures into each sheet, there were twenty-six sheets in each series, and we needed to make six series. Since we did this work alongside our normal activities, by 15 December 1938, we had succeeded in making only two series.

But, on that day, the Germans introduced a new change into the Enigma cipher. In all formations, including the S.D., they added to the existing three drums two more drums, IV and V. There were still three drums on the axle, but now three drums were to be selected from among five, and so, instead of six possible sequences, there were now sixty. But, leaving aside even the tenfold increase in the number of possible drum sequences, we did not know the connections in the new drums. How to obtain them? With the new system of encipherment, there were no characteristics. The cyclometer and card catalogs were useless. Fortunately, we had the S.D. net which, while it had introduced drums IV and V, retained the old system for enciphering the keys. Using the grill method, we sought for and found a day on which drum N happened to be one of the earlier, and therefore known, drums. Then we made the assumption that drums L and M included a known drum and an unknown one, and we found the connections in the latter drum the same way that, in 1932, we had found the connections in the third, then still unknown, drum.

Thus we were in possession of the connections in all five drums, and we could still read messages in the S.D. net. This was not easy, though, for although we sometimes knew which drum was in the N place—thanks to Różycki's clock method—the grill method, the only one that we could now apply to the S.D. net, sometimes failed, because, as of 1 January 1939, the Germans once more increased the number of letters changed by permutation S to seven to ten pairs. Nevertheless, the fact is that we did read messages in the S.D. net, and Calvocoressi was incorrect in saying that, at this time, no one in the world could read messages enciphered on the five-drum Enigma.

The reading of messages of military formations was a different matter. Though, thanks to the S.D. net, we knew the connections in drums IV and V, these drums needed to be applied to our bombs and perforated sheets. The AVA supplied a small number of drums IV and V for the machines with which the decipherers read messages of the S.D. net, but the bombs required thirty-six each of drums IV and V. And the work using the bombs should have gone on twenty-four hours a day, requiring the hiring of several additional operators.

As far as the perforated sheets were concerned, fifty-eight more series should have been made to go along with the two series that we already had. Though we did work out methods with which, in certain cases, we could determine with great probability which drum was in the N place, all the series of sheets were needed. Thus the situation presented itself as follows: leaving aside the S.D. net, we only read military messages when only the three original drums happened to be on the axle in the machine, as occurred on the average of one time in ten. Thus, the introduction of drums IV and V meant only quantitative, not qualitative, changes in our work. But when, as of 1 July 1939, the S.D. net shifted to the new way of transmitting message keys, the grill method ceased to be effective here, too.

Conclusion

That is how the situation stood when, on 25-26 July 1939, at the initiative of the Poles, a meeting was called in Warsaw, bringing together representatives of the British, French, and Polish intelligence services.

At that meeting, we told everything that we knew and showed everything that we had. We gave two Enigmas with five drums, produced by us, to Major (later General) Bertrand, who promised to pass one of the machines on later to the British, as he in fact did. From our guests we learned nothing. Neither the British nor the French had managed to overcome the first difficulties. They had neither the drum connections nor any methods.

The meeting, nevertheless, had very far-reaching consequences. Soon after the meeting, when the Germans without a declaration of war entered Poland, forcing the Cipher Bureau to flee to Rumania, Major Bertrand brought fifteen workers of that bureau, including its chief and its deputy as well as my two colleagues and me to France where, at the Château Vignolles, forty kilometers from Paris, he set up a workplace for us. But how to work there, when all our materials, equipment, machines (except for two Enigmas taken across the border in Lieutenant Colonel Langer's automobile) had been very painstakingly destroyed on Polish soil, so that no trace of our work would fall into German hands? It was then that the British sent us a complete set of sixty series, each of twenty-six sheets, of perforated Zygalski sheets.

The execution of this enormous job within a relatively short time was nothing extraordinary for the British. They had huge numbers of people at their disposal. At Bletchley, a town about sixty kilometers north of London where the British cipher bureau was at that time located, sixty cryptologists were already at work when the war began, and many more were employed as the war progressed. No wonder, then, that when using the perforated sheets, we began reconstructing the daily keys and sending them to each other across the Channel, for every one hundred keys found, eighty-three came from the British and only seventeen from us Poles.

When the French signed the armistice with the Germans in June 1940, Major Bertrand organized our escape to Algeria, and when, in the fall of the same year we returned to the unoccupied zone of France in order to act clandestinely under Major Bertrand's direction, we found that, in the interim, the Germans had once again changed the procedure for transmitting message keys. As a result, the Zygalski sheets became useless. We worked on other ciphers, no longer on Enigma.[5] For, as Calvocoressi correctly stated, in order to break this kind of cipher, two things are needed: mathematical theory and mechanical aids. And as the Germans refined the procedures for transmitting messages, the mechanical aids necessary to break the cipher became ever more complicated and expensive. Parallel with that, the amount of monitored material needed to deal with the cipher also grew. In our circumstances in France, in an unoccupied zone that was nevertheless controlled by the Germans, we were receiving little intercepted material, and we could not dream of designing, much less building, the complicated and expensive machines that would have been necessary. The British at Bletchley already in 1940 modified the Polish bombs of 1938 to suit the changed requirements, preserving the name "bombs" and their electromechanical character. Later they built ever more complicated machines for breaking the Enigma cipher, until, at last, one of them, which came into use at the very end of 1943, was—as Calvocoressi was assured—the first genuine electronic computer to be built in the world.

When the Allies landed in North Africa on 8 November 1942, and the Germans invaded the unoccupied zone of France in retaliation, Major Bertrand quickly evacuated us all to the Côte d'Azur in order to organize our transfer in small groups across the Pyrenees into Spain, and on to Great Britain. However, not all the expeditions turned out happily. In crossing the Spanish border, Lieutenant Colonel Langer, Major Ciężki, and engineer Palluth fell into the hands of the Germans. Palluth died on 19 April 1944 in a forced-labor camp when he was struck by a fragment of an Allied bomb dropped during an air raid on the camp. Lieutenant Colonel Langer and Major Ciężki were put into prisoner-of-war camps, from which they were liberated by the Allies only in May 1945. Jerzy Różycki had died earlier, on 9 January 1942, in the wreck of a ship that was carrying him across the Mediterranean. Thus, only Henryk Zygalski and I reached Great Britain. There, inducted into the Polish Army, we worked for a time at solving German ciphers (but not the Enigma cipher) until, under the terms of pertinent Soviet-British agreements, our small unit was disbanded.

NOTES

1. Bertrand, *Enigma.*

2. Fitzgerald, *The Knox Brothers.*—ED.

3. Cf. the "einwandfrei" episodes mentioned in the notes to chapter 5 and in chapter 15.—ED.

4. Calvocoressi, "The Secrets of Enigma."

5. The assertion that at Cadix the Poles "no longer [worked] on Enigma" is evidently in error. See chapter 10, note 11. Apparently the present paper by Rejewski took about three years to appear in print, and in the meantime he realized the error.—ED.

Appendix E

The Mathematical Solution of the Enigma Cipher
by Marian Rejewski

Introduction

Cryptology, the science of ciphers and codes, has long used mathematical methods. It was, however, only in the 1920s, with the introduction of cipher machines, that the application of mathematics to cryptology expanded greatly. This was so especially with permutation theory. Application of the latter, along with other methods of cryptological analysis, contributed to the breaking in Poland in 1932/33 of the German machine cipher, Enigma.

My two reports on the breaking of the Enigma cipher, the first dating from 1942 and the second from 1967, are to be found at the Sikorski Historical Institute (Instytut Historyczny imienia Generała Sikorskiego) in London and the Military Historical Institute (Wojskowy Instytut Historyczny) in Warsaw, respectively.

Part One: The Machine

1. *Description of the Machine*

Enigma was a device that served for the mechanical encipherment of plain texts. The photographs in the book and figure E-1 give an idea of the machine's appearance and permit an abbreviated description of its operation.

Enigma had a twenty-six letter keyboard and, beyond it, a panel with twenty-six letters illuminated by glowlamps beneath them. The main ciphering components, partly visible in the photographs, were three cipher drums or rotors (Chiffrierwalzen)[1] and a fourth, stationary reflector or reversing drum (Umkehrwalze), mounted on a single axle. The reversing drum could be moved to or away from the rotors with a lever. The three rotors had the

---

Translated from the Polish by Christopher Kasparek and originally published in Polish as an appendix to Kozaczuk, *W kręgu Enigmy*, on pages 369-93.

letters of the alphabet placed about their rims, the topmost letters being visible beneath little windows in a lid. Visible to the side, protruding somewhat, were serrated disks for manipulating the rotors. Each rotor had twenty-six concentrically arranged fixed contacts on one face and twenty-six spring loaded contacts on the other. The fixed contacts were connected with the spring loaded ones in irregular fashion by insulated wires passing through the ebonite heart of the rotor. The reversing drum had only spring loaded contacts connected among themselves in pairs on one face, likewise in irregular fashion. The connections in these four subsystems constituted the essential ciphering part and the secret of Enigma. The electric circuit of which the rotors formed a part is represented, functionally, in figure E-2.

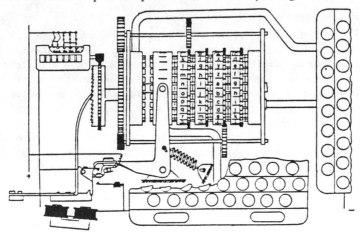

FIGURE E-1. Diagram of an Enigma with four rotors (type M 4).

To the right of the rotors was a battery that powered the machine. In front of the keyboard was the commutator. Six pairs of plugs connected with wires (Steckerverbindungen) made possible the interchange of twelve among the twenty-six letters of the alphabet.

Depression of an Enigma key caused the right-hand rotor to turn through one twenty-sixth of a revolution. At the same time, the circuit closed and current ran from the depressed key through the commutator, all three rotors, the reversing drum, back through the rotors, and once more through the commutator. A glowlamp lit under one of the letters, which was always different from the depressed key. If, instead, in the previous position of the rotor, the key marked with the same letter as the glowlamp that lit up had been depressed, then the glowlamp marked with the same letter as appears on the key initially struck would have lit. The Enigma machine thus served both for transforming plain text into cipher text and for the reverse operation, without any additional manipulations. Every successive depression of a key caused the right-hand rotor to move through one twenty-sixth of a revolution and yet another glowlamp to light. The middle and left-hand rotors likewise turned, but much less often, in accordance with a built-in program.

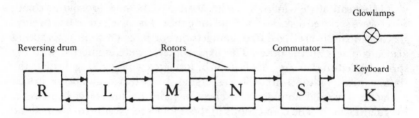

FIGURE E-2. Enigma's functional circuit.

2. Encipherment Procedure

The Enigma cipher machine could be operated in a variety of ways. In German military formations until 15 September 1938, and in the S.D. (Sicherheitsdienst) until 1 July 1939, the following instructions were in effect. The encipherer first set the rotors in the basic position (Grundstellung) established for that day and changed the letters in the commutator by placing the plugs in the appropriate sockets. Then he independently selected the individual key for that message, three letters which he enciphered twice. In this way he obtained six letters, which he placed at the opening of the message. Next, he set the rotors to the selected individual key and proceeded to encipher his message. The individual keys for a given day thus had two characteristics:

(1) Encipherment of all individual message keys began from the same basic position, which was unknown to the cryptologist.

(2) Each key was enciphered twice, and thus the first letter designated the same thing as the fourth letter, the second the same thing as the fifth, and so on.

If we have a sufficient number of messages (about eighty) for a given day, then, in general, all the letters of the alphabet will occur in all six places at the openings of the messages. In each place they form a mutually unique transformation of the set of letters into themselves, that is, they are permutations. These permutations, designated respectively by the letters A through F, are not known to the cryptologist, but the transitions from the first letters to the fourth, from the second to the fifth, and from the third to the sixth likewise form permutations, and these are known to the cryptologist. They are products AD, BE, CF of the previous permutations. They may be represented as disjunctive products of cycles and then assume a very characteristic form, generally different for each day, for example:

$$AD = (dvpfkxgzyo) (eijmunqlht) (bc) (rw) (a) (s)$$
$$BE = (blfqveoum) (hjpswizrn) (axt) (cgy) (d) (k)$$
$$CF = (abviktjgfcqny) (duzrehlxwpsmo).$$

This kind of set of permutations, obtained from the openings of messages, constituted the starting point for solving Enigma. Using such sets from merely a few days, we managed to reconstruct the machine's internal connections. Thereafter, following the construction of the machine's doubles, each such set made possible over a period of many years the reconstruction of the daily keys (Tagesschlüssel) and, hence, the reading of enciphered messages. Thus, in view of the importance of this set, we shall devote some more attention to it.

We know from the machine's description that, if striking a given key, for example "x," causes the "y" lamp to light, then, conversely, striking the "y" key will cause the "x" lamp to light. The cause of this is, of course, the reversing drum. That is what causes all the unknown permutations from A through F to consist exclusively of transpositions. If the encipherer, proceeding with the double encipherment of his key, strikes, in the first place, the unknown key "x" and obtains the letter "a," and by striking, in the fourth place, the same key "x" obtains the letter "b," then, by striking, in the first place, the "a" key, he would obtain the letter "x," and by striking, in the fourth place, the "x" key, he would obtain the letter "b." Thus, there occurs a successive action, first of "a" on "x," and then of "x" on "b." The successive execution of such an operation is termed multiplication of permutations. Thus, we see that, in writing the letters "ab" next to each other, we are writing a fragment of permutation AD, which is a product of the unknown permutations A and D.

Let us now consider the following example. Let

dmq	vbn
von	puy
puc	fmq

designate the openings, that is, the doubly enciphered keys, of three of some eighty messages available for a given day. From the first and fourth letters we see that "d" becomes "v," "v" becomes "p," "p" becomes "f." In this way, we obtain a fragment of permutation AD: "dvpf." Similarly, from the second and fifth letters we see that "o" becomes "u," "u" becomes "m," "m" becomes "b." We obtain a fragment of permutation BE: "oumb." And, lastly, from the third and sixth letters, we see that "c" becomes "q," "q" becomes "n," "n" becomes "y." We obtain a fragment of permutation CF: "cqny." The openings of further messages would permit a complete assembly of the set of permutations AD, BE, CF. Because of its configuration and fundamental importance, we shall call this set the characteristic set or, simply, the characteristic for the given day.

3. The Set of Equations

As we know, after a key has been depressed and before the current causes a given lamp to light, it first passes through a series of the machine's components. Each of these components causes a permutation of the alphabet. If we designate the permutation caused by the commutator with the letter S, and that which is caused by the three rotors respectively (from left to right) with the letters L, M, N, and that which is caused by the reversing drum with the letter R, then the path of the current will be represented by the product of permutations $SNMLRL^{-1}M^{-1}N^{-1}S^{-1}$. However, at the moment that the key is depressed, rotor N executes one twenty-sixth of a revolution, and, to take account of this movement, we must introduce a special permutation of one cycle that transforms each letter of the alphabet into the next one; we shall designate it with the letter P:

$$P = (a\;b\;c\;d\;e\;f\;g\;h\;i\;j\;k\;l\;m\;n\;o\;p\;q\;r\;s\;t\;u\;v\;w\;x\;y\;z).$$

Figure E-3, in which the rotors have been replaced with two-dimensional slides, enables us to follow the path of the current before and after the movement of rotor N.

The diagram makes it evident that the unknown permutations A through F may be represented in the form

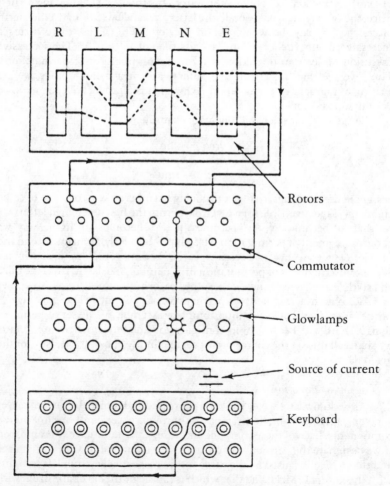

FIGURE E-3. Path of electric current through Enigma's components.

$$A = SPNP^{-1}MLRL^{-1}M^{-1}PN^{-1}P^{-1}S^{-1}$$
$$B = SP^2NP^{-2}MLRL^{-1}M^{-1}P^2N^{-1}P^{-2}S^{-1}$$

$$\cdots\cdots\cdots\cdots\cdots\cdots\cdots\cdots$$

$$E = SP^5NP^{-5}MLRL^{-1}M^{-1}P^5N^{-1}P^{-5}S^{-1}$$
$$F = SP^6NP^{-6}MLRL^{-1}M^{-1}P^6N^{-1}P^{-6}S^{-1}$$

and the known products AD, BE, CF in the form

$$AD = SPNP^{-1}MLRL^{-1}M^{-1}PN^{-1}P^3NP^{-4}MLRL^{-1}M^{-1}P^4N^{-1}P^{-4}S^{-1}$$
$$BE = SP^2NP^{-2}MLRL^{-1}M^{-1}P^2N^{-1}P^3NP^{-5}MLRL^{-1}M^{-1}P^5N^{-1}P^{-5}S^{-1}$$
$$CF = SP^3NP^{-3}MLRL^{-1}M^{-1}P^3N^{-1}P^3NP^{-6}MLRL^{-1}M^{-1}P^6N^{-1}P^{-6}S^{-1}.$$

The first part of our task is, essentially, to solve this set of equations, in which the left sides, and on the right side only the permutation P and its powers are known, while the permutations S, L, M, N, R are unknown. In this form, the set is certainly insoluble. Therefore, we seek to simplify it. The first step is purely formal, and consists in replacing the repeated product $MLRL^{-1}M^{-1}$ (it may be interpreted as a fictitious reversing drum) with the single letter Q. We have thereby temporarily reduced the number of unknowns to three, namely, S, N, Q:

$$AD = SPNP^{-1}QPN^{-1}P^3NP^{-4}QP^4N^{-1}P^{-4}S^{-1}$$
$$BE = SP^2NP^{-2}QP^2N^{-1}P^3NP^{-5}QP^5N^{-1}P^{-5}S^{-1}$$
$$CF = SP^3NP^{-3}QP^3N^{-1}P^3NP^{-6}QP^6N^{-1}P^{-6}S^{-1}.$$

4. Theorem on the Product of Transpositions

The next step is more important. From the known products AD, BE, CF we wish to obtain separately the unknown permutations A through F. As we have explained, these permutations consist solely of transpositions, and the expressions AD, BE, CF are their products. We may apply to them the following theorem:

If two permutations of the same degree consist solely of disjunctive transpositions, then their product will include disjunctive cycles of the same lengths in even numbers.

Proof: As an example, we designate the permutations to be multiplied by each other by the letters X and Y, and their degree by 2n. If, in permutation X, there happens to occur a transposition identical with a transposition occurring in permutation Y, for example (ab), then, in the product XY, there will occur a pair of uniliteral cycles (a) (b). With reference to transpositions identical in both permutations the theorem is, therefore, true. After rejecting these identical transpositions, we may without prejudice to generality assume that

in permutation X there will occur the transposition	in permutation Y there will occur the transposition
(a_1a_2)	(a_2a_3)
(a_3a_4)	(a_4a_5)
....	....
$(a_{2k-3}a_{2k-2})$	$(a_{2k-2}a_{2k-1})$
$(a_{2k-1}a_{2k})$	$(a_{2k}a_1)$

because the initial letter a_1 must finally occur in permutation Y. When we proceed to execute the multiplication XY, obviously we shall always obtain two cycles of the same length $k \leq n$:

$$(a_1a_3 \cdots a_{2k-3}a_{2k-1}) \quad (a_{2k}a_{2k-2} \cdots a_4a_2).$$

If, in this manner, we have not exhausted all the letters in the permutation, we continue our procedure until we have done so. At the same time let us note,

(1) the letters that enter into one and the same transposition always enter into two different cycles, of the same length, of permutation XY;

(2) if two letters that occur in two different cycles, of the same length, of permutation XY, belong to the same transposition, then the letters adjacent to them (one to the right, the other to the left) also belong to a single transposition.

Especially important for us is the converse theorem:

If a permutation of even-numbered degree includes disjunctive cycles of the same lengths in even numbers, then this permutation may be regarded as a product of two permutations, each consisting solely of disjunctive transpositions.

It is unnecessary to supply a proof for this converse theorem or to give a formula for the number of possible solutions for X and Y. It will suffice to mention that this theorem, when applied to the products AD, BE, CF, supplies for each of the expressions A, B, C, depending on the configurations of the products, between about a score and several dozen possible solutions, whereas permutations D, E, F are, in each case, determined uniquely by them.

Thus, for the whole characteristic set of three equations, we obtain anywhere from several thousand to several dozen thousand possible solutions, and extracting the one true solution would be very difficult. Therefore, the theorem on the product of transpositions does not bring us to our goal, but does bring us much closer to it. For, let us suppose that we know that in their messages, encipherers prefer, as keys, three identical letters, for example "jjj." Having before us the characteristic set and the letters "xqr gve" as the enciphered message key, and, assuming that in plain text these letters designate "jjj," we may conclude that the opening of a message "nfa qqb" must designate the letters "ppp," and that the opening "eug imf" must designate the letters "zzz," and so on. Thus, a knowledge of encipherers' habits, combined with the theorem on the product of transpositions, enables us to find the one correct solution, so that, finally, in the set of equations

$$A = SPNP^{-1}QPN^{-1}P^{-1}S^{-1}$$
$$B = SP^2NP^{-2}QP^2N^{-1}P^{-2}S^{-1}$$
$$\dots\dots\dots\dots\dots\dots\dots\dots\dots$$
$$F = SP^6NP^{-6}QP^6N^{-1}P^{-6}S^{-1}$$

we may regard the left sides as known. Of course, before he has broken the cipher the cryptologist generally does not know the encipherers' habits, but he tries to compensate for this with protracted trials, imagination, and sometimes the proverbial ounce of luck.

5. The Connections in Rotor N

Whether the foregoing set of six permutational equations with three unknowns S, N, Q is soluble without further supplementary data is not known to this day. However, it is known that this set would be soluble if the cryptologist had cipher material for two different days, with different plug connections, but with the same or nearly the same setting of rotors. At first glance, such a demand seems utterly fantastic, inasmuch as the number of possible settings of the rotors is 6 (26) (26) (26) = 105,456. Nevertheless, the laws of averages tell us that even within the span of several hundred, say five hundred, days, one may expect a couple of days with the same setting of rotors. And such a pair may be recognized by the fact that both have the same characteristic (but not the other way around: the presence of the same characteristic gives no assurance that both days have the same setting of rotors). But even having such a pair of days, the way to the goal would still be long and tedious, requiring the checking of many instances. In any case, a method of solving the set of equations existed, at least in theory. In reality, the necessary supplementary data were obtained by a different, far shorter way.

In December 1932 the French Cipher Bureau supplied the Polish Cipher Bureau with intelligence material containing German tables of Enigma keys, including the S commutator connections. Thus, it now became possible to transfer the S permutation, as a known, to the left side of our set:

$$S^{-1}AS = PNP^{-1}QPN^{-1}P^{-1}$$
$$S^{-1}BS = P^2NP^{-2}QP^2N^{-1}P^{-2}$$
$$\dots\dots\dots\dots\dots\dots\dots\dots\dots$$
$$S^{-1}ES = P^5NP^{-5}QP^5N^{-1}P^{-5}$$
$$S^{-1}FS = P^6NP^{-6}QP^6N^{-1}P^{-6}$$

thereby obtaining a set of six equations with only two unknowns, N and Q. This set is now soluble, but for various reasons, mainly in order to make certain whether within the six permutations A through F there does not occur a movement of rotor M, it is advisable to carry out certain transformations. Before we carry them out, we shall explain a certain question in permutation theory.

If we have three permutations G, H, T, such that $G = T^{-1}HT$, then we say that permutation G has been transformed from permutation H by the action of permutation T. As permutation theory demonstrates, it is not necessary to multiply permutation H on the left by T^{-1} and on the right by T in order to obtain permutation G. It is sufficient to execute, in the elements of permutation H, the changes indicated in permutation T. Hence, it follows that the two permutations G and H are similar. It further follows that if we consider T to be unknown, then the equation $G = T^{-1}HT$ is soluble when, and only when, the two permutations G, H are similar, and that we will obtain as many solutions for T as there are ways of writing permutation G beneath permutation H without affecting the value of permutation G. But, in the case when G (or H) consists entirely of transpositions, the number of solutions is very large, for example, with thirteen transpositions it amounts to 2^{13} (13!) = 51,011,754,393,600, and therefore is without practical importance. Yet, that is precisely the case that we have before us, since each of the permutations A through F consists of thirteen permutations. Hence, we carry out certain transformations in order, among other things, to free ourselves from these transpositions.

First, we transform both sides of the first equation by P, of the second equation by P^2, and so on, and, for short, we designate the left sides by the letters U through Z:

$$U = P^{-1}S^{-1}ASP = NP^{-1}QPN^{-1}$$
$$V = P^{-2}S^{-1}BSP^2 = NP^{-2}QP^2N^{-1}$$
$$\dots\dots\dots\dots\dots\dots\dots\dots\dots$$
$$Y = P^{-5}S^{-1}ESP^5 = NP^{-5}QP^5N^{-1}$$
$$Z = P^{-6}S^{-1}FSP^6 = NP^{-6}QP^6N^{-1}.$$

Next, we form products of each two successive expressions:

$$UV = NP^{-1} (QP^{-1}QP) PN^{-1}$$
$$VW = NP^{-2} (QP^{-1}QP) P^2N^{-1}$$
$$WX = NP^{-3} (QP^{-1}QP) P^3N^{-1}$$
$$XY = NP^{-4} (QP^{-1}QP) P^4N^{-1}$$
$$YZ = NP^{-5} (QP^{-1}QP) P^5N^{-1},$$

and, by eliminating the common expression $QP^{-1}QP$, we obtain a set of four equations with only one unknown NPN^{-1}:

$$VW = NP^{-1}N^{-1} (UV) NPN^{-1}$$
$$WX = NP^{-1}N^{-1} (VW) NPN^{-1}$$
$$XY = NP^{-1}N^{-1} (WX) NPN^{-1}$$
$$YZ = NP^{-1}N^{-1} (XY) NPN^{-1}.$$

Proceeding in this fashion, we shall obtain from the first equation several dozen possible expressions for NPN^{-1}, depending on the configuration of permutation UV (or of permutations VW, WX, XY, YZ, as all of them must have the same configuration, unless we have made a computing error or there has been a movement of rotor M). But we will obtain the same number of solutions for NPN^{-1} from the second equation, and one of these solutions must be identical with one solution for the first equation. The final two equations are now superfluous.

To the solution obtained for NPN^{-1} we apply the indicated method once again by comparing this expression with permutation P. We will obtain twenty-six possible solutions for N^{-1} that do not differ essentially, and, after selecting one of them, we will readily obtain N itself, the internal connections of the right-hand rotor.

6. *Example*

It seems appropriate to show how the foregoing theoretical deliberations were applied in practice to obtain the internal connections of rotor N. Let the characteristic already given in Part One, section two, serve as point of departure:

$$AD = (dvpfkxgzyo) (eijmunqlht) (bc) (rw) (a) (s)$$
$$BE = (blfqveoum) (hjpswizrn) (axt) (cgy) (d) (k)$$
$$CF = (abviktjgfcqny) (duzrehlxwpsmo).$$

We assume that thanks to the theorem on the product of transpositions, combined with a knowledge of encipherers' habits, we know separately the permutations A through F:

$$A = (as)(br)(cw)(di)(ev)(fh)(gn)(jo)(kl)(my)(pt)(qx)(uz)$$
$$B = (ay)(bj)(ct)(dk)(ei)(fn)(gx)(hl)(mp)(ow)(qr)(su)(vz)$$
$$C = (ax)(bl)(cm)(dg)(ei)(fo)(hv)(ju)(kr)(np)(qs)(tz)(wy)$$
$$D = (as)(bw)(cr)(dj)(ep)(ft)(gq)(hk)(iv)(lx)(mo)(nz)(uy)$$
$$E = (ac)(bp)(dk)(ez)(fh)(gt)(io)(jl)(ms)(nq)(rv)(uw)(xy)$$
$$F = (aw)(bx)(co)(df)(ek)(gu)(hi)(jz)(lv)(mq)(ns)(py)(rt).$$

Also known, thanks to materials obtained by intelligence, are the plug connections S for the given day:

$$S = (ap) \ (bl) \ (cz) \ (fh) \ (jk) \ (qu).$$

We, of course, also know permutation P and its powers:

$$P = (a \, b \, c \, d \, e \, f \, g \, h \, i \, j \, k \, l \, m \, n \, o \, p \, q \, r \, s \, t \, u \, v \, w \, x \, y \, z)$$
$$P^2 = (a \, c \, e \, g \, i \, k \, m \, o \, q \, s \, u \, w \, y)(b \, d \, f \, h \, j \, l \, n \, p \, r \, t \, v \, x \, z)$$
$$P^3 = (a \, d \, g \, j \, m \, p \, s \, v \, y \, b \, e \, h \, k \, n \, q \, t \, w \, z \, c \, f \, i \, l \, o \, r \, u \, x)$$
$$P^4 = (a \, e \, i \, m \, q \, u \, y \, c \, g \, k \, o \, s \, w)(b \, f \, j \, n \, r \, v \, z \, d \, h \, l \, p \, t \, x).$$

Thus, we may carry out the operations indicated in Part One, section five, to form the expressions U, V, W, X (expressions Y and Z will not be needed):

$$U = (ax)(bu)(ck)(dr)(ej)(fw)(gi)(lp)(ms)(nz)(oh)(qt)(vy)$$
$$V = (ar)(bv)(co)(dh)(fl)(gk)(iz)(jp)(mn)(qy)(su)(tw)(xe)$$
$$W = (as)(bz)(cp)(dq)(eo)(fw)(gj)(hl)(iy)(kr)(mu)(nt)(vx)$$
$$X = (ap)(bf)(cu)(dv)(ei)(gr)(ho)(jn)(ky)(lx)(mz)(qs)(tw),$$

and, next, their products:

$$UV = (a \, e \, p \, f \, t \, y \, b \, s \, n \, i \, k \, o \, d) \quad (r \, h \, c \, g \, z \, m \, u \, v \, q \, w \, l \, j \, x)$$
$$VW = (a \, k \, j \, c \, e \, v \, z \, y \, d \, l \, w \, n \, u) \quad (s \, m \, t \, f \, h \, q \, i \, b \, x \, o \, p \, g \, r)$$
$$WX = (a \, q \, v \, l \, o \, i \, k \, g \, n \, w \, b \, m \, c) \quad (p \, u \, z \, f \, t \, j \, r \, y \, e \, h \, x \, d \, s).$$

We see that the products have the same configuration of cycles, which is as it should be. Now we should (consistently with what we wrote in Part One, section five) write product VW beneath product UV in every possible way and, likewise, product WX beneath product VW. Of all these possible ways, one will give the same result in both cases. That will be the expression NPN^{-1}

that we need. Writing VW beneath UV, and WX beneath VW, in every possible way is rather tedious. However, there are various tricks and technical means that make this subscription unnecessary, but whose description and, especially, justification would take us too far afield. It will suffice to say that products UV, VW, and WX should be subscribed in the following way:

$$UV = (a\ e\ p\ f\ t\ y\ b\ s\ n\ i\ k\ o\ d) \qquad (r\ h\ c\ g\ z\ m\ u\ v\ q\ w\ l\ j\ x)$$
$$VW = (y\ d\ l\ w\ n\ u\ a\ k\ j\ c\ e\ v\ z) \qquad (i\ b\ x\ o\ p\ g\ r\ s\ m\ t\ f\ h\ q)$$

$$VW = (y\ d\ l\ w\ n\ u\ a\ k\ j\ c\ e\ v\ z) \qquad (i\ b\ x\ o\ p\ g\ r\ s\ m\ t\ f\ h\ q)$$
$$WX = (u\ z\ f\ t\ j\ r\ y\ e\ h\ x\ d\ s\ p) \qquad (c\ a\ q\ v\ l\ o\ i\ k\ g\ n\ w\ b\ m).$$

For, in both cases, we obtain for NPN^{-1} the same expression:

$$NPN^{-1} = (a\ y\ u\ r\ i\ c\ x\ q\ m\ g\ o\ v\ s\ k\ e\ d\ z\ p\ l\ f\ w\ t\ n\ j\ h\ b).$$

The rest is simple. Subscribing beneath permutation NPN^{-1} permutation P in all possible ways, of which there are twenty-six, we will obtain twenty-six variants for permutation N. For example, one variant is:

$$N = \begin{pmatrix} a\ y\ u\ r\ i\ c\ x\ q\ m\ g\ o\ v\ s\ k\ e\ d\ z\ p\ l\ f\ w\ t\ n\ j\ h\ b \\ a\ b\ c\ d\ e\ f\ g\ h\ i\ j\ k\ l\ m\ n\ o\ p\ q\ r\ s\ t\ u\ v\ w\ x\ y\ z \end{pmatrix},$$

after the upper row has been placed in alphabetical order, we obtain:

$$N = \begin{pmatrix} a\ b\ c\ d\ e\ f\ g\ h\ i\ j\ k\ l\ m\ n\ o\ p\ q\ r\ s\ t\ u\ v\ w\ x\ z \\ a\ z\ f\ p\ o\ t\ j\ y\ e\ x\ n\ s\ i\ w\ k\ r\ h\ d\ m\ v\ c\ l\ u\ g\ b\ q \end{pmatrix}$$

All the other solutions do not differ, essentially, from the above. The only consequence of adopting one or another solution is that the right-hand face of rotor N is turned by a greater or smaller angle with respect to the left-hand face. Which version of permutation N we accept as the true one will depend on such elements as the moments of rotation of the various rotors. But those details may only be established following the basic reconstruction of the connections in all the rotors.

7. Concluding Remarks to Part One

The description of the machine given at the beginning was purposely simplified in order to show, as clearly as possible, the process of reconstructing the connections in rotor N. In reality, the machine and its operation were considerably more complicated. For example, in addition to the three rotors and the reversing drum, Enigma also had an entry ring (Eintrittswalze) which made the breaking of the cipher much more difficult. Moreover, the rings on the rotors, with the letters of the alphabet engraved on them, may be moved with respect to the remaining part of the rotors, and, consequently, a knowledge of the basic position said nothing about the actual position of the middle part of the rotors. Not only rotor N rotated, but so, at less frequent intervals, did rotors L and M, a fact that also caused various complications. Finally, the order of the rotors could be changed, and, as a result, the number of possible combinations rose, given three rotors, sixfold, and, given five rotors, sixtyfold.

The last of the above-mentioned complications carried an implication not foreseen by Enigma's designers. It caused each of the three rotors to be located every so often on the right-hand side of the rotor set. As a result, the method described above for reconstructing rotor N could be applied by turns to each rotor, and thus the complete inner structure of the Enigma machine could be reconstructed.

Part Two: Keys

1. *The Cyclometer*

Reconstruction of the machine was a necessary but in sufficient condition for mastery of the Enigma cipher and for continuous decryptment over a period of many years. Methods also had to be devised for rapid reconstruction of the daily keys. In other words, the problem was the opposite of that presented in Part One. Whereas, in Part One, the task was to reconstruct the machine's works, given a knowledge of the keys for a certain period of time, now we wish to show how—having the machine—one can reconstruct the keys. Here, once again, permutation theory came to our help.

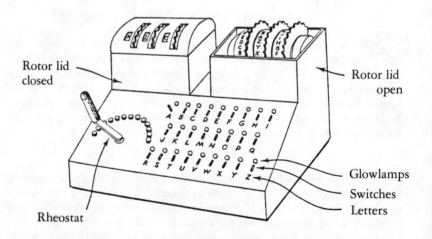

FIGURE E-4. Cyclometer

As the formulas for AD, BE, CF show, permutation S, as a transforming permutation, influences solely the letters within cycles comprising permutations AD, BE, CF, but does not influence the actual configuration of these cycles. Furthermore, permutations AD, BE, and CF have a characteristic form (see Part One, section two), and a set of three such permutations with the same configuration of cycles recurs infrequently.

Three rotors can be placed on an axis in six different ways, and the rotors themselves can assume (26) (26) (26) = 17,576 different positions. Therefore, if it were possible to design a device that gave the length and number of cycles in the characteristic for each position of the rotors, and if next the lengths and numbers of cycles were cataloged, then it would suffice to compare the products AD, BE, CF for a given day with products with the same configuration in the catalog to at once obtain the order of rotors and permutation S, while the remaining components of the daily key would be obtained by other methods.

It proved possible to design such a device, called a cyclometer. Figure E-4 will give a general idea of its appearance. The main part of the cyclometer comprised two sets of rotors suitably connected by wires through which electric current could run. Rotor N in the second set was three letters out of phase with respect to rotor N in the first set, whereas rotors L and M in the second set were always set the same way as rotors L and M in the first set. The operation of the cyclometer is depicted in figures E-5 and E-6. For greater

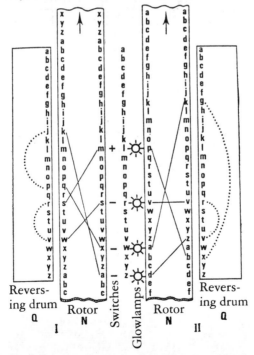

FIGURE E-5. Diagram of cyclometer.

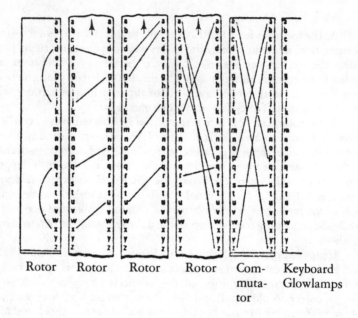

Rotor   Rotor   Rotor   Rotor   Com-   Keyboard
                                     muta-   Glowlamps
                                     tor

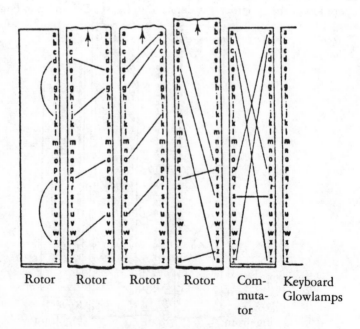

Rotor   Rotor   Rotor   Rotor   Com-   Keyboard
                                     muta-   Glowlamps
                                     tor

FIGURE E-6. Path of electric current through Enigma upon revolution of rotor N.

clarity, the order of the rotors in set II has been reversed in the diagram, but that does not alter the essentials of the matter. The reversing drums have been marked with the letter Q. They replace (in the diagram only) rotors R, L, and M. Between the two sets of rotors is a system of glowlamps with switches. If a source of current (symbolized in the drawing by the sign +) is turned on at any of the lamps, for example "l," then current will flow by turns through set I and set II of the cyclometer until, after a certain number of passes, it returns to lamp "l." At the same time, the lamps that lie in the current's path will light. Their number, always even, equals double the number of letters in one of the cycles of permutation AD. After a different switch has been thrown, that is, after the source of current has been turned on to a lamp that has not yet lit, further lamps will light, from whose number may be deduced the length of succeeding permutation cycles. In this fashion, with the help of the cyclometer, turning the rotors one by one and counting the lamps that light, one can determine the length and number of cycles in the characteristics for all 17,576 positions of the rotors for a given sequence of rotors.[2] And since there were six such possible sequences, the catalog of characteristics encompassed a total of (6) (17,576) = 105,456 entries.

2. Perforated Sheets

The catalog of characteristics based on the cyclometer fulfilled its task until 15 September 1938. Beginning on that date, in all German formations and units that used Enigma except for the S.D., completely new rules for enciphering message keys were put into effect. Henceforth, the Enigma operator himself selected the basic position, a new one each time, for enciphering the individual message key (Spruchschlüssel) and placed this basic position unenciphered (in clear text) at the head of the message. The individual message key, however, as before, was enciphered twice. Thus, the first letter of the key continued to designate the same thing as the fourth letter, the second the same thing as the fifth, and so on, although the basic position was now known to the cryptologist but was different for each message. Therefore, now there were no products AD, BE, CF characteristic for each day, whose configuration could be found in the catalog. Nevertheless, there continued to be a relation between the first and fourth, second and fifth, third and sixth letters of the key, and that relation had to be exploited.

It was sometimes the case that the individual message key selected by the encipherer assumed, upon encipherment, a form such as "pst pwa." This meant that the first letter was identical with the fourth (or the second with the fifth, or the third with the sixth), that is, in the language of permutations, it meant that in product AD, or perhaps BE or CF (if that was the case), there were uniliteral cycles, also called constant points, of the permutation. Since the length of the cycles in products AD, BE, CF was invariable with respect to the transformations produced by permutation S, the occurrence or nonoccurrence of constant points in the products was invariable with respect to those transformations.

Therefore, what was needed instead of a catalog of the cycle lengths of the products was to create a catalog of constant points for all the 17,576 possible products (for each arrangement of rotor sequence) and to compare them with the constant points appearing in the individual message keys during the given day. The difficulty lay in carrying out the comparison. To be sure, the basic positions for each key were known, because the encipherer now gave them in clear at the head of each message. But since the rings on the circumferences of the rotors were adjustable and their settings unknown for a given day, the only thing known was the relative distance of the constant points appearing in the keys for the given day.

Constant points occurred in the catalog in about 40 percent of all permutation products and, if transferred to a long tape, would have formed a distinct pattern. The constant points appearing in the keys for a given day, if transferred to another tape in accordance with their basic positions, would also form a pattern, and the task would be to find the place where all the constant points on the second tape coincided with the constant points on the first tape. But that task, at least with the existing technology, involved great difficulties. Besides that, the first tape would have had to be made double in length, so that the second tape could be moved over it. A different way was found, however (by Henryk Zygalski).

Fairly thick paper sheets, lettered "a" through "z," were prepared for all twenty-six possible positions of rotor L, and a square was drawn on each sheet, divided into 51 by 51 smaller squares. The sides, top, and bottom of each large square (it could as well be a rectangle) were lettered "a" through "z" and then again "a" through "y." This was, as it were, a system of coordinates in which the abscisses and ordinates marked successive possible positions of rotors M and N, and each little square marked permutations, with or without constant points, corresponding to those positions. Cases with constant points were perforated. Such a sheet (reduced in size) looked more or less as in figure E-7.

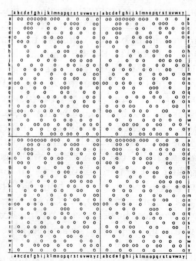

FIGURE E-7. Perforated sheet.

We see that each constant point had to be perforated as many as four times. This was a very time consuming job. When the sheets were superposed and moved in the proper sequence and the proper manner with respect to each other, in accordance with a strictly defined program, the number of visible apertures gradually decreased. And, if a sufficient quantity of data was available, there finally remained a single aperture, probably corresponding to the right case, that is, to the solution. From the position of the aperture one could calculate the order of the rotors, the setting of their rings, and, by comparing the letters of the cipher keys with the letters in the machine, likewise permutation S; in other words, the entire cipher key.

3. Concluding Remarks to Part Two

In addition to these two methods of reconstructing keys, still other methods and devices were used, as needed, in various circumstances and periods, often to supplement the cyclometer or the perforated sheets; some simple, for example, a method called the grill method (metoda rusztu), others mechanized and expensive, such as the cryptological bomb (figure E-8).

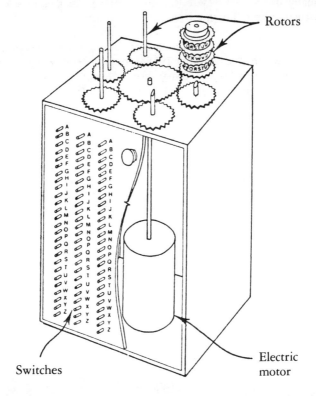

FIGURE E-8. Cryptological bomb. (For clarity, only one set of rotors is shown in the upper part of the bomb.)

These methods have not been described here, since they were based not on permutation theory but on the fact that the commutator connections did not change all, but only part, of the letters of the alphabet. It will suffice to say that the grill method, manual and tedious, was used primarily in the initial period, before the advent of the cyclometer. Later it was used rather sporadically. The bomb method, invented in the fall of 1938, consisted largely in the automation and acceleration of the process of reconstructing the daily keys. Each cryptological bomb (six were built in Warsaw for the Cipher Bureau before September 1939) essentially constituted an electrically powered aggregate of six Enigmas. It took the place of about one hundred workers and shortened the time for obtaining a key to about two hours.

A variety of methods and stratagems were also devised, of limited scope, to be sure, but which sometimes made possible great savings in time and effort. For example, there was the clock method (invented by Jerzy Różycki), which sometimes made it possible to determine which rotor was in the N rotor's place, that is, at the right-hand side, on a given day.

The German cipher service (Chiffrierdienst, or Chi-Dienst for short) continually introduced new difficulties designed to frustrate attempts at reconstructing keys. These moves had to be countered.

Thus, on 1 November 1937, the reversing drum was exchanged. The number of connections in the commutator was gradually increased from six to thirteen pairs. On 15 December 1938, the number of rotors was increased from three to five. From year to year the number of German radio communications nets also grew and, although each used the same Enigma devices, they used different keys.

In September 1939, nearly all the Cipher Bureau's equipment and most of its records were destroyed prior to and during evacuation. But at a meeting of Polish, French, and British cipher bureau representatives held in Warsaw on 25 July 1939, the Polish side made available all its methods and devices for Enigma decryptment to the future war allies, turning over to each, as well, a copy of the German cipher machine that had been reconstructed in Poland on the basis of the theoretical work that has been described here.

NOTES

1. In some Enigma variants used by the German Navy, four rotors (see fig. E-1).

2. The cyclometer was equipped with a rheostat since, with the continually changing number of light points, the lamps either would have failed to light or would have burned out.

Appendix F

Polish and British Methods of Solving Enigma
by Christopher Kasparek and Richard Woytak

It is only with the publication of mathematician Gordon Welchman's *The Hut Six Story* that we have begun to learn exactly what it was that Bletchley Park did during the war. Welchman's book is the first major publication to address extensively the *cryptological,* as distinguished from the purely *intelligence,* aspects of British work with Enigma.

Welchman is at his most valuable when he writes from personal experience. In general, when he had no direct experience, he candidly says so (there are many such cases in the book) and refuses to speculate. A glaring exception relates to the Polish origins of the Ultra secret. He writes (p. 13):

> there are different stories about what led up to the [July 1939] meeting [of British, French, and Polish intelligence representatives] in the Pyry forest [at which the Poles divulged their mastery of Enigma decryptment and promised to give Britain and France Polish-made replicas of the German military Enigma, together with all their methods for breaking Enigma ciphers]. On the whole I like the story, told in [William Stevenson's] *A Man Called Intrepid,* that in early 1939, when the new Enigmas were being delivered to frontier units, a German military truck containing one of them was ambushed. Polish agents removed the Enigma and put another machine in its place. They then made it appear that there had been an accident and that the truck had caught fire. Thus the Germans who examined the wreckage were led to believe that some charred bits of coils, springs, and rotors were the remains of their Enigma.... I am inclined to believe that something of this sort must indeed have occurred.

It is disconcerting to find such a cock-and-bull story repeated with approval in Welchman's otherwise sober and valuable book when so much documentation regarding Polish mastery of Enigma has been published in English.

Welchman goes on, however, to point out (pp. 15-16) that the perforated Zygalski sheets must have been the *forerunner* [emphasis throughout is that of Kasparek and Woytak] of the system developed in the Bletchley Cottage in the fall and winter of 1939/40. [The British, in fact, simply copied the Polish sheets.] The testing machine used by Dilly Knox's team must have been based on the [Polish] "Cyclometre." [—According to Marian Rejewski, "The Mathematical Solution of the Enigma Cipher," "the cyclometer, or rather the catalog of characteristics based on it, (had) served its purpose until September 15, 1938," when, except for the S.D. net, the Germans had introduced cryptographic changes that forced the Poles to invent the cryptologic bomb and the Zygalski sheets.] Rejewski's six-Enigma "Bomba" [bomba, or bomb] must have been the origin of the machine on which Turing was working in the fall of 1939. It must have used the idea of double-ended Enigma scramblers [that is, sets of cipher drums] that I describe in the Appendix.

Welchman presents Marian Rejewski with a backhanded compliment when he says (p. 16):

> Even Jean Stengers' excellent article ["La Guerre des Messages Codés (1930-1945)], does not explain how Rejewski came to know the internal wiring of [the] two new [cipher] wheels [that had been introduced by the Germans on 15 December 1938]. That he did [know the wiring] is evident from what followed. But as an achievement of pure cryptanalysis it is hard to believe; it seems to me that the Poles must have obtained the new five-wheel Enigma by capture or some other nefarious means. [The Poles, as Rejewski describes farther on, recovered the wirings in rotors IV and V by cryptological, not by nefarious, means.]

If Welchman is disoriented as to some aspects of the Polish contribution to Enigma decryptment, this is partly due to the secrecy, dissimulation, and compartmentalization that existed at Bletchley. Thus he writes (p. 17): "To my surprise, I now learn [from Stengers's article: Gustave Bertrand had already written about this in his *Enigma*] that an organization [the Polish-French Bruno] at Gretz [-Armainvillers, outside Paris] in France was collaborating with Bletchley for a time."

To be sure, he writes (p. 54):

> I knew very little about the "Green" traffic that appeared sporadically in the Chatham intercepts until I studied French intercepts and reports, which told me that this traffic came from the administrative network of the German army. [The "color" designations for the Enigma keys, for example, "Green," came from Welchman's underlining, in differently colored pencils on his charts, according to their keys, the daily discriminants in sets of four that were used with the same key.] It was not at all easy to intercept at Chatham, as most of it was on frequencies in the medium frequency range and did not carry far. Consequently the French intercept stations did a lot better than Chatham, and their intercepts gave me a good deal of Green traffic over quite a long period. When I analyzed the callsigns of earlier Green traffic I found that they were repeating from month to month, so I was soon in a position to give Chatham a forecast of callsigns that might be expected on the Green network each day.

To his credit, Welchman, unlike other Britons (for example, as in the appendix concerning Enigma, in volume 1 of *British Intelligence in the*

Second World War, edited by F.H. Hinsley), does not downplay the crucial importance of the methods and hardware that had been given to the British by the Poles (p. 14):

> The vital point is that the Poles managed to give us the details of the machine and the benefit of their expertise in time for us to exploit them early in the war. We would ultimately capture many Enigmas, but . . . everything was to depend on what we achieved in the first three months and later, in the very first year of the war. In fact, the Hut 6 balloon might never have gotten off the ground at all if I had taken six months instead of three to get things moving.

It was apparently the Poles, too, who were the source of the Enigma decrypts that Welchman received early in his work from Josh Cooper, in charge of air force operations at Bletchley Park. (Welchman does not say when or by whom they had been intercepted or decrypted.)

> It did not amount to much: decodes [that is, decrypts] of at most two or three days of intercepted traffic. At the time I did not know how the collection had been obtained. . . . However, the fact that Josh Cooper was able to hand them to me at that time was to have far-reaching consequences, for I believe it was the study of these decodes that gave me my first glimpse of what my job was all about.
>
> . . . As I studied that first collection of decodes. . . I began to see, somewhat dimly, that [w]e were dealing with an entire communications system that would serve the needs of the German ground and air forces. The callsigns came alive as representing elements of those forces. . . . The use of different keys for different purposes, which was known to be the reason for the discriminants, suggested different command structures for the various aspects of military operations.
>
> Even more important was the impression I got from the messages themselves. Although my knowledge of German was very limited, I could see that the people involved were talking to each other in a highly disciplined manner. They were very polite to each other. . . the originator of a message would be careful to give the full title of the officer or organization to which the message was to be sent. Furthermore, in the signature that came at the end of the message, the originator would be careful to give his own title in full. These early impressions proved to be of immense importance later. . . [pp. 37-38].

According to Welchman, a typical Enigma message comprised an unenciphered preamble, followed by an enciphered text divided into five-letter groups. The preamble in those days contained:

- The callsigns of the radio stations, first the sending station, then the destination(s).
- The time of origin of the message.
- The number of letters in the text.
- An indication as to whether the message was complete, or was a specified part of a multi-part message (for example, part two of four parts).
- The discriminant, a three-letter group that informed a receiving cipher clerk which, if any, of the keys issued to him had been used to encipher the text.

• A second three-letter group, which Welchman calls the indicator setting, that was related to the actual procedure for enciphering and deciphering the text.

Before this information in the preamble, the interceptor included two more items: the radio frequency used for transmission, and the time of interception.

Welchman states that a complete Enigma daily key comprised:

(1) The order of placement of the three cipher wheels (also known as drums or rotors) in the machine. With five wheels to choose from, there were sixty possible orders for the three wheels that were in use at any one time.

(2) The ring settings of the left-hand, middle, and right-hand wheels.

(3) Cross-pluggings on the commutator. Only ten or eleven cross-pluggings (Welchman is uncertain) were specified, leaving six or four letters unaltered (leaving four letters unaltered, curiously enough, would increase the number of possible cross-pluggings maximally, by a factor of twenty-six, thus giving a total of more than 2×10^{14}, or 200 trillion, cross-plugging possibilities).

In addition to the daily key, encipherment of a given message also required use of an individual message key. The cipher clerk would choose at random a wheel setting (Welchman calls it the indicator setting). Next he would set the cipher wheels to those respective three letters and then would encipher an individual message key (or text setting)—likewise comprising three letters which, similarly, he selected himself—twice, noting the resulting sequence of six letters that appeared on the lampboard (Welchman calls this six-letter sequence the indicator). He then would turn the cipher wheels to his chosen message key (text setting) and encipher the plain text, letter by letter. When the cipher text was transmitted, the indicator setting was sent at the end of the unenciphered preamble, and the six letters of the indicator appeared at the beginning of the message text, constituting the first five-letter group and the first letter of the second group.

"Fortunately," observes Welchman (p. 46), "when I arrived at the [Bletchley] Cottage on September 4, 1939, we already knew [presumably from the Poles] the [ciphering] procedure that the Germans were using."

Welchman subsequently states (p. 77), "A group of Polish experts had come to Bletchley and worked with [Alfred Dillwyn] Knox and [Alan] Turing on the concept of such a machine [the cryptological bomb] for a time before going to France." Unfortunately, he fails to say who the Poles were or when they visited Bletchley (Col. Gwido Langer, chief of the Polish Cipher Bureau, visited London in December 1939—too late to have helped with this stage of the work described by Welchman, even if he had known enough Enigma theory—although Turing did discuss Enigma decryptment with its actual originators while visiting them at Bruno outside Paris). Neither does Welchman say whether he had, at that time, met the Poles or known of their presence, or even (at least in that passage) unequivocally that "such a machine" had already been constructed by the Polish Cipher Bureau back in 1938. Indeed, the Poles remain a free-floating numinous presence throughout Welchman's book, even when he himself appears oblivious to that presence.

Welchman is most plainly aware of the Polish presence as he discusses "two somewhat startling breakthroughs" (p. 59) that he made during the second and third months of the war.

Welchman's study of the Germans' system of indicator settings and of indicators (doubly enciphered message keys), together with "the fact that it was not always possible for the same pair of letters to be the encodes [encrypts] of each other in scrambler positions three places apart in the cycle of machine positions" (pp. 78-80), led him to the idea that it was possible to create a system of appropriately perforated cardboard sheets whose suitable stacking would make it possible to discover a daily key after an average of 780 stackings. "[I]n great excitement," Welchman recounts (p. 71), "I hurried from [Elmers] School [on the Bletchley Park grounds, to which Knox had exiled Welchman after about two weeks "to study 'callsigns and discriminants' "] to [Bletchley] Cottage to tell Dilly [Knox] about it." He continues,

Dilly was furious. What I was suggesting was precisely what he was already doing, and the necessary sheets were being punched under the direction of my Cambridge friend and colleague John Jeffreys. Dilly reminded me that I had been told to study discriminants and callsigns, not methods of breaking the Enigma. He sent me back to the School without telling me how the testing and sheet punching were being done. Indeed I never did know whether Jeffreys designed his sheets in the way that had occurred to me. It is entirely possible that there may have been errors in my thinking at that time... [In fact, the "Zygalski sheets" had a capacity of 51 by 51 apertures, not 26 by 26 as Welchman envisioned.] One thing I did learn, however, was that the term "female," that I have used in my discussion [which had been coined by the Poles], had become established in the Cottage. The reason, no doubt, was the analogy between a punched hole, through which light can shine, and a female socket into which a plug can be inserted to make an electrical connection. [The term "female" (in Polish, "samiczka") may well have originated from a Polish play on words: "te same" ("the same," that is, an alignment of apertures) and "samiczka" ("a little female").]

The reader may find it hard to believe that I had not been made aware of so important a development. Dilly was notorious for not telling anyone anything, though he often thought that he had done so. Moreover Bletchley Park as a whole must have been pretty chaotic in October 1939 and for many months after that. Huts were being built all over the place....

As for the strange reaction of Dilly Knox, an explanation of this outburst has recently occurred to me. It is possible that Dilly did not know about the Germans' double encipherment of their text settings [that is, message keys] until the meeting in the Pyry forest [that is, the Kabackie Woods] in July 1939 at which the Poles had revealed that they knew "everything about Enigma." It seems probable that, at the same meeting, Dilly had been told about the identical method of breaking the Enigma [by means of the Zygalski sheets] that would occur to me a few months later in the School. If this was so, Dilly would not have had a chance to think up the idea for himself. It would have been infuriating for him to find that a newcomer, and one whom he had kicked off his Cottage team, had come up with an idea he had not thought of [pp. 71-73].

Welchman notes that, although this first of his two breakthroughs had already been thought of by others, "almost certainly [by] the Poles," he has no memory of having been frustrated by the fact that his idea was not new, or even of being particularly irritated by Knox's behavior. It was extremely important, he emphasizes, that the idea had come to him, too, "and so early in the game," for otherwise he might not have known about it for months. "And we didn't have months to spare. The planning for exploitation might have started *too late*." Any frustration that Welchman might have felt "must have been submerged in [his] delight at finding that the Cottage people believed, as [he] did, that the idea would work and that [Bletchley Park was] going to break into the Enigma traffic." Confirmation of his conviction about this at so early a date enabled Welchman to plan for exploitation of the coming decryption.

Welchman felt that Knox and his Cottage team regarded the "Jeffreys apparatus" (that is, Zygalski sheets) as primarily a cryptological success. No one seemed to be thinking about the organization that would be necessary for its systematic exploitation. With this in mind, Welchman formulated an organizational plan and submitted it to Comdr. Edward Travis, then deputy director of Bletchley Park under Alastair Denniston. Welchman's plan, which was immediately approved and implemented, postulated a twenty-four-hour operation of five closely coordinated departments: a Registration Room to perform continuous traffic analysis of Enigma messages, based on traffic registers received by teleprinter (that is, teletype) from intercept stations, both the existing ones and those that would be set up; an Intercept Control Room, in continuous touch with the intercept stations, which would help them concentrate on the most valuable traffic; a Machine Room handling the cryptologic aspects, in close collaboration with the Registration Room and the Intercept Control Room; a Sheet-Stacking Room, to be called into action by the Machine Room whenever a day's traffic on a particular key merited an attempt at a break; and a Decoding Room to handle the messages on any key that might be broken. (As it later turned out, there would be no need to produce duplicates of the German Enigma machine for the Decoding Room. British Type-X cipher machines, already in production, would be adapted with little trouble.) Welchman notes (p. 77): "in winning approval of this plan at so early a date I probably made my biggest single contribution to the war effort."

It is worth citing here, for the light that they shed on the perforated-sheet technique, the following observations (pp. 88-90):

> [T]he actual breaking of a key would depend on skilled work by the experts in the Machine Room. The sheet-stacking did no more than reduce the number of possibilities that had to be investigated. In the School days I did not attack this problem seriously. I was not told how Jeffreys proposed to solve it. When Hut 6 became operational, Jeffreys was in charge of Sheet-Stacking and Machine Room activities, while I worried about Registration, Intercept Control, Decoding, and relations with the intelligence people in Hut 3 [who handled German Army and Air Force Enigma decrypts]. I can see how the breaks might have been achieved, but will not discuss the matter.

According to Welchman, once the Machine Room had found a satisfactory set of females (giving priority to the operational Red key rather than to the training Blue key), the Sheet-Stacking Room staff would set to work. From time to time, they would obtain a "drop," which would be tested by the Machine Room. Most of the drops would prove false. (The Machine-Room decision to attempt a break was based on a calculation of the number of false drops that could be expected from the data that the Machine Room had given to the Sheet-Stacking Room.) When, with luck, the sheet stacking finally produced a true drop that would enable the Machine Room to determine the daily key, "a shout of triumph would be heard," and the Decoding Room staff would be activated. The shout of triumph for the key of a day's traffic would usually be heard in the early hours of the next morning.

The perforated-sheet technique was used by both the Poles at Bruno (Gretz-Armainvillers) and the British at Station X (Bletchley) until 10 May 1940 (the day of the German invasion of France), when the Germans "dealt us a blow that could well have been fatal" (p. 96). On that day, the Germans dropped the double encipherment of the message key—and the Zygalski sheets, whose use had depended on the message key's double encipherment, suddenly became useless. The German Enigma operator now set the cipher wheels to his indicator setting as before, but enciphered his message key only once. He then put the two three-letter groups—indicator setting and message key—in the message preamble (previously, only the indicator setting had appeared in the preamble, and the doubly enciphered message key had appeared in the first six letters of the message text).

Welchman's second breakthrough, likewise achieved under the auspices of the Polish numinous presence "before the war was three months old," had to do with the cryptological bomb, as it had been irreverently christened by Jerzy Różycki. Welchman writes,

> The name "bombe" seems to have been attached [to the device] by the Poles...but it was also applied to the machines [used by the British, based largely on the Polish design]. The term "bombe" [which was adopted by the British with that spelling] is simply the French for "bomb"; the connection with our machine is not clear to me, but it may have had to do with the idea of a mechanism that would go on ticking until it reaches a combination that will cause it to produce an output—in our case not an explosive one. Our "bombes" were said to make a noise like a battery of knitting needles.

Welchman's contribution to the British bomb was the addition of a diagonal board (as it was named, apparently, by Harold "Doc" Keen: p. 301), which as Welchman says (pp. 77-78) "greatly increased its power."

Welchman had been "influenced by those precious [evidently Polish] decodes [decrypts] that Josh Cooper had given [him]" when Welchman had started working in the School. At that time, Welchman noticed that stereotyped addresses and signatures appeared in the texts of the messages. He began to wonder whether this gave a possibility of using these as cribs to break Enigma keys. The British bomb, "as it was being developed by [Alan] Turing from Polish ideas," according to Welchman (p. 80) "depended entirely on being able to construct a diagram...containing three closed loops" of letters, for example, the loop "p" to "e" to "i" to "p." Welchman's breakthrough consisted of the idea that, by interconnecting the scramblers (that is, sets of rotors) in a new way, one need not depend on obtaining three closed loops; one loop, or no loops at all, would suffice.

When this new method of interconnecting the scramblers of a bomb first came to him, Welchman could not believe it. But he drew a simple wiring diagram and convinced himself that the idea would indeed work.

> Armed with this diagram I hurried once again to the Cottage, this time to talk to Turing [rather than to Knox]. Turing was incredulous at first, as I had been, but when he had studied my diagram he agreed that the idea would work, and became as excited about it as I was....

> With Turing's support it was not difficult to convince Travis that...the improved bombe was urgently needed... Again Travis wasted no time. Although I did not realize it then, Harold "Doc" Keen of the British Tabulating Machine Company, which was associated with IBM in America, must already have started on the design of the Turing bombe. Travis asked me to work closely with Keen...

> As is often the case with revolutionary ideas, mine, after it had occurred to me, proved extremely simple. It involved interconnecting a battery of scrambler units through what came to be known as a diagonal board....

> [T]he purpose of a bombe run was to determine whether, for one of the 60 possible wheel orders, a certain pattern of letter pairings derived from a crib could occur with a set of scramblers in relative positions corresponding to the positions of the letter pairings in the crib. The automatic test, of which I have talked, involved trying to prove that no combination of stecker [commutator-plug] pairings could allow the pattern to occur. It was accomplished in one fell swoop by electric current flowing to and fro between the battery of scramblers and the diagonal board. Thus the vast number of stecker combinations (around 200 trillion) on which the German cryptographers probably pinned their faith was of no avail against the bombe. In essence our automatic test could examine all possible stecker combinations in less than a thousandth of a second [pp. 81-82].

The diagonal board, Welchman explains (p. 306), made it possible to obtain a usable diagram of scrambler interconnections from a much shorter section of a crib.

By contrast with the six six-scrambler Polish bombs, which in 1938 had taken only a month to go from conception through manufacture, it took nearly a year for the first two ten-scrambler British bombs to come into operation in late 1940 (p. 295).

Thus, of the two crucial devices that were used to decrypt Enigma at Bletchley (the perforated sheets entirely based on Polish designs, and the British bomb very largely so), the first was in use only until 10 May 1940—the German invasion of France—and the second only came into use many months later the same year. (The world's first electronic computers, which were built for Bletchley Park, according to Welchman, were not used to break Enigma but to break a German radio teletype similar to the Siemens Geheimschreiber—pp. 176-77.)

During this hiatus of perhaps half a year or more (Welchman believes the two prototype bombs arrived only after the Battle of Britain had ended) how did the British—and the Poles—continue their decrypting? Welchman writes (p. 102):

> It was extremely fortunate that both the Herivel tip and the keyboard Sillies had been discovered before the Germans changed their indicating procedure and defeated our method of breaking Enigma keys with the Jeffreys apparatus. Had we been foiled then, we would not have been breaking at the time of the last Eagle Day [15 September 1940], and we would have lost the continuity that was to prove so essential later on in our use of cribs.

Just what were the "Herivel tip" and the "Sillies"? Welchman's explanations of these techniques might suggest that, as of 10 May 1940, Bletchley Park had involuntarily shaken off the Polish numinous presence. We would suggest, however, that this may not have been the case, and that Bletchley Park may, in fact, never have emancipated itself from that presence. We believe that a Polish priority can be established to the discovery of at least one—possibly both—of these techniques through comparison of their descriptions that have been set down by the Poles and the British.

The Poles

> [In and outside Paris, where the Polish cryptologists worked from 20 October 1939 until 10 June 1940, during the German invasion of France] the work was made more efficient by some new ideas and discoveries. For example, it was found that the German encipherers, after setting their Enigmas in the starting position and closing the metal lid, were selecting as the message key (Spruchschlüssel) the letters visible in the glass windows. Such carelessness cost the Nazis dearly. These letters were usually identical with the settings on the Enigma's internal rings. As a result, a few minutes past midnight [when the Germans routinely changed their daily keys] the duty cryptologist would already know the cipher key for that day, and the French could read Wehrmacht orders and reports broadcast that day at the same time as their intended recipients. [Kozaczuk, chapter 8, above.]

The British

> [John] Herivel's attention was drawn to a quirk in machine setup practice. When an Enigma operator was changing the setup of his machine to a new [daily] key, he had to choose the correct set of three wheels out of the five available, set the alphabet ring on each wheel, insert the wheels in the machine in the correct order, and close the cover. To set an alphabet ring on a wheel, he would probably hold the wheel in one hand so that the clip position was facing him, and then rotate the ring until the correct letter was opposite the clip position. There the clip would engage. Herivel's contribution was to realize that, when the operator inserted the wheel into the machine, the letter determining the ring setting would probably still be facing him, and when he closed the cover it was quite likely that the three letters appearing in the apertures would be pretty close to the ring settings of the new key. Indeed, if the

operator was lazy he might leave the wheels in their initial position when he encoded [enciphered] the text setting [message key] for his first message of the day. If so, the letters of the indicator setting in the preamble of this message would be pretty close to the ring settings in the new [daily] key. [Welchman, pp. 98-99.]

Welchman notes (pp. 164-65) that, had the British not made as early a start as they did on the development of the necessary organizational infrastructure for regular, large-scale Enigma decryptment,

We would probably not have been able to recruit the key people who made such important contributions later on. Herivel, in particular, might not have joined us, and it is by no means certain that anyone but he would have discovered the "Herivel Tip," without which we could not have used Sillies to break Enigma keys by manual methods. [Presumably, either the end of the foregoing sentence is untrue, or the Poles in fact discovered the "Herivel tip" earlier than Kozaczuk implies, that is, (as Rejewski says about "Sillies") "at the end of 1932 [or] the beginning of 1933," when the Poles first began using "Sillies." The first case would mean that the "Herivel tip" was not indispensable to breaking Enigma during the period from 10 May 1940 until the advent of the British bombs late that year; and the second case, that the "tip" had been discovered by the Poles seven years earlier.]

The Poles

[I]n the first period, only in the first period, that is, at the end of 1932 and the beginning of 1933—how things were before that, I don't know— ...the [German] cipher operators made certain mistakes.... As you know, for every message they selected an individual key...consisting of [three] letters. Well, they would make the mistake [of] favoring [message] keys such as "aaa," or "bbb," or "ccc," and so on. This made things easier [for us]. But after a few months they were forbidden [to do this]. Hm! it's funny that after a few months [they stopped].... But then they started choosing other [cipher] keys.... Do you have a typewriter? Do you type?... On a [German] typewriter...the keys go in a certain order: [top row:] QWERTZUIO [middle row:] ASD and so on. After a while, I knew by heart how they go. [T]hey would pick three letters ...three [typing] keys that stand next to each other. Or...diagonally [from each other] or like this...excuse me...But by then we already had them [the Germans] in our hands. So...it *availed them nothing* [*laughing*]...that they forbade them...to use [combinations like] "aaa," or successive letters "abc"—pft!—now they were using letters [picked] from the keyboard! Six of one to half a dozen of the other! That helped us too. To be sure, they had forbidden [certain combinations], but they hadn't forbidden using these letters... [And] when [eventually] they were forbidden [to use] three letters according to [the lay of] the keyboard,...we found another characteristic again.... There's no avoiding it... [W]henever there is arbitrariness, there is also a certain regularity. There's no avoiding it. For example, ...they didn't use letters with the same frequency...some letters were used oftener, the Germans didn't like certain letters, I don't know which they were, "x" or something.... [Rejewski, Appendix B, above.]

The British

Now for the "Sillies." [Welchman's footnote: "I have no idea how the term arose." Presumably it would have arisen from the fact that these were, as the Poles might have told the British, "silly" cryptographic errors.] Suppose the traffic register showed a three-part message whose indicator settings and indicators [that is, message keys] were [Welchman here gives an example set of three indicator settings and message keys]. Having observed the habits of Enigma operators in the traffic that we had decoded [decrypted], it was not hard to guess what the operator had done, from the arrangement of the Enigma keyboard.... He had obviously chosen as his indicator settings [for the three parts of the message, respectively] the alternate keyboard diagonals [from upper left to lower right] QAY, EDC, and TGB. We would conclude that his text settings [that is, message keys] would be the alternating diagonals [one place to the right on the keyboard]: WSX, RFV, and ZHN. If the text setting of the first part of the message was WSX, we knew that, with wheels set to QAY, MPR [Welchman's sample enciphered message key for part one of the message] was the encode [encipherment] of WSX. Similarly at setting EDC [indicator setting for part two], LIY was the encode of RFV, and at setting TGB [indicator setting for part three], VEA was the encode of ZHN. Thus this set of three "Sillies" gave us nine letter pairings. We knew that, at the wheel setting following QAY in the scrambler cycle, M and W were paired, that at the next wheel setting P and S were paired, and so on. It was, in fact, a form of crib.

Suppose that, in addition to this three-part message, we could find on the traffic register two single-part messages with indicator settings QWE [the three far-left letters in the top row of the three rows on the Enigma keyboard] and QAP [the letters of the far-left column]. Looking at the keyboard with an eye to pattern and the known habits of individuals, we might well guess that the corresponding message settings were ASD [the three letters just below QWE, in the middle row] and OKL [the letters of the far-right column, at the opposite end of the keyboard from QAP]. This would give us six more letter pairings which, combined with the Herivel tip, would probably enable us to break the Red key [used for the hot-war operational traffic of German ground and air forces: p. 88] for the day. Unbelievable! Yet it actually happened, and it went on happening until the bombes came, many months later. [I]t seems to me that we must have been entirely dependent on Herivel tips and Sillies from the invasion of France to the end of the Battle of Britain, right up to the final crunch on "Eagle Day," September 15, 1940. [Welchman, pp. 99-101.]

Welchman adds, concerning Sillies:

There were other types of Sillies that sometimes allowed us to guess a message setting. Occasionally, for example, a lazy operator would get in the habit of using the same three letters both for the indicator setting and for the text setting. This would mean that, having encoded [enciphered] his text setting, he would only have to move the right-hand wheel back three places to encode [encipher] his message. This type of Silly was known as JABJAB from the letters used in its first appearance, discovered by [Dennis] Babbage. But in JABJAB too our help came primarily from the use of keyboard patterns. If, for example, we found a three-part message in which the indicator settings were QAY, WSX, and EDC, it would be a good bet that the text settings were the same. [p. 102.]

The Poles and the British faced parallel problems arising from German changes of Enigma components or enciphering procedures. One of these problems involved coping with change of the reflector. The Poles solved this problem when the Germans exchanged the A reflector on 2 November 1937 to a new B reflector. The British had analogous experiences:

> One evening [during the Silly days, in the second half of 1940] when I came in to head the night watch in the Machine Room I found considerable excitement. A decoded [decrypted] message on the day's Red key had indicated that a new *umkehrwalze* [reflector] was to be used in the Enigma machine.... During the evening watch, headed by Babbage, a very long message had turned up. It was in at least six parts, and it wouldn't decode [decrypt], even though it used the Red discriminants for the day. Could this long message have been enciphered by a machine equipped with [the new reflector]?
>
> Babbage had studied the indicator settings and indicators of this multi-part message, and had found that the man who had done the enciphering was intensely lazy and a superb producer of Sillies. Babbage believed that he knew the text setting for each part of the message. If all this proved to be true, we would certainly be able to discover [the new reflector's] wiring in the morning [when an electrician could be called]. The assumption was that the text settings of all the parts of this... message had been enciphered on an Enigma machine fitted with [the new reflector], but that the operator had not been instructed to change the wheel order, ring settings, and steckers from those of the key for the day, which we already knew. In other words, we knew how to set up an Enigma, and we knew that if we set up the wheels to the indicator setting and enciphered the indicator for each part of the message we should get the text setting that Babbage had guessed.
>
> ...All we needed was an electrician who could disconnect the cross-connections of the standard German *umkehrwalze* on one of our Enigmas or modified Type-X machines. Then, with the machine set to the known key, we could easily find out what cross-connection of *umkehrwalze* terminals would be needed to produce each of the letters Babbage had predicted.... Fortunately I had David Rees with me. He had worked in the Cottage with Dilly Knox, and knew a lot more about the details of our Enigma studies than I did. He dug out the internal cross-connections of the movable wheels of the German Enigma, and from then on, though time-consuming, it was easy.
>
> With the help of the Registration Room staff I constructed a paper version of the Enigma machine for the known wheel order of the day. Once this was done I could trace the paths an electric current would follow from the keyboard key to the *umkehrwalze* and from the *umkehrwalze* to the light bulb that had to illuminate Babbage's predicted letter. Thus I could determine the cross-connection of two *umkehrwalze* terminals that would produce the predicted result.
>
> I went steadily through Babbage's predictions and when I got the same cross-connection for the second time (a confirmation), I was more than mildly excited. I had nearly finished the job at eight a.m. when Hugh Alexander dashed into the Machine Room to find out what had

happened. He had been present at the midnight conference, and one of my most pleasant memories is his remark: "I knew you would find a neat way of doing it!" [Welchman, pp. 113-15.]

Another parallel between Polish and British experience occurred when, in 1942, the Germans introduced their major proliferation of army and air force Enigma keys. John Monroe, a former Hut 6 worker, suggests (pp. 129-30) that this proliferation resulted from the Germans' becoming worried that their cryptographic security might be jeopardized if they passed too much Enigma traffic in any one key. Welchman feels that internal security may have been another important consideration for the Germans. The Poles had a similar experience of apparent German cryptological anxiety nine years earlier in January 1933, shortly after they had solved the Enigma machine. "[W]e had the impression," says Rejewski, "that the Germans had gotten jittery, as if they sensed intuitively that something had happened." [Chapter 5, above.]

Welchman divides the history of internal Hut 6 activity into four periods (p. 119). The preparatory period ended with the completion of the Zygalski (Jeffreys) perforated sheets, early in 1940. The second period, that of the Zygalski sheets, ended abruptly with the change in German operating procedures on 10 May 1940. The third period, that of dependence on Herivel tips and Sillies, ended somewhat less abruptly with the arrival of the first British cryptologic bombs, "probably not earlier than September 1940," which in turn opened the fourth and final period of Hut 6 history.

When the British Zygalski apparatus had begun to work, Welchman asked Stuart Milner-Barry to make a careful study of decrypts (p. 98). Welchman wanted him to develop an intimate knowledge of the correspondents on the German radio nets, as this might enable Hut 6 to find cribs, which eventually—when bombs became available—could lead to breaks. Milner-Barry had found what Welchman himself had discovered early in his work, upon examining the evidently Polish decrypts: that the addresses and signatures were often both lengthy and stereotyped. These potential cribs, however, were of no use without a bomb, just as a bomb was of no use without cribs (p. 120).

In the autumn of 1940, as the advent of the first bombs approached, Milner-Barry collected a small staff and founded a Crib Room. The bomb, Welchman emphasizes, did not break Enigma keys. If a crib could be found by the Hut 6 watch, the bomb simply reduced to a manageable number the assumptions of wheel order and scrambler positions that required further analysis.

Not long after the last Eagle Day, 15 September 1940 (the Germans had mounted an earlier Adlertag on August 13: p. 102), and after Hitler's abandonment of plans to invade Britain, decrypts began to show that German forces were being moved out of France, and, by the end of October, Welchman began to get indications from Hut 3 (army-air Ultra intelligence, which studied and processed the Hut 6 decrypts) that the area of operations of the German armies was going to expand substantially—into the Balkans and through Italy into Africa.

Welchman anticipated that the expanding German operations would involve the introduction of additional Enigma keys and more radio nets, and a much higher volume of Enigma traffic. He made an estimate of the numbers of Hut 6 staff, interceptors, and bombs that would be needed to cope with the anticipated traffic, and sent a handwritten memorandum to Travis. The latter was skeptical and returned the memo "with BALLS scrawled across the front page in a brown ink that [he] always used" (p. 121). However, when Welchman had improved his arguments, Travis was convinced:

> We got the additional supporting capabilities that we needed for the crucial developments of March, April, and May 1941. Although later developments were to show that my forecast. . . was grossly inadequate, I still feel that the speed with which I developed that initial approach to Travis got things moving [sooner] than would otherwise have happened, and so prepared the way for the major expansions of many Bletchley Park activities—not only those related to Hut 6—that were initiated early in 1942. This approach to Travis. . . may have occurred before the first prototype bombe actually became operational [in late 1940].

Welchman divides the bomb period itself into three successive subperiods with somewhat blurred boundaries. The first was roughly from September 1940 to the end of 1941; the second, roughly the year 1942. Both of these subperiods, especially the second one, saw substantial increases in numbers of Enigma keys and nets. The third subperiod ran from early 1943 until the end of the war (p. 123-24).

Shortly into the third subperiod, there were enough teletypes to carry virtually all the Enigma traffic intercepted in England. Bletchley was also receiving intercepts from overseas, enciphered on Type-X and sent by radio; having been enciphered twice—once by the Germans and once by the British—they contained fair numbers of garbles "and were not very popular in the Hut 6 decoding room," but produced much useful material (p. 124). By summer 1943, Hut 6, Hut 3, Hut 8 (naval-Enigma decryptment) and the teletypes had moved to the relative luxury of a specially constructed new brick building. (The various huts retained their original designations throughout the duration, despite numerous changes in their physical locations.)

By the end of the first bomb subperiod, Hut 6's cryptological problems had been considerably complicated by the number of new keys that they had a chance of breaking. Sillies had become rare, and the Germans had started to change the order of the wheels at midday. In the second subperiod, the big jump in number of keys caused still more trouble. But the worst cryptological problems began with the third subperiod and continued to the end, as the Germans introduced change after change in the machine itself, as well as critical changes of ciphering procedure. About two months before D-Day, they stopped using discriminants, and they had already begun to change periodically the frequencies of their radio nets. In February 1945, they began changing all radio frequencies daily and encrypting call signs by a simple method that the British could not break for lack of sufficient data. Still, about eighteen keys a day were broken with reasonable regularity.

How Hut 6 managed to do this despite the increasing obstacles being put in its way, however, Welchman is unable to describe. In May 1940 John Jeffreys, in charge of Hut 6's Machine Room and Sheet-Stacking Room, had been diagnosed as having both tuberculosis and diabetes (he died a few months later: p. 103). As a consequence, Welchman became *de facto* head of Hut 6, though Travis did not make him the official head for some time. From early 1943, however, Travis called on him increasingly for assistance in non-Hut 6 matters, so that the many problems of methodology and technology that arose thereafter were handled by other members of the Hut 6 staff. Near the end of the same year, Travis took Welchman away from Hut 6 completely, to be his assistant director for mechanization, a position that he held to the end of the war (p. 125).

The major proliferation of army and air force Enigma keys in 1942, during the second bomb subperiod, proved helpful in a strange way to Hut 6 (p. 30-31). The German producer of the monthly tables of daily keys had evidently kept records of all the key tables that had previously been prepared, and, apparently, it occurred to him that he could save himself work if he used either the discriminants, or the wheel orders, or the ring settings, or the commutator connections for a previous month. As it happened, Reg Parker of the Hut 6 Intercept Control Room had set himself the task of recording all discriminants and broken keys, and for some time had been looking at the discriminants and broken keys at the beginning of each month in the hope of finding repeats. In 1942 he began finding them. As a result, by the procedure of Parkerismus soon after the beginning of each month, Hut 6 might know, in advance, some part or parts of the daily keys for some types of Enigma traffic for the rest of the month. This was a tremendous boon. The problem of breaking daily keys would be greatly simplified. Sometimes Hut 6 would know all the components of the key from Parkerismus. Welchman believes that at one time Hut 6 knew in advance all the daily keys that Rommel would use in Africa for a whole month.

According to Welchman, it was also in 1942 that crib hunting, involving many kinds of cribs, developed into a major operation. There were still the lengthy stereotyped addresses and signatures that Welchman had noticed in the presumably Polish decrypts in 1939. These generally occurred in routine daily reports or routine orders, "which the Germans were kind enough to send at regular times of day, with the time of origin in the preamble to help us identify the message as soon as it appeared on the teleprinted traffic register," (p. 131). Such cribs were not without their difficulties. The command structure and the location of individual commanders could change. At the end of a message, where the signature appeared, some "x's" might be added on to complete a five-letter group. Enigma operators "delighted in peppering 'x's' throughout the signatures and addresses." Hence, in order to use this kind of crib, "it was necessary to be breaking a key pretty regularly, in order to follow people and habits" (pp. 131-32).

Another type of crib was based on the repetitious content of routine daily reports. For example, a certain German officer in the Qattara Depression in North Africa reported daily, with the utmost regularity, that he had nothing to report.

A third type of crib—"perhaps the most important of all"—resulted once again from the proliferation of Enigma keys. Sometimes a message had to be reenciphered in a second key for a commander who did not have the original key. Thus, if Hut 6 could break one of the two keys, it would have a crib to the other.

Hut 6 was "astonishingly successful" in its use of the various kinds of cribs. Welchman records as follows:

> But the thinness of the ice on which we were skating was a perpetual worry. German enforcement of elementary cryptographic discipline could have put an end to our cribs. If the Germans had discovered that a sufficiently long crib could enable us to break an Enigma key, they could have monitored their own traffic and admonished the people who were unwittingly helping us. [D]uring the African campaign, their cryptographic experts were asked to take a fresh look at the impregnability of the Enigma. I heard that the result of this "fresh look" appeared in our decodes [decrypts], and that it was an emphatic reassertion of impregnability.
>
> The precarious nature of our success was not obvious even to some of our close associates in Hut 3, whose knowledge of our activities didn't extend beyond the decodes they received. Hut 6 seemed to them to be breaking everything, and some of the Hut 3 people thought we were capable of doing anything they might want us to do. [A] member of the watch in Hut 3 might note that the decode of a particularly important type of report on one key didn't reach Hut 3 until late in the evening, although the report had been intercepted early in the morning. On investigation he might find that Hut 6 had been breaking another key in which he was not interested before even attempting to break his key. This seemed asinine behavior on Hut 6's part!...The truth of the matter could well be that our chance of breaking his [daily] key...depended on a retransmission on that key of a routine message that originated on the other key. If so we would have to break the other before we could break his [pp. 132-33].

Because a key that was producing uninteresting decrypts might at any time prove to be "the route into a much more exciting second key," or might itself begin yielding useful intelligence, Hut 6 for the sake of continuity often went on breaking seemingly unpromising keys. "[I]f we should leave off breaking such a key for a while we risked being unaware when and if its traffic characteristics changed. In that event we would find it hard to pick up the thread again if and when Hut 3 wanted us to do so." The entire German land, air, and naval communication system—Enigma as well as other forms of communication formed a single seamless fabric for the cryptologists.[1]

In time, U.S. Army and Navy personnel arrived to work at Bletchley Park. Welchman says:

> The U.S. Navy developed a large installation of bombes similar to but faster than our own, and, although their primary commitment was the handling of the German Naval Enigma, their bombes were sometimes put at the disposal of Hut 6. The U.S. Army had developed a machine of their own design that could handle at least one problem that we were unable to handle: the problem of using Sillies derived from periods of a

day during which different arrangements of the three wheels were in use [p. 135].

In addition to the regular round-the-clock shifts, there was often a daytime team engaged in research. To the very end of the war Hut 6, with an internal staff that peaked at around two hundred fifty persons, was still having to contend with new cryptological problems. In the last year of the war, two serious problems arose as a result of two mechanical adaptations of the Enigma machine. One of these made possible nonreciprocal commutator connections (that is, if "a" were commutated to "r," "r" would not necessarily be commutated to "a"). This, writes Welchman, "demolished the principle of the diagonal board of a bombe" (p. 137).

The other modification was the introduction of a new reflector, designated by the letter "D." When the German Army and Air Force began using this reflector, the Hut 6 researchers soon found that it was variable by cross-plugging.

It appears that by June 1941 the British had four to six bombs, including the two prototypes, and by early August 1941, they had eight to twelve bombs. Thus, production models were already being delivered at the rate of around three a month. Of the bombs that had been delivered by August of that year, half were housed at Bletchley Park itself (in Hut 11) and the rest in converted stables at Adstock, the village where Travis lived throughout the war. Another "bombe hut" was nearing completion in the village of Wavendon. Together, Bletchley, Adstock, and Wavendon must eventually have accommodated about twenty-four to thirty bombs. After Gayhurst Manor was requisitioned by the Admiralty, and a further sixteen bombs were installed there, bringing the total to about forty to forty-six, it was still felt that the limit would be about seventy bombs, which would require accommodations for about seven hundred Wrens who would operate them. In 1942, however, with the major jump in numbers of Enigma keys and nets, it was found that many more than seventy bombs would be needed. For reasons of security, housing for bombs had to be completely finished and ready for use before any bombs could be installed.

Eventually, further bomb sites were established in new brick office buildings at Stanmore, on the northern outskirts of London,[2] and in three new buildings in Eastcote, in the western suburbs of London. The third Eastcote block was erected in about six months and housed about eight hundred to nine hundred of the eventual total of two thousand Wrens. Bombs from Wavendon and Adstock were moved to Stanmore and Eastcote, but Gayhurst remained in operation to the end of the war. A few bombs remained in Bletchley Park, but were used only for demonstration and training purposes. Thus, Station X acquired the large bomb establishments that were needed for efficient operation at the dispersed sites that were needed as a precaution against possible air attack (pp. 138-41).

The two British prototype bombs were equipped with ten scramblers (sets of three cipher drums) each, and were followed by twelve-scrambler production models (p. 309). During a bomb run, the twelve scramblers were driven in synchronism through all $26 \times 26 \times 26 = 17,576$ possible positions of

the drums of each scrambler (p. 142). Harold Fletcher of Hut 6 recalls
(p. 144) that an average bomb run took about twelve to fifteen minutes.
When a run on a particular wheel order had been completed, another wheel
order would be tried. Allowing for the initial setup time, changing of drums,
and dealing with drops, it took one bomb something over twelve to fifteen
hours to run one menu on all sixty possible wheel orders. When there were
plenty of bombs, several could be put to work on the same menu, thus greatly
reducing the time required to achieve a break (p. 145).

Later in the war, according to Welchman, the German Navy modified its
Enigma by splitting the reflector into a fixed left-hand part and a rotatable
right-hand part, thus creating a machine with four rotating wheels instead of
three. The British countered by producing four-wheeler bombs. With little
additional effort, by driving the drums much faster than previously, "Doc"
Keen managed to build four-wheel bombs that could do twenty-six times as
many tests as the three-wheelers in only twice the time (p. 148).

The Bletchley operation was dependent on interception of German
radio transmissions. The big expansion of intercept facilities began in 1941,
when the RAF opened a large station at Chicksands, a little east of Bletchley.
Meanwhile, Station X depended almost entirely on the experienced interceptors at the army station at Chatham. However, since Chatham was too
exposed to air attack, most of its personnel were moved to Beaumanor, a
country estate in Leicestershire, about fifty miles north of Bletchley (however, a small group of interceptors remained at Chatham, for the sake of
diversified reception). Thus, by early 1943, Station X had four widely separated principal intercept sites: Beaumanor in Leicestershire, Chatham in
Kent, Chicksands in Bedfordshire, and Shaftesbury in Dorset (pp. 149-50).

The interceptors had to cope with the very poor frequency stability of
radio sets in those days. The drifting of German radio frequencies often made
it extremely hard to keep in touch with the stations of a net. However, by
following a net long enough, an interceptor could learn to recognize individual German radio operators by their "fists" (their characteristic ways of
sending Morse code), and this proved to be the most reliable means of
keeping in touch with all the stations of a net and avoiding confusion with
other nets (p. 153).

The Germans themselves faced the same problem of frequency drift.
The various stations in any German short-wave net used the same frequency
both for transmission and for reception. All the stations monitored this
frequency continually, one of them acting as net control. Stations could join or
leave the net as necessary, and the control function could be transferred from
one station to another. The German net controllers struggled to keep their
nets in working order by means of very short messages using the call signs of
individual stations and a so-called Q-Code. British interceptors recorded all
this chitchat in logs, which were systematically analyzed by a radio intelligence group known as the Central Party that, probably in 1942, moved into
Bletchley Park (pp. 153-55).

The various stations in a German radio net identified themselves by call
signs usually comprising two letters and one figure. These call signs, like all

the Enigma daily keys and their identifying discriminants, changed at midnight. When a net controller came on the air at midnight, his first task was to take roll call: using their call signs and the appropriate Q-Codes, he would ask each station to acknowledge if it heard him. This procedure gave Allied interceptors (British, and Polish and French before them) a chance to record in their daily logs all the call signs of the nets that they were monitoring (p. 155).

The traffic analysis experts of the Central Party studied the chitchat in the logs, used direction finding facilities to locate the German transmitters, and collected call signs used on successive days by the same stations so that, when the yearly repetitions appeared, log reading could begin to identify military units served by radio stations. (This identification became much easier when German call sign books were captured.) Presumably, when possible, they used interceptors' identifications of the German radio operators by "fist." The analysts studied the preambles of enciphered messages, especially retransmissions of the same messages on different nets (at Bletchley they were able to help the Hut 6 crib hunters), so as to piece together the structure of the German radio communications system, which, in turn, had to reflect the command structure and order of battle. From time to time, the logs would contain short messages in the clear, giving names of individuals or units. By getting to know the regular pattern of message traffic in relatively quiescent periods, the traffic analysts could hope to detect something unusual and to guess what it might mean (pp. 156-58).

The prime Polish and British sources on Enigma decryptment, Marian Rejewski and Gordon Welchman, are in agreement that the respective Polish and British successes were made possible by, among other things, an early enough start in working with Enigma, continuity of cryptological effort, luck, good guesswork, and incredible German cryptographic errors. The German errors remained much the same during the exclusively Polish, the transitional Polish and British, and the exclusively British periods of Enigma decryptment.

The Poles

[Success in] cipher and code breaking. . . require[s] an ounce of luck, a favorable coincidence. This thought will occur irresistibly to anyone who traces the struggles of the Polish cryptologists with Enigma in the years 1932-39. He will conclude. . . that, given a somewhat different sequence of events, Enigma probably would never have been solved. Whatever one may call it now, fate itself seemed to smile upon the Polish enterprise and to conspire against the Nazis.

When in November and December 1932 the most intensive work had been in progress in Poland on Enigma, German cipher clerks had committed outrageous blunders. They had often selected message keys (the first six letters at the beginnings of messages) in a perfectly stereotypic manner. For example, they would strike the same letter three times (AAA) or they would strike letters in alphabetical order (ABC). Or again, they would use letters that lay next to each other down or diagonally across the keyboard—which was also against regulations. . . [T]he crux of the matter would seem to have been blind [German] faith in Enigma. . . .

Nonetheless, the Polish mathematicians at B.S.-4 [the Cipher Bureau's German section]—thanks to the cycle principle discovered by Marian Rejewski... were able to quickly distinguish total chaos from the merely ostensible chaos that resulted when initially ordered impulses flowed through the machine....

About mid-January 1933, after Enigma had been solved, these German shortcomings disappeared. "So if we had set to work not in October 1932 but just a couple of months later, we would have had a lot more trouble. In fact we had the impression that the Germans had gotten jittery, as if they sensed intuitively that something had happened," says Marian Rejewski.

There were more coincidences that favored the Poles, beginning with French recruitment of Asche and [Gustave] Bertrand's turning over to the Polish Cipher Bureau in early December 1932 documents furnished by the German. In themselves Asche's materials were of little value, but when combined with the mathematical analysis that had already been done in Poland, they helped to form a completely new quality, reducing the number of unknowns in the equations that Rejewski had derived. Not long after that, Asche had been transferred to a different job and had lost all contact with Enigma.

When the Germans exchanged the reflector in their Enigmas on 2 November 1937 [from a reflector "A" to a new "B" reflector—this change was alluded to earlier], they would make the mistake of not changing the wiring in the three rotors at the same time. The Poles' work would also be facilitated by the S.D.'s tardiness in switching (finally, on 1 July 1939) to new procedures for enciphering message keys that had been adopted by other German Enigma nets on 15 September 1938. [Kozaczuk, chapter 5, above.]

[Soon after beginning work on Enigma in the fall of 1932] I succeeded in solving [the] first six letters [of messages] which constituted the [doubly enciphered] individual [message] key.... [Rejewski explains in Appendix D, above, that the Germans enciphered the message key twice as a hedge against radio-transmission garbles. A]nd thanks to my having decrypted these keys, I also had...as a bonus some additional material that later served me in solving the whole machine. So if the Germans ...hadn't enciphered these keys but had given them plain at the head [of the message] they would have come out better in the end. Because I managed to solve the keys anyway, and in addition [I got] this material on which I was able to work and solve the Enigma [machine] itself. [Rejewski, Appendix B, above.]

[Solution of] one of the secrets of the Enigma cipher, that of the message keys,...had not required a knowledge either of the drum connections or of the daily keys, of neither of the remaining secrets of the Enigma cipher. What was needed was a sufficient number of messages from the same day, about sixty, to make possible the formation of [a] characteristic set....

Also required was a good knowledge of the habits of encipherers regarding the selection of message keys. The first time, when I assumed that there would be many keys such as "aaa," "bbb" and so on, it was only a hypothesis that luckily panned out. Later, we followed very closely the evolution in the encipherers' fancies, and when before long they were forbidden to use as keys three identical letters, we always managed to discover other habits of theirs, if only that, since they were not allowed to use three identical letters, they avoided repeating any letter even once, and this trait also sufficed for us to determine what were the message keys prior to their encipherment.

We succeeded in working out several more methods of a similar nature. For it is a well-known phenomenon that man, as a being endowed with consciousness and memory, cannot imitate chance perfectly, and it is the cryptologist's task, among other things, to discover and make proper use of these deviations from chance. [Rejewski, Appendix D, above.]

What. . . were the connections in the entry drum? It turned out later that they can be found by deduction, but in December 1932, or perhaps in the first days of 1933, I obtained those connections by guessing. I assumed that, since the keyboard keys were not connected with the successive contacts in the entry drum in the order of the letters on the keyboard, then maybe they were connected up in alphabetical order; that is, that the permutation caused by the entry drums is an identity and need not be taken into account at all. This time, luck smiled upon me. The hypothesis proved correct, and the very first trial yielded a positive result. From my pencil, as by magic, began to issue numbers designating the connections in [the right-hand rotor]. [Rejewski, Appendix D, above.]

Placed on the circumferences of [the rotors] were adjustable rings with the letters of the alphabet engraved on them. How these rings should be set daily was given to the cipher clerks on the monthly tables supplied to them, along with the other components of the daily keys. We. . . had to find the settings of the rings.

From messages of September and October 1932 that had meanwhile been read, I learned that as a rule all messages, of course leaving aside the subsequent parts of messages comprising two or more parts, began with the letters ANX, from the word "an" (German for "to") and "x" to separate the words. One needed to select a suitable message, beginning, for example, with the letters "tuv," and depressing the "t" key all the time, rotate the drums, observing when the A lamp lit. Then he depressed the "u" key and, when the N lamp lit, depressed the "v" key. If the X lamp lit, there was a large probability that we had found the right case, and then one needed to set the rings appropriately. If not, he had to keep on looking until he succeeded. [Rejewski, Appendix D, above.]

[In the summer of 1934, in the period of Roehm's Putsch and the Night of the Long Knives, some German intercepts resisted decryptment by the Cipher Bureau in Warsaw. Eventually t]he cipher was found to be based on a hitherto unknown system of keys. In addition. . . (superencipherment) [of a code] had been used. . . . First to be solved were the openings of these messages, many of which began with the stock phrase Hoeherer S.S. Fuehrer (Higher S.S. Commander). These proved to be orders broadcast to S.S. and S.D. units from [Heinrich] Himmler's Berlin headquarters. Though the cryptography was complex, the primitive vocabulary made the cryptologists' work easier: it was mostly police jargon. . . . In some dispatches the names of cities in which the terror was known to have reached a particular pitch recurred.... Solution of this system, which was given the working name "S.D. cipher," was made possible by the recurring expressions. [Kozaczuk, chapter 4, above.]

[E]ncrypted messages might refer to mobilization preparations, to the deployment and composition of units, to armaments, to preparations for maneuvers. They might contain the recurring names of commanders or training grounds. Sometimes they would refer to S.D. or Abwehr operations on foreign soil. Thus, chances were that certain elements of a code or cipher could simply be guessed by substituting in probable words or phrases.

The cryptologists at B.S.-4 [the German section of the Polish Cipher Bureau] had a variety of reference aids at their disposal, including the Rangliste, an annual German Army publication that [appeared until 1932 and] gave the names of all regular Army officers, listed by rank and seniority.... A starting point could sometimes be obtained by studying the endings of enciphered messages, where the sender's signature usually appeared. [Kozaczuk, chapter 5, above.]

In September 1937, a couple of months before the change of reversing drums [that is, reflectors, on 2 November 1937], a new net had appeared on the airwaves. As it soon turned out, this was a net of the [Nazi] party's security service, the Sicherheitsdienst or S.D. for short....

The S.D.'s enciphering procedure differed little from that used in other nets. When for the first time a day's characteristic in this net was formed, it was located without any trouble in our card catalog. Thus, the sequence and position of the drums and permutation S [the commutator connections] were found, but when an attempt was made to determine the setting of the rings by the ANX method, it ran into difficulties. Apparently none of the messages considered had begun with ANX. Therefore, a fragment was chosen from the middle of one of the messages, and a start was made at tapping it out on the machine in all the possible positions of the drums, in the hope of thereby obtaining a fragment of the plain text. And indeed, fortuitously, after a relatively short time, the letters "ein" were obtained. This might be a fragment of the text, but, on the other hand, it might be a quite accidental occurrence of just those letters. When the whole message was tapped out with that position of the drums, no more fragments in German were found.

However, after closer analysis of this ostensibly senseless collection of letters, it turned out that certain repetitions of letters could be extracted from it, that these repetitions formed four-letter groups, and that the intervals between them were multiples of four; the entire message could be divided (neglecting the word "ein") into four-letter code groups. Thus what we had was a...superencipherment. First the sender of the message, doubtless an officer, encoded the text of the message, using a code book, into four-letter code groups—he had used the word "ein" only because he did not find that word in the code book—and it was only then that he gave the text, so prepared, to the cipher clerk for encipherment on the machine.

It was thanks to this slip-up—to the mixing of plain text with code—and to an ounce of luck that we were able to reconstruct the entire daily key, complete with the settings of the rings. [Rejewski, Appendix D, above.]

[O]n [15 December 1938] the Germans introduced a new change into the Enigma cipher. In all formations, including the S.D., they added to the existing three drums [that is, rotors] two more drums, IV and V. [These were the two "wheels" that Welchman finds it hard to believe the Poles could have solved by non-"nefarious" means.] There were still three drums on the axle, but now three drums were to be selected from among five, and so instead of six possible sequences there were now sixty. But, leaving aside even the tenfold increase in the number of possible drum sequences, we did not know the connections in the new drums. How to obtain them? With the new system of encipherment [that had been introduced on 15 September], there were no characteristics. The cyclometer and card catalogs [of characteristics, based on the cyclometer] were useless. Fortunately, we had the S.D. net which, while it had introduced drums IV and V, retained the old system for enciphering the keys. Using the grill method, we sought for and found a day on which [the right-hand] drum. . . happened to be one of the earlier, and therefore known, drums. Then we made the assumption that [the left-hand and middle] drums. . . included a known drum and an unknown one, and we found the connections in the latter drum the same way that, in 1932, we had found the connections in the third, then still unknown, drum.

Thus, we were in possession of the connections in all five drums, and we could still read messages in the S.D. net. This was not easy, though, for although we sometimes knew which drum was in the [right-hand] place—thanks to [Jerzy] Różycki's clock method—the grill method, the only one that we could now apply to the S.D. net, sometimes failed, because, as of 1 January 1939, the Germans once more increased the number of letters changed by [the commutator] to seven to ten pairs. Nevertheless, the fact is that we did read messages in the S.D. net, and [Peter] Calvocoressi was incorrect in saying that, at this time, no one in the world could read messages enciphered on the five-drum Enigma. [Rejewski, Appendix D, above.]

The British

That we managed to stay in the game until the end of the war was made possible only by a comedy of errors committed by the Germans. . . .

Perhaps the most spectacular single error was the Germans' failure to think of the principles of our bombes [based on the Polish design], which made an Enigma key vulnerable to a sufficiently long crib. But. . .our bombes, if we could ever have justified their development, would have been useless without cribs, and we would never have found our cribs if the Germans had not made a number of errors in procedure. At any time during the war, enforcement of a few minor security measures could have defeated us completely.

The double encipherment of each text setting [that is, message key], standard practice until May 10, 1940, was a gross error. It enabled us to attack the million-odd combinations of wheel order and ring settings without bothering about the vast number of steckerboard [that is, commutator] cross-connections (more than 200 trillion. . .) in which the German experts apparently had placed their trust. . . . Once we had our Jeffreys [that is, Zygalski] apparatus, an Enigma [daily] key became vulnerable whenever the volume of traffic on that key produced enough female indicators. About a hundred messages would be sufficient.

This gross error was compounded by a relatively minor mistake in procedure. In any application of the Jeffreys apparatus, we had to be quite certain that all the female indicators we were using had been enciphered on the same Enigma key. We could afford no mistake in determining which sets of four discriminants indicated the same key. And... we were greatly assisted in this... by the German procedural error of using different discriminants in the preambles of the successive parts of a multi-part message, and thereby indicating to us that these particular discriminants must belong to the same set of four.

I do not know whether the Germans abandoned the double encipherment procedure because they had discovered its vulnerability. However, this early error was extremely important to us, for without it the Hut 6 balloon might never have gotten off the ground.... First... if, in the early days of the war, we had not been developing [that is, copying] apparatus [the Zygalski perforated sheets] that would undoubtedly enable us to break Enigma keys, we would not have been able to obtain permission to build up Hut 6 quickly as an exploiting organization....

Second, if before the period of the Sillies we had not been able to use the females to break the Red and Blue keys for a few months, we would not have been able to make a thorough study of the habits the Germans followed in encoding [enciphering] message settings [that is, message keys]. Even if we had suspected the existence of the Sillies, which sometimes enabled us to guess message settings, we might have had far less confidence in them if we had never seen the actual decoded [decrypted] message settings.

Third, without decodes [decrypts] to study, we would have been unable to establish the cribs on which the bombes depended. And fourth, without the early successes with Red and Blue keys we would not have obtained timely support for the considerable expansion of interception and bombe capabilities that proved so essential as the number of German radio nets and Enigma keys increased.

The Sillies and the Herivel tip were two gross errors in operating procedure that should have been spotted if the Germans had been monitoring their own traffic adequately. [W]hen the Germans stopped using double encipherment of message settings [message keys] in May 1940... we were saved by these two types of error, perpetrated by a small number of German operators. Neither type of error would have been any help without the other, but in combination they brought our problem within the range of manual methods based on our modified Type-X cipher machines.

Thanks entirely to this combination of errors we were able to continue breaking the important Red keys with almost complete regularity. [Besides] produc[ing] valuable intelligence [this] also gave us the continuity that we needed to detect the cribs that we would use when the bombes came. [I]f the German errors had not allowed us to become well established as a valuable intelligence source by the end of 1941, we would not have been supported by the greatly increased interception, bombe, and intelligence processing capabilities that became so necessary in the remaining years of the war, and it might have proved impossible to find ways around the new obstacles that the Germans put in our path from 1942 on. . . .

After the advent of the early bombes and the subsequent proliferation of keys in 1942, we depended above all on continuity. [The bombs were useless without cribs, which, moreover, had to be of sufficient length.] Our best chance of finding cribs lay in examining the routine reports and routine orders. These might be expected to contain [long] stereotyped addresses and signatures. . . . The Germans helped us by establishing times-of-origin for such standard reports, and presenting these times in the preambles of the transmitted messages, which appeared on our tele[typed] traffic registers. Thus the Hut 6 crib experts, by studying the registers and watching the charts in the Registration Room, could usually spot without difficulty the messages in which they were interested. . . .

. . . It was often necessary for a message enciphered on one Enigma key to be retransmitted after reencipherment on another Enigma key. This was frequently done without any rearrangement of the text, with the result that, once we had broken one of the keys, we had a usable crib to the other key too.

There were two more errors. One was Parkerismus, and of all the errors that gave us our success, this must be the most flagrant. It is difficult to credit that the person or organization responsible for generating Enigma keys should have repeated entire monthly sequences of discriminants, ring settings, wheel orders, or steckers [sometimes, several or all of these daily-key components at once].

The Germans' biggest error of all was failure to monitor all their procedures. A team of German devil's advocates, analyzing their own Enigma traffic, could have discovered seven of the twelve errors I have identified: use of different key discriminants in multi-part messages, Sillies, Herivel tips, giveaways in routine messages, errors in message generation procedure and in message relay discipline and Parkerismus. . . . [S]uch monitoring. . . would have stopped us cold. Why didn't they establish it. . . ? . . . My guess is that the German theorists were dazzled by the enormous number of stecker connections. . . . [Welchman's footnote: ". . . the Sillies and Herivel tips had virtually disappeared by the end of the war, and Parkerismus flourished only in 1942, so perhaps the Germans did monitor some of their procedures. But the real damage had been done by the end of 1941."]

. . . The [Enigma] machine as it was would have been impregnable if it had been used properly. [Moreover,] modifications in the design of the Enigma could have defeated us completely in spite of the procedural mistakes. We would have been in grave trouble if each wheel had had two or three turnover positions instead of one. . . . It would also have been possible, though more difficult, to have designed an Enigma-like machine with the self-encipherment feature, which would have knocked out much of our methodology, including the females. . . .

[Finally,] at any point during the war, the Germans [might have] simply issued sets of single-ended connectors [for the commutator] to replace the sets of double-ended ones. This would have meant that the upper socket corresponding to each letter, say X, would be connected to the lower socket of a specified letter, say Y. The lower socket corresponding to X would also be connected to the upper socket of some specified letter, but this letter need not be Y....

The Jeffreys sheets would still [until 10 May 1940] have produced their drops, and the Silly menus would still have produced their output of jumbled letters, but what about the second stages of these key-breaking processes, the testing by the Machine Room people? We could no longer have deduced that if one letter, X, was steckered [commutated] to another, Y, then the second letter, Y, must be steckered to the first. In both eras, Jeffreys [Zygalski] sheets and Sillies, our ability to accomplish the actual [cipher-] breaking would have been almost, if not completely, washed out. In the bombe era, if we had gotten as far as that, the diagonal board would have been out of business, because it depended on being able to deduce B/A from A/B.

We were lucky. [Welchman, pp. 163-69.]

Gordon Welchman has given the first fully convincing general picture of British Enigma decryptment in World War II. Up to now, intelligence specialists such as F.W. Winterbotham have been able to argue authoritatively that Allied victory in World War II was touch-and-go and that Enigma decryptment was, in Eisenhower's word, "decisive." Now we can see clearly, from a cryptologist's account, that Enigma decryptment was itself touch-and-go, and that the Allies were simply lucky. Furthermore, we can now see better than ever that, without the Poles, the British would not have been able to read Enigma, even though without the British, the Poles' achievements might, ultimately, have been in vain. Virtually all the major cryptologic techniques that the British used to break Enigma in World War II had been thought of and used by the Poles earlier: Zygalski sheets, the cryptologic bomb, Sillies, and, possibly, Herivel tips. The chief British contribution was an expansion in scale of operations, to keep pace with the expanding requirements of the war. Welchman writes:

It should have been made known long ago that Hut 6 Ultra would never have gotten off the ground if we had not learned from the Poles, in the nick of time, the details both of the German military...Enigma machine, and of the operating procedures that were in use [p. 289].

Welchman argues persuasively that much that was learned in breaking Enigma remains valid today. (He has spent most of the postwar years as a consultant to the U.S. and British defense establishments, and devotes a third of his book to those present-day implications.) "[A]ssuming that the wartime records of the Central Party [the traffic-analysis group], Hut 6, and Hut 3 have been preserved...it seems to me urgent [that they] be opened up and studied" (p. 293).

Quite apart from the implications of what might be learned for contemporary military communications planning, we should support such a study for what it might add to our knowledge of what actually happened during the war. (After all, that war's outcome has helped shape our contemporary world. It seems likely that our ignorance of how the war came out as it did has also helped shape the present.) Indeed, we would urge that surviving Bletchley Park wizards and other staff be given an opportunity to reconstruct the equipment and techniques that they once used.

[M]y two ideas were by no means the complete answer to the often-asked question of "How did we do it?". . . . The methodology was worked out by others. . . . I think I can see how it could have been done, but I will not go into details. I might so easily be wrong. Perhaps some of the surviving wizards may provide a true account of what they did, pointing out any errors in detail that I may have made in this book. [Welchman, p. 305.]

One of the most intriguing questions that might be addressed concerns the nature and applications of the world's first electronic computers, which were developed for Bletchley Park. "[I]n spite of the continuing attempts to preserve secrecy, [Brian] Randell has been able to piece together a pretty reliable story of the relationship between some of the wartime developments and postwar computer technology" (p. 179). Is this secrecy really necessary?

NOTES

1. Thus, for example, Rejewski's and his colleague Henryk Zygalski's work on S.S. ciphers in Britain, during the final twenty-one months of the war, apparently was also tied in with Enigma decryptment. According to Col. Tadeusz Lisicki:

> Rejewski...did not know that when he was...attached [in 1943-45] to my [Polish General Staff signals] unit [outside London, in] solving...hand ciphers of SD, police, etc. [he was working for the Enigma team in Bletchley]. If you have read Dr Welchman's book ("The Hut Six Story...") you will see how important this work was for the "cribs".

Lisicki, Letter of 6 April 1982.

Though attached to Lisicki's unit, which was located at Stanmore, outside London, Rejewski and Zygalski actually worked at a Polish radio post at Boxmoor, likewise located outside London. However, Lisicki adds that during this period he "was in daily contact with" the two cryptologists. Lisicki, Letter of May 25.

2. Also located at Stanmore was the Polish General Staff signals unit, commanded by Tadeusz Lisicki.

Bibliography

Arbeitsstab Oppeln (Oppeln Working Staff). "Besondere Anordnungen für Nachrichten-Verbindungen, 23 August 1939" (Particular Directives for Intelligence Units, 23 August 1939). *Records of German Field Commands* Series T-312, roll 80. U.S. National Archives, Washington, DC. Microfilm.

Banach, K. *Zasady i metody pracy Oddziału II Sztabu Głównego* (Working Principles and Methods of Section II [Intelligence] of the [Polish] General Staff). Warsaw, 1938.

Beesly, Patrick. "The Operational Intelligence Centre in the Second World War." *Naval Review* (London), 1975, nos. 7 and 10; 1976, no. 1.

_____. *Very Special Intelligence: The Story of the Admiralty's Operational Intelligence Centre, 1939-1945*. London, 1977.

Bennett, Ralph. *Ultra in the West: The Normandy Campaign, 1944-45*. New York: Charles Scribner's Sons, 1980.

Bertrand, Gustave. *Enigma ou la plus grande énigme de la guerre 1939-1945* (Enigma: The Greatest Enigma of the War of 1939-1945). Paris: Librairie Plon, 1973.

_____. Extensive correspondence with Marian Rejewski, conducted for over two years before Bertrand's death in 1976. Rejewski's files.

_____. *Memoire relatif à* Enigma *contre* The Ultra Secret (Memorandum Concerning *Enigma* versus *The Ultra Secret*). Duplicated manuscript, 1976.

Betlewski, Czesław. Interviews given to the author.

Biegański, Witold. *W konspiracji i walce: z kart polskiego ruchu oporu we Francji, 1940-1944* (Underground Struggle: The Polish Resistance in France, 1940-1944). Warsaw: Ministry of National Defense Publications (M.O.N.), 1979.

_____. *Władze rumuńskie wobec internowanych i uchodźstwa polskiego* (The Attitude of the Rumanian Authorities toward Polish Internees and Refugees). Manuscript, Wojskowy Instytut Historyczny (Military Historical Institute), Warsaw, no. 5/22/81.

Boelcke, Willi A., ed. *Kriegspropaganda 1939-1941: Geheime Ministerkonferenzen im Reichspropagandaministerium* (War Propaganda 1939-1941: Secret Ministerial Conferences in the Reich Propaganda Ministry). Stuttgart, 1966.

Bonatz, Heinz. *Die deutsche Marine-Funkaufklärung 1914-1945* (German Naval Radio Intelligence 1914-1945). Darmstadt: Wehr und Wissen, 1970.

Braquenié, Henri. Interview recorded 9 July 1975.

Buchheit, Gerd. *Der deutsche Geheimdienst: Geschichte der militärischen Abwehr* (The German Secret Service: History of the Military Abwehr). Munich, 1966.

Calvocoressi, Peter. "The Secrets of Enigma." *The Listener* (London) 20 and 27 January and 3 February 1977.

——. *Top Secret Ultra*. New York: Pantheon Books, 1980.

Campbell, D. "Why is Britain's Wartime Code-Breaking Still Secret?" *New Scientist*, 12 February 1977.

Cieplewicz, Mieczysław, and Marian Zgórniak, eds. *Przygotowania niemieckie do agresji na Polskę w 1939 r. w świetle sprawozdań Oddziału II Sztabu Głównego* (German Preparations for Aggression against Poland in 1939 in the Light of Reports by Section II of the [Polish] General Staff). Wrocław, 1969.

Danilewicz, Leonard Stanisław. Memoirs about the founding of the AVA Radio Manufacturing Company. Manuscript in Rejewski's files.

Dank, Milton. *The French against the French: Collaboration and Resistance*. Philadelphia: Lippincott, 1974.

Davis, Nuel Pharr. *Lawrence and Oppenheimer*. New York: Simon and Schuster, 1968.

Deavours, C.A. Afterword to "How Polish Mathematicians Deciphered the Enigma," by Marian Rejewski. *Annals of the History of Computing* 3, no. 3 (July 1981):229-34. An incompetent translation of Rejewski's paper that originally appeared in *Wiadomości matematyczne* in 1980, and that appears, adequately translated, as Appendix D, above, under the more precise title, "How the Polish Mathematicians Broke Enigma."

——. "How the British Broke Enigma," *Cryptologia* 4, no. 3 (July 1980): 129-32.

"Einsatz von Abwehrtrupps im Fall 'Attila,' 21.1.1941" (The Task of Abwehr Units in Plan "Attila," 21.1.1941). *Records of German Field Commands* Series T-311, roll 251. U.S. National Archives, Washington, DC. Microfilm.

Farago, Ladislas. *The Game of the Foxes: The Untold Story of German Espionage in the United States and Great Britain during World War II*. New York: McKay, 1971.

Fitzgerald, Penelope. *The Knox Brothers*. London: Macmillan, 1977.

Foot, M.R.D. *Resistance: An Analysis of European Resistance to Nazism, 1940-1945*. London, 1976.

"Funkregelung im Kriege, 15 June 1939" (Instructions for Wartime Radio Traffic, 15 June 1939). *Records of German Field Commands* Series T-311, roll 42. U.S. National Archives, Washington, DC. Microfilm.

Garliński, Józef. *The Enigma War*. New York: Charles Scribner's Sons, 1980.

Gauché, M.H. *Le Deuxième Bureau au travail (1935-1940)* [The Second Bureau at Work (1935-1940)]. Paris, 1954.

Generalkommando II Armeekorps (Wehrkreiskommando II). Stettin, 16 September 1936, communication concerning fourth and fifth (mobilization) rotors for Enigma, and reply of 19 September 1936 from 12 Infanterie Division, Schwerin. Copies in the author's files.

German Army. *Heeressignaltafel vom 1. Februar 1941 (H. Dv. 425)* [Army Signal Table from 1 February 1941 (H. Dv. 425)]. Berlin, 1941. Copy in the author's files.

——. Order to destroy (burn) the tables of Army Enigma keys for February 1936 due to their having been compromised. Copy in the author's files.

German Supreme Command in the West (Ober-West). Report by the signals chief, 20 February 1945. Copy in the author's files.

Giessler, H. *Der Marine-Nachrichten und Ortungsdienst.* (Naval Intelligence and Location Service). Munich, 1971.

Giviérge, Marcel. *Cours de cryptographie* (Course of Cryptography). Paris, 1926.

Gondek, Leszek. *Działalność Abwehry na terenie Polski, 1933-1939* (Abwehr Operations in Poland, 1933-1939). 2d ed., rev. Warsaw: M.O.N., 1974.

———. *Wywiad polski w Trzeciej Rzeszy 1933-1939: Zarys struktury, taktyki i efektów obronnego działania* (Polish Intelligence in the Third Reich, 1933-1939: An Outline of the Structure, Tactics, and Effects of Defensive Operations). Warsaw, 1978.

Good, I.J. and C.A. Deavours. Afterword to "How the Polish Mathematicians Deciphered the Enigma," by Marian Rejewski. *Annals of the History of Computing* 3, no. 3 (July 1981): 229-34. An incompetent translation of Rejewski's paper that originally appeared in *Wiadomości matematyczne* in 1980, and that appears, adequately translated, as Appendix D, above, under the more precise title, "How the Polish Mathematicians Broke Enigma."

Guzicki, Stanisław. Interview of 16 January 1975.

Halder, Franz. *Kriegstagebuch* (War Diary). Edited by Hans-Adolf Jacobsen in collaboration with Alfred Philippi. 3 vols. Stuttgart, 1962-63.

Hamburger Abendblatt. 12 September 1978. Article on Allied anti-U-boat operations in the Atlantic.

Heeres-Gruppen-Kommando 4 [Army Group Command 4], August 19, 1939. "Betr. Steckerverbindugen der Chiffriermaschine 'Enigma'—Funkregelung im Kriege—und Wetterschlüssel" (Concerning Plug Connections for the "Enigma" Cipher Machine—Instructions for Wartime Radio Traffic—and Weather Key). *Records of German Field Commands* Series T-312, roll 80. U.S. National Archives, Washington, DC. Microfilm.

Hinsley, F.H., ed. *British Intelligence in the Second World War.* London: Her Majesty's Stationery Office, 1 (1979), 2 (1981). *See* Rejewski, "Uwagi do 'Appendix 1.' "

Jabłoński, Olgierd. *Żołnierze polskich sił zbrojnych w obozie koncentracyjnym Miranda de Ebro 1940-1943 (relacja byłego więźnia)* [Polish Military Personnel at Miranda de Ebro Concentration Camp, 1940-1943 (Account by a Former Inmate)]. Manuscript, Military Historical Institute, Warsaw, no. II/53/16.

Johnson, Brian. *The Secret War.* New York: Methuen, 1978.

Jones, R.V. *The Wizard War: British Scientific Intelligence, 1939-1945.* New York: Coward, McCann & Geoghegan, 1978.

Jordan, Peter, ed. *Aviation in Poland: A Brief Historical Outline.* London: Max Love Publishing Company, 1946. With foreword by the Rt. Hon. Sir Archibald Sinclair.

Jungk, Robert. *Brighter than a Thousand Suns: The Story of the Men Who Made the Bomb.* New York: Grove Press, 1958.

Kahn, David. *The Code-Breakers.* New York: Macmillan, 1967.

———. "Enigma Unwrapped." *New York Times Book Review*, 29 December 1974, 5. A review of F.W. Winterbotham's *The Ultra Secret.*

———. *Hitler's Spies.* New York: Macmillan, 1978.

Kasparek, Józef. Account of incident involving Gen. Bolesław Bronisław Duch given to the editor-translator.

Knox, Alfred Dillwyn. Letter to the B.S.-4 cryptologists of 1 August 1939. In the author's files.

Kozaczuk, Władysław. *Bitwa o tajemnice: Służby wywiadowcze Polski i Rzeszy Nie-mieckiej 1922-1939* (Secret Battle: The Intelligence Services of Poland and the German Reich, 1922-1939). Warsaw: Książka i Wiedza, 1967. A fourth edition was published in 1977.

———. "The Key to the Secrets of the Third Reich." *Poland* nos. 6, 7 (1975). A two-part article on Enigma.

———. *W kręgu Enigmy* (Enigma). Warsaw: Książka i Wiedza, 1979.

———. *Wojna w eterze* (War in the Ether). Warsaw: Wydawnictwo Radia i Telewizji, 1977.

———. *Złamany szyfr* (The Broken Cipher). Warsaw: M.O.N., 1976. Based on the author's articles on Enigma published in the Warsaw weekly magazine, *Stolica* (The Capital).

———. "The System of Command of the Polish Army Higher Formations in the East in the Final Period of the Second World War." *Revue Internationale de l'Histoire Militaire* (Göteborg) no. 47 (1980).

Kuratowski, Kazimierz. *A Half Century of Polish Mathematics: Remembrances and Reflections.* Oxford: Pergamon Press, 1980.

Langer, Gwido. Two wartime documents on Polish, French, and British Enigma-reading operations and on cooperation among the three. Copies in Marian Rejewski's files.

Leśniak, Jan. Interview recorded by Richard Woytak in London on 15 January 1976. *See also* Woytak.

Lewin, Ronald. *Ultra Goes to War.* London: Hutchinson, 1978.

Lisicki, Tadeusz. Appendix to *The Enigma War,* by Józef Garliński. New York: Charles Scribner's Sons, 1980, 192-204. Based on information and papers supplied by Marian Rejewski.

———. Two papers on Enigma. Copies in the files of Richard Woytak.

———. Materials enclosed with a letter of 30 August 1982 to the editor-translator.

———. Letters of 6 April, 25 May, 10 August, and 19 September 1982 to the editor-translator and Richard Woytak.

Lorentz, Leopold. *Caen to Wilhelmshaven with the Polish First Armoured Division.* Edinburgh: Erroll Publishing Company, [c. 1946]. An American soldier's account.

"Luftnachrichtentruppe, Betriebsvorschriften (L. Dv. 704/1), Mai 1941" [Air Intelligence Units, Operating Instructions (L. Dv. 704/1), May 1941.] Copy in the author's files.

McLachlan, Donald. *Room 39: Naval Intelligence in Action, 1939-1945.* London: Weidenfeld and Nicolson, 1968.

Majdalany, Fred. *The Battle of Cassino.* New York: Ballantine Books, 1957.

Masterman, John C. *The Double-Cross System in the War of 1939 to 1945.* New Haven: Yale University Press, 1972.

Mayer, Stefan A. "The breaking up [*sic*] of the German ciphering [*sic*] machine 'ENIGMA' by the cryptological section in the 2nd Department of the Polish Armed Forces' General Staff." Manuscript, Piłsudski Institute of America, New York, nine pages, written 31 May 1974, London. Also in the files of Richard Woytak.

———. "Supplement to the paper of 21 [*sic*].5.1974, 'The breaking up of the German ciphering machine "ENIGMA".' " Manuscript, Piłsudski Institute of America, New York, four pages. Also in the files of Richard Woytak. The earlier paper (above) was dated 31 May, and not 21, as noted in the title here. The supplement is dated 4 December 1974.

————. Interviews recorded by Richard Woytak in London on 11 and 15 January 1976.

Mazurowa, Kazimiera. *Europejska polityka Francji 1938-1939* (France's European Policies, 1938-1939). Warsaw: PWN, 1974.

Nord, Pierre. *L'Intoxication* (The Poisoning). Paris, 1969.

————. *Mes Camarades sont mortes* (My Comrades Are Dead). Paris, 1947.

Norman, Bruce. *Secret Warfare: The Battle of Codes and Ciphers.* Newton Abbot, England: David and Charles, 1973.

OKH, Az. E 13 AHA In 7. "Geheim. Betr.: Zuweisung von H.-Gebieten an die Horch-Kompanien und F.F.E.-Stellen (Secret, Concerning: Assignment of Zones to Monitoring Companies and Fixed Radio Intelligence Posts)." *Records of German Field Commands* Series T-311, Roll 42. U.S. National Archives, Washington, DC Microfilm.

OKW. Signals Commanders' Conference, late 1943. Minutes. In the author's files.

Oddział II Sztabu Głównego (Section II of the [Polish] General Staff). *Komunikaty o sytuacji wewnętrznej Rzeszy Niemieckiej w latach 1936-1939* (Reports on the Internal Situation of the German Reich in the Years 1936-1939). Manuscripts, Centralne Archiwum Wojskowe (Central Military Archives), Warsaw.

————. *Niemiecka służba wywiadowcza od czasu zawarcia traktatu wersalskiego do chwili obecnej* (The German Intelligence Service from the Conclusion of the Versailles Treaty to the Present Moment). Manuscript, 1927. In the author's files.

Paillole, Paul. *Services Spéciaux 1935-1945* (Special Services 1935-1945). Paris: Robert Laffont, 1975.

Pawłowicz, Zofia. Interviews granted to the author in 1982. Prewar director of the B.S.-4 secretariat.

Pertek, Jerzy, *Wielkie dni małej floty* (Great Days of a Small [that is, Polish] Navy). 7th ed. Poznań, Poland: Wydawnictwo Poznańskie, 1972.

Peszke, Michael Alfred. "The Polish Armed Forces in Exile: Part 1. September 1939-July 1941." *The Polish Review* 26, no. 1 (1981): 67-113.

Polski czyn zbojny w II wojnie światowej (The Polish Armed Effort in World War II). Vols. 1, 2. Warsaw: M.O.N., 1979, 1981.

Randell, Brian. "The COLOSSI—Britain's Secret Wartime Computers." Based on a much longer paper presented at the International Research Conference on the History of Computing, Los Alamos, NM, 10-15 June 1976.

Records of German Field Commands. Series T-311, T-312, U.S. National Archives, Washington, DC. Microfilm. *See also* specific titles.

Reile, Oscar. *Geheime Ostfront: Die deutsche Abwehr im Osten 1921-1945* (The Secret Eastern Front: The German Abwehr in the East, 1921-1945). Munich, 1963.

————. *Geheime Westfront: Die Abwehr 1935-1945* (The Secret Western Front: The Abwehr 1935-1945). Munich, 1962.

Rejewski, Marian. "An Application of the Theory of Permutations in Breaking the Enigma Cipher." *Applicationes Mathematicae* (Warsaw) 16, no. 4 (1980).

————. Interview recorded by Richard Woytak in Warsaw on 24 July 1978.

————. "Jak Matematycy polscy rozszyfrowali Enigmę" (How the Polish Mathematicians Broke Enigma). *Roczniki Polskiego Towarzystwa Matematycznego, Seria II: Wiadomości matematyzne* (Annals of the Polish Mathematical Society, Series II: Mathematical News) 23 (1980): 1-28. Appears above as Appendix D.

————. Letters to Richard Woytak of 26 October 1978, 1 March 1979, 15 April 1979, 25 November 1979, and 2 December 1979.

_____ . "Matematyczne podstawy rozwiązania niemieckiego szyfru maszynowego 'Enigma' " (The Mathematical Foundations for Solution of the German "Enigma" Machine Cipher). Appendix to Kozaczuk, *W kręgu Enigmy*. Warsaw: Książka i Wiedza, 1979, 369-93. Covers much the same ground as the paper "An Application of the Theory of Permutations in Breaking the Enigma Cipher," above. Appears above as Appendix E.

_____ . *Sprawozdanie z prac kryptologicznych nad niemieckim szyfrem maszynowym Enigma* (Report of Cryptological Work on the German Enigma Machine Cipher). Manuscript written in Uzès, France, 1942. Copy in the author's files.

_____ . Transcript of confidential military service record issued by the War Office Records Centre (Polish), Bourne Avenue, Middlesex, England, 8 November 1957. In Rejewski's files.

_____ . "Uwagi do 'Appendix 1'. . . książki: *British Intelligence in the Second World War* prof. F.H. Hinsley'a." A single-spaced, four-page manuscript prepared by Rejewski for Richard Woytak on or before 2 December 1979. "Remarks by Rejewski on 'Appendix 1, The Polish, French, and British Contributions to the Breaking of the [*sic*] Enigma,' to *British Military Intelligence in the Second World War: Its Influence on Strategy and Operations, Volume One, by F.H. Hinsley.*" London: Her Majesty's Stationery Office, 1979, 487-95. Appendix is on pages 487-95. Published complete in an English translation by Christopher Kasparek, in *Cryptologia*, 6, no. 1, January (1982) 75-83.

_____ . Virtually continuous interviews given to the author over many years running.

_____ . *Wspomnienia z mej pracy w Biurze Szyfrów Oddziału II Sztabu Głównego 1932-1945* (Memoirs of My Work in the Cipher Bureau of Section II of the General Staff, 1932-1945). Manuscript, Military Historical Institute, Warsaw (1967) no. I/2/44.

Renauld, Gen. P. Notes appearing in *Bulletin Trimestriel de l'Association des Amis de l'École Supérieure de Guerre* (Trimestrial Bulletin of the Association of Friends of the Ecole Superieure de Guerre), Paris, 1978 or 1979. Made available by Linda Y. Gouazé, who received them from General Renauld.

Report of German Army Signals Chiefs. *Records of German Field Commands* Series T-311, roll 18. U.S. National Archives, Washington, DC. Microfilm.

Rohwer, Jürgen. *"Special Intelligence* und die Geleitzugsteuerung im Herbst 1941" (Special Intelligence and Convoy Steering in the Autumn of 1941). *Marine-Rundschau* (Hamburg) no. 11 (1978).

_____ . "Vorläufige Bemerkungen zur Frage Sicherheit der deutschen Schlüsselmittel" (Provisional Remarks on the Question of the Security of German Keys). *Marine-Rundschau* (Hamburg) no. 9 (1975).

Rohwer, Jürgen, and Eberhard Jäckel, eds. *Die Funkaufklärung und ihre Rolle im Zweiten Weltkrieg (Eine internationale Tagung in Bonn, Bad Godesberg, und Stuttgart vom 15.-18. November 1978)* [Radio Intelligence and Its Role in the Second World War (An International Conference Held at Bonn, Bad Godesberg, and Stuttgart, 15-18 November 1978)]. Stuttgart: Motorbuch Verlag, 1979.

Różycka, Maria Barbara. *Wspomnienia żony mgra Jerzego Różyckiego z okresu 1-9 września 1939 r.* (Memoirs, by Mrs. Jerzy Różycki, of 1-9 September 1939). Manuscript in the author's files.

Rygor-Słowikowski, M.Z. *W tajnej służbie: Polski wkład do zwycięstwaw II wojnie światowej* (In Secret Service: The Polish Contribution to Victory in World War II). London: Mizyg Press, 1977. Reviewed by Richard Woytak in *The Polish Review* no. 3 (1979): 106-07.

Sadowski, Ludwik. *Oddział II Sztabu Głównego (Rezultaty pracy pokojowej i udział w przygotowaniu do wojny)* [Section II of the Polish General Staff (Results of Peacetime Work and Participation in Preparations for War)]. Manuscript, Military Historical Institute, Warsaw, no. 1/3/60.

Santoni, Alberto. *Il vero traditore. Il ruolo documentato di Ultra nella guerra del Mediterraneo* (The Real Traitor: The Documented Role of Ultra in the Mediterranean War). Milano: Mursia, 1981.

Schlüsselanleitung zur Chiffriermaschine Enigma vom 8.6.1937, Geheim (H. Dv. g. 14; M. Dv. Nr 168: L. Dv. g. 14) [Keying Instructions to the Enigma Cipher Machine from 8.6.1937, Secret (H. Dv. g. 14; M. Dv. Nr 168: L. Dv. g. 14)]. Berlin, 1937. Copy in the author's files.

Schramm, Wilhelm von. *Der Geheimdienst in Europa 1935-1945* (The Secret Service in Europe, 1935-1945). Munich, 1974.

Schuschnigg, Kurt von. *Im Kampf gegen Hitler* (In the Struggle Against Hitler). Zurich, 1969.

Shirer, William L. *The Rise and Fall of the Third Reich: A History of Nazi Germany.* New York: Simon and Schuster, 1960.

Smoleński, Józef. Interview recorded by Richard Woytak in London on 16 January 1976. Smoleński was the last prewar chief of Poland's Section II, from January 1939.

Sobczak, Janusz. *Propaganda zagraniczna Niemiec weimarskich wobec Polski* (The Foreign Propaganda of Weimar Germany against Poland). Poznań: Wydawnictwo Poznańskie, 1973.

Stengers, Jean. "La Guerre des Messages Codés (1930-1945)" [The War of the Coded Messages (1930-1945)]. *L'Histoire* no. 31 (February 1981).

Stevenson, William. *A Man Called Intrepid.* New York: Harcourt Brace Jovanovich Inc., 1976. On Enigma, at least, most charitably characterized as history-fiction.

Strumph Wojtkiewicz, Stanisław. *Sekret Enigmy* (The Enigma Secret). Warsaw: Iskry, 1979. A fictionalized account.

Suszczewski, Tadeusz. *Wspomnienia z lat II Wojny Światowej* (Memoirs of the World War II Years). Warsaw, 1975. Copy in the author's files.

Szumowski, Tadeusz. Account of escape and evasion networks in France. Manuscript, Military Historical Institute, Warsaw, no. V/22/88. Szumowski was the prewar director of the Western Office—Samodzielny Referat "Zachód"—in Section II of the Polish General Staff.

_____ . *Sprawozdanie* (Report). Manuscript, Military Historical Institute, Warsaw, no. 1/3/94.

Ścieżyński, Mieczysław. *Radiotelegrafista jako źródło wiadomości o nieprzyjacielu* (The Radiotelegrapher as a Source of Information on the Enemy). Przemysl, Poland: 1928.

"Tätigkeitsbericht für die Zeit von. 1.7.-30.9.44—III Funk" (Report of Activity for the Period from 1.7 to 30.9.44—III Radio). *Records of German Field Commands* Series T-311, roll 18. U.S. National Archives, Washington, DC. Microfilm.

Ulam, S.M. *Adventures of a Mathematician.* New York: Charles Scribner's Sons, 1976.

U.S. Department of State. *Documents on German Foreign Policy.* Series C, vols. 1-4, and Series D, vols. 5-7. Washington, DC, 1949.

Watt, Richard M. *Bitter Glory: Poland and Its Fate, 1918 to 1939.* New York: Simon and Schuster, 1979.

Welchman, Gordon. *The Hut Six Story: Breaking the Enigma Codes*. New York: McGraw-Hill, 1982.

Wiadomości matematyczne (Mathematical News) (Poland) 23 (1980). Includes obituary of Marian Rejewski.

Winterbotham, F.W. *The Ultra Secret*. London: Weidenfeld and Nicolson, 1974.

Wojewódzki, Michał. *Akcja V-1, V-2* (Operation V-1, V-2). 3d, ed., rev. Warsaw: Pax, 1975.

Woytak, Richard. *On the Border of War and Peace: Polish Intelligence and Diplomacy in 1937-1939 and the Origins of the Ultra Secret*. New York: Columbia University Press, 1979.

_____ . "Wywiad z Pułkownikiem Dyplomowanym Janem Leśniakiem (fragmenty)" [Interview with Col. Jan Leśniak (fragments)]. *Studia historyczne* [Historical Studies], Kraków, 23, no. 1 (88) (1980): 109-14.

_____ . Review of *W tajnej służbie* (In Secret Service), by M.Z. Rygor-Słowikowski. *The Polish Review* no. 3 (1979): 106-07.

Zakrzewski, Tadeusz. *Relacja attaché wojskowego w Bukareszcie (1939-1940) ppłka dypl. T. Zakrzewskiego* [Account by the (Polish) Military Attaché in Bucharest 1939-1940, Lt. Col. T. Zakrzewski]. Manuscript, Military Historical Institute, Warsaw, no. V/21/17.

Zygalski, Henryk. Diary. In the author's files.

INDEX